MY LIFE AS A SAILOR

Sea Stories of a Cold Warrior

Commander Robert Bartron
U. S. Navy (Retired)

M. Cave Publishing
Sacramento, CA

ISBN: 1499627335
ISBN-13:978-1499627336

DEDICATION

To all my grandchildren
...a record to be read when they are old
enough to be interested in the past.

Books by Robert Bartron

Crew Eleven

The Autobiography of
Terry Ryan, A Shooter
(with Pat Bartron)

Nearcus Versus the Gods

To Steal a Million

To Murder a Ghost

To Clear Datum

You Can't Give Up On Love

Wylie Finds His Special Place

My Life as a Sailor

All titles available at MCavePublishing.com
and other on-line book sellers.

ACKNOWLEDGMENTS

I wish to acknowledge all my classmates and shipmates who made my life as a sailor so interesting and fulfilling. Each one played a big role in my maturing and my enjoyment of my time in uniform.

Preface

On June 29, 1969 I raised my right hand and swore to "protect and defend the Constitution of the United States against all enemies, both foreign and domestic." A quarter century later I retired from active duty, having never been in combat or fired a weapon in anger. I spent by service as a "Cold Warrior."

When summarized as I did above, it could sound rather uneventful—perhaps even boring. However, I look back on my time as a sailor as anything but boring. It was a tremendous amount of work every day, but I truly enjoyed it. I was one of those "lifers" who was a great fit with the Navy. I honestly appreciated every day I got to serve, and the reason I did was because of my shipmates—of sailors who were always the antithesis of boring! This volume is full of true stories about sailors and their common approach to life in the Navy. Serving on a seemingly constantly deployed frigate and then flying in land-based patrol squadrons gave me a sea chest full of "sea stories."

Looking back, I have come to realize that my life as a naval officer was during a peculiar time in the history of our country, yet most aspects of my experience are practically identical to what nearly all sailors endure...and enjoy. Wartime and peacetime in the Navy have much in common...because the peace is "fought" by the same sailors that go to war when the balloon goes up.

If the reader is seeking stories of heroism in battle or magnificent tales of being victorious against all odds, I recommend reading other histories about naval wars. What I share in this book are just real-life vignettes of life in a Cold War ...oh, and I might mention ...we won that war. And please note that as Sergeant Joe Friday would say, in many cases "the names have been changed to protect the innocent"...and the guilty.

When I was assigned to teach new commanding officers how to achieve success I had ten golden rules of leadership. The one that applies to this preface is simple:

"Rule Number 8: Love your sailors. Invest yourself in their success and happiness. Never miss an opportunity to praise them...but never ignore the need to correct them when necessary. And above all else, *whenever you hear of a sailor doing something so outrageous and unbelievable that you think no human being would even ever attempt such an act or stunt...remember they are sailors,* ***so believe it!*** The best quality in our sailors is their robustness—their fearlessness in trying the impossible. No regulation or any amount of common sense can ever stand in the way of a sailor expressing his robustness, and that is a good thing. We raise them to be risk takers, independent thinkers and men of action who can overcome any obstacle to achieve victory...contrary to what some of your sister services believe about their enlisted members, in the Navy we want sailors with a swagger, a confidence, a pride in self, ship and service and if this means they go overboard now and again,...well, we accept that. Always remember you are leading *sailors* ...it is a rare privilege few in history have had the honor of exercising...so take care of your Sailors—*love your sailors*—protect your sailors....you're "the old man" now, so don't screw it up.

P.S. In case you did not pick it up from the above advice, always remember that you work for your sailors and they take precedence over the commodore and admiral. Invest your best efforts in *their* success and *your* career success will be a given."

In closing, some of these stories might appear to be far fetched, but I can assure you from personal experience they are all true sea stories featuring robust American sailors.

Chapter One

Boat School

The best definition of the experience of attending the U.S. Naval Academy was given by an upperclassman to a little old lady one day. He was hustling back to Bancroft Hall from morning classes with his arms full of text books and a slide rule case clipped to his belt. He was about to complete his "Melville Mile" (the distance from Melville Hall back to Bancroft Hall) when this elderly tourist stopped him near the statue of Tecumseh. This was not an unusual occurrence as the Academy Yard was open to the American public who paid for it. Midshipmen were part of the "Tourist Attractions" at Annapolis, so we were required to stop for pictures with Aunt Millie or little Freddie if asked to do so. The conversation on this encounter went something like this.

The old lady demanded, "Young man, I want to talk to you."

The mid slowed and smiled as he quickly said, "I'm sorry, ma'am, but I will be late for formation."

"Just one minute young man!" she insisted, "I have something to ask you!"

The mid stopped and faced the tourist,

She continued, "Are you taking your education seriously? I sure hope so! I'll have you know that it is my tax money that pays for your *free* $40,000 education! I hope you appreciate that and work your hardest!"

Of course, she was wagging her finger in the mid's face while she pressured him to appreciate how *her* particular tax dollars were making it possible for him to earn a degree. The mid nodded and said thank you the first three times she ranted about his *free* $40,000 education. But he was late for his formation and he was in no mood to absorb any more verbal abuse, so he ended the encounter by locking the old lady's eyes in an intense stare and replying through clinched teeth...very politely, of course,

"Yes ma'am, I'm getting a *free* $40,000 education crammed up my ass a nickel at a time. Do you want any of it back?"

As far as he knows, she is still standing next to Tecumseh with her mouth hanging open.

Of course, today's cost to the taxpayer is closer to $400,000, but I am willing to bet the current members of the Brigade identify with this feeling of how it is taken onboard.

*****

When I was a mid ("and please, never call me a 'middie'") it was an all-boys school. Once women were finally admitted, much of the gross aspects of the experience were sanded smooth and modified to accommodate the new Brigade composition. This was a good thing. I can illustrate that by the following true stories of how the upperclassmen treated plebes (freshman.) Please note that none of these events taught a plebe anything about how to become a leader, unless it was in a negative sense—as in, this is how *not* to inspire anyone.

A plebe had only five responses to any question asked him by an upperclassman: "yes, sir"; "no, sir"; "no excuse, sir"; "aye, aye, sir" and "I'll find out, sir." In fact, you can answer about any question in life with one of these five responses. Please note that "I don't know, sir" is purposely absent from the list.

About a month after the Brigade came back from summer training and the academic year had started, I was serving the Second Class (juniors) at our dining table when I was asked a question which put me in an awkward bind. At the Naval Academy, twelve midshipmen eat family style at each rectangular table. Four plebes along one side, four "youngsters" (sophomores) opposite them and then two first classmen (seniors) on one end and two second classmen (juniors) at the other end. All food was dished out in order of rank. The first classmen got first pick, then the dishes were rapidly passed by the plebes to the second class end. Then the youngsters could dish up and whatever food might be left over was split between the four plebes. (For an entire year, with one notable exception, my classmates and I never tasted the ice cream occasionally served for dessert.) It was my turn to be the plebe nearest the second classmen with the responsibility to ensure they were served quickly and completely.

Meal times really sucked for plebes. You had four tormenters at the table with nothing to do but harass you (the youngsters were not allowed to play with plebes.) If the upperclassmen were in a foul mood (a daily occurrence morning, noon and night) then the plebes were in for a tough thirty minutes of having questions thrown at them one right after another. Get an answer wrong and you were in a world of hurt. If you confidently answered a question with the correct answer, the upperclassmen would go to great lengths to make you doubt your knowledge. If you stuck to your guns, then invariably you would be asked if you wanted to "bet your ass" on being correct.

That was not a bet to be taken if you had any doubt whatsoever in your answer or if there was any chance—even one-in-a-thousand—that you could be wrong. Because if you were wrong then you would lose your ass—almost literally. You would have to bend over and put your elbows on your desk while standing, and hold this pose while the upperclassman took your heavy push broom and whacked it across your butt. I can remember betting my ass and losing over the first name of a classmate in my company. We were required to know the first names of all of our company classmates, about thirty of them. I confidently gave the first name to a classmate who lived just two doors down from me. How was I to know that he always went by his middle name? He did not like his first name, Herbert, and never admitted to it. I can tell you that I, too, did not like his first name later that evening.

It was Sunday evening when I was asked the question that could not be correctly answered by the five authorized responses. It was near the end of the meal and the second classman—let's call him Tony—was having a discussion with his classmate about Tony's girlfriend. Tony noticed I was interested in the conversation (remember that with the exception of one afternoon during Parent's Weekend, I had not been near a girl in nearly four months.)

So Tony asked me *the* question. "Tell me Bartron, do you think my girl is pretty?"

How do you answer such a question? "Yes, sir," would get him in my face asking if I had designs on his girl. "No, sir," would be insulting. Obviously, "No excuse, sir" and "Aye, aye, sir" did not fit, so I responded with my only other choice.

"I'll find out, sir," I said while I kept my eyes in the boat (straight ahead,) hoping this topic would pass quickly.

"Yes, you do that, Bartron," Tony said in a totally emotionless voice, "Come around to my room after study hour and I'll show you her picture."

That did not sound too bad to me. Upperclassmen could not play with plebes from 7:15 PM to 10 PM six days a week. That was designated study hour for the freshmen. So I would just "chop" (plebes ran everywhere they went in Bancroft Hall; this trot with eyes straight forward and a ramrod straight back was referred to as "chopping") down the hall to Tony's room at ten. However I got an inkling that it was not going to be such a "piece of cake" when Tony stood up to leave and added one additional requirement to this command.

"Oh, and Bartron, come dressed in only your clacks [flip-flop type shower shoes] and your B-robe [officially issued Navy bathrobe.]

"Aye, Aye, sir," I responded as my mind raced with confusing thoughts.

Well, at 10 o'clock sharp I rapped on Tony's door and announced my presence. He ordered me to come in and to brace-up (locked at attention with my chin pulled in as much as possible) against the interior wall adjacent to his door. I stood there for a minute and then Tony and his roommate pulled their desk chairs to a position right in front of me. Tony went to his locked desk drawer and removed two slick, all-color magazines and brought them to me.

I soon learned that Tony and his roommate had done their earlier summer cruise to Copenhagen. Before the internet, hard-core pornography was extremely rare to come across. Playboy and the like were prevalent but true hard core porn was really an exception—except in Copenhagen and other European cities. I know at 18, I had never seen any.

"Untie your B-robe, Bartron and open the front," the roommate ordered and I complied. This was turning very weird very quickly.

Tony handed me the porn magazine and ordered, "Here is a book of pictures of my girlfriend with her friends. You are to look at each and every picture— "

Then his roommate completed the sentence, "And we had better not see anything move below your waist!"

So for the next five minutes I stood there looking at a porn magazine while two upperclassmen sat just inches from my exposed lower body and laughed and laughed.

Trust me. Nothing moved.

Did I mention it was an all-boys school back then?

*****

I might as well share other perverse "fun and games" that went on after the officers went home at night before I move on to other topics.

During plebe summer training we were instructed by members of the Class of 1971 who were new second classmen and in charge of the Plebe Detail. They were a good group on the whole and recognized that levity and laughter were important outlets for the immensely intense training for those two months. For instance, one afternoon my entire platoon of 39 plebes was squished together along the bulkhead of the hallway in front of our rooms. Our second class leaders were lecturing on something forgettable when one of their classmates came walking down the hall in his clacks, V-necked t-shirt, white bell-bottom trousers and carrying a paperback book in his hand. And he was whistling, which interrupted our training session. Our leader knew his classmate and asked him, "Why are you down on this deck? You guys are up two flights."

"I gotta use the head."

"Well, you have heads on your deck, why come down here to use ours?"

Without slowing or breaking his brisk stride he answered very quickly and calmly, "I don't want my plebes to know I'm human."

In fact, that was the very first time that summer that it occurred to me that our upper class might also be human.

Well, one night about five weeks into Plebe summer training our entire platoon was ordered to assemble in the main hallway of our deck in Bancroft Hall. It was after taps (10:30 PM) and only minimal lighting illuminated the hallway. It was the right mood for our platoon leaders to engage in their form of "positive leadership." We were ordered to report dressed only in our clacks and B-robes and to bring our official Academy velum stationary and "Quality Blind Made Skilcraft" black pens we were issued at the start of the summer.

Once assembled with our backs pressed against the hall walls, the upper class started the instruction.

"Now we have been receiving reports that some of you men have not been writing your mothers and girls with sufficient frequency. All of you lie down on the deck in front of you. Now take out your stationary and write what I tell you."

We all promptly complied without saying a word. He then continued.

"Dear Mom. I am sorry I haven't written as often as I should but we have been very busy here learning important and vital things. I am especially impressed by the caring and professionalism of my platoon leader. He takes wonderful care of me. He ensures I get plenty of good food to eat and fresh air and exercise. In fact, I have never known a nicer and more helpful human being than...fill in the name of your platoon leader here. Now sign it, your loving son and add your name."

The other platoon leader now took charge of this training session. "Remove one envelope from your Academy Velum box and insert the letter. Now get out a second piece of stationary. Now everyone roll over onto your back. And remember you are at attention. Now in a smart, efficient and military manner, everyone untie their B-robe and pull it back so you can air out your precious equipment."

There were groans and chuckles as we all complied. Then in a room adjacent to the hall we heard music playing. It was a version of Marilyn Monroe's "Kiss Me Tiger" with heavy breathing and sighs. In fact the lyrics are:

"Hey, Tiger, teach me tiger, how to kiss you, oooh-ahhh
Show me tiger, how I kiss you, oooh-ahhh
take my lips, they belong to you, but teach me first

teach me what to do
Touch me tiger when I'm close to you, oooh-ahhh
help me tiger, I don't know what to do, oooh-ahhh
I know that you could love me too, but show me first,
show me what to do"

About two lines into this recording, a platoon leader barked, "Okay you horny mids, flip over onto your stomachs!"

Of course we complied, and let me tell you, even in August, that tile floor was cold!

"Now once again, write what I tell you. Dear fill-in-your-girl's first name. I miss you so much! It is so hard here because I am away from you."

Now the other two platoon leaders took positions at each end of the row of bodies and gave new directions, "Okay you horny creeps I want to see everyone of you hump the deck! That's right; we want to see those butts going up and down—and you better do it together in a good military, orderly fashion. Up! Down! Up! Down! Schmuckatelli, you're out of rhythm—get with it! Up! Down! Up! Down!"

By this time, there were 42 midshipmen laughing almost uncontrollably. The absurdity of the situation made it hysterical...but it was definitely nothing you would admit to officers or your mother that you did it! The song ended and we were all admonished for being eunuchs and sent to our rooms. Just another perverse night of tension relief by the Class of '71.

*****

Most mids have stories about learning the "gouge." For instance, when the brigade returns at the start of the academic year, many plebes will be asked "How long is the mess hall?" The only proper response in the list of five answers is, of course, "I'll find out, sir."

The typical reply from the upperclassman was, "You do that, Bartron...and use the six-inch ruler you were issued on your first day here to find the exact length. And don't try any shortcuts because I know the answer."

This was no easy task before the internet that now has

nearly all information known to man available at your fingertips. Four thousand men ate in the cavernous mess hall three times a day. The only time available to a plebe to use a six-inch ruler to measure it would be after taps by sneaking out of his room and finding a way to get into the mess hall. Like many idiots before me, I managed to do this at 1 AM. It took me nearly two hours and then I still was not sure I had done it exactly and precisely as was required. However, as I prepared to go to breakfast the next morning where I knew I was expected to answer the question to the satisfaction of the upperclassman, I learned "the gouge" — the traditional right answer to the question, "How long is the mess hall?" My classmate told me the trick. The answer is somewhat racist, but it saves having to measure the length of the mess hall with a six-inch ruler.

"How long is the mess hall?"

The correct response is, "No sir, 'How Long' is a China man."

The other very popular "trick question" for a plebe was, "How many bricks did it take to complete Tecumseh Court?" Once again if you did not know the correct answer, you must respond, "I'll find out, sir."

The first week the Brigade is back, you can see many plebes slowly walking around the brick court yard in front of the entrance to Bancroft Hall. It is at least a quarter mile square and the bricks follow no geometric pattern so it is impossible to count rows and bricks and multiply to get the correct answer. I was all set to start my count one Saturday afternoon before another classmate gave me the "gouge."

"How many bricks did it take to *complete* Tecumseh Court?"

The correct reply, "One, sir."

Sometimes an upperclassman asked a question that could not be answered by the "gouge." I was asked at a "come around" one evening, "What is the General Sherman Airborne Amphibious Assault Vehicle?"

And despite what I was thinking at the time, the correct answer was not, "Who knows and who cares?" It took away from precious academic study time to research this off-the-wall question. What did I learn from the research that benefited me as a naval officer? Absolutely nothing.

But then "come arounds" were not meant to be educational in the specific sense. Rather, the purpose of the "come around" system was to place a plebe under stress in order to condition him to handle pressure and to think when every notion in his brain is to quit—yet he never gives quitting the status of being a true option. I recently read of a Navy pilot who described being in combat in Iraq (or was it Vietnam?) where missiles were incoming, warning lights indicated his engine was failing and his G-suit was malfunctioning and he smiled because he had the thought, "Hell, I've had come arounds tougher than this."

When told to "come around this evening" by an upperclassman it meant you were to report to his room at 6 P.M. Then he would play games with you until the evening meal formation at 6:30 P.M. During this thirty minute period you could expect to be put at a brace against the bulkhead and receive questions that you were expected to answer precisely, quickly and correctly. The four basic questions—or basic plebe "rates"—were: the current officers-of-the-day; what movies were playing out in town; how many "days" (to include the number of days to the next Army competition, the number of days to the next leave period, the number of days to the second class ring dance, and the number of days to graduation for the first classmen); and the menu for the next two meals served in the mess hall—verbatim! To this day, nearly forty-five years later when I ask my wife what are we having for Thanksgiving and she answers, "Turkey," I immediately correct her by repeating the precise description that was used on the mess hall menu, "Roast young tom turkey."

Beyond the basic rates, often you were required to report on what you learned about some other matter that had been assigned at a previous "come around"...such as the details and employment of the General Sherman Airborne Amphibious Assault Vehicle. In my plebe company there was an atmosphere that the Class of 1973 was having it too easy and it was incumbent upon the Class of 1970 to "make men" of us. The only other company of the thirty-six which comprised the entire student body that had it tougher than us was Twenty-Third Company. That was one company area in Bancroft Hall that every member of our class avoided. Now that I look back on how we were treated as plebes in my company I can see more humor in it, but I concluded years ago the particular group that were responsible for leading us, by and large, were rather lazy. It did not take any effort to treat plebes with distain and to use humiliation as a form of first classmen entertainment. Shouting at the top of your lungs just inches from the nose of a plebe braced-up against the wall was not really leadership or character building. However I remember that some did it with style—meaning without every other word being a profanity. The one that still sticks in my mind was by my initial squad leader. Remember that this was 1969 and four years before "Roe v. Wade" when he screamed at me about some supposed shortcoming, "Bartron, you are the absolute best reason I have ever met to justify legal abortion! The world would be a better place if you had never come out of your mother's womb alive!"

"Come arounds" were not only stressful mentally. There was usually a physical stress attached to it. The perfect example is the "beer run. The first "beer run" you do as a plebe is very educational; so much so that the next time it was a piece of cake.

At 6 P.M. you report to the upperclassman ready to do emotional battle. But instead of shouting humiliating insults, the mid casually asks that you do him a favor. "Of course, sir," you reply.

"I want to go on a picnic this Saturday with my friend. Will you go over to his room and ask if he is interested?"

You get the room number of the friend and you smartly chop through the 4.3 miles of corridors in Bancroft Hall to locate the friend and ask if wants to go on a picnic. It was not unusual for it to be over a half-mile to the other room.

The friend indicates that he would like to attend. You chop back the half-mile to your squad leader and the conversation goes something like this.

"Sir, Midshipman Friendly reports he would enjoy going on a picnic with you."

"Great, Bartron, did he say who should bring the beer?"

"No, sir."

"Well go back and ask him if he will bring the beer or should I"

"Aye, aye, sir."

But before you can turn to start your return trip, your squad leader would add, "Oh, yeah, Bartron it took you nine minutes to get your last answer. You best beat that time on this run."

You chop much faster and return with the answer that the friend wants the squad leader to bring the beer. So, the squad leader has you run back to ask "What kind should he bring?" And you must beat your previous time. This ping-pong game of sending a plebe running back and forth takes up the entire half-hour "come around."

And it is much later when you realize that your squad leader and his "friend" had never specifically planned this little game. But it was just something they had endured as plebes so they knew what was expected when some confused plebe showed at their door asking if they wanted to attend a picnic this weekend.

It was times like this when you realized the truth in the midshipmen's definition of life at the Academy: "130 years of tradition, unhindered by progress."

Personally, I had such a high opinion of myself that I would rather the squad leader yell insults at me than make me do the running or push-ups in a double-breasted suit and tie. But I had classmates that preferred the physical challenges because it left their self-esteem alone and it did not require any thinking—and with it the chance of choosing a wrong answer.

Other physical "indoctrination"—you see, hazing was forbidden—included such painful traditions as the green bench and hanging around and listening to music.

"Mr. Bartron, you look winded. Maybe you should take a rest. Why don't you sit on that green bench over by the bulkhead?"

Of course, there were no green benches in Bancroft Hall. You would go to the imaginary bench and place your back against the wall and slide down to a sitting position, holding yourself at right angles between your shins and your thighs by the tension in all your leg muscles. You would sit ramrod straight on this "green bench" until your legs started to quiver and you were about to collapse. That is when a particularly cruel upperclassman might say, "You need to relax, Mr. Bartron. Put your leg up on your knee so you are more comfortable." Upon complying with that order you now put the entire weight of your body on one leg and it would not be long before you fell to the deck.

You learn to be suspicious of any seemingly nice or humane gesture by an upperclassman. A favorite ruse was to invite a plebe into the upperclassman's room to "hang around and listen to some music." Radios and stereos were forbidden in a plebe's room. This was long before the invention of ipods or cell phones or any other devices current students use to listen to popular music. So when a relaxed upperclassman smiled and casually asked if you wanted to hang around and listen to music in his room for the scheduled "come around," it sounded very attractive.

It was only after you accepted that you learned the key words in the invitation were "hang around." In each midshipman's room in Bancroft Hall were a sink with mirror and next to these a single-stall, tile shower. You were required to grasp the shower curtain rod like a pull-up bar and suspend yourself from it while the upperclassman played music on his stereo. Of course, the shower curtain bar was not high enough to permit you to leave your legs extended, so you bent your legs at the knees and stayed in this position until one of three outcomes occurred; either your grip failed or the shower curtain rod failed from your weight on it or the upperclassman got tired of the joke and dismissed you. I never experienced the third outcome and I never had to worry about the first because invariably the rod would break after just a couple of minutes. The painful part of this game was when you fell from the rod. Your knees would slam onto the tiled threshold of the shower entrance. It was not enough to cripple you, but it did smart for a few minutes.

But the upperclassmen could be very concerned about your morale. I remember one night after the evening meal and before mandatory study hall commenced, two upperclassmen came into our room. They asked if we had talked to our mamas recently. No? Well we should make time to call home right now. We were confused on how we would do that when the only pay phones were in the basement of the fifth wing and we lived five stories above them. There would not be time to run down to the phones and return before mandatory study hours began. No problem! The upperclassmen explained that we must have forgotten that we had a pay phone installed in our shower earlier. So my room mate and I took turns "calling home." We stepped into the shower fully dressed in our Service Dress Blue uniforms and pretended to call home. This was before push-button phones so we were directed to use the rotary dial in front of us which, of course, was the handle used to turn on the water. So we took turns stepping into the phone booth and shouting greetings to our mama over the sound of the water drenching our good uniform suits and flooding our good "inspection" dress shoes. The upperclassmen nearly split their sides laughing at us and, honestly, once we accepted the fact that this was going to happen, we started laughing too!

Once again proof that boredom can lead to much mischief.

*****

Another event that evidenced the anxious boredom of midshipmen occurred just prior to the start of Christmas leave plebe year. During the noon meal a particularly unpopular company officer was eating with the staff at the head table which was located at the intersection of the three wings of the mess hall. A group of mids rushed him and hoisted him in his chair on their shoulders and then paraded him through the mess hall. Unfortunately for this Marine, two events combined to his misfortune. That meal was served with rolls and the loud speaker system played the Animals tune, *"We Gotta Get Out of This Place."* Four thousand mids sang along with the lyrics that perfectly matched their attitude that day. The emotions of the singing soon led one mid to throw his roll at the disliked officer being transported up and down the wings. Soon another roll was slung and then another. In a matter of seconds the entire mess hall had erupted into the largest food fight I had ever experienced. Not just rolls, but the main course and side dishes were thrown by four thousand students. Like a Keystone Kops pie fight, one table was hit by food from another table so they retaliated which led to more food being thrown. This daisy chain went on throughout the entire mess hall.

Sitting in the middle of this free-for-all were many plebes, erect in their assigned chairs and getting pelted with food but not moving because no one had given them permission to join in the fun. However, there was one table where the plebes had disappeared.

That meal's desert was ice cream served in two large frozen aluminum mixing bowls. As all the upper classmen were engaged in the food fight, it was the perfect opportunity for my three classmates and me to grab the forgotten ice cream and our spoons and then climb under the table. The four of us huddled beneath our table and rapidly crammed as many spoonfuls of the delicious ice cream as possible into our mouths.

That was the only time I remember getting any ice cream during my entire plebe year mess hall experience.

*****

For every five demerits a mid received he had to walk one hour of punishment. For the first three years you did this with an M-1 rifle and marched back and forth on the terraces behind Bancroft Hall, out of sight of the tourists. These punishment tours were marched for one hour on Wednesday afternoon and three hours on Saturday afternoon. Since plebes were not allowed off campus with the exception of Saturday afternoon, you would basically loose your entire week's liberty if you had 15 demerits to work off on Saturday.

Knowing that plebes would make mistakes their first year, each was allowed to receive 345 demerits before being considered for a conduct discharge. Like a reverse graduated income tax, the number of allowable demerits decreased each year until you were allowed only 75 your senior year.

I received only five demerits my entire plebe year. I was given an "A" for my conduct grade. However, I marched extra duty tours almost every time they were conducted for the entire year. I remember having one Saturday afternoon liberty my entire first year at the Academy.

Why did I march all those hours? Because I "volunteered" to do so!

The conduct system was structured such that a plebe could

either be placed on report using a "Form 2," or for a lesser offense he could admit his mistake on a "Form 3." The "Form 2" report was formal and processed through the chain of command and if an investigation showed that you were guilty of the transgression, demerits were awarded and added to your permanent record.

Ahh! But often the upperclassmen would report your misdeed on a "Form 3"—which meant no officers would review the transgression! It would be handled by the midshipman chain-of-command at the Battalion level. Technically, the offending mid, recognizing his error and need for correction would voluntarily submit a "Form 3" on himself and be assigned one or two or three hours of extra duty to provide an opportunity for the plebe to reflect upon his misdeed.

The "volunteering" usually took the form of an upperclassman saying, "You really screwed up Bartron! You have a choice of bringing around a Form 2 or Form 3 and placing yourself on report."

I really needed a lot of time for reflection I guess because I marched the four hours a week every week. To this day I can still do the manual of arms in my sleep...halt ...order arms...about face...left shoulder arms...forward march..."

The first Saturday after the Brigade returned from summer leave and training I think every plebe in the battalion was in line in front of the Battalion Office prior to the start of extra duty tours. In two lines were over a hundred plebes all dressed in our white sailor uniforms with blue-rimmed Dixie cups on our heads, leggings neatly laced around our ankles, a web belt with a bayonet sheath around our waists and our M-1s held firmly in our right hands with the butt of the rifle resting on the deck. We were ready for the pre-march inspection.

Down the line of identical plebes came the midshipman battalion officer of the watch (BMOW or as he was always called, the "Bow-wow.) He had a complaint about every plebe in the line. As he approached my position I heard him speaking to my classmates. In my peripheral vision I recognized the upper classman. It was "Cap" Parlier, a green-dyed Marine wantabe; hair cut high and tight, perfect uniform and perpetual scowl on his face.

"Mister, *say* the Star Spangled Banner!"

The plebe got three lines into it before he had to stop to sing it in his head to remember the next line.

During that pause, Parlier shouted, "What kind of American are you? Are you a Commie trying to serve in my Navy? *No credit!*"

Those last two words sealed the plebe's fate for the next hour. He would march his extra duty but not receive credit for doing it, meaning he would have to walk the punishment tour again to get credit.

Parlier inspected the next plebe in line and this time demanded, "*Say* the Star Spangled Banner...backwards."

My classmate got four words out before he was stumped.

Parlier went ballistic, "What? Another pinko Commie? Is this whole class full of Commies and hippies? *No credit!*"

The next plebe in line for inspection was surprised when Parlier ordered him to "present arms" and then snatched his rifle from his hands and inspected the piece.

"Did you oil this weapon before coming down here?"

"No, sir."

"*No credit!*"

Parlier took one side step to his left and inspected the next plebe. Looking at the plebe's rifle he asked, "Did you oil this weapon before coming down here?"

The plebe stuck his chest out a little farther and answered confidently, "Yes, sir!"

"Too much oil. *No Credit.*"

Next in the line was me. As Parlier started to move to a position directly in front of me one of his classmates walked past. Parlier turned to his right and said hello and then continued his right hand turn to inspect the next plebe. In doing so he pivoted right in front of me and finished his turn facing the plebe to my right. He had skipped me! It was something very easy to do when all plebes looked alike.

Soon the entire extra duty muster had been inspected and we were taken to the terrace to march. Upperclassmen with demerits to work off were in charge of the plebes to insure we followed the proper military manual of arms with each turn. If you screwed up or started skylarking (not paying attention to what you were doing) then you could here the dreaded words "no credit" and you would have to march the entire hour over again.

I made it through the entire first hour "with credit." One down and only one more to do this Saturday. It had been a good week and I had only "volunteered" to work off ten Form 3 demerits.

We were taken inside the third wing and muster was taken as follows.

"Allen?" "No credit, sir."

"Ames?" "No credit, sir."

"Baker?" "No credit, sir."

"Bartron?" "Credit, sir."

With my unexpected response the upperclassman left his position and hustled down the line to get two inches from my face. "What do you mean, 'credit?'"

Eventually he resumed the muster and when it was all said and done, I was the only plebe who had received credit for the first hour of marching.

I know it will come as no surprise that I marched the next two hours without credit. In fact, I think it was three Saturdays later when I finally worked off that last hour, but by then I had a dozen more that needed to be completed.

*****

Some "outsiders" felt that we suffered from being compelled to perform "plebe servitude." However, the vast majority of mids understood and accepted that some of our plebe duties were more in the sphere of paying dues to get the later benefits of club membership. The best three examples were chow call, window closing, and forming funnels.

All meals were mandatory during the week. The entire Brigade would form up by companies and then march to the mess hall. No matter what your class, freshman to senior, it was extremely obvious if you were late to fall into the formation. Consequently, in every hallway of massive Bancroft Hall stood a plebe shouting at the top of lungs informing all that it was ten minutes before formation time. This "chow call" included a recitation of the menu (verbatim, of course), the number of days, and the location (inside or outside) and uniform of the formation.

After the ten-minute call, the duty plebe would then go by each room assigned to his location and check to insure no one was asleep and had missed hearing the "chow call." All of this had to be completed in time for the plebe to return to his assigned station and make the five-minute call. After waiting for the clock on the bulkhead to click to the next minute he would yell the four-minute script then the three- and two-minute calls. The last one—the one minute call—was done very quickly because the plebe had to recite the required information and then hustle to make it to the formation before the clock clicked to the next minute. If you were on the fourth deck and had to go down five flights of stairs to reach your outside formation location you had a real race on your hands. To this day when I am running late to a meeting or appointment I can hear my own voice in my head shouting, "THERE IS NOW ONE MINUTE TO NOON MEAL FORMATION. TIME, TIDE, AND FORMATION WAIT FOR NO MAN—I AM NOW SHOVING OFF, SIR!"

Taking turns doing "chow calls" during plebe year was a small price to pay to have a safety net to keep you from sleeping through formations for the next three years.

The same perspective was taken about the formation of a funnel for the football team to run through at the start of each game. There were no assigned seats for individual midshipman at the stadium and so your vantage point was determined by the "first come, first served" system within the allotted seats for the Brigade. The Brigade seating area was not the best for watching the game and the seats closest to the field were the worst of the bad. So tradition demanded that all the plebes left their seats to run to the end of the playing field and form two lines for the team to run through as they entered the stadium. Of course, all the upperclassmen immediately moved higher in the stands to fill the seats vacated by the plebes who were out forming the funnel.

Again, having bad seats for the first season was a small price to ensure you had much better seats the next three years.

And another example of supposed "plebe servitude" was the window closing requirements during the fall and spring. Air conditioning is a relatively new addition to Bancroft Hall. Prior to its installation, the only way to get air in the rooms was by opening the windows. In the late autumn and the spring, it was too hot to have the windows closed at bedtime, but overnight the temperature would drop and a chill would fill the room if the window remained open. So to avoid stuffy noses and chattering teeth in the morning, the open windows needed to be shut during the middle of the night. So this duty was assigned to the plebes. When it was your turn to have the window closing detail, you would silently enter the upperclassmen's (and also your own classmates') rooms and slide the windows shut at about 2 A.M. This could be done efficiently by three plebes servicing the entire company of 110 mids.

That is, it could be done efficiently if the upperclassmen did not make a game of trying to catch us doing it. The mission was to silently open the door, and then using the light from the hallway that seeped under the door to navigate across the room and shut the windows. All windows were covered by horizontal Venetian blinds, so you would have to reach through the blinds and slowly push the window down. The key was not to snap one of the blind segments because this small noise could wake the sleeping lion in the den. Upperclassmen truly hated to be awakened and you would feel their wrath at breakfast.

However, some of the upperclassmen thought it would be a fun game to booby trap their dark rooms to ensure they caught the poor plebe doing this duty as best and silently as he could. Some of the snares were sneaky—the corn flakes on the deck to cause a crunch when you walked, the fish line tied across the room at ankle level and attached to a metal clock, or the dark covered books strewn across your path which were nearly impossible to spot in the dark. Even if you reached the window successfully, you had to make certain the blinds and windows were not sabotaged. A popular trick was to leave the blinds in a horizontal position and then place quarters on them. The slightest movement of the blinds would send the coins crashing to the deck and wake the occupants.

Of all the dumb things of plebe year it was this booby trapping to catch the window closer that I never understood the reasoning behind. How did the upperclassman "win" if he was awakened from a good sleep? The plebe was already up in the middle of the night, so he didn't suffer by the booby trap—only the sleeping upperclassman did. And if the upperclassman wanted to trap the plebe so he could run him at "come around" that was stupid because he could just arbitrarily order the plebe to report for "indoctrination" with no other reason than the upperclassman felt like playing with the poor schmuck.

Once again, window closing benefited the upperclassmen but it also was a good thing for the plebes for all four years there.

I am sure there were cases of plebes being required to do some work for the upperclassmen—to have been forced into "plebe servitude"—but I don't recall anything like doing homework for them or shining their shoes and things like that. Any academic help could be construed as an honor offense and it was not worth the risk to an upperclassman just to avoid doing something he had already mastered the first years he was there. On occasion an upperclassman would stick his head into a plebe's room and "ask" the plebe, "I'll buy if you fly?" The soda machines at that time were located in the basements of Bancroft Hall so many a plebe "volunteered" to run down to get a soda for an upperclassman...but his reward was a free soda for the plebe (hence the "I'll buy" part of the question above.)

However, during the fall semester of my plebe year I did have a job that bordered on "plebe servitude." Over forty years later it sounds a little bizarre, but you must remember that for four years Bancroft Hall was our home. You moved to many different rooms within its eight wings during your time as a mid, so it could be a challenge to consider one particular location as your "home." Everyone likes to be surrounded by the familiar and favorite things that give you a sense of center and "home." To many mids that place was a certain stall in the group heads located at the end of each hallway in each wing. In fact, I distinctly remember walking into the head on the first deck of the eighth wing to use a urinal and having to step over two of my classmates engaged in a no-holds-barred wrestling match at the entrance to one of the stalls. They both insisted it was *their* stall and were not going to let the other occupy it. Our company had moved from the fifth wing to the eighth wing after our plebe year and we stayed there for the remaining three years. This longevity in one area meant that many company members had developed a preference for which stall was "their" private area to contemplate the universe. There was no attachment to any specific urinal, but the commode was a matter of choice. I remember more that once a classmate pounding on the door of a stall and demanding it be vacated immediately! The other five stalls were unoccupied, but some interloper was keeping him from using his favorite!

Knowing the attachment a mid could get for a favorite "home" to do his business, the following should not sound so weird. The first semester of plebe year my squad leader wanted to be able to get up at the reveille bell and shuffle down to the head and gain immediate access to "his" stall. Since it was an all-boys school, there were over 70 mids who arose at the exact same time and all had to answer nature's call immediately (the 35 plebes in the company had risen an hour earlier and had used the toilets long before the rest of the company greeted the morning.) So my tasking during the first months of the academic year was to arrive at my squad leader's favorite stall and sit on the toilet. I was required to wear my B-robe and to never actually use the toilet and to be in place no later than 5:45 A.M. (reveille was at 6:15 A.M.) I used this time to study the front page and sports page of the *Washington Post* since we were required to be able to share the major stories with the upperclassmen at breakfast. This little duty accomplished two objectives for my squad leader: it reserved his favorite stall and it warmed the toilet seat for his use. I guess you could have called that plebe servitude.

****

The biggest lesson learned at the Academy was time management. I am sure that is a lesson most college graduates have learned, yet, as with most things at the "un-college" it was taken to the extreme.

It was easy to lose sight of proper priorities when you are assailed from all sides as a plebe. In order to fend off the wrath of the upperclassmen, my shoes were well polished, my brass belt buckle gleamed in the sun without a hint of a smudge, I could recite the days and all other plebe rates precisely and I could function on just a couple of hours of sleep per night. It took something shocking for me to realign my vision and reorder my priorities properly in order to graduate.

Normally a mid will receive two grade reports a semester,

a mid-term and a final grade. However, knowing the demands placed on plebes a third grading report was given them after the first quarter of the semester. It was an excellent policy. It saved me from flunking out.

My first grade report shocked the crap out of me. I had a grade point average (GPA) of 1.94. The minimum to remain at the school was a 2.0. I was surviving the military indoctrination, but it didn't matter how well I could do the manual of arms, because I was bound to be sent home for academic failure.

That first grade report reminded us that we were attending a college and not basic training. It worked. I had always been a "B" student in high school and now here I was *failing!* So I found five minutes to sit in my room and evaluate how this could happen. I came to the conclusion that I was wasting my time throughout the day. I needed more time to attend to the academic work. I examined my typical day and realized that there were minutes where I was unemployed. If I arrived five minutes early to a class, I would shoot the breeze with classmates until the professor showed. After mandatory sports in the afternoon I had fifteen minutes free after I prepped for the "come around," and the half-hour between the end of mandatory study time and taps I would engage in end-of-the-day socializing with my classmates who were free to visit my room during that time. This analysis revealed to me that I could capture nearly ninety minutes a day that I had been unknowingly frittering away.

My wife and children have seen what happens when I flip a switch in my brain to the "1.94" setting just as I did that first semester at the Academy. My focus and drive become sharper and stronger than they care to remember.

I was a history major at the Academy. It is an engineering school and all of us "bull" majors were in the distinct minority. One of the disadvantages of being a history major is the assigned reading compared to science, math and engineering students. We were expected to read about 250 to 300 pages a night. I computed that I read at a pace of one page per minute. That meant I needed nearly six hours per day to complete the required reading. So finding ninety more minutes that I could use to read my history books was a big deal.

I want to point out that the Academy is a military

institution with an academic mission. And like everything in the military it is organized to yield the most efficient results. If you have the student body held captive on campus then it would be highly inefficient to have their academic endeavors limited to twelve to sixteen semester hours per term. So every mid took at least 18 academic hours per semester. Now these were true academic courses—no credit for the mandatory physical education (golf, tennis, boxing, squash, etc.) and no academic credit for military functions like marching drill.

I once had a job where I reviewed naval officer training applications from candidates across the United States. I read about 3,000 transcripts a year from hundreds of universities and it took me a couple of months to get over the minimum academic loads required to graduate from most colleges. Most required completion of 120 academic hours to earn a bachelor's degree. But these credits included such things as "Introduction to Dance," "Volleyball" and "ROTC Drill." I reviewed my Academy transcript and converted it to what I saw on these civilian reports. The result was the equivalent of over 180 semester hours at a civilian institution.

The opportunity to get an "ivy league" education was available to every midshipman. Unlike large state universities across the nation where 300 freshmen are seated in an auditorium and taught English literature by a Teaching Assistant, our classes were never more that thirty students and always taught by an accomplished and engaged professor. The only exception was when professional subjects such as navigation and shipboard engineering were taught by credentialed fleet officers.

We had access to fully equipped labs and to one of only two university owned and operated digital computers on the east coast (the other being Princeton in 1969.)

I had a roommate who had the same access to these education tools and I often questioned if he got the "ivy league" education available, or if his attitude yielded an advanced junior college education when he graduated. His favorite motto was "Anything over 2.0 is wasted effort; we all get the same commission upon graduation." Max did work hard and I am sure I am stretching his real experience when I joke about his attitude, but he did spend a considerable amount of time down in the T.V.

lounge during our upper class academic years.

We took classes six days a week back then. Classes were either Monday-Wednesday-Friday or Tuesday-Thursday-Saturday. The standard set by the school was that each student was expected to study forty hours-per-week *outside* of the classroom. Some of us actually did that, some even did more (especially the chemistry majors—what gluttons for punishment!)

As I previously mentioned, the Academy was primarily an engineering school. Our class was the first (and last) in its history to permit all mids to freely choose their own major. When over half of our class picked non-science and non-engineering majors, that policy was quickly reversed. Currently around 65% must be science and engineering majors. To correct this one time error in sanity, our classmates were encouraged to switch their "bull majors" to science, math or engineering. My academic advisor was sure I would want to change my major from history to engineering in a year or two, so he insured I was academically prepared for that choice. That meant I could not take "fruit juice" (easy version of electrical engineering) or "physics for poets" or any other lesser challenging engineering courses. So I took calculus for math majors, physics for physicists and chemistry for chemists. At the time I felt put upon to have to wade through these courses when easier, less challenging courses were available. But in hindsight I am forever grateful he made me do that. Later in my career, believe it or not, I actually used what I learned in those courses.

However, as a "bull major" I was also required to earn three years credits in a foreign language. In high school I could do the math and science well enough, but having only one right answer to any problem seemed boring to me. I preferred the social sciences where you could argue for your own solution to a situation. Consequently, I was challenged and my ego fed in these courses. The only subject that I struggled with was foreign languages. I was embarrassed when I tried to speak another language and it came out terribly. So I earned my high school language requirements by completing two years of Latin—a dead language my teacher did not make us verbalize. When I sat down with an academic counselor during plebe summer and he informed me I would have to take six-semesters of a foreign language I was in shock and frightened. I remember the exact conversation on that day.

"Which language are you going to take?" he asked and when he saw the panic on my face he paused and then added, "You're not very strong in language, are you?"

"No, sir."

"What did you take in high school?"

"Latin, sir."

"Well then," he continued with a sympathetic tone, "I'm not going to let you take German, French or Spanish."

A look of confusion came over my face.

"Mr. Bartron, most of your classmates have taken one of those languages in high school and many will purposely tank the placement exams to be placed in beginning classes so they can coast the first semester as the Prof reviews what they already know. The profs know this and race through the material so if you have never taken these languages you would have difficulty keeping up."

Immediately I liked this guy. He knew mids and he knew the system.

"And if language is not your strong suit, I don't recommend Russian or Chinese for obvious reasons."

I nodded in total agreement and then asked, "What do you have left?"

He answered, "Portuguese or Italian."

"Which is easier?"

"Italian."

"Sign me up," I said with false bravado.

And that is how I came to take three years of Italian when in college.

It might have been easier than some languages but it was enough to kick my butt. Especially when the entire class for the three years consisted of about eight students, each (except me) with a last name that ended in a vowel. All had spoken some Italian while growing up, if not with their parents then with uncles and aunts. At the start of the third year I was tired of being the odd man out, so I had a new uniform name-tag made that I wore in the class. I changed my name at 10 A.M. every Monday, Wednesday and Friday to "Bartroni."

Later I will share some recruiting command sea stories about sales experiences, but I learned early that there was always a way to close the sale. I was struggling in Italian until one day at the Midshipmen Book Store I came across a Catholic calendar. Being the only Protestant in the class I was unaware that every day was a "Saint Somebody Day." I invested three dollars in the calendar and took it back to my room. Those three dollars got me an "A" in Italian the next five semesters.

Our professor was an exchange officer from the Italian Navy. Comandante Cordaro was a devout Catholic. And he loved to share his knowledge of the church with whomever would listen. For the next couple of years whenever I had not found the time to translate the assigned pages from Dante's *Inferno* prior to class, I would steer the conversation to the Comandante's favorite topic.

"Mr. Bartroni, you look puzzled. What is the matter?"

"Gee, Comandante, I am confused. I noticed that today is Saint Ignatius day and I don't remember why he is celebrated?"

"Oh! I clear that up for you!" and then he would spend the next 35 minutes of the class relating the history of Saint Ignatius and how it fit in with the acts of other saints. My classmates knew immediately what I was doing and would sit there and listen with one eye on the clock.

Since the Catholics celebrate many, many saints I was able to do this many, many times. In fact, on one occasion some months later, Rick Borro actually kicked me under the table because he really wanted to improve his Italian!

I remember one day after one of my inquiries about saints, the Comandante hit his forehead with the palm of his hand and blurted out, "Mr. Bartroni is a Protestant and yet he is the best Catholic among you!"

Half way through the final semester, even Comandante Cordaro caught on. I was walking in a hallway in Mahan Hall where the professors' offices were located when Comandante Cordaro stepped out of his office and we made eye contact. He stopped me and asked, "Mr. Bartroni, I do not think an 'A' would hurt you? No?"

It took me a second to reconstruct his question in my head—his English required that little mental drill at times. I finally answered, "No, Comandante, an 'A' would not hurt me."

"But I give you 'B' because you are *lazy* and *shiftless*!" he snapped and then he walked on.

I stood there and smiled. It is hard to be angry at the truth.

He did give me a "B" for the midterm report, but he relented and gave an "A" for the final grade.

The 1.94 GPA did its motivational job and reprioritized my efforts. At the end of my first semester I had a 2.78 GPA and had mastered the study techniques needed to graduate.

*****

After surviving plebe year and getting a solid handle on the academics during youngster year, other areas of interest surfaced. One was the transition to an "upperclassman."

At the end of my short summer leave period between Youngster year and the start of Second Class year, I went to the civilian barber at home and had him give me a "high and tight" Marine style haircut. The next day I reported along with 3,000 others as the Brigade reformed at Annapolis.

I assumed a deep scowl and walked totally erect with my heals clicking on the tile as I marched the halls like one ticked-off Marine. I wanted the plebes to fear me and never realize that I was a human being. I would lock them in a mean stare and give a faint growl of disapproval whenever I passed a plebe.

It was actually quite effective. I once caught my own reflection in a hallway window and it scared me—and I'm fearless!

However, my rough, tough, no-nonsense facade was not supported by my classmates. During one of the first meals in the Mess Hall I was deep into my act, sullen and sending out mean-as-a-stepped-on-snake vibrations, when I asked a plebe to pass the salt. But the plebe was totally overwhelmed by the noise and activity of the Brigade being back, with all 4,200 eating and talking at the same time. The plebe failed to respond to my request and since his sole job for this meal was to ensure all my wants and needs were met, his inaction was totally unacceptable. So I asked for the salt once again, this time in a louder voice. The plebe remained frozen and lost in what we called a "clutch." I actually asked a third time and even used the word "please" in my request. The plebes at the far end of the table had heard my request and promptly passed the salt and pepper down the line and the classmate next to the plebe who had the "second class duty" was hitting the arm of his buddy trying to get him to take the shakers. But the plebe just sat there mesmerized by the surroundings and totally unresponsive to his simple tasking.

It was time for me to make an unforgettable impression on this plebe and his classmates. I jumped to my feet, ramming my chair back four inches and then I leaped onto the chair and shouted at the top of my voice, "What do I need? A special request chit approved by the Commandant to get some salt?"

All conversation at the surrounding tables stopped for an instant and in that fleeting moment of silence I shouted, "Pull your head out and give me the salt!"

Before the plebe could respond, the silence was broken by my classmates in my company. They yelled at me, "Sit down, Bart! We're trying to eat here! Get your own friggin' salt if you want it!" And all these comments were accompanied by rolling laughter from others in my company. It seems as hard as I tried to appear the hard-nose, Cap Parlier Marine wantabe, they saw through my thin acting skills.

But I had a tough reputation with the new plebe class...for maybe one day.

If you had a sense of humor and perspective about the challenges at the Academy then I was not the upperclassman you would fear in 31st Company. I played with the plebes, but the emphasis in my interactions was not necessarily education as it was fun. If you did not see the humor in the act, then I had no time for you.

A classic example was when I burned a plebe at the stake. His crime was not displaying a positive Christmas spirit. It was early December, 1971 and this plebe came chopping down the shaft on 6-1. It was the hallway where I lived and it was after evening meal but before study hour. The plebe was not from our Company and had obviously wandered into our spaces by mistake. Any plebe with an ounce of sense would have immediately recognized his error and reversed course and cleared datum (distanced himself from the area.) But this plebe was just standing in the narrow hallway in front of my room's open door. I took notice of him.

"You lost plebe? What are you doing in my shaft?"

"No, sir, I'm not lost. I just don't where I am for sure," he responded in typical sea lawyer logic.

Nothing I detest more than a sea lawyer, so I shouted, "Up against the bulkhead, plebe! And brace up!"

He hesitated and this ticked me off a little, so I stepped outside of my room and locked him in a glaring stare.

"You have the Christmas spirit, plebe?" I inquired.

"Yes, sir" came the tentative reply.

"Then how about a little caroling since you trespassed in my shaft? Let's hear Little Town of Bethlehem."

"Aye, aye, sir," he said and then tried to sing the carol only to falter on the fourth word, so I interrupted his feeble attempt.

"You know what an honor offense is, mister? I sure hope you weren't lying to me when you said you had the Christmas spirit, because that lame attempt at caroling makes me doubt you were telling the truth."

He stood there in silence, totally confused about how to select a correct response to my attitude. He had yet to learn that there is no correct response when an upperclassman was just playing with you.

"You stay here. I'll be right back," I ordered as I returned to my room. I came back with my can of lighter fluid we used to remove built-up shoe polish on our shoes and a small box of wooden matches.

"I think you are probably a pagan, plebe. And you know what we do to pagans in this neighborhood?"

He did not reply, but just remained at a brace against the bulkhead totally confused and wishing he had never turned down the 6-1 shaft.

I popped open the spray top of the lighter fluid can and proceeded to squirt a nice arc on the floor around his shoes. Once it was very wet, I sprayed a small squirt over the tops of his toes. He kept his "eyes in the boat"—staring straight ahead into space while he wondered what I was doing down around his shoes. Once I was satisfied that the fluid was appropriately placed, I stood up and showed him the matches.

As I lit one match, I said, "Around here we burn pagans at the stake." I dropped to my knee and moved the match closer to the flammable liquid, saying, "I wouldn't move if I were you or there could be some pain attached to this."

As I lit the lighter fluid and small blue flames grew to a couple of inches, my classmates started to take notice of my fun in the hallway. They did not need any explanation of what was happening...Bob was playing with a plebe again...nuff said.

Soon the lighter fluid had burned out and the plebe who was now sweating something awful, finally smiled at the creative harassment he had endured. Everyone in the hall had a good laugh; after all, burning a pagan at the stake wasn't done that often, even at the Naval Academy.

The episode ended when I got close to the plebe's ear and whispered, "Are you going to pay attention in the future and not get lost anymore?"

He nodded.

"Well, I doubt you will be coming back down this shaft anytime in the near future. Lesson learned; now carry on and return to your room for study hour."

He dropped his brace and rather than chop back to his room he was able to stroll because I had granted him "carry on" for the rest of this journey.

And I am willing to bet that he tells the story about the time he was burned at the stake to his grandkids.

*****

Sports were mandatory at the Academy. I had played Pop Warner and high school tackle football, but I weighed only 155 pounds so playing varsity football was out of the question. However during Youngster year I earned a varsity letter playing second string on the "150-pound football team." As only three sophomores made the traveling squad on that team, I was proud of making the team.

However, I was 20-years old and my body wanted to weigh 170 pounds on my six-foot frame. But I forced it to operate at 155 pounds in order to make weight each week.

I remember the extreme measure I chose at the end of my

first season on the team. I had made weight throughout the season the old fashioned way—starving myself and running in a plastic jogging suit to sweat off the last couple of pounds before the game weigh-in. But the last game of the season I had over three pounds to lose in less than two days. So I took the "modern" method. Big mistake.

Now remember I had not tasted anything sweet such as ice cream or chocolate in nearly four months. So when I opened the box of Exlax at the start of study hour the night before weigh-ins, I was craving anything sweet.

Did you know that those little squares of chocolate-flavored Exlax resemble little Hershey candy bar pieces? So, per the instructions on the box, I put two little squares in my mouth and then waited. But while I waited, the sweet taste seemed to radiate around my tongue and as I sat there reading a history book and waiting for the laxative to take effect, all I could do was think on how wonderful those squares had tasted. After twenty minutes I did not feel any need to use the head, and the taste was still in my mouth...so I took two more squares...and waited...and enjoyed the sweet after taste on my tongue...and after twenty more minutes with no reaction to the laxative, I convinced myself that I needed to taste two more squares. (This is why I know you should always believe it when you're told a sailor did something unbelievably stupid.)

I did not have to wait for an immediate reaction to the triple dose of laxative I had taken. I jumped from my desk and raced from my room, across the hall to the 6-1 head. This time I did not even attempt to make it down the line of stalls to my "favorite." I slammed open the first available stall door and barely got my trousers clear before I commenced a high altitude bombing run over the toilet. I arrived at this, my new home, at approximately 8 P.M. I did not leave the safety of that toilet seat for more than five minutes the rest of that night. The next morning I was able to drag my totally dehydrated body to class, but I remained for only the first ten minutes of each session before I excused myself and found the nearest head.

I made weight that afternoon.

I don't remember having a regular bowel movement for the next three months.

Sailors do stupid things.

*****

Midshipmen have been known to act like sailors on occasion. I remember the development and utilization of "flaming tennis ball cannons." By the assembly of steel cans with the tops and bottoms removed then duct taped together to form a four-foot long tube a rather creative plaything can be made. The end of the bottom can is retained and then shredded cotton balls soaked in lighter fluid are rammed into the bottom to act as wadding. A small hole is punched near the bottom and more lighter fluid is sprayed through it. A tennis ball, also soaked in lighter fluid, is rammed down the tube, providing a rather tight seal by its perfect fit. The cannon is then aimed at the selected target and a match is touched to the hole at the base. The compressed lighter fluid flashes and the tennis ball flies out the cannon end for a distance of fifteen to thirty feet. Of course, the fuzz on the exterior of the tennis ball is now aflame as well.

The tennis ball cannon was just one of several home-made weapons used in the inter-company wars we fought off and on over the years between our classmates who lived in the eighth wing and we in the company who lived in the sixth wing. The two wings were connected by an enclosed bridge that spanned the roadway that ran by the mess hall. I don't know how the wars started, but the battles provide fond memories of fun times in Bancroft Hall. Of course, these battles were always in the evening, long after the officers had gone to their homes.

One sight I will never forget is when a friend suffered collateral damage between two warring rooms.

Jim was a varsity wrestler and nearly competed in the Olympics after graduation. He would need to relax and, I guess, air himself out after being confined in wrestling tights all day. He made it a habit of wearing nothing but a half t-shirt and shower shoes for most of study hours. He lived down the 6-1 shaft and he would stop by the ice machine down by the mess hall on his way back from evening meal and bring a large stein full of ice to his room. Then after he got undressed and comfortable, he would shuffle down the shaft and buy a couple of cans of soda at the vending machine that had been moved from the basement to the first deck by our second class year. He would pop the tops on his soda then pour the contents over the ice in his giant stein.

One evening he was making his coke run dressed in nothing but his standard t-shirt and shower shoes when a battle heated up between the eighth and sixth wing classmates. Jim was caught in the crossfire with his hands full of soda and his hairy butt exposed. A flaming tennis ball hit his butt. I never laughed as hard as I did at the image of Jim trying not to spill his stein full of precious soda while simultaneously using his hands to slap out the fire burning all the hair off his butt. Of course he was hopping as he did it and he kept juggling the full stein from one hand to the other as he tried to put out the butt fire that had spread to both cheeks.

Ah....good times and great leadership training.

On another occasion I was introduced to another effective weapon used in these "wars"—the shaving cream can grenade. I was asleep about an hour after taps. I heard our door fly open and then a pop and a high pitched whine as if the air was being expelled from a balloon. Then I heard my roommate, Mike, shout, "We've been hit!"

When he turned the light on, the entire room, including my sheets and face, were covered with shaving cream. Our classmates across the hall had taken a nearly full can of "Foamy," shook it up to build maximum internal pressure and then used a metal beer can opener (aka a "church key) and the rim around the bottom of the can to puncture it. The key in using a shaving cream can grenade is the same as using a live, war reserve grenade. You want to get it out of your hands as quickly as possible. So you point the bottom towards your mark and then pierce it quickly and toss it immediately. It will spin around and spread the shaving cream in a 360 degree arc until all the pressure is relieved. So it behooves the assailant to toss the grenade and then immediately retreat to cover less the spray cover him as well. Our classmate in the room across the hall had waited until our lights were off and then kicked the door open and threw the grenade, ducking back to the safety behind the hall bulkhead as soon as it left his hand.

The war had resumed only this time the perpetrators were

our sixth wing classmates. A new phase of the war had begun.

After cleaning the shaving cream off our faces, Mike and I grabbed our cans of "Foamy" from the medicine cabinet and church key openers and crossed the hall to return fire. Our target was a three-man room and although only two of the tenants actually participated in the raid, the entire room would suffer the consequences.

So goes war.

We tried to slam open their door but in violation of regulations they had locked it. So our next thought was to throw a grenade through their window. We got into a company officer's office that was situated right next to our target's location. I climbed out on the four-inch wide ledge that ran along the exterior wall, about twenty feet above the ground below, only to discover they had locked their window as well.

Our next action was to break into the janitor's cleaning locker located in the head. There we found two plastic bottles of straight ammonia. We took the janitor's bucket and diluted the ammonia to a 50/50 mix with water. It was still exceedingly pungent as I sloshed the fluid under the door. While I did this, Mike positioned himself outside their window with grenade in hand. After only five minutes the fumes in the room were so intense that they had to open the window in an attempt to get fresh air. As soon as it was lifted six inches, it was POP! and SWOOSH! And their room was filled with a swirling shaving cream can. A successful counterattack!

*****

A key component in the education of a midshipman occurs during the summer. His first summer is the radical conversion from civilian to a military lifestyle. The second summer is when a mid goes to sea to learn the life of an enlisted member of the Navy. During "Youngster cruise" you have the opportunity to sleep in jammed berthing compartments, wait in excessively long lines for chow, stand enlisted watches in engineering spaces, the Combat Information Center and the bridge. You have a cruise book full of questions that you are supposed to find the answers to while on-board a big grey floating thing.

Our Youngster cruise was in the summer of 1970 when the Vietnam War was still being fought. Nearly half the class was assigned to two amphibious ships out of San Diego and the other half served aboard another two large amphibious ships out of Norfolk. My brother (and classmate) and I served aboard the USS Vancouver, a Landing Ship Dock (LSD) home ported in San Diego. We left California and transited the Pacific Ocean to have liberty in Yokosuka, Japan, then Hong Kong and then a quick stop at Da Nang, Vietnam to pick-up a group of Marines and their equipment.

Similar to my normal practice through plebe year, I managed to get in trouble and become about the only commissioned officer I met in my career who had a "Captain's Mast" on his record.

At Da Nang the mids were allowed to attend a picnic on China Beach. The refreshments available for the 600 mids were 300 cases of beer and ten cases of soda. It was a very hot afternoon and the soda disappeared very quickly, but there was no way the mids were going to drink a half case of beer each in a couple of hours. So at the end of the party, much beer was returned to the ship's storerooms and locked away, as all U.S. Navy vessels are "dry" and no alcohol consumption is permitted.

However, a couple of cases of beer ended up in an unused berthing compartment down in the bowels of the ship. The Vancouver was capable of transporting over a thousand Marines and even with the small detachment we picked up in Da Nang and the mids, there were many berthing compartments that were not in use. So some crew members thought it would be convenient and low-risk to stash beer in a compartment so they could refresh themselves on the long transit from Vietnam to Hawaii, our next port.

By this time in the cruise I had completed the required written questions and, like most of my classmates, I just wanted the time to pass quickly to end the training and commence our first long leave in over a year. The best way to have time whisk by was to sleep it away. I was getting nearly fourteen hours of sleep a day while at sea. Chow lines were long and slow and that took two hours of the day and watch standing took another eight hours, so the rest of the time I slept.

The ship's officers and the Academy staff officers onboard took a very dim view of this waste of time, but there were just too many mids to keep track of all of us. I found a nice secluded, dark, quiet, and comfortable spot to kill time. About six of my classmates and I would go down to the lowest level of troop berthing compartments and crack the escape shuttle hatch open and slide down the ladder to our "den." The compartment was obviously not on any normal inspection cycle by ship's company because there was trash strewn all over the deck in the largest open area near the main ladder to the space. There were old issues of *Stars and Stripes*, empty soda and beer cans, and cigarette butts extinguished on the deck. For the next week, I used a lower bunk in the far corner as my hiding place between chow lines and watch standing.

I was awakened from my unauthorized afternoon nap by the sound of a dogging wrench loosening the locks on the main hatch to the compartment. I was the slowest to react to this intrusion to the "den." My six classmates had scurried to the far corner and used the escape scuttle to get away. I was at the bottom of the ladder about to climb to the top and freedom when I heard the gruff voice of the ship's warrant officer order me to halt.

I was caught. An examination of the compartment by the warrant and master-at-arms uncovered a half-case of unopened beer in one of the lockers. It seems members of the crew had used this lair as well and were the ones responsible for the trash and empties that littered the space.

Then my real trouble began. I was accused of smuggling the beer back aboard after the China Beach party. I denied it much to the astonishment and anger of the salty old warrant. Next I was accused of an honor offense for lying about my innocence. This was serious business now. I could be kicked out of the Academy for sleeping during duty hours because I was assumed to be guilty of lying about smuggling the beer.

The threat of an honor violation "scared me and I'm fearless." My classmates and my reputation as a "teetotaler" came to my defense and the honor offense was dropped. Now I was given a choice on how the conduct offense would be handled. The Academy officers said I could either wait to have the offense judged when I returned to the Academy after summer training, or to go to Non-Judicial Punishment ("Captain's Mast") before the ship's captain immediately.

It did not take me long to decide my fate. At the Academy you could be placed on report for "intending to whistle at a woman"—you did not even have to whistle to get ten demerits! The thought of what kind of punishment I would receive from such a system had me picturing myself marching for another year. I would be better off standing before a regular Navy commanding officer on the charge of sleeping during working hours. And I figured, in the "fleet," standards of behavior for a sailor are not as absolute and strict as for a mid at the Naval Academy.

So that is how I ended up standing tall in front of Captain Brown on the USS Vancouver. He was a "Mustang" (prior enlisted) who was about to finish his thirty-plus years and had seen about everything a sailor could do. I got a lecture and then restricted to the ship until we returned to San Diego as well as extra duty that consisted of cleaning that hideaway compartment well enough to pass a white-glove inspection each day by the warrant officer.

I took my "B" grade for summer training and got real good on the business end of a floor buffer and at making restricted men's muster four times a day both at-sea and in-port.

So my very first visit to Hawaii was hampered by my restriction to the ship...but I still managed to see all of Oahu in a six hour period! The Command Duty Officer (CDO) noticed my attendance at restricted men's musters while we were in Pearl Harbor. Being the only midshipman among the crew's restricted men, I was rather easy to notice. We were scheduled to depart Hawaii and return to California on Monday. I had spent the whole port visit watching my classmates hit the beach while I remained aboard and waved to them from the ship's flight deck. The CDO took pity on the poor mid who was going to visit Hawaii and yet never leave the ship. He pulled me aside after the noon restricted men's muster and asked if I could be back by the 6 P.M. muster if I went ashore. I assured him I could.

You'd think that you couldn't see much of Hawaii in less than six hours, but if you know sailors then you know that is a challenge and not an obstacle.

My brother was 21 years old and back then that was old

enough to rent a car. He had a car and along with a couple of classmates we completed a clockwise tour of Oahu from Pearl Harbor, through the pineapple fields, swam at Waimea Bay on the north shore and hiked to Waimea Falls, stared out from the Pali Lookout and absorbed a lot of eye-ball liberty on Waikiki Beach as I ate my fresh pineapple purchased earlier. It was a great liberty thanks to my brother!

*****

Rules at the Academy were not really that hard to follow...if you cared to. And I was a real "straight arrow" six days a week. I would never go over the wall for "French liberty"...I'd fold my laundry within 24 hours of its return, and all my socks would have "happy faces" if you inspected my locker...I never was late to class...I never disrespected my seniors...in short, I followed the letter and spirit of the "laws" all week long.

Except for many Sunday mornings.

Attendance at chapel was mandatory for all midshipmen every Sunday. You had your choice of the Protestant or Catholic services at the beautiful Chapel or Jewish services on campus. The justification for mandatory chapel was that, per the mission of the Academy we were supposed to be mentally, physically and *morally* prepared to serve our country. Chapel was a key element in our moral preparation. If you were not religious, the chain-of-command developed an alternative to attending a chapel service. You could choose to attend an ethics class on Sunday morning. So, a mid had the choice of sleeping in one day a week beyond the normal 6:15 A.M. reveille and attending chapel at 10 or 11 A.M. or presenting himself to a classroom at 6:30 AM for the ethics class instruction. Obviously, the separation of church and state was not a real concern for a mid if the choice was to sleep or not to sleep. No more than a very small handful ever attended the ethics training.

After plebe summer there was another option for church attendance. You could meet the mandatory chapel requirement by joining a church party that marched to a local denomination out in town. I was raised a Methodist, so I signed up to attend the local Methodist Church located on Church Circle in downtown

Annapolis. It was a ten minute march from the front gate in good weather and a brutal twenty minute trek through blowing snow and sleet in the winter. On more than one occasion the dozen mids would show up in formation only to discover the services had been cancelled due to terrible weather. That evidenced a lack of faith or a great deal of common sense by the civilians who were not mandated to attend.

It did not take long for me to learn church party etiquette at this very old Methodist congregation. Midshipmen were welcome because we made the best ushers you could imagine. After all, we were there every week in our own formal usher attire with high, stiff collars and two rows of shiny gold buttons down the front of our full dress uniforms. The inside of the church was a very old colonial design, with high backed pews on the main floor and a half-balcony that ran along three walls above the large windows. One Sunday I took a seat on the main floor and nearly caught my death of cold by the icy stares the other attendees shot my way. I quickly realized that midshipmen were expected to be fine decoration by sitting in the balcony away from other worshipers, required fixtures in this centuries-old church like the cross and pulpit and pews.

I also learned the tradition of the church party from the mid's perspective. The advantage of attending was it got you off campus one additional morning and made a plebe feel almost human for a short period. Additionally, it did not start until 10:40 A.M. so your morning was not as brutal as the regimented demands of attending chapel on campus. And then, there was the tradition unique to the Methodist Church party.

Every Sunday the Methodist Church party would assemble on the Fourth Wing terrace just outside of the Fourth Battalion office. The senior midshipman, usually one of the two First Class mids would call the roll and mark attendance on the "Church Boards." Attendance at formations was done by referring to a large piece of heavy stock cardboard six inches wide by eighteen inches long with the names of mandatory attendees listed on it. Once the attendance was complete and accurate, the senior church party member would give the order to "fall out and go down the steps and reform at the base of the ladder. I will turn in the muster board and possibly catch up with you as you march out to town."

Notice how this order was given. Nearly every time the senior member would go inside to the Battalion Office and turn in the muster board and then return to his room to have the rest of the morning free. He was careful to state in his order that he *might* catch up with the party and attend the service, but he had not given his word that he would. If he did say he would and then did not show up it would have been an honor offense.

Well, for nearly three years I broke formation and assembled at the base of the ladder with the other dozen and we marched out to Church Circle, rain or shine, heat or snow. But by the second semester of my junior year there was only one First Class member of the Methodist Church party, and sometimes he would have the duty or be on weekend liberty and that made me the senior man in the party! And one thing you are taught at the Academy is that tradition is very important. So one Sunday morning I took an accurate muster of all who fell into formation for the Methodist Church party and then I took the Muster Board into the Battalion Office and watched the Third Classman smartly march the squad across the parking lot towards the main gate as I strolled back to my room.

In our company the First Class let the Second Class have wardroom privileges on weekends. It really wasn't a "wardroom" as such, just one room with the bunks replaced by two rows of sofas facing a 25" television mounted on the wall. My plan that morning was to get out of my full dress and then see what my classmates might be watching on the tube.

My room was in the sixth wing and the T.V. room was at the end of the main hall in the eighth wing. When I entered my room my roommate was lounging on his bunk wearing his full dress blouse reading the paper. He had just returned from his early chapel services and hadn't changed his uniform yet. I quickly got out of my full dress and placed the blouse over my desk chair, slipped on some bell bottom white trousers, an athletic T-shirt and my clacks.

As I departed our room I stopped and turned to tell Mike something rather unusual, "Mike, you don't know where I am going right now. I am *not* telling you where I am going."

"You're weird, Bob. Just get out of here," and then he

shook his head and returned to reading the Sunday funnies. My stating something weird was not an unusual occurrence, so he just shrugged it off.

In the wardroom I joined five of my classmates as we watched sports and sipped cold sodas for a half-hour. Then Bill had to use the head and left the room only to return ten seconds later with panic in his eyes!

"The OOD has church muster boards in his hand and is checking rooms to find those who cut out of chapel!"

Immediately all six of us dove behind the sofas and hid. We remained in hiding until a voice cut through the silence and said, "Why am I hiding? I already went to early chapel this morning!"

"Then get up and peak down the hall and let us know if the OOD is coming here!"

He did and soon he reported, "Now's your chance! He just turned down the shaft!"

The eighth wing is shaped like an "H" and we were trapped in one corner of the letter, but when the OOD started down the cross hallway it gave us the opportunity to race down the hall to the center of the "H" where the stairs were located.

Now this was not my first time running from an OOD or upperclassmen who wanted to catch me and write me up. Earlier that year I was returning from an event in the Field House before it was dismissed and the OOD sent his "Mate' (the plebe on duty who was always one step to the right and one step behind the OOD) running after me and a classmate to get our names. After a brisk walk around the Eighth Wing corner pretending not to hear the shouting plebe who was closing us at a fast jog, we broke into a competitive sprint once we were out of sight. That plebe could run, but he became befuddled when we split up after getting inside the building.

Another time, as a plebe, I was part of a make-shift group of mids who had taken the spirit of a pep rally a little too far and we ended up outside the campus walls. We were being marched back to the Main Office by three First Classmen. Their intent was to have us placed on report. I was resigned to my fate when a Youngster who was positioned next to me tapped my hand and said, "There are only three of them. They can't come after us or the whole group will bolt!"

As we made the turn from the Main Gate to Captains' Row he took off running towards Dahlgren Hall. I hesitated only a short second and then joined him in the run for freedom. He had been right; the "guards" did not run after us less the whole group escape.

As we five cutters of mandatory chapel took our window of escape that Sunday morning the noise of our shower shoes echoed down the halls as we scrambled to make the stairs before the OOD retraced his steps. "CLACK–CLACK–CLACK–CLACK" It sounded like a herd of frightened water buffalos stampeding on a tiled floor. I was certain that this would prompt the OOD to quickly exit the shaft and catch us running for our lives. So I picked a door at random and entered a room. Sitting at the desk was a Youngster in our company studying an engineering text book. I quickly sat down across from him in the other desk chair and opened another text book. A set of stereo earphones were resting on the desk so I slipped those on as well to make it appear that I belonged in the room.

As a mid you learn not to question too much that happens. This Youngster looked up at me and then returned to his studies, not questioning for a second why I might be in his room pretending to belong there. After a short minute a thought occurred to me.

"Where is your roommate?" I asked.

"He's at chapel."

CRAP! That means the OOD will soon be here to ensure the roommate had not cut chapel! I had picked the wrong room to hide in!

I peeked down the hallway and then started a quick but casual walk to reach the stairs about twenty feet in front of me. Upon reaching the doors to the stairs I pushed them aside and immediately bounded up the steps, taking two at a time. I made my way to the third deck and then cautiously peered down the hallway and not seeing the OOD or his Mate, I went to the elevator which was normally off limits to mids. I got on the elevator and went to the mezzanine level which most officers did not know existed in the Eighth Wing. The back doors of the elevator opened and as I stepped out I pushed the button to send it to the basement. The mezzanine was only a small patio-like space that provided a way for the janitors to drop trash down into a dumpster below. I stayed there for ten minutes then re-boarded the elevator and rode to the first deck. The coast was clear. Once again I had successfully avoided being nabbed by the OOD.

I returned to my room and Mike related how the OOD had popped his head in looking to see if I was there instead of at chapel. Mike smiled as it relayed what happened. My proper prior planning had proven effective.

The OOD had stepped into the room and asked Mike, "Do you know where your roommate is?"

Mike had answered truthfully, "No, sir."

The OOD had then noticed my full dress blouse on my desk chair and Mike was wearing his so it was obvious that I was not at chapel, but he just smiled at Mike and left.

My silly insistence on telling Mike that he did not know where I'd gone meant his answer was not an honor offense. If the OOD had asked, "Is your roommate at chapel?" Mike would have had to acknowledge that I was not at chapel.

So another day of "cops and robbers" was completed that Sunday.

But Monday follows Sunday and the game started over again.

When I returned from Monday afternoon classes a message written in very large letters covered the entire chalkboards of the 31st Company area. The notice ordered five members of the company to report to the Company Officer. It seemed an urgent matter as this type of communication was highly unusual. As was my usual experience as a mid, my name was prominent on the list of those obviously in trouble.

I was completely in the dark about how I could be grouped with two of our leading classmates and a couple of other relatively "high greasers."

During the academic year there were three sets of midshipmen leaders who were in charge of the brigade. A new set was installed about every three months. There was one "six striper" (pronounced "stripe-er" and not to be confused with a bass or a lady who undresses near the San Diego Boot Camp) who was the brigade commander, then a handful of "five stripers" who held Regimental command or other senior positions within the Midshipman chain-of-command. There were more "four stripers" and even more "three stripers" who commanded battalions and companies. The lowest ranking first classmen were designated as "MIRs"—meaning "Man In Ranks." These midshipman officers and the regular commissioned officers on the staff would rank the underclassmen by professional competence each set. I had tried hard over my first three years at the Academy to be invisible. If no one knew you were there, then no one thought to pick on you. Consequently, I found myself in the bottom five of my 30 or so company classmates each set when the rankings were made. I was comfortable with that. This ranking was known as the "grease." I always had very low standing when the upperclassmen "greased" me and the Company Officer, not knowing me, simply relied on the first classmen's ratings. Everyone in the infamous "Five" ordered to report to the Company Officer on that Monday afternoon were high greasers compared to me.

By the time I walked from the sixth to the eighth wing where our Company Officer's office was located, I heard the rumors swirling around the company area. The midshipmen listed on the chalk board soon came to be known in our company as the "Chapel Five." Rumor was that a *classmate* had turned us in for missing chapel the day before. A classmate! That just wasn't done! Classmates stick together—you *never* bilge a classmate over a conduct offense! That was the ultimate bond of being classmates—short of murder or rape or theft or any other honor offense, you NEVER ratted out a *classmate*!

I was the last to report to Captain Matthews, USMC the 31st Company Officer. I waited my turn to be called into a closed door session. The first four each took about thirty seconds and then came out. Their interviews consisted of Captain Matthews saying he had reason to believe from a valid source that the mid had skipped chapel on Sunday and then the Marine asking if that was true. The other four answered, "Yes, sir." Matthews then asked, "Will you tell me why you did that?" Each mid answered, "No, sir." The interview was complete and the mid left and sent in the next in line.

I was the fifth and last to enter. Two hours later, my

interview was over.

It was the very first time my Company Officer had ever had a discussion with me, where there was honest give-and-take. I had nothing to lose—it wasn't like he could really lower my ranking more than it already was. So, I explained how I had a girlfriend in California, so I got good grades by devoting my time to study and had no where really to go on weekends. I tried to make this non-Academy grad understand what it was like to live 24/7 with the silly regulations imposed on all midshipmen and how some days you just need to set your own rules to maintain sanity. I tried to give him insight into the game of "cops and robbers" played by midshipmen, where today you might be the robber trying to get away with ignoring a regulation and tomorrow you might have the duty as a BOW-WOW and be required to catch robbers and put them on report. If you approached this situation with a balanced sense of humor and an understanding of what parts would be important to an officer and what parts were strictly apropos to Academy life, then life at the Academy could make sense. Without this humor or perspective, you could really go crazy.

Now, the next part of this true story I am a little hesitant to share, but after forty years have passed, what the heck? Why not!

During this extended interview, Captain Matthews offered me the chance to relax from standing at attention in front of his desk and have a seat on the government-issued fake leather sofa in his office. The springs were worn on it, so when I sat down, my knees were in my chin. I was in a position requiring me to look up at Captain Matthews as if he were behind a high judge's bench. Sitting to his left in a straight backed metal chair was our Midshipman Lieutenant Company Commander and to Matthews's right in another chair was my classmate, let's just refer to him as "Jack." Jack was the source of Captain Matthews's knowledge of our indiscretions on Sunday.

The conversation consisted of Captain Matthews asking questions about how a mid thought and my answering bluntly and truthfully. No one else participated in the conversation. My answers troubled the Marine and this led to more questions as he tried to warp his perspective to see my point of view. The biggest problem that bothered him was his perceived violations of the honor concept when we fell-out of chapel formations. I had trouble connecting his understanding of the honor concept to what we lived by. It took awhile for me to see that in his eyes, by our presence at the muster we were giving our word that we would attend the scheduled event. Once I was able to grasp his misunderstanding I was quick to give him evidence that falling out of formation was a conduct offense and not an honor offense.

I crawled out of that broken sofa and grabbed the "Cook Book" sitting on his desk. (It was the Conduct Manual, but since the vernacular for placing a mid on report was "to fry" him, the Manual became known as the "Cook Book," because it gave directions on how to "fry midshipmen.") I flipped through this thick tome and showed him that "Missing formation, but attending event was ten demerits" and "Making formation but missing event was a "Class A" offense and resulted in the awarding of at least 40 demerits."

I closed the book and in a rather forceful tone said, "See! It was a conduct offense, so give me my Class A and stop with this nonsense about an honor violation."

We got that issue settled in the first half-hour. But then he was concerned about the effect on company morale when it was learned that Jack had turned in his classmates. During the course of discussion on this topic I was asked if I personally had any hard feelings towards Jack for turning me in and getting me a Class A.

"Truthfully, no I do not, sir."

The Company Commander who understood the midshipman culture leaned forward with a greatly puzzled expression on his face. He looked at the Marine who then looked at me and asked, "Why not?"

Again, I answered truthfully. "Because my father taught me that you can't hold a crazy person responsible for things they do, and we all know that Jack is crazy."

Jack had been in Bethesda Naval Hospital the end of the previous semester for symptoms of a nervous breakdown. The pressure of the death of his father and of getting his first "B" in Chemistry after carrying a 4.0 GPA had made him crack. I had watched the corpsmen escort him out of the company area in a straight jacket between classes.

Jack just sat there with no response to my assessment of

his mental and emotional state, but the Company Commander had a hard time stifling a laugh.

That night, after evening meal and study hour, the Company Commander came to my room and asked me an unexpected question. He wanted to know if I would let Jack move into our room for the rest of the Academic year for the "good of the company." You see, Jack had turned in his own *roommate* who just happened to be a Brigade boxer and was exceedingly upset with our classmate. I agreed but with one condition, that Mike move out. I didn't see any reason to make Mike subject to the deal.

I lived to regret agreeing to this solution.

For the next two months God taught me patience, if not compassion. Having Jack as a roommate was an ordeal. He had "found God" while on drugs at Bethesda and that was why he felt we had to be punished so he had called the OOD to report our cutting chapel. When the OOD did not catch us he went to the Company Officer and reported our sins. But I had no problem with that—remember, in my judgment he was crazy already. However, I am a verbal person and it was torture not being able to make even a light comment to pass the day without being emotionally lectured on what was wrong with me and other midshipmen. One example:

"Wow, Jack! Did I just come from a boring class. I really had trouble staying awake in that snooze-fest."

"THAT'S THE PROBLEM WITH YOU GUYS! YOU HAVE THE CHANCE TO LEARN AND ALL YOU WANT TO DO IS SLEEP! THEY SHOULD KICK OUT GUYS WHO DO NOT TAKE ADVANTAGE OF THE EDUCATION HERE!" he shouted.

What I left out of this example was the use of eight four-letter words sprinkled in those short sentences. Jack had a religious awakening, but it sure did not affect his ability to curse. In fact, his speech was much dirtier after he came back from the hospital.

The end of this story illustrates the unique nature of life at the Academy.

About a week after Jack had become my roommate I was standing in the hall talking with my classmate, Marv. We were approached by a group of three Youngsters who said they had something to say to me and my classmates. It was close to mutiny for the underclassmen to assemble and elect classmates to voice an opinion about the upperclassmen, but apparently that was what had happened. These three Youngsters drew the short straws to come forward and speak for their classmates.

These representatives wanted to express their disappointment in the manner in which we took revenge on a classmate who had bilged his roommate and four others. We were dumbfounded by their attitude. After all, there are traditions on how to handle a disloyal classmate, such as hiding his dirty laundry bag on pick-up day then returning it on delivery day with his clothes still dirty; going down to the press shop and when no one was looking cutting off the sleeves and legs of his dress uniform; even blanket parties where the offending classmate is beaten; and the all-powerful shunning. But the Class of '73 did none of these traditional things. So Marv and I were confused by this delegation's comments.

"What you did to Jack was just cruel and uncalled for and we, the Class of '74 want you to know of our disappointment in what you're doing."

Marv replied, "What are you guys talking about? Nothing has been done to Jack, even though he deserves it."

"Don't tell us that! We know what you did, and we don't think it is right!"

It took a couple of minutes before we discovered what they were referring to...it seems they were convinced that we arranged for Jack to room with me so I could drive him totally insane! Marv was the first to pick up on their meaning and he nearly fell over from laughing so much.

Such was my reputation with the underclass mids.

*****

One result of the Chapel Five incident was that I was no longer invisible to my company officer. I went from being ranked in the bottom five to the top five in the company. This meant I was picked to be the company commander the next summer for plebe training and then act as company commander for the first set of our academic year.

It just goes to show that mothers do know their kids best. All my life, Mom told me that I had a habit of going into a situation dirty as sin, but coming out smelling like a rose.

The second month of plebe summer training is much different than the first month. The first set leaders were stuck teaching the plebes how to transition from being a civilian to becoming a midshipman—how to march, salute, wear the uniform, respond to questions, etc. Our job in the second set was to stress the plebes even more to teach even greater time management and solidify their cohesion as classmates. We on the second set detail were warned that the plebes we received from the first set would be so well trained that if we lined them up along the sea wall and shouted "jump," each of them would be in the water without any hesitation. We were warned to think before we spouted off some idiotic order, because these new sailors were so finely honed that it could spell trouble if we abused our new authority.

I discovered this was true.

It was during the company marching competition that I first encountered the power of "the voice." Now sailors are not known for their marching skills. No one travels to Washington D.C. to see the Navy's silent drill team perform—that is strictly a Marine skill or precision displayed by the Army at the Tomb of the Unknown Soldier. So watching three platoons of plebes going through drill practice was torture to a mid who spent many, many hours marching off extra duty tours. It was really a group gaggle when all three platoons formed into a mass company formation and were ordered through a series of movements. We had to endure this mass of non-precision each day as we prepared for the company drill competition.

The competition required the completion of an exact set of commands given in a required order. Like most companies, we had given the order list to the plebes and told them to memorize the drill, step-by-step. Unfortunately, if just one of the 100 plebes in the summer company forgot or skipped a step, it would foul-up the entire formation. I came to the conclusion that this must be corrected. So I gave my best Patton speech the day before the competition.

"Listen you idiots!" I bellowed as I strutted back and forth in front of the assembled company, "Stop trying to THINK! You can't do it. Why? Because we haven't trained you to think! You cannot remember the twenty-three steps in the precise order because it is beyond your feeble capacity! So don't think out there! It will only confuse your little minds and one of you will make a mistake and ruin it for the entire company. So stop anticipating the next order and just listen and respond to my orders. I WILL DO ALL THE THINKING FOR THIS COMPANY! AND I WILL NOT MAKE A MISTAKE! I GUARENTEE IT!"

Of course, while I am swaggering in front of the company, my classmates—the company platoon commanders and sub-commander are doubled over behind the company trying to stifle their laughter at my act.

So competition day arrives and I lead my company onto the parade ground. The first two steps in the required routine are simple enough: "halt" and "at close interval, dress right, dress." The grading started as soon as the company entered the designated area. The first step was to insure the drill would start with everyone in the right position. It called for all the plebes to snap their left hand to their left waist and then take proper interval between the mid next to them using the bent elbow as the correct distance.

The competition did not start so easily for our company.

My first order was "halt," and that went well. But the very next order I broke my guarantee and screwed up. I shouted (with great confidence in a truly inspiring command voice) "Dress right, dress!" Immediately the confused little obedient plebes started to slap each other as they tried to open their spacing to regular interval by fully extending their left arms to the side.

I had forgotten to say, "At close interval." And half of the plebes did exactly what I commanded and attempted to place three feet between them instead of the close interval of only fourteen inches. The other half, knowing the expected command to be "at close interval," tried to establish the shorter spacing.

Second command out of my mouth and the chance of doing well in the competition evaporated. So much for braggadocio.

*****

The lesson to watch what you say when in charge was learned another time on a less public scale. Mike McDonough was the plebe summer company sub-commander when I was company commander. One day we were walking by a three-man plebe room on the third deck of the first wing, which was our company area. We stopped in when the sloppy hospital corners on the bunk nearest the door caught our attention. The three plebes came to attention and Mike, who was a true blooded Marine even before graduation, berated the lousy bed making skills of the roommates. We were leaving when I opened my mouth and said something I regretted.

"If I come in here again and see your bed made so sloppily, I will throw it out your window and you can find something else to sleep on."

The day went on and after noon meal, Mike and I strolled past the same room when the plebes were out at a class. Sure enough, the bed was still not made to satisfactory standards. Crap! I had painted myself into a corner and there was only one way out.

Luckily the plebes' room faced "Goat Court," a small inner patio surrounded by the first wing. So Mike opened the window and we threw the offending plebe's mattress and bed linen out the window. It was fun, so we figured it was a teaching moment to emphasize how each plebe should support their classmate. We figured that if his two roommates could not take the time to assist their classmate in meeting standards, then they should lose their beds as well. So flying out of the fourth story window two more mattresses and accompanying linens went floating down to soft landings in Goat Court.

Mike and I then retired to the vacant room across the hall and waited the five minutes until the roommates returned from their training class. It was hard not to laugh loudly when we heard the roommates' conversation.

"Hey? Where's my bed?"

"Where's my bed?"

"What happened to all our beds?"

"You don't suppose he really..."

Mike and I then entered the room to see all three plebes

looking out of the window to the bottom of Goat Court.

"You pinheads have exactly fifteen minutes to retrieve your bedding and prepare this room for inspection!" Mike bellowed in his best Marine voice.

The look on their faces makes me laugh to this day. But I learned to think before I spoke to subordinates that day.

*****

The responsiveness of plebes after six weeks of training came in handy for Mike one Saturday afternoon. I had left campus on liberty that afternoon while Mike stayed behind in Bancroft Hall to "baby sit" the company plebes. Bancroft Hall houses up to 4,300 midshipmen, but during the summer only 1,200 plebes and another couple hundred upperclassmen undergoing training are present. This means there are many rooms vacant and whole decks of certain wings are empty. Mike was at his desk when the plebe Mate of the Deck (MOD) knocked and entered. Each occupied deck in a wing had one fourth classman staffing a desk in the hall to act as a messenger, answer the phone, and be a fire watch. The MOD wasn't sure he should report a rumor he heard, but he made the right decision and shared it with Mike.

"Sir, I heard that Midshipman Fourth Class Schmuckatelli was looking to end his plebe summer."

Mike responded casually without looking up from his *Sports Illustrated*, "Well, if he wants to bilge out have him report to me and I'll help him get the paperwork started."

"I heard he wasn't going to go through the paperwork, sir."

"He plans on going over the wall?"

"No, sir. I heard he was thinking of taking a dive into T-Court."

This got Mike's attention and he looked up and saw the MOD was serious. Mike ordered the plebe to follow him and they went upstairs to the vacant fourth deck looking for Schmuckatelli. On the top floor of Bancroft Hall there is a ledge nearly three feet wide that is accessible from room windows. Mike located the distressed plebe standing on the ledge and peering over the side.

From his location, if the plebe jumped he would land at the basement level, approximately five stories below.

Mike had an instantaneous choice to make on how to handle this situation. The normal option would be to talk gently to the plebe to relax him while the MOD ran for professional help. But Mike was going Corps and so he used a slightly different approach.

Mike barked orders to the well-trained plebe, "PLEBE! ATTENTION! Now come here immediately."

The plebe had no control over his conditioned response. He obeyed impulsively and without thinking. He came to attention and took two steps towards Mike's position in the nearest window. That was all the closer he had to come for Mike to reach out and clamp onto the young man and pull him into the window. Mike sat on him and sent the MOD to get the men in the white coats down in the Sixth Wing basement clinic.

When I got back from my short liberty, Mike was at his desk reading the *Sports Illustrated* again. When I asked if anything had happened while I was out, he replied by shaking his head, then he added, "Oh, yeah. Schmuckatelli bilged out this afternoon."

I had to get the rest of the story from the MOD.

Those future Marines knew how to maintain an even keel.

*****

A couple of weeks before the upperclassmen of the Brigade returned to start the new academic year, a late night meeting was called of all the company commanders in the room of the regimental commander. I remember we all squeezed into that two-man room and listened as our classmate showed his emotion over being ignored about a seemingly trivial matter. Earlier, during the evening meal, he had announced to the regiment that the bell used to call order in the mess hall had been "liberated" as part of a plebe prank. He had announced that the bell could be returned with amnesty granted to the high-spirited and light-fingered thieves, provided it was back in place by 10 P.M. Well, it was 10 P.M. when the commanders' meeting commenced and the bell was still missing.

I believe I remember the exact words used by the regimental commander at that short meeting. I do not believe he was personally mad at being ignored, but he was upset that the authority of his position had been challenged. He told us, "I want that bell back tonight. Find it." When another classmate asked what we were authorized to do to find the bell, the regimental commander responded, "Tear 'em up."

Okay, I spent my plebe year in 9th Company. We were still chopping during Dead Week before finals. Unlike the experience of some of my classmates who had reasonable, skilled leaders directing their Plebe year companies, we in the Ninth knew the darker side of leadership techniques. When I heard, "Tear 'em up," I knew exactly what to do.

From 10 P.M. until 10:45 P.M. the Class of '76 plebes in our company, for the first and only time that summer, experienced a very little taste of what my initial training had been three years prior. I watched as the platoon commanders proceeded to stray from the enlightened leadership of demanding performance to the ineffective, but memorable, techniques of humiliation and "playing with their minds, just 'cause we can" style of bossing.

It all started with the 120 plebes of our Company at a strict brace against the passageway bulkheads. Then each platoon commander tried to best the other two in "playing" with his charges. To this day I laugh out loud when I recall the diabolical technique of one who shall go un-named when he held a traditional "snow flake" drill in the hall. He sent his platoon back into their rooms and told them to return with all of their white socks and then he ordered them to throw all the socks into the air, and then kick them into a big pile in the middle of the passageway. Then he asked, "Are these all of your white socks?" Before any could answer, he added, "I see a great big pile of white uniform socks, but I don't see any athletic socks here."

Immediately, all of his plebes raced to their rooms and returned with all their athletic socks which were added to the pile.

Now came the diabolical part of his plan. Next he said, "Gentlemen, it looks like we might be up all night, so it is probably better that you change from your sleeping attire to a uniform. So, let's have an easy uniform race to see how fast you can get properly dressed. As soon as the clock on the wall clicks to the next minute, you beat feet for your rooms. I will call out as you go which uniform you will put on. And remember gentlemen, you will have exactly two minutes to be back against that bulkhead in a *complete* uniform or we will be here having fun all night."

On the next movement of the minute hand of the clock, the forty plebes in his platoon bolted for their rooms. As they vacated the hallway, the platoon commander bellowed, "Service Dress White! GO! GO!"

It took nearly five seconds before the first moan and expletive could be heard from each room. The plebes were in a predicament that I'm sure most faced many times in their future careers. They were in a no-win situation. All of their white socks were sitting in a pile in the middle of the hallway and without them, it was impossible to don a complete and proper set of whites. And they could not go back out in the hall until they had on the complete prescribed uniform and if they did have a complete uniform, then it would be confessing that they had disobeyed the first order to bring all white socks.

While this platoon was wrestling with the impossible, down the hall another group of forty plebes was having their own night to remember. Each had been sent to bring back proof that they had not lost one of their jock straps. As the laundry had been returned the day before and was not to be picked up for another couple of days, each plebe should have both his G.I.-issued jock straps in his possession, one clean one in his locker and one dirty one in his laundry bag. So I watched when they all returned and held a jock strap in each hand as they braced against the bulkhead. Then the platoon commander directed each plebe to pass one jock strap to the person on his right and to drop his remaining jock strap. Still totally confused, the plebes did as they were directed. Next the platoon commander decided that since all were holding a nice harness in their hands, then "greyhound races" would be a good thing to do.

The plebes formed three lines at the end of the hall and when directed, the first man would don his harness by putting his neighbor's (possibly dirty) jock strap over his face like a dog muzzle and get down on all fours. The second man in line would grab the first plebe's feet and then the pairs raced down the hall. At the end of the hall, they changed places and raced back. This gross relay went on until every plebe had been forced to wear his classmate's jock.

The remaining platoon was undergoing a quiz while the snowflake drill, uniform races, and greyhound relays were happening. The platoon commander wanted to know if any plebe could state, without any doubt, the exact number of shelving supports that were in his locker. Each shelf was adjustable by means of removable clip supports and so sometimes the clips were lost, making the answer much more difficult than a mere multiplication problem. Of course, the only proper response to a question that you could not answer with certainty was, "I'll find out, sir." So the platoon commander gave them permission to go find out. And he added as he dismissed them, "And I'd like you to bring all of your clips out here in the hall to show me how many you actually have. Everyone back here in one minute. GO!"

One minute later, forty plebes were standing at a brace against the hall bulkhead with a stack of metal shelving clips cradled in their hands or shirt tails. During the previous sixty seconds, every shelf in every locker had fallen to the bottom of the closet and all the very neatly folded clothes and other properly stored items were in total disarray, spilling out onto the deck in what appeared to be the results of a mini-tornado touching down in their inspection-ready rooms.

Of course, all the clips were next thrown into a giant pile in the middle of the hallway and the platoon commander proceeded to conduct uniform races that were hindered greatly by the plebes' inability to find the right clothes in the piles of confusion that had previously been their precisely organized, squared-away lockers.

Forty years have passed, and I have trouble remembering all the other "fun things" that were done with the plebes that night. But I do remember how the night ended. The Regimental Commander approached our company area across the enclosed bridge from the adjoining wing. I met him before he had a chance to enter completely.

"Hi, Gary. Any word on the bell yet?" I asked very innocently.

"No. I just came by to ensure that you have your plebes in bed now. The OOD is patrolling. He's looking for any plebe indoctrination violations. You didn't do any of that old school stuff did you, Bob?"

"Old school? What do you mean?" I responded to his question with another innocent question.

"You know, stuff like clip counts and things like that," the Regimental Commander said, his eyes growing wider as he looked over my shoulder.

Just then, two plebes were pushing dozens of locker clips with big brooms across the hallway where we were talking.

There was a long pause in our conversation as I thought about how to answer that question with what he had hoped to hear. Finally, I decided it was best if I just ignored it altogether.

"So, no word on where the bell is, huh Gary?" I asked.

"Bob, I figure the OOD will be coming through here in about five minutes. I would appreciate it if he left satisfied that the little plebes are safe and sound and tucked into their beds."

"No problem," I said over my shoulder as I turned and hustled to prep for the OOD's tour.

I remember Gary shaking his head as he turned and went back the way he came.

When the OOD came by a few minutes later, he strolled through our spaces and glanced through the open door of each room. He left confident that our Company had not participated in anything unusual before taps. All appeared to be secure, so he continued his rounds and entered the adjacent wing.

If he had stepped into any room he would have seen everything the plebes owned heaped in a big pile in and by the shower, out of the sight line from the hallway. Once it was clear, the platoon leaders and I pretended we did not see the flashlights scanning the plebes' rooms after taps as they worked through the night to have their rooms inspection ready before breakfast.

So what did I learn about leadership that evening? Well, one lesson I had learned earlier in the summer was reinforced. Don't say it, unless you really mean it. People have a tendency actually to take you at your word!

The second lesson I learned on the "Night of the Stolen Bell," was you have to trust those to whom you delegate. Gary did, and that was the right thing to do. And the third lesson I learned was that you must back up those same subordinates if they did what they thought you had directed. Gary did not attempt to "cover his own six" when he saw the plebes sweeping the clips. He did not turn into a screaming, "holier than thou" superior yelling, "How could you?" He did not try to "dump" on me for misinterpreting what he had said. Rather, he was loyal down the chain and asked only that I take whatever action was right and necessary to correct the problem as it was then—not worrying about what had happened previously to arrive at the current dilemma.

I watched Gary through the coming academic year and he never failed to impress me with his level-headed approach to tasks and his talent at inspiring those he led. He was made Brigade Commander and represented our class very well in that position.

Of course, my classmates know who I am describing in this sea story. The Plebe Summer Regimental Commander and academic year Brigade Commander was Gary Roughead. Later in my career and after I retired from the Navy I would hear of Gary being given command of a fleet, and then another fleet, and then becoming the highest admiral in the Navy, the Chief of Naval Operations. Each time I read of his promotions and his extremely important assignments, I felt good inside. I actually would go out of my way to share with shipmates and family how I felt about Gary's assignments, telling them, "The Navy did something right. The fleet is in good hands."

Yeah, it was forty years ago this summer, when Gary and I were both just 21-year old midshipmen, but I still remember the leadership lessons I was personally taught by the (future) CNO.

Oh, yeah...later it was discovered that the bell had been taken as a prank by members of the Class of 1974 who were undergoing second-class training that summer. Go figure.

*****

In addition to training plebes during the summer prior to the start of senior year, I also completed my First Class Cruise in the Mediterranean Sea. It was aboard a large amphibious cargo ship and rather than hundreds of mids aboard, there were only a dozen. On this cruise we worked as junior officers rather than enlisted. What you did and where you went on the cruise was purely luck-of-the-draw. I happened to be on a ship that spent two weeks in Naples and then steamed a couple of days to Barcelona where we were in port for another week then we cruised to Sardinia.

My favorite sea story from this cruise took place in Naples. The ship was anchored in the harbor and we rode the boats to the pier where you had to run the gauntlet of pick-pockets and shoe shine boy scams once ashore. I learned very quickly to carry nothing in my pockets but my government ID card and folding money in a clip with my left hand stuffed in my front pocket protecting it from rather aggressive children who forcibly tried to take whatever was in your pockets. No subtle attempt to lightly lift a wallet, these wharf rats just rushed you and rummaged your pockets. You were tempted to fight back, but the Italian police were in force and watched this happen, just waiting to grab an American sailor who might push back. The assault only lasted a few seconds and then you were clear of these pests. The next thing you had to do was to dodge the spit coming from bus passengers passing near the curb. Then when you made it across the busy street you were surrounded by three shoe shine boys all trying to get an American's business. You learned never to let them touch your shoes if they are working in front of a cobbler shop. In just a matter of seconds they could use a razor hidden under the shine rag to cut all the thread that held your sole to the body of your shoe. "Luckily" your shoe happened to fall apart right in front of his uncle's shoe repair shop!

I also learned you never ignore the "buddy rule" when on liberty. One evening my classmate and I were invited to the enlisted men's club to socialize with some of the crew. We agreed to stop in at the "Bluebird Club" which was located on a very narrow street near where the liberty boats landed.

The place was absolutely packed when we arrived. A rock band was completing a USO tour of dates around the Mediterranean and it was knocking out live and loud music which drew the big crowd. They were playing from a very narrow raised stage that was barely wide enough for the drummer to fit his instruments on one end. The entire club floor was packed with sailors and local dates crammed together around two dozen small round tables. It was so crowded that it was a real effort in logistics to move between the tables and boisterous sailors to make it to the crowded bar.

We spied our hosts from the navigation department and made it to their table which was located very near the end of the stage that held the drummer. As we made small talk I noticed that the drummer was surrounded by more than a half-dozen large empty beer bottles and there were two more balanced near his cymbals that he would chug from as the beat permitted. The drummer's eyes were rolling and he was having trouble staying upright on his stool, but he never missed a beat and kept pounding away on his drum set. A real rock-and-roll band traditionalist.

Then it happened. No more beer could make it down his throat, and what he had previously consumed erupted like a great volcano! He puked all over his snare drum and filled the rim and it just kept coming! But he never stopped banging on his drums and this splashed his vomit all over those sitting next to the stage. They immediately shouted and jumped up, which caused them to bump into the patrons behind them...who jumped up and rammed those next to them....and this daisy chain of angry sailors and dates started throwing bottles and fists. It instantaneously turned into a better bar fight than Hollywood had ever captured on film.

Being sober, my liberty buddy, John, and I quickly extracted ourselves from the melee and like many others trying to avoid the flying puke, beer and glasses we pushed our way to the only exit. Just as we were getting clear of the front door a squad of a dozen Shore Patrolmen, batons waving over their heads, waded into the little riot. John and I started down the narrow street towards the pier when we saw a platoon of Italian police racing up the street right towards us. Immediately we reversed course and ran the other direction.

After zigging and zagging through the narrow streets made narrower by the garbage piled everywhere (there was another garbage strike going on in Naples...I guess it is a common occurrence) John and I finally had cleared the area sufficiently to determine we could no longer hear the ruckus...and we were lost in the nearly black back streets of Naples. I remember the streets were paved with something like cobblestones because with each step we took a loud clacking echo bounced through the air.

We were making our way back towards the water when we came to an alley off to our right. Down the alley at about fifty yards was a small street light. Under that light was a very attractive woman of the night. She motioned for us to join her under the light. John was more than willing to investigate this invitation, but something just did not feel right to me so I said no. Well, John had stopped thinking with the head above his shoulders and said he was going down that alley. I told him he would do it on his own.

"Whatever," he replied and started down the slightly uphill, narrow alley.

I stood there totally conflicted. I knew going down into the dark was a stupid thing to do, but it was my duty as a "liberty buddy" to stick with him. I was debating if that "liberty buddy" stuff meant I should do something stupid. It was the old question your mom always put to you, "If Johnny told you to jump off the bridge, would you do that?"

My dilemma was solved just ten seconds later. John and the woman had walked up the alley and left the bright spot light made by that street lamp. I was still deciding if I should follow when I heard rapid clicks on the cobblestones and rushing into the light from the far side was John, and he was screaming, "RUN, BOB! RUN!"

It took a second for me to comprehend John's direction, but when I saw this large Italian man follow John into the spot light and glistening in his hand was a silver straight razor he was waving over his head...well, I hesitated no more!

John and I won the Naples summer sprint championships that evening and John followed the buddy system for the rest of his liberty excursions. I have proof that two scared midshipmen can out run any Italian thug.

And who said all those beer runs as a plebe were without benefit?

*****

Each year the reserve squadron stationed at NAS Alameda conducted "sleigh rides" for mids to get to the west coast and Hawaii for the Christmas leave period. A couple of C-118 aircraft would fly from Andrews AFB in Washington DC to Alameda the day our leave started. One of these C-118s would continue on to NAS Barbers Point in Hawaii so our classmates from the 50th state could afford to get home for Christmas as well. On the last day of our leave period, they would fly back to Andrews. Now the Navy C-118 was the military version of the DC-6B flown by airlines in the 1950s and each would carry about 65 passengers who sat facing backwards in the standard military flight manner. It was a lumbering old airliner propelled by four reciprocating engines that could pull it through the air at a cruise speed of only 170 knots. But it was sturdy and had very long legs. It might take ten or more hours flying west to cross America, but it could do it without refueling.

I had ridden these "sleigh rides" previously, so I was able to get my name on the list senior year and save the cost of an expensive airline ticket to California. Most of the mids on the manifest were plebes and youngsters with a small percentage being juniors and seniors. This last "free ride" from Andrews turned out to be rather exciting.

The weather in Washington DC in December was overcast and drizzly. The flight was scheduled to depart in the late afternoon, just before dark. I took an aisle seat over the port wing and settled in for a long flight. Next to me sat my classmate, Mike Carrigan who occupied the window seat. I knew Mike from our days on the Plebe fencing team and so it would be a pleasant ten-hour trip.

After takeoff we slowly climbed into the foul weather and turned to the west. We were airborne for maybe fifteen minutes when some mids on the right side of the airplane made a few excited comments about the number four engine stopping. The propeller had stopped and we all felt the plane make a gradual turn to reverse course. Obviously there was engine trouble and we were heading back to Andrews to make an instrument approach and landing in minimally acceptable weather conditions. Mike and I just shook our heads, because mechanical problems on the C-118 were nothing new for these "sleigh rides," but it was hard to complain when the only charge to fly home was $1.65 if you wanted to purchase a box lunch for the flight.

The flight became anything but normal when Mike and I spotted something that was really bad out our side window. A small river of oil was leaking across the wing from the cowling of the number two engine. Just a matter of minutes later, flames were shooting out of the cowling openings all around the engine. A couple of seconds later, fire retardant dust billowed from the cowling openings and the flames went out and the prop stopped.

Walking down the aisle came the LT(JG) reserve copilot. He stopped at my seat and bent over me to get a good look at the number two engine. As he did this, he said, "That should take care of it."

Just then the flames returned and started dancing through the cowling openings. The copilot immediately hustled back forward and entered the cockpit. While he was gone, some mids on the right side started a rumor that the other starboard engine had been shut down. This got our attention very quickly. Mike and I could count and we knew that at this gross weight, loaded with maximum passengers, baggage and fuel load, no C-118 could remain in the air for very long with only one operable engine.

I reached for my overcoat and put it on over my Service Dress Blues, and grabbed my hat. I wanted to be ready to exit this airplane at the first opportunity. Mike did the same.

A few seconds later we got the true gouge that only number four engine was out on the starboard wing. Another puff of extinguisher dust floated from the cowling of number two engine. The flames were knocked down again.

Again the copilot returned to lean over me to get a visual on the number two engine. This time he said, "The fire's out now."

He should have put that in the form of a question rather than a statement. Just as he looked out our window the flames returned and the oil on top of the wing caught fire, sending a giant flame down the length of the port side. The entire interior of the passenger compartment was illuminated for a couple of seconds.

I looked at the copilot and made a classic midshipman understatement of the situation, "I don't think the fire is out."

The copilot did not react with steely-eyed confidence that would settle our rising fears. I saw complete terror in his face and heard him mumble, "Uh-oh." Then he ran back to the cockpit.

For the next ten minutes we felt the plane yank and bank and drop from the sky. Mike and I tried to look forward through out window, but all we saw were blackness, clouds and rain drops. Soon we were low enough to descend through the bottom of the overcast, but all we saw were roads and trees and farmers' fields. Both of us just knew that the pilot was about to set this burning plane down anywhere he could. We got lower and lower and then we saw the threshold fence and taxi-ways and, just before the wheels touched down, the Andrews runway slid under our wing.

As we rolled out on the runway I saw something I never saw again in my life. As we slowed on the runway, running alongside the airplane was a fire truck spaying foam on our inboard port engine even before we had come to a complete stop.

When all motion finally stopped, the crew chief stood up and directed that the starboard aft door and over-the-wing hatches be opened and for everyone to immediately exit.

At this moment the standard midshipmen attitude kicked in for the passengers. Most of the mids stood up and started to find their belongings before they exited.

"Is that my overcoat?" "Hand me my hat," "Do you see my book bag?" and other shouts were heard as the mids were getting ready to deplane.

Except for Mike and me. We had our overcoats on, our hats on, and I was clutching my $1.65 box lunch before the main mounts even touched down. In fact, there were ten mids between us and the opposite over-the-wing hatch, yet the first one to emergency egress from that burning plane was Mike. I was right on his heels. To this day, I don't know how he got past me to get out first.

Just as I ducked my head to exit through the hatch, I heard the crew chief yell in exasperation over the reaction of the mids, "NOW I DON'T WANT TO PANIC YOU GUYS, BUT THIS BABY COULD BLOW AT ANY SECOND!"

Immediately, coats, hats and scarves flew into the air as all rushed for the exits.

Mike and I exited the wing using the lowered flaps as a slide. As soon as we hit the ground, we took off in a sprint. After thirty yards we stopped and turned around. We saw the fire trucks still pouring retardant on the number two engine. We looked at each other and shook our heads. We both had the same thought. We were still too close in the event this plane exploded. We turned and ran another thirty yards. At sixty yards from the burning plane we nodded to each other, satisfied we had put enough distance between us and the plane. I opened my box lunch and shared one of the cold fried chicken legs with my classmate. We stood there at a safe distance and munched on my box lunch and watched the show in front of us.

That is what first class midshipmen do.

The show was being put on by the underclassmen. As they each slid off the wing, they put their hand out and noticed the light rain falling. Rather than stand in the rain, they begin to huddle under the right wing. Not the smartest move when the left wing is on fire. But then, when we're only 19, all of us are "ten foot tall and bullet proof, and will live forever."

I believe Mike waited in the hangar along with nearly all of the other mids for the mechanics to fix the engines and the flight to be started again.

I drove to Friendship Airport in Baltimore and caught a stand-by seat to Sacramento on American Airlines. I had experienced enough Navy excitement for the day.

Chapter Two

Life on a Fast Frigate

First Lieutenant

The orders my classmates and I received coming out of the Boat School were late being generated. The Chief of Naval Personnel (CNP) came one Saturday morning to give a professional lecture to select midshipmen in the late spring. The "select midshipmen" consisted of underclassmen ordered to fill the seats and any first classmen who had the duty and couldn't find a way to avoid another talk by another admiral. The lecture was okay, but it got real interesting when the admiral opened the floor to questions upon its completion.

Midshipmen are truly the "spoiled and pampered pets of Uncle Sam" and a first classman in the back of the room raised his hand to fill the silence.

"Admiral," he asked "we had service selection night months ago and we graduate next month. When can I expect to see my orders to my new assignment?"

It was not exactly the type of question the CNP expected to receive. He was ready to continue to share insights on how to lead sailors and complete a successful career, which had been the subject of his speech. His facial expression revealed irritation at being asked such a specific question about one midshipman's trouble with his Bureau of Naval Personnel.

"Give my aide your name and he will look into the delay in your orders and get an answer for you. Are there any other questions?"

Two hands shot up from two more first classmen. The admiral nodded at one, a smile returning to his face at the eagerness of these mids to pick his brains about career suggestions.

"Admiral," another of my classmates asked, "When will I receive my orders?"

The admiral looked at his aide and then at the other mid with his hand raised and asked, "Do you have the same question?"

The mid nodded. The admiral's neck around the collar started to turn red and his change of complexion showed he was becoming quite irritated and embarrassed by these inquiries. After a second of thought, he asked the assembled group two questions.

"How many here are first classmen?" About twenty of us raised our hands in response. Then he asked, "How many of you haven't received your orders yet?"

All but the three going Nuclear Power raised our hands.

The Chief of Naval Personnel was professionally embarrassed that May Saturday morning. He left the lecture wearing a scowl that told me I did not want to be on his staff.

I don't know what he did upon returning to Washington D.C., but I wouldn't be surprised if members of his staff were called in over the weekend to attend to the needs of "Uncle Sam's pampered pets." The admiral was that embarrassed.

Less than a week later we all had orders. Over my career I had multiple sets of orders and all of them were multiple pages long—with one exception. Here, in its entirety, is what I was issued on May 9, 1973:

"Upon graduation and when directed proceed port in which USS Schofield (DEG3) may be, arrival report CO duty."

We waited months to get these complex orders? I guess they figured I was an Academy graduate and could find my own ship and arrange my own way to get there. Of course the most important line in the orders was one at the bottom that read: "ACCTG DATA." With the money authorization attached to the orders, all could be managed.

I wrote the Executive Officer (XO) of the ship and we arranged that I would take graduation leave of 30 days to get married and move to San Diego where the Schofield was home ported. So in July I checked aboard my first ship.

I look back on that time and shake my head when I remember what a raw, raw rookie I was. I was the embodiment of the "dumb ensign."

*****

The USS Schofield was 414 feet of "twisted steel and sex appeal." It was a very beautiful ship...but like many beauties, it could flatter much but deliver little. It was built to find submarines with active sonar, to shoot down incoming aircraft with a missile, and to bomb shore targets. And it could do all of these missions...with minimal effectiveness. Rather than build a dedicated anti-submarine warfare (ASW) or anti-aircraft (AA) or gun ship, America had built a class of frigates that could do all of these things (as my chief said) "half-assed" and not one thing really well.

We had the AN/SQS-26AXR active sonar on the bow. It was the "most powerful sonar in the world." It was designed to locate submarines in what is known as the Convergence Zone (CZ), a narrow swath of sea about thirty miles from the ship. However, there were two drawbacks to this detection system. First, it put enough noise in the water when it pinged in the active mode to tell submarines located 200 miles away exactly where we were. So if we were doing ASW escort duty for a carrier task force, we acted like a beacon to attract every submarine in the ocean. The second problem was even if we located a submarine in the narrow CZ we did not have a weapon that could reach it. Our Anti-Submarine Rocket (ASROC) launcher had a range of about five miles.

Our AA warfare weapon was a single Tartar missile launcher amidships. It was a very, very accurate weapon and quite deadly if we could somehow attract an enemy airplane to fly within seven miles of our ship. Its limited range made it very...limited. Quite sexy, but really nothing more than a "tease."

We had one five-inch gun on the fo'c'sle. The ship was designed to have the more modern 5"/54 gun, but due to labor troubles during the Schofield's construction, the old World War II 5"/38 was substituted. It was a very effective duel purpose (air and surface) gun and extremely reliable—mostly because nearly everything was done manually. It was a very personnel-intensive gun system. Of course, other frigates in the class had no missile and two guns, one forward and one amidships where our missile launcher was located. If I was a Marine ashore and called for gunfire support, I would have preferred the frigate off-shore to have two guns to hit the target with twice as much ordnance.

I came to understand the chief's assessment of the ship...it could do a lot of things half-assed but not one thing very well.

The first day onboard was a lot like "Induction Day" at the Academy. A lot of go here, see this guy, do that, etc. However, after lunch I was scheduled to meet the Commanding Officer (CO) for my "Welcome Aboard" one-on-one interview. It was this short interview that put me on an unexpected path of leadership training.

The captain asked about my major at school and then he said he had two junior officer vacancies and wished to know which I might prefer. He put it this way.

"I have the Sonar Maintenance Officer position where you would act as the *assistant* third division officer, "and then his voice grew more enthusiastic like a huckster on an info-commercial as he continued, "Or...I can make you the First Lieutenant and you would *command* a division of 45 sailors all by yourself! Which do you prefer?"

He knew just the right button to push. Coming from the Academy where we were indoctrinated in the belief that command was the ultimate objective of a naval officer, I immediately answered, "I want my own division, sir!"

"Great! That's settled then."

I returned to the wardroom where a half-dozen fellow officers had just completed a short meeting with the XO, who looked up and asked me what job the Captain had given me.

"I'm the new First Lieutenant, sir," I said with enthusiasm and pride.

As soon as the words crossed my lips I heard many guffaws emanating from my fellow, more senior officers. The XO hushed them and told me to report to his cabin in ten minutes and he departed the wardroom.

As soon as he left, a lieutenant junior grade ("J.G.") put his forefinger in his mouth and pulled it like a hook, indicating that the Captain had snagged a gullible fish.

The J.G. was right.

I reported to the XO's cabin and he invited me in. On his little secretary-type stateroom desk he had a stack of naval tactical and technical publications that was nearly two feet high. He slid the pile an inch towards me and said, "This is your job. Go learn it."

I took the books to my stateroom and got on with the job.

Normally, during a three-year tour on a ship a junior officer might have two or three primary duties, often in two separate departments. He might work a year in the weapons department and another year or so in engineering or operations. Knowing this, I was a little shocked to learn that I would be the *sixth* First Lieutenant on the ship over the last *two* years. It seems that one had been normally rotated, two had been "relieved for cause" (i.e. politely fired and moved to another position), one had developed ulcers and been transferred for medical reasons, and the current First Lieutenant was a warrant officer filing in until a new ensign would report and be thrown in the fire.

"Welcome aboard, Ensign Bartron!"

When I checked aboard, the ship was being retrofitted with a retractable hangar and a slightly larger landing deck to accommodate the addition of a Light Airborne Multi-Purpose System (LAMPS.) As a result, we were in port for the first few weeks of my time onboard. During this period I tried to affect a turnover with the warrant and assume duties as First Lieutenant. Every time I tried to sit down with him and review the division personnel, maintenance, and inventory records he would find something else to do and send me off to inventory the Boatswain's Locker (the first one done in years) or suggest I read some of the material the XO had given me.

After a week of learning my way around the ship, one morning I came to the wardroom as breakfast was finishing and everyone was sitting around the leather covered table reading message traffic and drinking coffee. I asked where the warrant was and again guffaws echoed down the table.

The joke was that the previous evening he had bet the duty officer that he could clear all of his stuff off the ship in less than five minutes. He won the bet by taking handfuls of his clothes and tossing them onto the pier. He packed his sea bag and a couple of boxes on the pier and departed the ship. Oh, it was a funny way to check-out, alright...but it left me with no kind of turnover to assume duties as the First Division Officer.

After breakfast, officers' call was held on the deck just outside the wardroom. While the entire crew went to quarters, the officers lined up in front of the XO and listened to his directions for the day. Then the officers broke out into departmental groups and listened to the day's orders from the department head. Then the division officers went to where their divisions were mustered for quarters to continue passing information and direction down the chain-of-command.

That last part of the morning shipboard ritual caused a slight problem for me. I had no idea where my division mustered. I knew the entire Weapons Department assembled on the fo'c'sle, so after dismissal by the department head, I faked re-tying my shoe to stall so the other two weapons division officers would reach the fo'c'sle before me. I assumed that the only division without an officer in front of it must be mine.

It worked. I pretended I knew what I was doing and quickly strode to the front of my rag-tag assembly of non-rated sailors (E-3, or seaman, and below.) I introduced myself to the Boatswain Chief and he announced to the sailors that I was their new division officer...for now.

That week I used most of what I had learned at the Academy in a matter of six days. The first direct order I gave, the seaman told me to shove it where "the sun don't shine." I had my first racial incident between crewmen, I attended my first "XO's screening" and "captain's mast" with my accused sailors, and I put in the first of many, many 80-hour work weeks. If I expected the "fleet" to be less stressful than the Academy that expectation was immediately put to rest. All of a sudden the intense schedule of the Academy...the six-days of classes each week, the mandatory sports in the afternoon, the 40 hours of study outside of the classroom, the marching, the twenty semester-hour academic loads, the full summers of training...all of that now made sense to me. Going to sea on a frigate was *hard work.*

*****

During our first underway period the weather was rough the first night. When I reported for the 20-24 bridge watch the wind was kicking the sea spray over the bow and onto the bridge windows. I had yet to adapt my stomach and brain to the rolling of the ocean and I felt queasy as I assumed the watch. As part of the Junior Officer of the Deck (JOOD) turnover with the only other ensign onboard, I volunteered that I wasn't feeling too well.

"Don't feel lonely," he said, "I've been puking my guts out all watch."

"What is the duty bridge wing?" I asked in order to know which side I should choose in case I had to throw my cookies overboard.

"Starboard," he answered and then he went below to get some rest and maybe sleep a few hours.

I managed to keep my uneasy stomach under control for the majority of the watch. But around 11:30 PM I lost control. Remembering the gouge that had been passed down, I rushed through the closed door that led to the starboard bridge wing. I reached the chest level side wall and immediately the entire contents of my stomach erupted and I pointed them over the side...only to have the wind throw them back right into my face. I had been tricked and told the windward side was the "duty seasick" side. But once my body had started, there was no stopping. The best I could do was to hurl and then quickly duck to avoid the returning puke, then hurl and duck and then hurl and duck. Eventually, I had nothing left in my stomach to come up.

My foul weather coat and face smelled terribly and the watch team wouldn't let me come in from the wet night by re-entering the enclosed bridge. Luckily, my relief showed early and it was only ten minutes before I could secure to my stateroom.

However, I did not go directly to my room. I stopped at the officer's head and took a quick shower to wash my face and hair. Then I did something that I had learned during the Academy Wing Wars...I got even.

I quietly opened the door to the stateroom of the other ensign and placed my stinky foul weather coat on his desk chair. Then I shut his door and found the switch to turn off the ventilation to his room. The next morning when he and his roommate awoke, the smell was enough to cause them to gag.

I almost regretted that his roommate had to suffer the prank...almost.

*****

Boatswain Chief Williams was my mentor the first year in the fleet. It was his last eight months before he retired with twenty years completed. He spent eighteen years of his career on sea duty and he shared with me that the worst two years of his service was when they gave him shore duty. Chief Williams was a sailor who knew what was expected of him when aboard a ship, but ashore it was frustrating for him. On a ship there is a rhythm to life. For the first half of your career you stand watch eight or more hours a day, plus put in another eight hours of work at your assigned job. The norm is a sixteen-hour day with maybe two hours of leisure time and six hours of interrupted sleep. The second half of your career you are senior enough to often times drop the watch standing duties and then be able to devote twelve hours a day to your primary job. Chief Williams had two primary jobs. The first was to organize and lead his division and the second was to train and manage his young division officer.

However, onboard the Schofield he had become bitter his last months in the Navy. As I look back, I am actually amazed that his attitude was as professional as it had been. Onboard this frigate the chain-of-command had failed him. He was a sailor of the "old school." As a very young man during the 1950s he had been a rabble-rouser, but his career progression had been initially enabled by more than one trip to the scullery in the middle of the night. The Chief said his Boatswain Chief "back in the day" would take a young sailor who thought he could scam the system by ignoring the commands of his senior petty officers to a midnight meeting with the "enforcer." The largest, meanest member of the division was given the special billet of being the chief's "enforcer." If you got out of line, the enforcer would grab you by the nape of the neck and drag you to the empty scullery and beat respect into your attitude under the watchful eye of the division chief.

Of course, under Admiral Zumwalt's "new Navy" this sort of traditional physical discipline was outlawed. And then there was "Project 100,000" instituted in the military in the 1960s by Secretary McNamara. Part of President Johnson's "Great Society," this program was sold as a "boot strap" opportunity to break the generations of poverty and hopelessness in America's slums. By loosening the enlistment (and draft) standards to include those young men who failed to pass the military entrance examinations and physical requirements two benefits could be gained. First, since the military is a powerful tool in forming pride, mission focus, and maturity in men, a whole generation of welfare dependents could be trained to become contributing members of society. Oh, yeah, this project also contributed one other benefit to the Johnson Administration. It provided a source of manpower to fight the Vietnam War while allowing the politicians to retain draft deferments for the suburban kids who enrolled in college.

Johnson's "whiz kids" in his administration never served in uniform and failed to grasp the essential purpose of having a standing Army and Navy. The military is there for the sole purpose of fighting and winning wars when called upon to do so. It is not a social program to advance the "Great Society."

This program was ended in 1971 and primarily effected the Army, however all services had learned to be flexible in administering enlistment standards over that period. When the "All-volunteer Force" was created by the elimination of the draft in 1972, the enlistment of "Category IVs" was an automatic waiver in all the service recruitment commands. There were five categories on the enlistment exam. If you showed for the exam and could get half your name right on the answer sheet, you were a Category V. If you could get your entire name right and scratch an answer in every blank on the testing sheet, then you scored as a Category IV. Now these exams were not perfect instruments of determining a young man's ability to serve his country well. It was especially difficult for non-English speakers and poor readers to achieve minimum standards. However, being able to make yourself understood in English and the ability to read instructions keeps you from being a burden on your shipmates.

There are many jobs in the Navy where you do not want a Phi Beta Kappa. A really intellectual sailor gets bored when shining the brass work or chipping paint, yet these duties must be performed and are no less important than operating nuclear reactors or fixing complicated electronics. All the jobs on a ship must be done to have an effective fighting vessel and that is why for centuries pay was never dependent on your assignment, but rather on your proven experience to do your assigned job well.

And a bored sailor gets into trouble, so you want members of your crew who find ship preservation a mental challenge at times.

In fact, Boatswain Chief Williams left school after completing the eighth grade, yet he had a very successful career and contributed substantially to his ships and shipmates. But that was in the "old Navy", when a rowdy young sailor could be made to tow the line by the "leadership tools" his chief had in the person of the "enforcer."

The Navy had changed from 1954 to 1973. The leadership, both civilian and military, had instituted new rules which left Chief Williams feeling powerless to control his rowdy sailors on the deck plates of a sea going frigate. On the Schofield two other factors had also contributed to the Chief's bitterness. They were the merry-go-round of division officers over the previous two years and the decision by the commanding officers to use First Division as the "laundry" outfit.

For a spell prior to my arrival, the attitude aboard was that if another division had a "problem child" infecting the performance of the team, he was threatened with reassignment to First Division. So when I assumed duties as First Lieutenant there were forty-five division members. It consisted of the chief, an alcoholic second class boatswain mate, two very junior third class petty officers and 41 non-rated sailors. Of these non-rated, some were designated strikers in ratings other than the deck force. They had screwed-up in the missile or engineering or ships' service divisions and then, despite their training, were sent to First Division to chip paint.

The attitude in the wardroom was, "If you have a problem child, send him to First Division where he could be straightened out. And once the sailor had seen the benefit of his home division and got his act together and became a contributing member of the crew, he could be pulled back to his rating area." In other words, my division was like the laundry. Send me your soiled sailors and I was to clean and press them and return them to you.

That process stopped the second week I was aboard. In fact, I changed it so the door only swung one way—the opposite way. If another division scouted a non-rated sailor in my division and thought he would make a good gunnersmate or mess specialist or engineman, then I was more than willing to transfer him to the new assignment. By striking for another rating a sailor could make petty officer and get a start to a good career. But every other division officer onboard realized I was serious about my rule of the door only swinging one way. If I sent a squared-away sailor to another division and their leadership failed to keep him squared away, I would not accept the screw-up back into First Division. It took more than one long and heated discussion with the Executive Officer to get him to agree with this policy.

The laundry division was closed. No more attitude of, "Well, we'll try the sailor out as an electrician striker and if he doesn't work out, we can always return him to First Division." And if the Bureau sent a screw-up to your division, then fix the leadership problem yourself—Bob was not going to accept your cast-offs any more.

I quickly determined that it was the chief and I against the world. The second class boatswain mate was sent off to alcohol rehab and the two BM3s were unable to influence their recent peers. However, at the end of the first week in my assignment I committed the egregious sin of ticking-off my chief...or so I thought.

It was 5:30 P.M. and the end of a very long day in port that had started poorly and gone quickly downhill for me. Every department head on the ship and the XO had taken a chunk of my hide for what they considered my shortcomings. Now I found myself standing on the catwalk outside the captain's in-port cabin waiting to get my butt chewed by the "ol' man."

As Chief Williams and I leaned against the life-line on the 0-2 level, he took a long drag on his ubiquitous cigarette and then started to lay into me.

"Now, Ensign, when you get in there with the captain you tell him this and you insist on that and take no heat from him...be a real officer and stand-up to him...don't be a weak Nellie—do this and do that."

Something welled up within me and before I knew the words were escaping my lips I heard myself interrupting the chief and saying, "Okay, that's enough! I gotta take it from all the department heads and the XO and the CO in there, but I don't have to get my butt chewed by you *chief,* so just put a sock in it! Okay?"

It went silent on that catwalk as we both altered our views to look out over the San Diego piers. Inside I was saying to myself, "Well, you really blew it now, Bob. The one thing they stressed at the Academy was to develop a good relationship with your first chief, and what did I do? I insulted him and put him in his place. I'm screwed now."

Chief Williams took another two long drags on his cigarette and then the captain's stateroom door opened and we were invited in.

I always remember the dynamic of that meeting, if not the exact words. The captain was sitting in his desk chair and I stood at attention about three feet from him. In between the captain and me was Boatswain Chief Williams pointing his finger in the CO's face and saying, "And captain you gotta do this and you gotta do that!" I stood behind my shield and kept nodding in agreement with the chief. Inside I was shouting, 'Yeah! Get him, Chief! Tear him a new one you old salt!"

We left that meeting, my butt still in tact, and we enjoyed a wonderful ensign-chief relationship until he retired a few months later. I don't know for sure, but I think Chief Williams was tired of ensigns who allowed themselves to be stepped on or something like that, because he took care of me as I learned how to serve at sea.

*****

In fact, Chief Williams really took care of his ensign when later in my first WESTPAC deployment the Schofield "crossed the line." Whenever a ship crosses the equator and travels into the southern hemisphere a "crossing the line" tradition was still observed in 1973. Once again, I found that some of the stupid experiences I had endured as a midshipman had actually prepared me well for fleet service.

There are two types of sailors in the Navy. There are trusty Shellbacks and slimy Pollywogs. Shellbacks had been initiated into the royal order of the deep; pollywogs had yet to be admitted to the Shellback community. Onboard the Schofield we observed this ancient maritime tradition with admirable gusto. On the day we crossed the equator the entire plan of the day was devoted to the scheduled initiation of Pollywogs.

I actually felt blessed to do this "ceremony" as an ensign. I would hate to have to do it as a more senior officer.

The day started with the Shellbacks of the crew, dressed in pirate attire, rousting the Pollywogs out of the rack and having them crawl to breakfast which was served on the mess decks. The "breakfast" consisted of cold spaghetti with sardines and hot sauce and cold oatmeal and anything else the cooks had lying around the galley. Of course, Pollywogs were not permitted the use of utensils or tables and chairs. We were to crawl through the chow line and be fed like dogs.

The uniform of the day for Pollywogs was Navy issue boxer shorts worn backwards, a white T-shirt and shower flip flops. Having been previously required to meet stupid demands such as the crew was enduring this day, I was quite comfortable with the initiation steps. In fact, I decided that it would be appropriate if I really got into the fun. So, starting at breakfast, I decided to enthusiastically accept the challenges the Shellbacks had designed for the initiation. I took my paper plate of disgusting food in my mouth and set it on the floor in the middle of the mess deck. I then attacked the food with growls and head bobs just as a mean, hungry dog would do. Then I growled at the sailors next to me who were pretending to eat but were hesitant about what was happening. I pushed the sailors out of the way and barked at them like a big dog stealing a Dachshund's food.

This little show made the Shellbacks laugh and they got a leash to keep me from attacking other "dogs."

The next part of the morning was the search for Davy Jones. Most of the Pollywogs were herded to the bow and told to scan the horizon for the "captain of the deep." Knowing what was going to happen next, Chief Williams took care of his ensign. He had me assigned to look-out duty high in the mack (our combination mast and stack.) There I put my hand against my forehead and pretended to scan the horizon looking for Davy Jones. What I really did was use my perfect perch to watch the Shellbacks break out the fire hoses and spray the Pollywogs as if they were Black freedom marchers in Alabama in 1963.

Eventually, I joined the Pollywogs on the fo'c'sle in time to make the trip down the starboard side enroute to the fantail helo deck. For this trip we were forced to crawl on our hands and knees along the very rough non-skid surfaced deck. About every fifteen feet a Shellback would yell for me to "assume the position" and I would raise my butt in the air. I had heard that command as a plebe when I had bet my ass and lost, so I was familiar with the drill. The Shellback would then raise his "shillelagh" which was a 30" length of 2 1/2" fire hose that had been wound with electrician's tape on one end to form a handle. Down his weapon would come to slap my behind. This was done the entire length of the starboard side as all of the Pollywogs crawled aft in single file.

Upon reaching the flight deck, we each had to pass through the "royal court" members. The first one was the "Royal Dentist" where you opened your mouth and he used a spray bottle to squirt down your throat the vilest tasting stuff the Shellbacks could create. Then you moved to kneel in front of King Neptune who would judge your sins. This meant you could be ordered to revisit the "conga line" of butt beaters or, as was more common, you had to kiss the baby's belly. Sitting next to King Neptune was the fattest sailor onboard with his bare belly rubbed in heavy axle grease. You were ordered to kiss his belly and as your face got close to him, he would grab both your ears and pull you into his greasy flesh. It was a good idea to take a deep breath before this happened as you never wanted to need air before he released you!

Then you would crawl over to be "washed in the blood." Now I have been to many church services where the preacher asked "Have you been washed in the blood?" I am pretty sure that I was the only one in the congregation that could say, "Yes! I've been washed in the blood...literally!"

As part of the initiation on the flight deck, the bottom half of an ASROC container was placed on the deck. The container was just a fiberglass shell about 30 inches high, 30 inches wide and nearly twelve feet long. At the beginning of the initiation it had been filled with fire fighting foam. The Pollywogs were to crawl into one end of the container and then submerge under the foam and swim to the other end. However, by the time it was my turn the form had returned to its natural state. Before ships were equipped with Aqueous Film-Forming Foam (AFFF) we were supplied with protein based foam extinguishers. This protein was often no more than whipped ox's blood. So when I crawled into the ASROC bath it was just a pool of ox blood. I got "washed in the blood" and came out the other end.

The next stop was the stocks. You stood up and put your head and hands in the stocks and then a Shellback slathered axle grease over your hair and face and then finished this "tar and feathering" by using the stuffing of a few pillows.

From the stocks I crawled over to the "garbage chute." The bottoms of two of the crew's very long divisional laundry bags were removed. The two bags were sewn together to form a sixteen foot long tunnel that a man could fit in. All the wet garbage from the galley had been saved for a couple of days and then thrown into the chute. I was ordered by a Shellback to enter one end of the chute and to crawl through the garbage to the other end. Being a well trained Naval Academy graduate I did so quickly and without any reservation.

As I came to within three feet of the opposite end my way was blocked by a Shellback's foot. Then we had the following conversation by shouting at each other.

"STOP! Who goes there?" the Shellback demanded.

"A slimy Pollywog," I answered with what had been drilled into us all day long.

"WHO GOES THERE?"

"A slimy Pollywog," I shouted again.

His foot remained in place and I was stuck. I couldn't go forward and there was no way I could back up.

"ONE MORE TIME, ENSIGN...*WHO* GOES THERE?" When I heard that a light finally went off in my head.

I shouted back with pride and anger, "A TRUSTY SHELLBACK—NOW LIFT YOUR STINKIN' FOOT AND LET ME PASS!"

Suddenly my way was no longer blocked and I exited the chute to the big smile of Chief Williams.

So in the Navy where there are two kinds of sailors...*I was now a loyal Shellback.*

*****

I went through four pairs of Corfam shoes that first year onboard. When the only leadership for the division was the chief and me, I spent hours and hours everyday, at sea and in port, walking the decks. The non-skid covering on the decks wore a silver dollar sized hole in the sole of my shoes right on the pivot point of my constant turning.

I had to learn my job, so I spent the few moments when I was not circling the deck checking on my working gangs, memorizing my duties required for the next deck division evolution on the Plan-of-the-Day. During our first at sea period that was my first underway refueling. I had memorized what was to happen as it was explained in the Naval Warfare Publication 50 (NWP-50), my Bible of deck evolution standards. As we pulled alongside the oiler, at night of course (everything is more challenging at night), I pulled Chief Williams around the corner from the refueling station onto the newly completed helicopter flight deck. Out of sight of the rest of the division, I started to go through the steps of what was about to happen. I shared my memory work about how the shot line would be passed between ships and the length of cord that would draw back a larger diameter line which was attached to an even larger size and so on until the main cable was brought aboard.

Before I could recite all that I had memorized, the chief was smiling very widely and then calmly said to the nervous ensign, "Mr. Bartron, don't worry about it. Just watch me. You're the safety officer on the station, so you are just expected to watch. If something goes wrong you will be the first to know—just listen to my screaming."

I will always remember that first of many, many underway replenishment evolutions. We slid alongside the oiler at about 65 feet spacing and then for the next forty-five minutes twenty sailors worked as a team to haul over the cable and then the five-inch refueling hose that rode on it. All of these people and these actions were confined to a very small space on the deck that measured maybe seven feet by twelve feet. Water came over the gunnels to make our footing very slippery and the life line had been removed to make way for the refueling hose to reach the bulkhead behind us. And it was night with poor lighting and we all wore bulky kapok life vests that made each man occupy a space twice that of normal. I was standing next to my two sound-powered phone talkers, one connected to the bridge and the other to the oiler via a phone line passed between ships. I was sure that at any minute I would be directing them to pass the "man overboard!" call to have the ships break away to look for a lost sailor who had been jostled over the side.

But the chief did not let that happen. He would anticipate a sailor's poor choice of location or foot placement and give positive direction before the sailor got in extremis and fell overboard. I was proving to be a very effective safety officer on the station. I had learned to keep quiet and watch the chief.

Some months later I got an insight into his sense of humor because of what occurred during a daylight refueling evolution.

We had been in Subic Bay in the Philippines and were scheduled to go out on an operation as an escort for the USS Oriskany, the oldest carrier in the fleet at that time. I had dinner with a couple of classmates at the officers' club the night before we got underway. During the dinner conversation they related how it was nearly impossible to refuel from the Oriskany because its STREAM refueling hose was improperly mounted on the cable. It meant that the probe they sent down the cable was at an awkward angle that prevented it from seating in the receiving bell onboard the frigate. They shared (quite angrily, by the way) how it took many attempts to get the probe to seat properly and that the carrier claimed it was always the frigate to blame for the problem.

I left that dinner forewarned and if I wasn't ready if a problem occurred when the Schofield was alongside the Oriskany, then it would be my own fault.

The next morning I met with the Main Propulsion Assistant, LT (jg) Jensen and we reviewed the NWPs and came up with an alternative way to refuel should it be impossible to use the standard STREAM probe method with the Oriskany. We read up on how to use the NATO refueling method. This required the receiving ship to unbolt the bell hose from the main refueling pipe and replace it with a NATO approved flange. Then the refueling ship would pass over a hose with a matching flange and quick disconnect weak link that would be bolted to the refueling pipe.

Of course, although the Schofield had been fitted with this flange years ago, it had never been used since the ship spent its service in the Pacific and far from any NATO navies. However, Jensen did a search of forgotten storerooms and found the flange and the bolts. They were cleaned and oiled and readied for use, and then prior to our first refueling evolution with the Oriskany they were positioned inside the helo hangar for quick access should they be needed.

As expected, we went alongside the Oriskany to refuel and it proved impossible to seat their probe. After nearly an hour alongside without receiving even one drop of fuel, the evolution devolved to a point where simultaneously I was asked by both my phone talkers the same question from two different sources.

"Ensign Bartron, the bridge wants to know what you suggest on how to fix this and complete the refueling?"

The ship-to-ship station phone talker told me the lieutenant commander First Lieutenant on the Oriskany had the exact same question.

I stood there with a sick smile on my face as I considered this rare and absurd situation. The captain of the frigate and the first lieutenant on the carrier both wanted to know how an ensign could solve this dilemma. Yeah...I was that important to the fleet...

I responded with a suggestion that had never been heard previously by these two Pacific Fleet officers. I recommended that we break away and re-rig to use the NATO coupling method to refuel.

The only response to my suggestion was by the announcement on the loud speakers of both ships that the Schofield was breaking away and to cease all refueling operations. So we sent the probe and cable back to the Oriskany and then the chief and I headed for the bridge to explain why there was a problem with the carrier's rigging.

The last line to be sent back in a breakaway is the bridge-to-bride phone line. Just as the chief and I arrived on the port bridge wing the captain was finishing his last conversation with the Oriskany's bridge personnel. In fact, later I came to realize that he had been listening to disparaging remarks about the Schofield from the admiral embarked on the carrier. The captain's tail feathers were smoking when he turned to face me. It was not a pleasant conversation for me.

"Captain, the problem is in their support rigging for the probe hose. They do not have a support at—"

That was as much as I could get out before his red face exploded and all his embarrassment spewed from him and he shouted at the closest target, me, "Look mister! Get off this bridge before I kick you off!"

This loud outburst caught me and the chief, the weapons officer and the XO who were standing behind me all off guard. What had the ensign done to deserve such a threat?

I came to attention, clicking my heels together and responded promptly, "Aye, aye, sir." It seemed the best of the five responses the Academy had engrained in my head.

Then I turned and slide down the steep ladder leading from the bridge wing to the main deck. As I did so, I noted the looks of shock and surprise on my department head and the XO. The chief just followed me down the ladder.

By the time I had reached the main deck, the shock was wearing off and I was becoming angry at the captain and the situation. As I ripped apart the knots tying my kapok life preserver I heard the chief laughing as he lit his first cigarette in an hour.

"What's so funny, Chief?" I wanted to know.

Between chuckles and pulling a long drag on his butt he was able to push out, "That's the difference! That is the difference between you Academy grads and other officers!"

"And just what is that, Chief?" I asked in an angry tone, not appreciating being laughed at in this particular circumstance.

"Oh," he replied as he continued to laugh, "You Academy grads sure know how to take an ass chewing."

"Thanks a lot. You make it sound like that is all we learned at the Academy."

"Pretty much."

I could see his point of view, but it didn't make me feel any better, so I stormed away saying, "I'm putting myself in hack. If anyone wants me I will be in my stateroom."

I had reached my stateroom and had just enough time to sling my life preserver on my rack when an announcement blared over the 1MC. Now normally an officer is called to the bridge by the Boatswain Mate of the Watch announcing over the ship's loud speaker system, "Mister Bartron, your presence is requested on the bridge." But that is not what the entire ship's crew and sailors topside on the carrier still within earshot heard.

The captain's distinctive voice blurted out, "BARTRON! LAY TO THE BRIDGE ON THE DOUBLE!"

Now even an ensign has his pride. So I casually strolled through the mess decks and passageways as I leisurely made my way to the bridge. Every sailor I passed gave me a look that he might share with a condemned man walking the "Green Mile." I kept this deliberate pace all the way to the last four steps leading from the Combat Information Center to the bridge. I made a loud display on these steps as if I were running and then I flung open the aft bridge door and breathed heavily as if out of breath from sprinting to see the captain.

Surprisingly, the captain had regained his calm demeanor and sat in his raised chair and asked me to explain what a NATO coupling refueling included. I gave a quick outline of how it worked.

Then he asked me, "How long to refit to use this method?"

Feeling cocky—after all I was an ensign and they can be quite cocky—I replied, "We can be ready to go alongside again in ten minutes, sir."

His only response was to note the time on his watch and say, "Now you have less than ten minutes."

"Aye, aye, sir," I said and turned around and walked slowly to the aft door. As soon as I shut the door behind me I am sure the entire bridge team could hear my running to the helo hangar.

Proper prior planning worked its magic that day. Nine minutes later I notified my bridge phone talker to report "ready to go alongside." Of course we were still a good quarter hour away from having the new flange completely installed, but I figured it would take quite a while for the Oriskany to find their NATO coupling gear and that would give us time to complete our installation. I was right. They didn't clear us to approach for another hour.

*****

For the first twelve months onboard I operated in a very intense leadership school. Of the 41 non-rated I had in my division, I personally did the paperwork to get the Navy to kick out a dozen—for "frequent and discreditable involvement with civil and military authority." In the early 1970s, it took four solid drug busts to get a sailor discharged as undesirable. This was before the "zero tolerance" policy instituted by the CNO in the mid-seventies. And even with the old standard, I was able to process a dozen in one year—that equates to 48 instances of catching them in the act of using drugs on the ship.

Yeah, I'd say we had a drug problem in the fleet back then.

One of the leaders in the drug culture was a seaman apprentice (SA) who came to us from the nuclear powered navy. Onboard submarines the "zero tolerance" policy had been in force since the early days of Admiral Rickover. In fact, SA Harold told me that he only mentioned to his division chief that he was *thinking* about trying marijuana and they kicked him out of submarines and sent him to the Navy's Drug Rehabilitation Program. They call it Drug Rehab, but for sailors who attend with the wrong attitude because they are forced to be there, I came to think of it as "Drug Postgraduate Training." SA Harold graduated with a very widespread knowledge of how to use hard drugs without being caught while onboard a ship.

Harold was different from nearly all the other seaman in my division. In the crew we actually had rocket scientists who operated and maintained our Tartar missile system and acoustic engineers that could bend sound in water to find submarines. But in first division, often derided with the term of "knuckle-dragging deck apes," Harold's Nuclear Navy intelligence made it easy for him to influence his shipmates in Compartment 106.

Harold had checked into my division during a very busy time in port as we prepared to get underway for a fleet exercise. I was unable to have my standard check-in one-on-one interview with him during his first week aboard.

I got to know him later that first week when rumors reached me that my division was on a "haircut strike." It did not take long to find the "brains" of this labor action. It seems that Harold had convinced most of the junior seamen that it was unfair that women in the Navy could wear their hair long if they kept it in a bun on their head during working hours, yet male sailors had to have short hair. So the sailors in my division were not going to get a haircut until the Navy changed the regulations to where male sailors could have the same length of hair as the females.

What SA Harold had not counted on was my Academy experience. For my last three years there our company officer was Captain R. R. Matthews, U. S. Marine Corps. While serving with him I picked up some practical attitudes about enforcing rules.

I went to the work party on the fo'c'sle and found SA Harold. I did not ask about the haircut strike or exchange any light banter with him. I identified myself as his division officer and ordered him to follow me. He must have thought we were going to my stateroom/office to conduct the check-in interview because he was totally surprised when I ushered him to the ship's small, one-chair barbershop.

Our ship's barber previously was assigned to First Division and I had helped him transfer to the Supply Department to work to become a Ship's Serviceman petty officer. He was now assigned as the ship's barber, despite having never gone to barber school or possessing any prior haircutting experience. He was definitely undergoing "on-the-job" training in the tonsorial arts.

SHSN Johnson greeted my entrance into the tiny barbershop with a large smile. He liked his new duties on the ship. They were a real step up from chipping paint and standing bridge watches. Johnson was just finishing his latest victim so I exercised my "head of the line" privileges with my former sailor. I ordered Harold to take a seat in the chair. He started to protest, but my tone and demeanor convinced him that the consequences of failing to follow this legal order by a superior would be worse than anything Johnson could do to his hair.

Fifteen minutes later Harold was back to work with the fo'c'sle gang with the worst haircut I had ever seen in my life. On one side of his head the hairline was a good two inches above his ear and on the other side it touched the top of his ear. The back was nearly shaved to the crown and the top was totally uneven. When his shipmates saw him and realized what was in store for members of First Division that failed to meet Navy haircut standards, the strike came to a quick end.

And Johnson's business in the ship's barbershop fell way off as most sailors opted to have their haircut out in town rather than be a practice dummy for an inexperienced barber.

*****

A few weeks later on one Sunday morning while in port in San Diego, SA Harold tried to test me again. On Sundays the duty section had a morning muster and then household chores were done prior to having the rest of the day free from non-urgent work details. On this particular Sunday, I had the duty and so Harold came to me after the muster and informed me that he could no longer work on "the Sabbath."

He said to me, "Mr. Bartron I recently had a religious experience and now my religion prohibits me from working on the Sabbath."

"You mean you cannot pull your own weight with sweeping and swapping the decks this morning?" I responded.

"I believe it is my Constitutional right to exercise my religion and it forbids me from doing labor today."

"Let me ask you this, Harold. If you take a dump today will you wipe your butt?"

He just looked at me with a confused expression.

"Well, doing sweepers on Sunday morning is the same thing. We have to keep the ship clean or it will rust out from underneath us. Don't you think you can do that on the Sabbath?"

"No, sir," he shared, "My religion is quite strict on this tenant. No labor on the Sabbath."

He had my interest so I continued the conversation. "I'm a pretty religious guy, Harold and I could refer you to many classic scholars who struggled with how a man of faith could still serve in the military. I am interested, what exactly is your church or faith or denomination?"

"Oh, sir, I am now a devout Seventh-day Adventist," he answered with an innocent and serious face.

I busted up laughing and told him to get to work. "Nice try, Harold, but next time you might do a little more research on the religion you profess. The Seventh-day Adventists observe the Sabbath on Saturday."

"Really? Oh...okay," he replied sheepishly as he went to get a broom and join his shipmates.

*****

I look back at my first couple of months aboard Schofield and refer to them as my "prune days." I would rise way before dawn and shower in my apartment in Chula Vista prior to my twenty minute commute to work. While I was in the shower I was safe like a babe in his mother's womb. Surrounded by hot water and secure in my privacy, it was a form of withdrawal from what I knew lay ahead during the long day. When I stepped from the shower, I had to start a day filled with confrontation and disappointment. This job was not what I had imagined when I was a senior at the Academy. I knew I would spend the entire day striding around the non-skid decks ensuring my little band of seaman kept at their assigned tasks and this routine would only be interrupted by department heads and the XO who demanded explanations of why their expectations were slow in being met.

Knowing what was in store for the rest of the day, I stayed in the security of that shower as long as possible...so long that when I stepped out, my fingertips looked like dried up prunes...hence, my "prune days."

This stress almost got the better of me one morning and ended my young career, save for the intervention of Chief Williams...

SA Jakeups shuffled to quarters late again and he failed to wear a cap and his boondockers were untied and his shirt tail not tucked in his trousers. I could see that this was like waving a red flag in front of a bull—the bull being the chief.

We dismissed the division from quarters and I was besieged by nearly half the men with request chits for special liberty to get out of work. By this time I had developed the "fastest signature in the west" and had a real talent at checking "denied," scribbling my name and handing it back to them. Yet, the slackers continued to rush me most mornings with their best excuses...like "my cat is sick and I gotta take it to the vet" or "my wife, she...(fill in any emergency here)" or "my car, it needs (fill in any emergency here.)" I have to admit that later, when I was Third Division officer I got a chit from a truly superior first class petty officer that read simply, "I don't have a cat and I don't have a wife and I don't have a car. I just want the day off." It was a pleasure checking "approved" and sending him on his special liberty.

As I signed the onslaught of chits, I watched the chief lead Jakeups around to the front of the gun mount, out of sight of everyone on the fo'c'sle. From the stiff body language and the way the chief was attacking his cigarette I sensed the "counseling" about to take place forward had the real possibility of going "old school" and getting physical.

I managed to reach the two sailors just as the chief's butt chewing was reaching a peak. The two were facing each other, about two feet apart when I approached and took a position that placed me facing that space between them. Jakeups just stood there, totally un-touched by the rage in the chief's voice and demeanor. That sailor just looked past the chief and chewed his gum with his mouth open. Just a half-minute after I arrived I noticed the chief's right hand fold into a clinched fist and his knuckles were turning white. As he brought that fist up to strike this slovenly sailor I caught his forearm with my left hand and prevented the chief from striking.

As if we were a well rehearsed team, we switched positions without saying a word, and now I was face-to-face with Jakeups. I started to express my displeasure in his performance as the chief watched and cooled down a little.

To this day I have no recollection of what Jakeups said to me, but I do remember what I was thinking. Inside of me, all the stress and tension I had been absorbing in this job bubbled to the front of my brain. I had only one thought and desire at this very instant. I wanted to punch this sailor in the face so hard that my fist wouldn't stop until it reached the back of his skull. He had gotten under my skin in a royal fashion. Before I realized it, all the anger and disappointment and frustration in my life became concentrated in the two square inches on the surface of the knuckles on my right hand. I raised my hand to hit Jakeups just as hard as I could. However, before I could get my arm higher than a couple of inches, a hand grasped my forearm and stopped me. This time it had been the chief's turn to keep Jakeups from getting what he truly deserved.

"Get out of here, sailor and turn to. There's too much to do today to spend any more time with you. Now scat!" Chief Williams directed.

Once alone, the chief and I went to the lifeline and looked out over the ships tied to the piers at the Naval Station. We both started to laugh and shook our heads. We recognized that we made a good team and had kept the other from getting in deep trouble.

We turned around and both happened to glance up at the very high bow of the USS Samuel Gompers, a destroyer tender tied inboard in our nest. Looking down on us, having interrupted his morning exercise routine was Rear Admiral Gravely, Commander Cruiser-Destroyer Group Two, and it appeared he had witnessed the entire confrontation with Jakeups. The chief and I recognized the only Black admiral in the fleet and since he was looking right at us, we both came to attention and saluted before we hurriedly left the fo'c'sle.

Thanks chief, you saved me again from another career ending move!

*****

I had "head of the line" privileges when it came to the weekly XO's Screening and Captain's Mast. Some division officers would go months and months without one of their sailors being placed on report, so their attendance at XO's screening and Captain's Mast was a rare occurrence. But with the majority of non-rated in the crew working in my division, I had to take time out of my work week every time screening or mast was held. So the XO insured I could get in and get out rapidly.

Funny thing is that, with one exception, I never resorted to placing my sailors on report. I could usually find a more creative way to get their attention. Yet, they would return late from liberty, or lip-off to petty officers in other divisions, or do something stupid ashore that would get them placed on report by others. So, I regularly found myself outside the XO's stateroom waiting to enter with one or more of my charges to hear the case against them. If the XO thought it was a viable case, then the sailor was referred to Captain's Mast which was held on the bridge while in port.

I was taught a lesson in loyalty down the chain-of-command when I did personally place one of my sailor's on report.

One Sunday evening while tied outboard of another frigate at one of the San Diego Naval Station piers we were ordered to shift berths. This was to be done "cold iron," meaning we would not have our steam turbines on line. Our electrical power would be supplied by our diesel generators and the duty section would man the lines as the tugs yanked us from our current berth and slid us to another one farther up the pier.

As the duty Weapons Officer, I was in charge of the line handling crews composed of sailors in the department. The amidships and stern lines would be handled by Second and Third Division personnel. My division would handle the forward lines.

Earlier, I had foolishly let one of my division sailors go ashore to take care of some personal business before this unexpected evolution was placed upon the ship's duty section. I had just enough men to handle the forward lines, but the

Command Duty Officer wanted me to supply a phone talker on the bridge. My solution was to take the phones from my talker and send him to the bridge, meaning I would supervise while wearing the headset. I directed SA Harold to hand me the headset and to report to the bridge.

For the next fifteen minutes everyone stood around, both on the Schofield and the tugboats while we waited for Harold to reach the bridge. If he had gone directly there it would have taken him less than a minute. For that quarter of an hour I had to listen to the Operations Officer who was the CDO nag me about how slovenly my sailors were and how the entire evolution was screwed up because my men could not do the job smartly.

Finally, Harold decided to end his aimless tour of his ship and he reported to the bridge. As soon as he got on the phone line I informed him that I was placing him on report for failure to carry out an order. He started to argue with me, but I cut him off and told him we would discuss the matter after the berth shift was completed.

It may have taken him fifteen minutes to travel from the fo'c'sle to the bridge at the start of the evolution, but he was able to reach me in less than thirty seconds when we secured from our stations. I remember how agitated he was and the exact conversation.

"What do you mean I'm on report?" he demanded.

"You failed to carry out my order and go directly to the bridge. You're on report."

"You can't do that! You told me to go to the bridge and I went there."

"Okay, you're right," I replied in a surprisingly controlled voice, "Then you are not on report for failure to carry out a direct order. You are on report for being slow in carrying out an order."

With that, Harold finally understood that the ensign had about enough of his attitude and poor performance.

What happened after this incident was the teaching moment for me.

Our XO permitted the division officer or department head to suggest what we thought might be an appropriate punishment for a sailor that transgressed enough to be placed on report. On the reverse of the report form were a series of blocks the CO could use to assign punishment. The XO let the junior officers and department heads the privilege of using a light pencil check in the boxes of the punishment we felt appropriate. In this case, I thought a $50 fine was about all the punishment that was needed, and I so indicated on the reverse of the report chit.

So I was surprised when the entire XO screening went as follows.

"Seaman Apprentice Harold, I see here that Ensign Bartron has placed you on report," the XO said without looking up from the report chit.

"Yes sir," Harold spoke up to defend himself, "but it wasn't fair—"

The XO cut him off in mid-sentence, "Shut-up Harold. I didn't ask to hear you say anything. The matter is referred to Captain's Mast. Now depart."

About an hour later mast was held on the bridge. It is a formal affair with saluting and proper military bearing by all present. A normal mast (and I had been to a lot on the ship!) would start with the Master at Arms reading the charge and then the captain asking the accused sailor to explain what happened. If there were conflicting stories then the petty officer or officer who had placed the sailor on report stated his side. Then the captain would ask the accused sailor's division chief and division officer what kind of contributor the accused was to the effectiveness of the division.

My first dozen mast cases I would usually expand on the very terse assessment Chief Williams gave of the accused sailor. Invariably, the chief would say something to the point such as, "He's a bum" or "He's a good shipmate" or "He's a scraper." However, after a couple of months of standing before the captain on behalf of my sailors, I had learned that the chief had really told the complete truth when asked, so my response was normally, "I concur with the chief." Just learning to say that was a big step in my professional development and to this day, ensigns should learn this lesson.

Knowing how captain's masts were conducted, as did Harold who had been before the "ol' man" previously, what happened next left an impression on me.

The only one who spoke at this mast was the captain, "I see here Ensign Bartron has placed you on report. Guilty. You are fined one-half month's pay for two months and restricted to the ship for thirty days. Dismissed."

Harold's jaw slacked and he was totally confused. An accomplished "sea lawyer" he was ready to plead his case before the captain, but the Master at Arms immediately directed him to replace his cover, salute the captain and march off the bridge. Chief Williams and I followed him to the port bridge wing as we exited.

That is when I heard the chief summarize what had happened in one sentence for the confused seaman apprentice, "I guess you learned: don't mess with the ensign."

*****

Chief Williams was not able to pick an enforcer to take wayward sailors to the scullery in the middle of the night and beat the fear of the chain-of-command into them. Yet he was still able to impress his very junior sailors.

We had one of our less than stellar sailors turn over a new leaf after he fell in love and got married. Seaman Fisk soon came to the conclusion that he could no longer remain a seaman and make enough money to support the family he wanted. So he went to the chief and asked for help in becoming a petty officer in the deck department. The chief had doubts that Fisk possessed any real leadership talent which was very necessary to be an effective boatswain mate. Many petty officers in other ratings are effective technicians and earn promotions based upon this book knowledge which is fine because a third class sonar tech is considered the workforce and no one really works for him. However, in first division, a third class boatswain mate can be responsible for the daily performance of a ten-man working party.

I always thought that Chief Williams might have seen a little bit of himself in Fisk. The chief had dropped out of school after finishing the eighth grade. This was before the military instituted the Armed Services Vocational Aptitude Battery (ASVAB) so being a healthy young man with a minimal criminal record, Chief Williams was allowed to enlist. His first few years in uniform were a time of maturing...to include multiple midnight visits to the scullery. Eventually he worked for a chief that saw through the youthful antics and got him on the path to success in the "old Navy." So when Fisk came to him and asked for help in making petty officer, Chief Williams was open to being a mentor...a hard-tasking mentor, but also a man willing to help the boy mature.

Fisk got to work on his practical factors (prac-facts) for third class boatswain mate. This was a list of proficiencies a sailor must evidence to be eligible for advancement. One of these required prac-facts was to demonstrate knowledge of how to rig and un-rig underway replenishment equipment. On our next underway period we came alongside a stores ship. On our fantail flight deck, hidden beneath cover plates was a large, foldable kingpost. Once it was tipped upright and secured by guy wires, it was about fifteen feet high. It was exceptionally sturdy because it had to support the cable between the stores ship and our vessel. Once alongside the supply ship, the cable was attached to the top of the kingpost and through a system of hydraulic rams the line was constantly held taut with great tension as the ships rocked back and forth. A pulley was attached to the cable with a hook underneath. Cargo pallets were netted and then slung from the hook. On each side of the pulley were two smaller wire cables known as the in-haul and out-haul ropes. The palleted supplies would be suspended under the main cable and then the out-haul wire would be pulled to transit the load to the receiving ship. Once over the right spot on our flight deck, the main line's tension would be slacked to lower the stores to the deck. Immediately the load was unhooked, then tension reapplied to the cable and the in-haul line activated to withdraw the pulley back to the supply ship. Dozens of sailors would descend on the pallets and before the next load could be rigged on the supply ship, the newly delivered stores would be moved into the hangar or below decks. It was an all-hands evolution to move the stores this rapidly.

Of course, boatswain mates were the sailors who climbed the kingpost to attach the main cable and scrambled on top of the newly delivered pallets to unhook the load. Fisk had to evidence he could complete these dangerous tasks prior to being recommended for promotion to BM3.

I was standing in the open helo hanger watching the evolution with fellow Weapons Department officers and a couple of chiefs from the "goat locker." Things went well and Fisk was getting his prac-facts signed off right up until the last step in the transfer evolution.

Fisk had to climb the kingpost one more time to unhook the main cable. It was obvious that he did not want to do this. It took a lot of nerve to climb up a very narrow ladder to reach the top of a tall pole as the ship rocked back and forth in the seas. I do not like heights, so I empathized with Fisk regarding the terror in his assignment. As we all stood about twenty feet from him, something dramatic and totally unexpected happened. When Fisk reached the top of the kingpost his shipmate gave the signal via hand paddle for the supply ship to give slack to the line. However, for some reason the sailor on the other ship got confused and actuated the hydraulic ram to give massive tension on the in-haul/out-haul line. The half-inch wire cable broke apart and the free end came whizzing through the fitting on the top of the kingpost and whipped across the helo deck of the Schofield. Luckily, most of the crew had already cleared the area and those few of us still there were all paying attention to the evolution. So when that deadly line came whizzing across the deck we all dove to our bellies in an attempt to save ourselves.

As I hit the metal deck I tried to make myself as flat as possible. When I felt a couple of shipmates land on top of me my only thought was, "Yes! More bodies please! Maybe enough bodies will slow down that killer cable so I can survive what is coming!"

In a matter of seconds the cable had whipped across the deck and over the side. Miraculously, no one on deck had been hit by it. When the bodies had climbed off of me I immediately looked to the top of the kingpost where Fisk had been when the accident happened. I expected to see his decapitated corpse hanging from his life line he had clipped to the pole. But when I looked to the kingpost my heart sank a little. Fisk was not there. We had forced him to go up there and do something he was afraid to do, and now he was gone.

I was feeling pretty low for a few seconds until I saw a terrified face peak out from the opposite side of the post. Fisk had no blood north of his shoulders—I have never seen a person with a whiter face and vacant, fear filled eyes. The cable had come within fractions of an inch of cutting off his head and that event was evident in his expression.

With shaky hands, Fisk unhooked his safety line and started to climb down the kingpost to a safer position.

That is when I witnessed the true depth of leadership in a sea-going senior petty officer. Chief Williams went to the base of the kingpost and shouted up to his seaman.

"Where do you think you're going, sailor? You haven't finished the job yet. Get back up there and disconnect the main cable."

Right then I realized that Fisk was more afraid of disappointing the chief than he was of the dangerous cables. He climbed back up the kingpost and successfully completed the job.

As a footnote let me share that Fisk did complete all his prac-facts and passed the written test for promotion and made petty officer. Yet, I can assure you he never climbed another kingpost that was still attached to a STREAM cable.

*****

Fisk had his prac-facts to complete for promotion, and I had my own. In order to qualify as Officer of the Deck (OOD), I had to learn the entire ship as well as gain ship handling experience.

During my time as First Lieutenant I was required to accomplish a rather steep learning curve. In addition to learning how to listen to my chief while not totally abdicating my responsibilities, I had to qualify as an OOD. This meant I physically traced all steam, electric, weapons, alarm and high pressure/low pressure air systems on the ship. While in port I would spend twelve hours a day trying to get my division's assigned spaces and work completed by constant supervision of my very junior sailors and then go home to see my new wife. While at sea, I would manage my division's work assignments, stand eight hours of bridge watches and then use every other free moment in fan rooms and other odd spaces tracing the systems of wires and pipes that ran through the ship. I would diagram what

I found which often did not match the ship's official class diagrams because of a twist in the building schedule for the Schofield. There was an extended strike in the shipyard when the three ships of this class were built on the West coast. When the strike was over after many years, parts and equipment were robbed from DEG-2 and DEG-3 to complete DEG-1 and then the systems in DEG-3 were robbed to finish DEG-2. The Schofield, DEG-3, was then fitted out with whatever the builder had lying around his shipyard. The plans and drawings of systems for the DEG-1 class of ship did not reflect this fact, so the only way for me to learn the ship was manually to follow the pipes and wires.

It took me nine months to gain a solid understanding of how the systems worked sufficiently to estimate where a problem might be causing a system to fail and to have sufficient knowledge to grasp how to bypass a failure should it occur in wartime. I put all my research of the systems and summaries of how to operate the detection equipment and weapons into a binder and submitted it through the chain-of-command to the CO as part of my OOD training program. That binder, along with actively seeking the chance to drive the ship whenever possible, got me designated as an OOD in record time onboard that ship. In less than nine-months I was standing OOD watches underway.

In order to accomplish this I had to demonstrate how to take the ship into port and that was a challenge because many other officers had been aboard longer than me and there was only one chance to do this with each at sea period. When I did get my chance, it was not much of an effort.

On our way home from my first Western Pacific deployment we stopped at Pearl Harbor. As I had but one more ship handling "prac-fact" to complete, I was given my chance to drive the ship to our berth. As it turned out, I got the "check in the box" for the evolution although there was no real ship handling involved. We boarded the pilot before entering the throat of the harbor and for the entire evolution I stood at the centerline compass mounted at the front of the bridge and the pilot stood at my left shoulder and the captain stood at my right shoulder. Once we made a turn prior to Ford Island it was a straight shot to our assigned berth at the refueling pier. The conversation on the bridge was almost comical.

I'd say to the pilot, "I think I will come left three degrees."

The pilot would nod and then I would look at the captain and he would nod. Then I'd announce to the bridge team, "Come left three degrees, steady new course zero-eight-two."

When we got closer I'd say, "I think I'll slow ten turns."

The pilot would nod and then captain would nod, then I would announce to the lee helmsman, "Drop ten turns."

If the pilot had a different suggestion he would whisper to me and I would check it with the captain and then implement the suggestion.

And that is how I completed my last ship handling requirement. Not much to draw on later when I had actually to maneuver the ship in tight quarters!

*****

I once made the effort to add up my sea time during my frigate tour. This was right after the end of the Vietnam War and the military was drastically reduced. In fact, the draw down for the Navy was rather substantial as most of the World War II combatant ships that had been kept in service to use on the gun line off the Vietnam coast were retired. Although the number of ships decommissioned during this time was high, the number of Navy commitments was not correspondedly reduced. The common phrase heard onboard ship was, "We have a three ocean commitment and only a one and one-half ocean Navy." This meant our deployment cycles did not decrease with the end of hostilities.

Like most frigates out of San Diego, the Schofield was practically "port and starboard" with the Western Pacific. A "normal" ship deployment cycle is one year operating out of your homeport and then six-months overseas. Like other San Diego based "small boys," we would spend eight months operating out of San Diego and then another 7 1/2 months overseas. This cycle combined with local operations and duty days resulted in my sleeping in my own bed with my new wife less than ten months during our first 2 1/2 years of marriage.

And I had it good compared to the ship's company on a carrier! Flat-tops were cycling with seven months out of San Diego and then nine months over seas.

This much sea time meant the ship was run hard. Our engineering plant was not the most reliable ever made. It was one of the first high pressure maritime steam plants and ran at 1,200 PSI rather than the normal 600 -750 PSI plants that propelled earlier ships. This increase in pressure meant minor leaks became major problems. In fact, the reliability of the plant was so suspect that around the piers we were sometimes denigrated by being referred to as "DIW-3" (Dead in the Water) vice DEG-3. One thing you learned to do in Deck Division was how to rig for towing.

On my first deployment we steamed around the Indian Ocean for nearly two months as one of only four American Navy ships there. We were supported by an oiler and patrolled with the USS Bainbridge, a nuclear powered cruiser. The only other American ship in what was then considered the back waters of the world was the USS LaSalle, dubbed "The Great White Ghost of the Arabian Coast" that steamed in a command ship role near the Red Sea and Arabian Gulf.

Our semi-reliable power plant quit on us one afternoon and we went DIW. The Bainbridge steamed to our rescue to tow us to a port. Luckily the Indian Ocean in the winter is calmer than a quiet lake. In the summer it can have the worst seas in the world with gigantic waves pummeling a ship from all sides. But our stay in the IO during this deployment was very calm and flat.

Out on the sunny fo'c'sle my division rigged for towing once again. We unhooked the anchor from its chain and rigged a heavy hawser to the end of it. The evolution would require the Bainbridge to pass slowly across our bow where we would fire a shot line to its fantail. The deck crew of the cruiser would then haul the hawser aboard and use the aft wench to bring the heavy chain up to their deck. Once sufficient anchor chain had been let out and securely attached to the towing ship, the cruiser's OOD would very slowly get underway, increasing the shaft RPMs just a few turns at a time to very slowly pull an additional length of the heavy anchor chain from our storage locker in the bow so that the appropriate spacing between the ships was established. Then we would secure the chain with pelican hooks before the towing ship increased to transit speed.

At least that was the method used by the other ship that had towed us previously. I should have known that the bridge handling team of the Bainbridge would not know how to do it properly. They had little experience in maneuvering in close proximity to ships at sea. All fossil fueled combatants and supply ships would steam alongside each other at least once every three or four days to facilitate refueling and store passing. But the Bainbridge did not accumulate this expertise since most of their stores were loaded via helicopter and they never went alongside to get fuel.

I should have known there would be a problem because a week prior we had participated in a naval gunfire exercise where live rounds were shot at a sled target towed behind the ship. The Bainbridge shot first as we towed the target. Then we were to pass the tow line to the cruiser who would tow it for our gun crew's turn to shoot. Three times the cruiser had attempted to take station abeam of us close enough to shoot a shot line and affect the tow line transfer. Each time they slid on past and could not settle into a good position. We finally told them to hold course and speed and despite towing a target, we adjusted our speed to come alongside her to affect the transfer.

On the Bainbridge's first pass to cross our stationary bow to commence the tow, they had to veer off at the last second to keep from ramming our pointy end. On the second pass they were so far in front that the shot line could not reach them. On the third attempt they got their course and speed right and came to a stop in a good position. We passed the shot line and their deck crew was able to wench over the end of the anchor chain and fasten it properly. So far, so good.

Then life got very exciting and dangerous on our fo'c'sle. Instead of very slowly and gently getting underway to pull the proper length of chain from our anchor tackle locker below decks, their OOD cranked on five knots vice five turns. The anchor chain came barreling out of our locker and jumped from the groves in the windless. It started to whip across the deck at high speed. If it hit anyone he would be minus his legs from the knees down in an instant.

The chief remained in position behind a small chariot-like metal protective wall and attempted to regain control of the chain by using the windless brake. I was standing behind the chief and a few feet aft of the opening to the chain locker. One of our sailors was forward and to the side of the windless watching the chain play out. However, when that massive chain jumped the windless and started whipping across the deck that sailor had to be quick to survive a deadly game of jump robe. It was noisy as the chain smacked against the steel deck and ran through the bull nose out of control. Our sailor barely made it to safety behind the ASROC launcher while the chief keep working the break wheel in an attempt to regain control of the runaway chain. I saw the danger and immediately turned and ran from the fo'c'sle to the weather break at the aft end of the bow.

Our bridge team was able to communicate to the Bainbridge to stop accelerating and the chain links fell back into the windless groves which gave the chief the ability to slow and then stop the chain.

I returned to the fo'c'sle and after the excitement was over the chief laughed as he asked me where I had run so quickly.

"Oh, I was going below decks to set the compressor to stop the chain," I answered with complete sincerity. The compressor was a contraption that would squeeze the chain as it ran from the locker to topside and was located a deck below the weather deck. All that study of shipboard systems paid off.

This made the chief laugh louder and I started to join him. We both knew that I had removed myself from the danger because I did not want my legs removed at the knees and there was nothing I could do to help.

As his laughter began to die down a little, Chief Williams said, "Well, I don't know about that, but Ensign, you are not only quick on your feet, but also quick with an excuse!"

As it turned out, our engineers were able to repair the power plant and the Bainbridge tow lasted only a short time.

*****

During our cruise in the IO we had only two liberty ports, the first one being four days swinging at anchor off the coast of

Bandar Abbas, Iran. The liberty in Iran was different than any other I experienced on the frigate.

As First Lieutenant I was assigned as the boat officer for the liberty boats we operated from the ship to the waterfront dock. The officers and chiefs used the Captain's Gig to be ferried back and forth from ship to shore. The rest of the crew had to wait their turns to ride the Motor Whale Boat. The liberty sections for the crew totaled about 145 sailors. It was nearly an hour round trip to the dock and about 30 sailors could be crammed into the boat. So it took nearly six hours of constant running to get the entire liberty parties ashore. As soon as the morning runs were done, then getting them all back to the ship by 11 PM meant we started shuttling the boat at 5 PM. And I rode that boat for every trip but one for the entire four day stay.

Being the ensign First Lieutenant meant you were given this kind of duty. "Oh, gee it was fun."

The unusual aspect of this liberty in Iran was that it was "old school" with regard to the wearing of uniforms. Admiral Zumwalt had granted civilian clothes privileges to all ranks when he became CNO, but in Iran the local politicos decided that all first class petty officers and below had to wear their dress white "Crackerjack" uniforms ashore.

I noticed on more than one occasion the impact this requirement had on the sailors in the boat. When everyone is in civilian clothes there is no obvious rank among the liberty party. If a junior sailor started to get out of hand and violate the accepted standards of behavior it was often times too easy for a senior petty officer to pretend he did not notice so he would not have to reprimand the kid. However, when a first or second class petty officer is sitting there with his "crow" (petty officer rating) very visible on his arm, it was harder to shirk the responsibility to exercise expected leadership over junior shipmates.

One example of many occurred during a shuttle trip from the dock to the ship around 9 PM on the second night in port. Despite Iran being a Muslim country where drinking alcohol was supposedly forbidden, our sailors still managed to locate some booze. One young seaman, (who surprisingly was not in my division!) had imbibed to excess and was quite verbal with his opinions. He specifically thought all officers—especially ensigns—were wastes of human tissue and if he could have his way there would be a pile of dead bodies in the wardroom. This sailor was starting to talk himself into some very serious trouble. I could see where this was going and I was sure the senior petty officers on the boat also knew where the situation was headed. I did not want to have to confront this 18-year old young sailor who was on his first liberty drunk. But I could not maintain the position my rank demanded if I ignored his threats. I looked over my shoulder and stared at the sailor and gave him my best "evil eye," in the hope he would shut-up and that would be the end of it. And he was quiet for close to fifteen seconds, but then he got loud and belligerent once again with even more inappropriate threats.

This time when I turned to face him I let my eyes stop long enough to lock on to the eyes of a first class boiler technician (BT). The petty officer next to this burly first class pointed to the water ahead of the boat as if he spied a problem. I looked forward to see what could be there. As soon as my head was turned I heard a "whack!" behind me that sounded like a fist hitting a cheek. Then I noticed that the loud young seaman was quiet now. I turned around and saw the seaman with his head rolled back and his eyes shut and the BT was rubbing the knuckles on his right hand.

I guess the troublemaker must have just fallen asleep due to the booze and the swaying of the boat. Ahh...problem solved...no report chits or court-martial write-ups...just a warm bunk for the seaman when he was carried up the ladder to the ship.

Booze was not the only distraction our sailors sought after a month at sea.

On the third day in port all officers were expected to attend a late luncheon being hosted by the Iranian Navy at their Bandar Abbas base. So that afternoon I relinquished my boat officer duties long enough to ride the Gig ashore with a half-dozen other officers to attend this mandatory social function.

However, once we reached the dock we discovered that none of us knew where the Iranian Navy Officers' Club was located. We thought we could just catch a cab and the driver would know where the base was. It was then that I discovered that Bandar Abbas was what you might call, "A one camel town."

There were no cabs or other public transportation that we could find. After walking a half-mile in what we hoped was the right direction we were able to finally flag down a small pick-up. The driver did not speak English and when we pooled all the language skills of this gaggle of officers we found that although we could converse in a rudimentary fashion in Spanish, Italian, French and Russian, none of us knew anything about Farsi. Despite this communication handicap, we thought we got the driver to understand that we wanted to go to the naval base. When he saw the twenty-dollar bill we waved in front of his face he nodded vigorously and we took that to mean he understood our desires. So Denny Walsh climbed in the cab in the shotgun seat and the rest of us piled into the truck bed.

Off the driver sped as if he knew exactly where he was going. However, when we left the outskirts of the town and whizzed by the airport and kept heading inland towards the desert, our discussion in the bed of the pick-up began to center on the possibility that perhaps the driver did not understand our request. Soon a large 1955 black Cadillac filled with six mean looking Iranians passed us going the opposite direction. When we watched that car pull a quick u-turn and race to catch up with our overloaded pick-up, we all got nervous. Those with wallets took them from their pockets and started to stuff them in their socks for safe keeping. We looked around the bed of the truck for any wrenches or other items that could possibly be used as weapons. There was nothing.

Just then the driver swerved off the paved road and started racing up a dirt road that curved around some small hills. We were certain that we were about to become victims of an anti-American slaughter. The pick-up kicked up so much dust that we lost sight of the Cadillac that had been behind us. Thoughts of jumping from the truck and looking for hiding places were some of the options we were all considering. But the truck was going too fast for that to be a good choice.

When the driver turned around a small hill and came to a flat area that was covered in great piles of rock, as if the slag of a mining operation was grouped together, some of us in the truck started to laugh. We recognized the destination from a description the XO had given the crew before we arrived in port.

The XO had spent a tour as aide to the Middle East commander before he transferred to the Schofield. He was quite familiar with Iran and the way the Shah took care of his sailors and troops. The XO had told the crew about a place called "the rock pile." It was a state-run whore house to service the needs of the Iranian sailors stationed at the base located in provincial Bandar Abbas. Muslim women wore veils and were totally off-limits to sailors—both Iranian and American, so the Shah had established the "rock pile" out of town to meet the lusts of his armed forces.

The pick-up truck driver naturally assumed that any group of sailors would want to be transported to this facility. Actually, it was not a bad assumption on his part!

So we gave the driver his twenty and he sped off. As the Schofield was the only ship in port, we had provided shore patrol petty officers to ensure that the whore house was run in a most efficient and military manner. The shore patrol van was making a run to the docks, so we officers had to wait for it to return before we could be shuttled to the Iranian Navy Officer's Club for our mandatory socializing.

While we were waiting, I observed how this efficient service was organized. The facility was a long narrow building with small "bedrooms" right next to each other like a very cheap, old roadside motel. There were about six rooms on one end and six on the other with a large waiting room in the center. The shore patrol would supervise the waiting room where sailors would "take a number for better service" from a device that could have been used at a deli. The sailor would take a seat in one of the plastic chairs placed against the walls and in an isle down the middle of the room. Once one of the hookers sent a customer from her room, the shore patrol would call the next number. The sailor would pay the clerk his $3 and proceed to the available room. The sailor had no choice in girl; he just got the next one available.

I stood in the door and chatted with the petty officers who had drawn this duty and with some of my divisional sailors as they waited their turn. During the twenty minutes I waited for the duty van to return, I noticed that sailors were only spending ten or twelve minutes in each room. This made sense to me since we had been at sea for over a month. I watched as the sailors returned to the waiting room with a smile and then tore another number from the machine and sat down to wait for another turn. At only $3 a visit and over a half-hour wait for another turn, they were ready to cycle through the facility three or more times.

The duty van returned and the officers got in and we were deposited at the Iranian Officer's Club. All of us were hungry so we decided to eat a late lunch prior to the start of the social gathering which held the probability of only serving finger foods. It was at this meal that I was schooled in how to order from a restaurant in a third world country. There were four of us at our table and none of us had eaten fresh meat or vegetables in weeks. So seeing "thick steak" on the menu, three of us ordered that and waited in anxious anticipation for the delivery of a wonderful meal.

The fourth officer at our table ordered the chicken dinner. He then proceeded to berate us for our order by saying, "You fools! What? Do you think the Iranians have herds of cattle out grazing on the desert? You are not going to get anything like what you hope to eat! You should always order chicken because it is universal. Practically every county raises chickens!"

Well, he was right about our steak orders. When they were finally delivered to our table they looked like a deep fried, thin pancake. I don't remember finding any real beef under the thickly coated disc we were served. Our shipmate just laughed at us and said, "I told you so!"

Five minutes later the waiter brought him his chicken dinner. It looked exactly like our pancake steaks only there was a small pigeon-sized drumstick stuck to one side.

I guess we got the last laugh.

*****

The calm seas in the IO led to one of my sailors doing something stupid, which led to me doing something as dumb.

I was down in the Weapons Department office looking at some classified material that I had no real "need to know" about, but my boss had it out of the safe and thought I might be interested in the message traffic. Most of it was classified "Secret," but there was one sheet in the pile stamped "Top Secret."

Just as I was reading the Top Secret page the excited voice of the Boatswain Mate of the Watch came over the 1MC loudspeaker system.

"MAN OVERBOARD! MAN OVERBOARD! THIS IS NOT A DRILL. ALL HANDS TO MAN OVERBOARD STATIONS!"

The announcement caught me off-guard and I reacted immediately by running top side to my Man Overboard station. In the event of a man overboard, I was assigned as the boat officer in the Motor Whale Boat. In a matter of less than a minute I arrived at the upper level, just below the signal bridge. It was there that we would climb into the Motor Whale Boat and be lowered to the rail in anticipation of being set in the sea.

I went to the kapok life preserver locker near the boat and pulled one out to don quickly...and it was there that I noticed for the first time that I still had the Secret and Top Secret papers clutched in my hand.

I had a real dilemma. If I returned to the Weapons Office to replace them in the safe it would delay the boat being lowered and possibly risk the life of a shipmate floating in the shark infested Indian Ocean. There were no other officers nearby with sufficient security clearance to hold the papers for me. In fact, other than the enlisted boat crew who were focused on getting it ready to be lowered, there was *no one* around me. Noticing this, I made a (bad) split-second decision.

I re-opened the top of the life preserver locker and stuffed the papers under the bulky jackets and then secured the top of the locker. I climbed aboard the Motor Whale Boat and gave the order to lower it to the rail.

We sat in this position and waited to hear from the bridge what to do next. The delay told us that the ship was being maneuvered in an attempt to retrieve the sailor using a temporary davit positioned on the fo'c'sle which could be used to pull him directly from the sea to the deck. We knew this procedure had been successful when the order was received to raise the Motor Whale Boat back into its davits.

As soon as I was able, I scrambled from the boat to the deck and made a bee-line for the life preserver locker. I had to retrieve that classified material before it was missed. I quickly opened the heavy top access hatch to the locker and started flinging kapok life jackets to the deck as I frantically searched for the papers I had hidden there. But I could not find them! I broke out in a cold sweat of fear and panic. I dug deeper and deeper into the locker—but they were not there! Crap! I was in deep kimchi!

I was bent over with my head and upper torso buried deep in the locker and my toes barely touching the deck. Soon I realized that the papers were gone and I managed to back out of the locker. As I stood there convinced that my career was over, I looked up to the signal bridge. There was the XO with a handful of papers in his left hand and a very sinful smile on his face.

He waved the papers at me and asked, "Mr. Bartron, are you missing something?"

I thought my goose was cooked, but the XO had seen the whole thing and truly enjoyed making a silly junior officer squirm. He gave me back the papers with a simple suggestion that I take better care of classified material in the future.

The XO was cool.

However, the CO had a much different reaction to the entire man overboard event.

I found out later that he had been on the bridge and witnessed my sailor earn the nickname of "Divin' Dan Hills." Hills had been assigned the task of painting the bull nose on the very front of the bow. The bridge team, including the captain who was sitting in his underway chair, had observed Hills at work. The weather was clear and the temperature warm so no one thought much of it when Hills put his paint brush back in the bucket and stood up to remove his dungaree shirt. However, things got more interesting when he kicked off his boondockers and then slipped out of his trousers and socks. Hills then shocked everyone when he waved to the bridge team and proceeded to dive overboard.

Sometimes sailors do some really stupid things.

I thought it only fair when during the course of his rescue from the sea that the forward davit was used. Whoever designed this class of ship had installed the base for the davit right above the overboard discharge outlet for the forward crew's head. As

Hills placed the rescue horse collar under his arms and his shipmates started to hoist him aboard, some one flushed a very large deposit from the forward head. Hills received a full shower in raw sewage as he was hoisted aboard. Poetic justice, I thought.

Soon after he was cleaned up, Hills and I were standing in front of the captain who really wanted to know why Hills would do something so stupid. The captain had a hard time believing what Hills answered. But knowing Hills better than the captain, the seaman's answer seemed to fit my impression of the sailor.

"Captain," he explained, "for weeks I have been looking at the calm waters out here and had the urge to go swimming. I just couldn't fight the urge anymore."

The captain asked if he was aware of the multiple Great White sharks that had been spotted the day before feeding on our wet garbage thrown off the fantail, and Hills answered, "Oh, yeah...I guess I forgot about that."

It was during this year as First Lieutenant that I learned that sailors can do some really stupid things.

After Hills was dismissed, the captain had me remain to give me about the dumbest order I remember receiving in the Navy. And remember, I had been ordered to do some pretty silly things as a plebe.

The captain was certain that Hills had been attempting suicide when he gave himself an unauthorized swim call. Consequently, he ordered me to prevent him from committing suicide. This really confused me. What was I supposed to do? Assign two sailors to the "Hills watch" 24/7? Was I supposed to handcuff Hills to his rack down in Compartment 106? Just what could I realistically do for the remaining weeks we were scheduled to be at sea? If someone was determined to kill himself onboard a Navy ship, there were many means to accomplish this goal with ease.

My solution was to have Hills watched for a couple of days and then I had the chief order him not to commit suicide. Hills assured the chief that dying was the farthest thing from his mind; especially when the chief outlined the pleasures due the crew in our next liberty port, the Seychelles Islands.

*****

Victoria on Mahe Island in the Seychelles is located about 900 miles to the east of Africa. Our visit was only four days, but that was enough to take in the sights and experiences of this small island.

In 1974 the Seychelles reminded me of what Honolulu must have been like in 1915, before it was developed into a tourist destination. Of special interest to me was the plethora of Great White Shark jaws displayed in curio shops. This was before "Jaws" had been released, but after we had viewed onboard the ship the film "Blue Water, White Death" about how Great Whites hunt. From the number of dried Great White jaws that had been retrieved by the local fishermen, it indicated that the island was surrounded by a Great White habitat.

On Mahe Island was the most perfect beach I have ever visited. So a couple of fellow officers and I spent one afternoon lying in the shade of palm trees on pure white sand. There were no crowds and the water temperature was just a couple of degrees cooler than the air temperature. This meant you could rush into the surf without having to get used to the water, yet it was just cool enough to give you a break from the heat. Down the beach a distance was a shack where divers could check-out equipment to explore the reef a few hundred yards off shore. Many crew members took advantage of this opportunity.

The beach sand ran out at a shallow angle into the water. No rocks or seaweed to trip you up, just a soft carpet of sand on the bottom. I decided to walk out to where it was deep enough to swim. I got through the surf and did a dozen strokes out into the wide cove. I was about 100 yards from the beach and in water too deep to touch the bottom. I treaded water and scanned the horizon for a minute and turned my head to start back to my spot on the beach when my attention was drawn to movement in the corner of my eye. I thought I had seen something break the water's surface about fifteen yards out to sea from my position. It was just five seconds later when I saw first one fin-shaped object break the surface and then another matching shape follow it. The ship had been escorted by enough dolphins when we cruised that I had learned that they only had the one dorsal fin. Two fins only meant one thing—a shark—and in these waters that meant a Great White shark!

I immediately started the smoothest, splash-free stroke I could manage as I hurried towards the beach. I knew I could not out swim a Great White, but I wasn't going to hang around to be his lunch without trying to make an escape. At any second I expected to feel the thud and rip of his massive jaws as they tore at my legs. The thought of this made me abandon the smooth, splash-free strokes and just start pulling as hard and as fast as I could for the shore.

I made the shallow surf and pulled right through the waves and soon I was in thigh deep water. I swam and ran in the water until its level was knee deep and then I sprinted for the safety of the beach. I did not stop when I reached the shore. I continued to run another twenty yards just in case the mean beast tried to grab me from the water's edge. Finally I stopped and noticed that about a minute earlier I had stopped breathing! I could feel my heart pumping and thumping in my chest. I turned to face the water, fully expecting to see my nemesis gliding back and forth in the shallow water just baiting me to enter the ocean again.

I stared at the sea and scanned it thoroughly. A minute into my search I saw the double fins again. And right after they broke the surface I saw a head wearing a face mask pop up. It became clear to me that I had run from a skin diver just off the shore.

Just the same, I enjoyed that sunny day on the beach about ten yards from the waters edge the rest of the day.

*****

While in the IO, I was still under the mistaken belief that it was my duty to serve every one of my sailors. A couple of months later I had learned a valuable lesson in leadership that freed me from being the doormat for my screw-ups. I can thank SA Jakeups for that lesson.

While we were in the IO we received a message from the Red Cross saying that Jakeups' dad was very sick and the sailor should be given the opportunity to see him in case his father should pass away soon. The XO and I had to do some rather intricate finagling to arrange his transport from the middle of the Indian Ocean via a passing merchant ship to Africa and then transport to Europe and finally back to New York City. And what was the payback for bending over backwards and accomplishing the nearly impossible? Serious embarrassment was our reward.

Jakeups had been a screw-up since the first day he checked aboard the Schofield. Back in San Diego I met him and two other very recent graduates from Boot Camp on their first day aboard. As I welcomed them to the ship and division the other two young sailors had bright eyes and an eagerness to find adventure in the Navy. But Jakeups refused to make eye contact with me and kept shuffling his toe against the deck. I had dismissed the other two and asked Jakeups to accompany me back to my stateroom. I sat him down and asked what was bothering him. The conversation had gone something like this.

"I just can't take living on a ship," he said with a cold tenseness in his voice.

"When did you check aboard?" I asked.

"Last Friday late."

"This is Monday, so what happened over the weekend that led you to the decision that you can't live on a ship?"

"I was on liberty all weekend."

"So you haven't slept one night aboard the ship yet?"

"Yeah, that's right, but I just know I can't do it. I gotta get off this ship," he offered in a rather surly tone.

There was a long pause in the conversation as I quickly reviewed his very small personnel file. I noted his ASVAB scores were in the "Cat IV" range. Jakeups was practically a "certified idiot." And our conversation was proving this fact. But I had a job to do with the sailors that were assigned to my division, so I continued the counseling session.

"Well, Jakeups, the situation is this. You are assigned to this ship and to our division so we are going to have to work out some sort of arrangement that you can live with. As I see it, you have three options. One is to go kill yourself...and I don't think the situation is a bad as that, do you?"

He shook his head in response.

"Your second option is to desert, but you will be caught and spend a lot of time in a much more cramped space than this ship as you serve a long stretch in the brig," I paused as he considered this option momentarily. Then I continued, "Or we can work together to help you adapt to the current situation and get you started on a good solid career as a sailor—be it for four years or more. Now don't you agree that this final option makes the most sense?"

He gave a little...a very little...nod and then I dismissed him.

The next morning when the roll was called at quarters, Jakeups was absent. In fact he was absent every day.

Back in those days, the crew was paid twice a month in cash. It was a very orderly system. The two disbursing clerks and the disbursing officer would sit at a table on the mess deck. A line of sailors formed and one by one they approached the first disbursing clerk and identified themselves. The clerk would verify how much pay the sailor was to receive and tell the disbursing officer sitting next to him. The disbursing officer would count out the exact amount from the money in a cash drawer sitting in front of him. Then he would hand the senior disbursing clerk the money who would then count it again to be sure there were no mistakes. The senior disbursing clerk would hand the cash to the sailor and have him sign a receipt. Then the sailor would move two paces to his left and stand in front of a chief who was collecting for the ship's fund. Based upon the amount the sailor received, a levy would be assessed and the sailor would "volunteer" to donate that amount to the chief's slush fund. This fund was kept by the Chiefs' Mess and was used to help shipmates in financial trouble. If a sailor was in dire financial need, he could go to thc chiefs and request to be funded from this unofficial account. Most often it was used on things like paying for a plane ticket to help the sailor to get home in an emergency situation. The Navy would pay to get a sailor back to San Diego from overseas, but then it was the sailor's responsibility to find money to pay for a flight to Des Moines to visit his sick momma. Sailors did not have the funds for such unexpected expenses. For true emergencies, often times the money drawn from the slush fund was a gift and did not need to be repaid.

However, if a sailor needed money to pay the rent to keep his family from being evicted because the sailor had gotten drunk ashore and got taken by some wharf rats or he had lost it gambling, then the loan had to be repaid. The chiefs, all having been in similar situations as junior enlisted, knew the wives and kids of the sailor should not have to suffer because their husband and father was a screw-up. So the loan would be repaid via the bi-monthly payday collections.

Well, SA Jakeups was listed as being an "Unauthorized Absence" on the daily muster sheets submitted to the in-port OOD for weeks. He was broke now and showed up in the pay line and told LT (JG) Jim Bonafede the Disbursing Officer he expected to get paid. Jim had no idea who this sailor was, having not met him on the one day Jakeups had been aboard. However, Jim did recognize the name from the muster lists he had seen while standing in-port OOD watches.

Jakeups demanded, "I'm in the Navy, so I want my pay!"

Bonafede answered, "Sailor, if you don't work, you don't get paid."

Jakeups said, "No, you gotta pay me."

Bonafede said, "I don't have any money for you."

Jakeups then decided he would show this pork chop officer his knowledge of Navy Regulations and said, "Well, I'm not assigned to this stinkin' ship anymore anyways. I am a deserter so they're gonna transfer me to another shore command."

But the officer had the last laugh. "Tell me Jakeups, why do you think you have been declared a deserter?"

"I've been gone thirty days and after thirty days you are declared a deserter!"

Jim smiled and gave the sailor the bad news, "You had better learn to read a calendar better, shipmate. You have been gone only 29 days, so you are still attached to this command."

Jakeups was mad and flustered and snapped back, "Then I'll leave and come back in two days!"

"No good," Jim informed him. "Since you were onboard today, the clock is reset and you will have to be gone another thirty days to be declared a deserter."

"But I'm broke! I gotta have some money!" Jakeups said with tears starting to form in his eyes.

I had been summoned by the junior disbursing clerk while this conversation was taking place. When I arrived, the sailors in line waiting to get paid were pretty upset at this idiot delaying the proceedings. I took Jakeups to Chief Williams and we explained the facts of life to the young sailor.

Jakeups had been assigned to the ship only a month and already he was placed on restriction and fined money he did not have.

Now months later in the IO, the XO and I worked to "take care of a shipmate" by making difficult arrangements for Jakeups to get to New York to see his sick father. The payback for this extra effort was a string of messages from every ship and port and plane he took that reported Jakeups's bad behavior. He was able personally and individually to smear the name of the USS Schofield from the IO all the way to New York.

When we returned from deployment, Jakeups rejoined the ship. The first thing he wanted was my help in arranging a humanitarian transfer to the New York metro area so he could be near his sick father.

As a good division officer, I considered it my duty to "take care of my sailors." So, I sat down with Jakeups and we covered what the requirements were for a humanitarian transfer. I would do all the paperwork and all he had to do was stay out of trouble for a few months, because the Navy would not approve the request until a sailor had remained clear of captain's mast and civilian arrests for a matter of months. Jakeups acknowledged what we each would do in this plan to help him.

You guessed it. Two weeks later he lipped off to a senior petty officer in a very disrespectful manner and got himself placed on report again. It was then that I experienced a rather big awakening concerning my duties as an officer towards my sailors.

I gathered the multiple personnel manuals and instructions in my arms and carried the load from my stateroom down to Compartment 106. Jakeups was standing by his rack. I took my arm full of publications and dumped them on his bed.

I told him, "Here, you do it yourself. I am not going to work for a sailor who won't work for me."

Then I turned and left the compartment, a wiser junior officer than I had been a week before. That phrase became a motto I shared with every subordinate ever assigned to me the next twenty years. "You work for me and I will work for you."

I remember the last time I ever saw SA Jakeups. A couple of weeks later he had gotten off of restriction and gone out on liberty in San Diego. When he came back in the early evening, I had the duty as in-port OOD on the quarterdeck. Jakeups was drunk and I ordered him to go below and sleep it off and directed a couple of his shipmates who were standing near the quarterdeck to help him get to bed.

About an hour later my relief showed to take over the in-port watch. It was Master-At-Arms Chief Peoples. Just prior to effecting the turn over we saw Jakeups standing on top of the helo hangar doors. He was outside the safety lines and swaying as he tried to keep from falling the twenty feet to the steel deck. Chief Peoples was shocked by the dangerous situation. I was just irritated and tired.

I shouted up to Jakeups, "Okay sailor get off of there."

He responded in a drunken slur, "I'm okay. It's fine right here."

The anger in my voice was obvious when I put on my best "command voice" and shouted, "Look, Jakeups, get back behind the safety line right now. I don't care if you fall, but I don't want it on my watch. I am not about to spend the rest of this evening doing paperwork because you are a dumb ass. Now get back behind that safety line until I am relieved!"

He mumbled something under his breath and slowly started to step over the safety line behind him. His stalling got under my skin a little more.

"Say, Jakeups! You remember the deal you had with Chief Williams? Well that same deal goes with me!" I shouted.

Jakeups stumbled away from the edge. I looked at Chief Peoples and his mouth was hanging open. I guess he wasn't used to ensigns speaking to their sailors in quite that cavalier of an attitude.

We relieved the watch and I never saw Jakeups again in my life. I guess he understood my meaning when I told him the same deal he previously had with Chief Williams was in effect with me. Before Chief Williams had retired a month earlier, he had shared with me that there were a handful of bad eggs in our division that he had promised that he "would help pack their sea bag any time they wanted to leave and never come back."

I know how to read a calendar and so 32 days after Jakeups disappeared, I phoned the Third Navy District in New York and gave them Jakeups' parents' address and requested they send shore patrol petty officers to pick him up as a deserter. I never heard back from the District, but I like to think that Jakeups was arrested and spent some time in the brig.

*****

I should clarify that First Division had many excellent sailors and shipmates; men such as "Wolfy" Bland and Darryl Shattuck and petty officers such as BM3 Goldsberry and BM3 Baker. It just seems that the most memorable sea stories centered on the screw-ups.

One of these sailors who would have been eligible to enlist under the "Project 100,000" program was SA Johnny Lajewdice who hailed from Brooklyn, New York. One day I asked him what he thought it would be like to be in the Navy. I mean, why did he enlist if he chaffed at carrying out any and all orders? He answered in all truthfulness that his recruiter had told him that onboard ships the crew got to enjoy swim call every day at sea. Later I spent four tours in recruiting and I know that Lajewdice had employed "selective listening" when he put that thought in his small brain.

How limited was his thinking? How big a deficit did he possess in exercising forethought and judgment in making decisions in his life? On another deployment, one of our liberty ports was Hong Kong. The day before we were to pull out of port I was touring my division's sleeping compartment and the only one present was Johnny Lajewdice. He was standing in front of the small mirror mounted on the bulkhead by the base of the ladder with his shirt off, admiring the art work he had gotten at a local tattoo parlor the day before. Unlike today when more people sport tattoos than those who refrain from getting inked, back in 1974 only criminals, bikers and sailors got tattoos. And what did this genius get permanently scrawled on his chest? Above his left nipple was the word "hot" and above his right nipple was "cold." Below the left nipple was the word "Sweet" and below the right nipple was "Sour." Then on a crooked line unevenly spaced between the nipples across his chest were the words, "Brooklyn Bomber."

It was the worst ink I have ever seen. Yet, he stood there so proud and admiring his choice of design.

On another instance, we pulled into a port overseas and Lajewdice gave himself permission to visit the petty officers' club on base. This wasn't too hard to do when all hands had civilian clothes privileges for liberty. My sailor proceeded to break the seal on a brand new bottle of Tequila and chug-a-lug its entire contents. Of course he dropped dead on the spot, but lucky for him a corpsman was at a nearby table and jump started his heart and got him vomiting the booze from his system. An ambulance came and rushed him to the local clinic where they pumped his stomach and got him stabilized. They decided to keep him for observation with the hope of possibly returning him to our ship in the morning.

However, they did not post a guard over my sailor. So he got up and found his clothes and got dressed. He then made his way back to the petty officers' club where he proceeded to eat a glass glass to prove how tough he was. The ambulance came again and they pumped his stomach for the second time that night. This time they put a watch on him and in the morning they delivered him to the quarterdeck of the Schofield with the recommendation that Lajewdice not be granted liberty in this port again.

This was a sailor whom I was planning on boxing when we arrived in Subic Bay, the Philippines. The men in my division had found out that I had boxed one year at the Naval Academy so immediately there was talk of arranging an interdivisional boxing smoker once we arrived in Subic for an upkeep period.

I was frightened, honestly frightened, to get in the ring with Lajewdice. He could keep both his arms down at his side so I could land my best punch and I was convinced the only result would be broken knuckles on my punching hand and he would merely shake his head and say, "Gee, Mister B, is that the best you got?"

Luckily, our operations tempo was too great to permit time to organize a smoker and Lajewdice got hepatitis from sharing a bad dope needle and was sent back to San Diego.

*****

All WESTPAC ships visited Subic Bay. My first trip to Olongapo City outside the Naval Station gate was very educational. The XO had the reputation of being a real "steamer" and he felt obligated to take the fresh, innocent ensign across the infamous river to experience liberty in what many called the "sailors' sexual Disneyland." For the equivalent of five dollars American, there were hookers who would meet any fantasy a young sailor had ever imagined. Not every sailor sought out this wish fulfillment, but a great number did.

The XO took me in trail and led me across the bridge just outside the main gate of Subic Bay Naval Station. The street was lined with bar after bar after bar. The first one we entered was packed with sailors on liberty, each being attended to by their "girlfriend" for the evening. As soon as we stepped through the front door, every girl in the place took notice of the XO's arrival. They left their current escorts and rushed to surround the XO and since I was right behind him, also me. They all shouted with glee, "The XO! XO is here!" Before I knew it one girl had her hand in my left front pocket another had her hand in my rear pants pocket and another was searching my other rear pocket. Yet another girl pushed her hand down the front of my trousers searching for something else.

I had learned how to go on liberty in Naples, so my ID card and money were in my clinched fist stuffed tightly in my right front pants' pocket. That left me just one hand to fend off the many girls attacking me. They were all smiling and giggling so it was hard to get mad at them, but trying to remove four groping hands with only one arm was a real challenge. It did not take long for me to slip back out onto the street, leaving the XO to fend for himself with the amorous young ladies of his favorite Olongapo bar.

The next night I was the ensign offered up to the base security force. When there were many ships in port, the regular shore patrol (SP) had to be augmented by sailors assigned from ships. One officer was given the duty to coordinate the SP patrols each evening. I was the "expendable ensign" in our wardroom, so I got the duty when the Schofield had to supply the officer.

I put on by Tropical White Long uniform and reported to the main shore patrol office near the main gate. A squad of sailors composed of petty officers from various ships in port reported for the evening's duty. The first thing I did was have the twelve men fall in according to height. I then went to the end of the line that had the tallest and biggest sailors and pointed at the first two. They were to accompany me on patrol that night. The other ten paired up and I sent them out on walking patrol.

The two biggest petty officers took positions on my right and left and we started our patrol of the bar district. It was a long, but uneventful night. That was probably due to my policy of how shore patrol should be conducted. As we walked along the side of the street, if we saw a fight or disturbance ahead, I would lead my two bodyguards across the street to avoid the trouble.

It worked, because at the end of the patrol my white uniform was still clean—no puke or blood stains anywhere! The two petty officers liked my approach to this dirty duty and said so as we turned in our SP brassards, "That was the best shore patrol duty I ever pulled. I will stand the duty with you ensign anytime."

*****

I was truly the "expendable ensign" my first year aboard. This provided me with opportunities to experience rather interesting assignments. We needed to provide an exchange officer for a joint exercise with the Taiwanese Navy. Of course, I was picked as the one least likely to be missed aboard the Schofield during a fleet exercise, so I was sent to ride the Chinese ship.

For years I had heard the expression "that was as fouled up as a Chinese fire drill." Well, I got to witness a real Chinese fire drill and I discovered the phrase has some basis in fact.

I rode an old World War II relic that we had given the Nationalist Chinese about 1965. Since they did not have a blue water navy, but spent all of their time patrolling the Taiwan Strait, they had modified the original design of this small destroyer. The mess decks were converted to berthing spaces because they carried a full war complement of sailors. In fact, since they were still technically at war with Communist China, they kept one gun mount manned and loaded with war reserve rounds at all times. Additionally, their deck mounted torpedo tubes were loaded and charged with live torpedoes.

With the mess decks now devoid of tables, the crew was fed a bowl of rice and a little fish four times a day. Each sailor would go through the line and have the food plopped into his bowl and then he would go out on the main deck and find a spot to squat down and shovel the food into his mouth with chopsticks.

The Chinese were not well practiced in alongside underway replenishment techniques, so one of the evolutions scheduled for my at-sea period onboard was for this Chinese ship to come alongside a U.S. Navy supply ship and pass pallets between the two vessels. This type of evolution was done every week by the Schofield and other "small boys" in the U.S. fleet, but it was a truly new experience for these Chinese sailors. Usually, if they needed supplies, they would just pop back into Kaohsiung or Keelung and load them aboard while pier side.

I stood back and watched the ship's crew prepare to pass stores from ship to ship using their kingpost mounted amidships. I saw what had to be chiefs barking orders at the sailors and this gave me confidence that these "old salts" knew what they were doing. So I was caught flat footed when the entire evolution started to unravel.

The first thing I noticed was the lack of preparation by the sailors who were assigned to pull the in-haul line aboard. Every one had the ends of the long ties used to fasten together their kapok life preservers flapping in the breeze. I used sign language to try and communicate to the chiefs that for safety reasons the sailors should tuck in the ties to prevent them from wrapping around the in-haul lines. The chiefs nodded and smiled as if they understood my advice, but not one sailor secured their ties.

The evolution proceeded and soon it was time to let the supply ship retrieve its line. The sailor with the signal paddle gave the "haul in" wave and the American ship began rapidly pulling the large line back. Just then, the life preserver loose tie of a Chinese sailor got wrapped around the line. In an instant he was off his feet and being pulled overboard. At first his shipmates tried to grab him and hold him from being dragged over the side, but soon they just let him go to suffer his fate! The chief standing next to me just stood there, frozen from taking any action to help his sailor.

Having been a safety officer for many of these evolutions during my ten months as First Lieutenant, I knew what had to be done. I raced to the seaman with the signal paddle and grabbed it and started giving the "slack off" signal. The supply ship immediately stopped pulling the line back and we were able to free the seaman from the line.

For a few tense seconds there, it truly had been a "Chinese fire drill."

*****

However, what I remember most about the days aboard this foreign ship was experiencing the "Great Chinese Watermelon Torture." For this joint exercise a U.S. Coast Guard lieutenant was to ride another Chinese ship, but that ship could not get underway. So he was transferred to ride the same ship as me.

Now the Chinese were absolutely wonderful hosts...and that is what caused me such trouble. When I came aboard, their one English speaking officer asked if I would prefer Chinese or western cuisine at dinner. As I was not a fan of Chinese food and since he asked, I told him that I would prefer western cuisine. Big mistake.

The cooking staff on this ship was not too familiar with American food preparation. And since the Coast Guard officer had said he preferred to eat Chinese food, our hosts thought it only proper to serve me everything he received *plus* a full American meal. Consequently, I would eat three courses of Chinese food and then my specially prepared western dishes would be set before me. Of course, to be polite I had to eat them as well. However, that posed a little problem. The cooks had made the fried chicken and potatoes and some sort of greens before they cooked the Chinese food which was served hot from the wok. Every piece of western food served me was deep fried in thick grease, and since it had sat around for nearly an hour before it was served, this grease had congealed into a layer of fat around each piece of meat. I felt the thick grease slide up my teeth and ooze over my gums with each bite. I managed to eat it all and had the urge to find my rack and let everything settle in my stomach, when the CO said something to me through the English speaking officer.

"The captain has brought onboard a watermelon from his own garden," the interpreter relayed, "He wants to know if you would like some?"

The thought of a thin slice of cool, crisp watermelon to cleanse my greasy mouth resulted in a broad smile on my face. A minute later a slice of watermelon was set before me and I ate it and it was good. It really hit the spot. I smiled at the CO sitting at the far end of the table to acknowledge his generosity.

A moment later, there was another slice of watermelon set in front of me. Although I was exceedingly full, I ate that one too...after all, it was a personal gift from the CO's personal watermelon. Since I seemed to enjoy it, another slice was placed in front of me. I ate and smiled three more times before I figured out that the watermelon would keep coming as long as I smiled. My stomach felt like it was about to burst by this time.

I remembered this meal a couple of years later when I was water boarded as part of my POW training. I think that torture was easier than the polite stuffing I received at the hands of the Chinese.

Anti-Submarine Warfare (ASW) Officer

At the end of my first year of sea duty, we had a change-of-command aboard the Schofield. The change in CO was dramatic and traumatic to many of us. Our new CO was from the surface nuclear navy.

Believe me when I tell you that nukes are a different breed of officer. I know, my brother is one.

Commander T. A. Almstedt, Jr. would drive himself (and his men) to make two stars before he retired. Before I share the perspective of what it was like to serve as a junior officer under him, let me state that of all the COs in my career, he is the one I would want in charge if we went to war. He knew his ship and how to fight it—well and effectively. His focus and drive would ensure that we came through battles victoriously because he had trained us completely and he understood every system and weapons platform on the Schofield.

However, as the following stories will indicate, his people skills were not the best I experienced from a leader.

*****

We were in port in San Diego and I had not had a day off in nearly three weeks. The combination of duty days and mandatory Saturday projects just happened to keep me on the ship during waking hours. I had promised my wife to try and get the next Saturday free so we could visit an amusement park. On Friday, about two days after the change-of-command the CO called an "all officers meeting" for Saturday morning. When I heard this I asked for special liberty to miss it and the XO approved my absence.

I had forgotten the tickets to the amusement park in my stateroom aboard the ship, so I left my wife in the car as I hurried down the pier to board the ship. I was in civilian clothes and made the turn to head down the ladder to Officers' Country that was near the rear door of the wardroom. At that exact moment the wardroom door opened and ten officers all gasped when they sighted me. Quickly, the XO came to the door and pushed me out of sight and with a panicked look on his face shut the door behind him.

"Bob, get below and get your uniform on, then I will take you to the captain's cabin. Be sure to bring all your paperwork on the lost pneumatic tools," he said as he guided me towards the bottom of the ladder.

I was about to become the sacrificial lamb given to appease the new commanding god. Later I discovered that the captain had just spent ten minutes berating my professionalism and lack of dedication for missing this "important" meeting. He kept harping on my inexcusable absence and he did not accept the protestations of my department head and the XO who tried to explain that it was my first day off in weeks and that I had received prior permission to miss the meeting.

So when, as usual, my timing was perfect to be seen that morning, he stormed out of the wardroom and told the XO to have the Weapons Officer haul my butt to the captain's stateroom.

Somehow I figured right then that we were not going to be enjoying an amusement park today.

When I arrived at the captain's cabin, my department head, LT. Hall, escorted me into the room. The captain sat at his desk and we were directed to sit on the sofa which at night folded down to be his bed. I remember the feeling more than the actual events of this meeting. It was as if I was standing on the edge of an active volcano with the heat of the bubbling lava hitting my face...and huddled behind me was LT. Hall, trying to find protection from the heat coming our way.

"I understand you lost $1,500 in pneumatic tools that were checked out from the naval base. Is that right, Ensign?" the captain asked through angry, clinched teeth, his face squeezed into what I discovered was a perpetual scowl.

"Sir, there are presently $1,500 of tools unaccounted for, but I know where they went," I replied with the truth in an even voice, not wanting to appear flippant or contrary.

"So just where exactly are they!" he almost shouted as an exclamation and not a question.

"I have a signature of the sailor who signed out each tool right here in my records. Most of them were signed out to members of the engineering department," I said not knowing then the special affinity this nuclear trained officer had for engineering personnel. His reaction seemed to be a rise in his anger, if that was possible.

"A signature! That doesn't ensure a sailor will return the property! Why didn't you do something like make them leave their ID card as a deposit when they checked out a tool?"

"Initially that is exactly the program I had in place, but the Ops Officer told me it was illegal and directed me to cease the practice. I objected, but the chain-of-command backed him, so I went to a log-out chit system."

Suddenly, the captain's harsh demeanor seemed to ebb away. It was hard really to fault me if I had actually done it his way.

In a very even and professional tone he continued, "Well, what have you done to track down the missing tools?"

"I have given lists to each division officer and department head and requested they find the tools and have them returned to the First Lieutenant's storeroom."

Now for the first time, the CO broke eye contact with me and looked at my department head cowering behind me. "Lieutenant Hall, work with the other department heads and let's recover these tools."

Hall nodded and replied, "Aye, aye, sir."

The CO turned to face his desk and we stood to get out of there as fast as we could. Just as my hand grasp the doorknob, the captain turned again and locked his gaze on my eyes and said, "Everyone down in the wardroom thinks that I just tore your ass off...and I don't want them to think any differently. You understand, Ensign?"

I nodded and replied, "Yes, sir."

As I walked back down the pier to my exasperated wife in our car I thought about what had just happened. The CO wanted to intimidate the officers by "killing a crow and hanging it on the fence." He did not want to have to kill a second crow, so I was to pretend he had threatened me with career murder so his intended objective had been met.

*****

The next thing the new CO did to get the wardroom members attention was take the last at-sea bridge watch bill and review it. He drew a line through every OOD's name and told the XO that all OODs were now disqualified and that they must be re-qualified to Captain Almstedt's standards. Having a brother who was my classmate and who worked in Admiral Rickover's navy, this sounded familiar to me—a typical "leadership" technique of the nukes.

Unfortunately, the Schofield received a change of orders and we were told to put to sea for a ten day period soon after he disqualified all the OODs. As it happened, there were still two OOD qualified officers who were not listed on that old watch bill and consequently, the captain had not yanked their OOD qualifications.

One was the senior watch officer, LT. Hall, because the senior watch officer had been exempt from standing watches. The other was Ensign Bartron because I had finished my qualification for OOD at that last at sea period and was designated by the previous CO just before he was relieved.

So we put to sea and the OOD watch bill had Hall standing six hours as OOD and then Bartron standing six hours for the entire ten day period. It was tiring and absurd. Absurd because my JOODs were the chief engineer and operations officer and other senior watch standers who had been training me the last time we left port. But since we had so many officers available to stand JOOD watches, they got to rotate the assignment with a five section watch while Hall and I were port and starboard. So not one of them complained about having to stand watch as a JOOD.

*****

With the new nuke captain onboard, I tried to revert to my Academy Youngster year persona....stay out of sight! I cannot watch the movie "Mister Roberts" without identifying with Jack Lemmon's character, Ensign Pulver. In the movie he would run and hide whenever the captain came his way. I tried to do the same thing to avoid having to come into direct contact with Captain Almstedt.

One day I was walking down the passageway that ran alongside the wardroom when I saw the captain coming right for me. I immediately tried to duck into the wardroom and use the back door to exit and avoid a meeting with the CO. I tried the door but it was locked; the stewards were cleaning the wardroom. I went ahead two steps and tried the door to the wardroom scullery, but it was locked too. Now it was too late, the captain was upon me. I turned sideways to let him pass and greeted him.

"Good morning, captain."

He stopped, turned to me and with our bellies nearly touching and, due to his tall stature his face towering over mine, he snarled something in a low growl that must have been on his mind as he toured his ship, "When you junior officers get off this ship you're gonna be the best trained sons-of-bitches in the fleet!"

Then he turned and strode away.

I stood there with a bewildered look on my face, then shrugged my shoulders and went on with my business. Such unexpected outbursts from the captain were just something you had to learn to live with.

*****

One day we put to sea to conduct engineering casualty control drills while steaming just off of Southern California. Now being an officer who had spent the formative years of his career standing engineering watches "down in the hole," these drills were quite exciting for the captain. In fact, he, in essence, spent the entire few days at sea trying to drive the ship from the deck plates in engineering. The big drawback to this, of course, is that you can not see as there are no windows down there!

Now my department head, LT. Marshall Van Sant Hall was the most laid back officer I have ever known. Nothing seemed to rattle his even keel. In fact, his formal calling card that back then all officers had to possess read, "Lieutenant M.S. Hall, United States Navy, *The man and the legend.*" So when I arrived on the bridge to relieve him of OOD duties I was shocked by who I saw there. The relaxed and confident Weapons Officer had been replaced by a nervous, tense and frightened shell of a man!

The weather was good and although there was a lot of ship traffic in the area, it was nothing we couldn't avoid easily. So what had Hall in this terrified state? The answer came as soon as the X1JV sound powered telephone circuit from the engineering spaces squawked loudly near the captain's elevated chair. Marshall turned and faced the phone and I saw all the blood drain from his face and it looked like he was about to pass out. I could tell that my boss needed to be relieved in a hurry. He looked at me with pleading eyes and then back to the ringing phone.

"I'll answer that, boss," I said as I moved to the front of the bridge.

It was the captain on the line, screaming that the engineering drills were being sabotaged by an inept bridge team. I identified myself as the oncoming OOD and he replied, "Well, you had better get it right, mister!"

That was the first of many degrading conversations I had with the captain over the phone that afternoon. The one I remember the best was him shouting at me because I had changed course to avoid ramming an amphibious ship operating in the same section of ocean. I guess the movement of the rudder affected some drill the engineers were running.

During the course of that "conversation" the captain screamed, 'DO YOU WANT TO BE AN OOD ON MY SHIP?"

I paused as I thought about that question. In my head I answered, "No sir! As a matter of fact, I would rather be anywhere else than here driving your ship!"

I guess I took too long thinking of what I would like to say, so the captain continued in an even angrier voice, "WELL, DO YOU?"

"Yes, sir."

"THEN STOP SCREWING UP!" Then he slammed the phone down.

The quartermaster of the watch came up to me and having overheard the screaming on the phone said, "Yeah, Ensign. Stop screwing up. Next time run into that gator ship."

It made me feel a little better.

*****

I had other "adventures" with the captain while standing bridge watches. One day we were scheduled to get underway from the San Diego Naval Station but due to problems with the power plant our departure was delayed until after dark. Normally a ship tries not to transit San Diego Bay in the dark, but we had to leave to make some sort of commitment. We left the pier easily enough and got turned to head north in the channel. However, just as we passed under the Coronado Bridge a very thick fog bank rolled in. It was so thick I could not see the bull nose from the bridge. However, we had a great radar picture and we were getting good fixes from known locations ashore.

I was OOD and I noticed on the radar an exceedingly large shadow moving rather rapidly around the top of North Island. This ship coming our way was big, real big and moving too fast for the conditions. Watching the radar return on the bridge I gave the order to slide the Schofield to the right side of the narrow channel. It was obvious that this ship approaching would need a lot of space to get by.

"What are you doing?" the captain asked me.

"I'm moving to the right side of the channel and I intend to run buoy to buoy leaving the markers very close to our hull," I answered.

"Nah, we're fine where we are," the captain opined.

This is where I showed my inexperience as an ensign and made my biggest error of the evening. Looking back, I should have announced to the bridge crew, "Navigator, log it. The captain has assumed the con."

That is what I should have done, but in actuality I just gave orders to the helmsman that took us down the center of the channel.

As we approached a position abeam of the Broadway Pier both the captain and I were out on the port bridge wing straining to see this huge ship through the fog. Just then the phone talker for CIC shouted, "CIC RECOMMENDS ALL BACK EMERGENCY FULL AND SOUNDING FIVE SHORT BLASTS ON THE SHIP'S WHISTLE!"

Down in the dark, windowless compartment of the Combat Information Center the large blip of the approaching ship merged with the close-in blur of our radar. From what they could tell, all of their instruments indicated an imminent collision.

"What are they talking about?" the captain asked as we peered into the fog.

Just then the captain and I saw why the CIC watch team was so excited. Out of the fog and night the large, menacing bow of the *Japan Bear,* 768-feet of fully loaded container ship appeared and loomed over the captain and me on the port bridge wing. Both the captain's and my immediate reaction was to scream orders to the helmsman and lee helmsman.

The captain shouted orders first from the port bridge wing, "ALL AHEAD FLANK! HARD RIGHT RUDDER!"

Just then, as if we had rehearsed it many times, we shouted a simultaneous command, "SHIFT YOUR RUDDER!"

I look back and am amazed that we each gave the same rudder order, which was counter-intuitive. The container ship was rapidly approaching our port side and so the first order had been to turn away from it, but then when the situation became more recognizable, we saw that it was too late to turn away. The merchant ship was so close to us that our only hope was to pivot the Schofield to the left in an attempt to swing our stern free from the on coming mass of steel.

For the next few seconds there was nothing to do but watch what developed. As we stood there with that massive bow heading for us, neither of us considered running to avoid the imminent impact. In my mind were two thoughts. First, "I think it will cut us right along the dotted helicopter approach line that runs diagonally down the flight deck." That thought was replaced by the question, "So this is how a collision at sea happens? Who would have thought it could occur in San Diego Harbor?"

It had always seemed nearly impossible to me that ships on the ocean can somehow manage to collide. I mean, if one fellow was given an 18-wheeler and I was given another one and both our engines had governors that restricted our speed to 20 MPH, and then we were put in a massive parking lot and told to drive around without hitting each other...well, it would be rather easy to avoid a collision. And the Pacific Ocean is the largest parking lot in the world.

Those thoughts passed instantaneously and I turned to the captain and asked, "Should I sound the collision alarm?"

He shook his head and calmly replied, "Nah."

Somehow the *Japan Bear*'s bow slid down our port side and passed our stern with a clearance of less than nine feet. As I later learned in naval aviation...."an inch is as good as a mile as long as you don't touch." But there were a couple of casualties in this near-collision. The port side amidships phone talker saw that bow suddenly appear out of the night fog and he quickly turned to run away from where he was sure would be the point of impact. But he forgot that there was a bulkhead right behind him and he nearly broke his nose when he hit that wall in a panic. On the fantail, the after-lookout was sitting on the capstan located on the aft port corner of the flight deck. Seeing that container ship pass within feet of him put him into temporary shock. His division shipmates had to go pry his hands from the capstan and help him to his rack.

On the bridge, as our stern apparently just missed being ripped apart by the container ship, I was fully aware that now we had our rudder hard to port and a flank bell rung up to the engine room. The captain remained on the port bridge wing and watched the high, white hull of the *Japan Bear* slide past him. He said to me, "Rudder amidships."

I ran into the bridge and shouted, "RUDDER AMIDSHIPS!"

I ran to the radar repeater at the front of the bridge and tried to determine where we were in the channel. As fate would have it, at that exact moment the forward radar repeater failed. It went completely dark. I was without any visual references and we were shooting across the bay with a flank bell rang up and no course given and completely blind. It seemed to me that the situation had just gone from really bad to really badder.

"All stop!" was my order to the lee helm as I raced to the back of the bridge and shoved the quartermaster to the side to enable me to look at his master radar console. I was relieved to see that his scope was still operating correctly and tried to get my bearings and determine our location in relation to the channel as it curved around North Island.

Just then the CIC phone talker shouted, "CIC RECOMMENDS ALL BACK FULL AND HARD LEFT RUDDER!"

Oh, great! More back seat driving from the guys with no windows. Just then my attention became focused on the little remembered phone talker who connected the bridge with the sonar man manning the fathometer during the sea and anchor detail.

"Thirty-five feet under the keel," he said in a dry monotone.

Just a few seconds later he reported, "Twenty-seven feet under the keel."

This was bad news. I knew the channel had been dredged to an average depth of 60 feet, so if we were in the channel our depth under the keel should be around forty feet.

"Now only twenty feet under the keel and decreasing rapidly!" was the next report.

"Hard left rudder," was my next order.

"Fifteen feet under the keel."

The picture in my mind had us swinging to the left to get back in the channel, but the turn was not tight enough to keep us from running aground near Harbor Island. Since I had already cranked in the maximum rudder available, my only other choice was to increase the speed of the turn. It worked when driving a car...so I thought it might work in driving a ship.

"All ahead flank!"

"Ten feet under the keel."

"C'mon you beast, get through this turn and headed for the channel again," was my only thought for the next half-minute.

"Twelve feet under the keel."

Yeah! Dodged that bullet.

"Rudder amidships!" Things were starting to work themselves out...but then I made my second mistake of the evening. Since there was no visual reference to give me clues on our speed through the water, I forgot my last engine order was all ahead flank. Oops.

I was feeling clean, being bathed in the reports from the fathometer crew.

"Thirty feet under the keel...forty feet under the keel...forty-five feet under the keel."

Then I started to get dirty again.

"Thirty feet under the keel...twenty feet under the keel and decreasing rapidly...fifteen feet under the keel..."

Crap! I had shot right through the channel and now I was approaching the beach on North Island!

"ALL STOP! RIGHT FULL RUDDER!"

I was staring at the master surface search radar console by the quartermaster's table when the CO returned to the bridge. Much to my surprise he just went to his chair and picked up the ship-to-ship handset and started talking to the captain of the *Japan Bear*. This gave me a chance to get us back in the channel before he became aware of how I was racing at flank speed from one side of the harbor to the other.

Using the good picture on the radar, I was able to re-establish our position in the center of the channel and we navigated out of the harbor without further incident.

Almost.

As we approached "1-S-D" (the number of the first buoy as you enter the channel to arrive at San Diego,) the captain left the bridge to eat a late dinner in the wardroom. About ten minutes later we entered an area that appeared to be choppy sea clutter return on the radar. I found out this was not the case when bright lanterns appeared in the dark fog. We had steamed into the night fishing fleet. I slowed the ship immediately, but it was too late to avoid running through their nets.

I made the call to the wardroom to report to the captain. He was on the bridge a minute later and wanted to know just how in the world his ship could cut the nets of professional fishermen. I thought it a rather obvious answer if he would just look out of the bridge windows and note the black, thick fog.

I took the butt chewing like all good Academy graduates, and he left the bridge. I noted the time, and right then I knew I had gotten the shaft. It had been a very eventful sea and anchor detail to leave port and it took over two hours crawling through the fog and night to get where we could establish the normal underway watch team. It was 8 PM and the first section to go on duty was the 20 to 24 watch. This, of course, was my bridge section. I was emotionally exhausted and hungry, but I still had the "pleasure" of another four hours as OOD.

*****

The captain was not too adept at inspiring the best from his crew leaders. In fact, he once called a mandatory meeting for all officers and chiefs in the ward room. During the course of this meeting he shared his belief about our contributions to the Navy and his ship. The following is nearly an exact quote from this nuclear trained captain to the assembled leadership of his ship.

"Let me tell you that there are only two important jobs in the entire United States Navy. The first are engineers because without them this ship cannot move. The second is supply because they get the parts for the engineers.

"And there is only one difficult job in the entire United States Navy and that is engineers. Hell! I could get trained monkeys to do the rest of your jobs!"

Well, I don't know where he got it, but Ensign Todd Lowe, USNA Class of '74, who worked with me in the Weapons Department and was my roommate, somehow came up with a bunch of plastic bananas and hung it in our stateroom that very afternoon.

The entire crew was aware of the captain's honest beliefs within hours. During our next underway period I was standing the mid-watch (midnight to 4 AM) on the bridge. We were doing independent steaming and it was a very quiet night. The next thing I knew, I was hanging by one arm from the lifeline strung across the bridge at a height of about seven foot. With the other arm I was scratching my underarm while I made rather accurate sounds of a monkey. It was a rather good imitation, I thought. The bridge team enjoyed it and had a good laugh. I sensed something was up when the laughter immediately cut-off. I dropped to my feet and assumed the standard OOD pose with my hands resting on the "500-pound" binoculars hung around my neck.

I turned and noticed the captain standing there. "Good morning, captain."

He just grunted and left the bridge.

I don't think he was too impressed or surprised. In an earlier instance he had once appeared on the bridge to find the OOD, me, missing. It was a beautiful day at sea. Calm waters and good visibility and no other ships in sight as once again we were doing independent steaming. As the captain scanned the bridge to see where his OOD might be, he heard my voice bellow through the voice tube positioned in front of the helmsman.

"Ahoy, matey! Mind ye helm and steer 2-7-0. Keep a sharp eye out for them mermaids. They gots to be near, arrggh!" I said in my best pirate voice.

I was a little shocked to hear the captain's voice come from the voice tube near me on the flying bridge where I had moved my watch position. He said, "Mr. Bartron can I see you on the starboard bridge wing?"

There he suggested that I stand my watch from the main bridge. I agreed.

*****

The lessons of hard work and effective time management that I learned at the Academy were extremely valuable when Captain Almstedt assumed command. It was time for me to rotate to another assignment onboard the Schofield about the time he came aboard. My next job would still be in the Weapons Department, but I would assume duties as the Third Division officer. This is the ASW division and is comprised of sonar technicians, ASROC gunner's mates and torpedo men. To assume these duties I had to attend a couple of schools. The first was the six-week ASW Officer's Course at Naval Base Point Loma and the second was a course in the care and feeding of nuclear weapons held in a compound on NAS North Island.

My relief as First Lieutenant was not due to arrive until a week after I completed my scheduled ASW Officer's Course. So the captain and my department head thought if I truly wanted to move to Third Division, I should be able to lead both First and Third Divisions while simultaneously successfully completing the school located 25 minutes from the ship.

To do this, I had to flip my "1.94 GPA" switch and really get serious about keeping a packed schedule. So I would report to the ship at 6 AM and get my divisions started on their daily work by reviewing the schedules with the chiefs, complete any paperwork my department head wanted for that day, and then rush over to Point Loma to be in class at 7:30 AM. The school finished around 4 PM and then I would rush back to the ship to check on how much of the scheduled divisional work was completed, counsel any sailors who might need a word or two, complete whatever administrative work was required, and then head for home about 7:30 PM. After dinner I would do any homework and study for the course, which included mastering the movement of sound in the water and Soviet submarine tactics and American Navy ASW procedures and doctrine. This schedule was maintained Monday to Friday, and that left me Saturday to work exclusively on my division officer duties, and every other week I would have the duty on Sunday as well.

Technically, I was assigned full-time to the ASW Officer School house, but the CO felt I should be able to carry my own weight onboard the ship, to include standing weekend duty. About three weeks into the school, I was so tired that I fell asleep in class. My instructor knew the workload I was under, and he thought it best to mention the impact my schedule was having on my training to the school commanding officer.

That is when I became the rope in a CO tug-o-war contest.

It was like the refueling episode when the captain and carrier First Lieutenant wanted to know what to do and they turned to the ensign. Now once again, I was such a "valuable" asset that two commanding officers were fighting over my services...well, that is one way to look at it. In reality each CO was engaged in a "mine is bigger than yours" silly contest. The school CO felt he owned me and insisted my captain keep his hands off until I graduated. My CO felt he owned me and he would pull me out of that school just to spite the school house skipper. In the end a compromise was reached. I'd belong to the school house during the work week and to the ship on weekends. I was not happy with this solution because I still worked the same number of days, plus now my CO expected me to be the top of the class because I had so much time to study during the week!

*****

After graduation from ASW Officers School, I assumed full-time duties as Third Division Officer while maintaining responsibility for First Division. A week later the new lamb to the slaughter arrived and was made First Lieutenant. Almost immediately I learned that Third Division was totally different than First Division and that I would need to modify my leadership techniques.

A couple of days after taking over the division, I was walking through a passage way that was assigned to my division for cleaning and upkeep. Third Division had the reputation for keeping the best looking spaces on the ship. As I walked through this heavily traveled passageway on the main deck I noticed a single crushed cigarette butt lying in the corner. That was the only flaw in an otherwise outstanding space.

I turned to Sonarman First Class Jones who was the leading petty officer in the division and was walking with me and mentioned, "Petty Officer Jones look at that butt. We should pay more attention when we conduct sweepers after knock-off. Third Division has a reputation to keep up."

His only response was, "Yes, sir."

It was an off-hand comment and if I had said it to a sailor in First Division it would have been forgotten as quickly as I said it. But this was Third Division and pride ran high with these dedicated sailors.

I left the ship about 6:30 PM and went home. When I arrived at 6:30 AM the next morning I was shocked by what I found. That passageway had been prepped and painted and properly stenciled overnight. New tile was laid on the deck and waxed and polished to a beautiful shine. Plus, the couple pieces of brass fittings were shining brighter than the sun.

Immediately I remembered my casual comment the afternoon before, and I realized that I had better choose my words carefully when dealing with these professionals. It was my first pleasant encounter with the standards these sailors maintained for themselves and for the next eighteen months I enjoyed leading talented, intelligent, and motivated sailors. Gone were the days of having to stand over my men to ensure the work was done and done to a proper standard.

*****

One further example of how great it was to be supported by great sailors occurred just before we were set to deploy to the Western Pacific once again.

Four times during the week before our departure the captain asked me if I had enough expendable bathythermographs—"XBTs". That seemed like a peculiar question coming from the CO, but I had learned that his micromanagement nuclear style of leadership resulted in many oddly timed questions so I just shrugged it off and went on with the long list of prep items to be done before we deployed.

It was like the time he broke the unwritten rule of wardroom dining when he talked business during the luncheon. Lunch was to be a break in the long work day and a time to socialize and relax a little. Captain Almstedt just viewed it as an opportunity to reach out and connect with his worker bees and take reports on systems and operations preparations.

I had my soup spoon about to touch my lips when he loudly asked from his seat at the far end of the table, "Mr. Bartron, do you know the salinity content of your sonar cooling water?"

Reverting to my plebe training I automatically cycled through my five acceptable responses and settled on, "I'll find out, sir."

And I intended to do that as soon as we finished lunch. I slurped my spoonful of soup before I noticed that all the other officers at the table had stopped eating and were looking at me. I set down my spoon and made eye contact with the captain.

"Well?" he said, indicating that for some reason he needed to know the salinity content of our sonar cooling water right this instance while we sat in port, moored to the pier.

Being the good ensign Academy graduate, I pushed back from the wardroom table and mumbled "Excuse me," as I departed.

Turns out that our salinity content had been high in a test three days earlier, but currently my techs had properly controlled it and it was well within operating limits.

So when the CO repeatedly asked me about my supply of XBTs no bells or whistles went off in my head. However, the day before our scheduled early morning departure from San Diego I finally received the message from the Fleet Weather Center (FWC) that had sat on my department head's desk for two weeks. The message said that we were to help collect data on sea water temperatures at depth during out transit from San Diego to Pearl Harbor. Normally, a single XBT was used to do this twice a day when under way, or some days we did as many as one every four hours. The information was used to help the FWC develop accurate models of ocean temperatures in different areas of the world. We carried enough XBTs in our assigned stores to drop one every four hours for the four day transit to Hawaii.

However, I panicked when I read this tasking the Schofield had received for our next transit. We were to drop an XBT every hour of the transit. That meant we were to use nearly 100 on this trip! Now the captain's question about our stock made sense!

I was in a real bind. We had maybe forty XBTs aboard and somehow I had to locate sixty more late in the afternoon before we sailed the next morning. The base supply office was closed and I knew I was screwed. So I did what any smart ensign does before he falls on his own sword. I took my problem to the division leading petty officer.

I explained the screw-up and my assurances to the captain that we had enough XBTs for our transit. STG1 Jones was not the best sonar tech aboard the Schofield, but he was the best leader in Compartment 29, the Third Division berthing space.

"Can you get me the duty truck, sir?" was all he asked.

"You got it," I responded and raced to the quarterdeck. The OOD was the new supply department ensign and I told him to give me the keys to the pick-up assigned by the base motor pool while we were in port. He started to object, but the panicked look on my face was enough to convince him that my demands for the truck out weighed the other twenty sailors and officers who needed to use it.

I gave the keys to Jones and he drove off with a third class sonar tech. I paced the quarterdeck for an hour hoping that somehow Jones could get enough XBTs somewhere on base—even if he had to steal them—to get me out of this jam.

Before long, the duty truck came gliding quickly down the pier and stopped in front of our brow. In the bed of the truck, stacked higher than the cab, were Styrofoam boxes filled with XBTs. Jones gathered a Third Division working party and unloaded the truck in a matter of just a few minutes.

He had returned in under an hour with over 75 XBTs. I asked him where he got them and he gave the traditional senior petty officer answer when an officer asks about something that is best left unsaid, "You don't want to know, sir."

And, as usual, he was 100% right.

Yes, being Third Division officer was a special privilege on this ship.

*****

When I was First Lieutenant I decided to do what I asked my sailors to do on a regular basis. It was a real pain and slightly dangerous to frap the bow lines in port. Frapping is wrapping twine around the two or three large hawsers that were the mooring lines. This kept the lines looking neat and ship shape. There is only way to frap a set of lines. You have to climb out onto the lines and with your legs wrapped about them, slide down to the pier tying the twine in a half-hitch as you go. While doing this you were balanced about thirteen feet above the dirty, slimy port water. If you were a circus performer this would be a piece of cake, but doing it while wearing a bulky kapok life jacket and a safety line tied around your waist was more of a challenge. And it didn't help any if you were afraid of heights...like me. But I made it a point to frap the bow line...once. Although, I did let the seaman attach the rat guards which required the ability to climb back up the line to the ship.

So when we received a message to check the structural integrity of the ribs inside our bow mounted sonar dome, I thought it would be appropriate if I was involved in this unusual chore.

Again, not a good decision. Especially for anyone who suffers from any amount of claustrophobia, which, of course I do.

To reach the inside of the sonar dome all the water must be pumped from it and then a single, very narrow ladder is exposed by opening a hatch on the fo'c'sle. Anyone more than 220 pounds will not fit down the cramped and exceedingly deep hole. The hole was so tight that my shoulders rubbed against both sides and my back was pressed against the wall all the way down. I followed one of my sonar techs down the rabbit hole. We carried rubber mallets to use in testing the ribs. A second petty officer followed us carrying a large wrench.

Upon reaching the bottom it was dark except for the light from our small flashlights. At the end of the ladder is a small room about the size of a little closet. Only two men could stand in this space where you were surrounded by the cables that were attached to the large array of transducers. To reach the ribs that supported the rubber dome you had to wiggle to get on your back and then slide under the drooping electrical cables. Of course, you were moving through the wet sludge that was left by the sea water that had been pumped from the dome.

Once in the narrow space between the transducers and the bulbous exterior dome, there was just enough room to stand in a bent over position. We each started at opposite ends of the dome and began whacking the interior side of the ribs. If we heard a thud instead of a whack that meant the structural integrity of that rib was suspect. It took us about ten minutes to thump all of the ribs. Each one passed the test.

Now there were two ways to exit the dome. You could either climb back up the long, long narrow ladder, or exit through a hatch at the rear of the dome. When reviewing this option by studying the schematics of the ship's design it appeared that it was a simple crawl of maybe fifteen feet to reach the Louis-Allis Power Supply (LAPS) compartment deep, deep down in the ship. A hatch had to be unbolted from the dome side, so it was not possible to enter the dome through this hatch. The second petty officer had a wrench to remove the hatch bolts and open it so we rib whackers could take the short exit and then he could bolt the hatch behind us.

Ever since my experience climbing through that tight tunnel to escape the dome I have very closely identified with Charles Bronson's character in "The Great Escape." It took every bit of my conscious mind to control my fear once we entered that crawl space. It was so tight that after the first four feet it was impossible to crawl on your elbows. You slithered along like a snake, with your arms stretched before you and your toes pushing your undulating stomach forward. And once you commenced the passage, you were committed. It was impossible to back out of there. It was dark and our clothes were wet and slimy and there was no light yet at the end of this tunnel.

As I followed the petty officer, my fingers touching his shoes, a really bad thought struck me. The sailor behind us was bolting the hatch shut from the outside. In front of us the hatch that leads into the LAPS compartment was also bolted from outside the tunnel. Just what if my sailors had decided that it would be a good joke to keep us locked in this coffin-like prison?

The thought of being trapped in this tunnel was almost enough to induce a panic attack. However, I calmed my building fears by reminding myself, "I've had come arounds tougher than this." One such memory came back. I recalled being rolled down the stairs from the top floor of Bancroft Hall locked in a cardboard cruise box with instructions to change uniforms while I was inside the 3′ x 2.5′ x 2.5′ container.

Things were getting under control in my mind...until we hit the turn. About half way down the tunnel there was sharp "S" turn that we had to squeeze through. The only way I was able to contort my body to pass through this obstacle was the feeling of fresh air hitting my face from the open LAPS compartment hatch that was visible around the bend.

I am proud to say, that I have never met another officer who can say, "I'm an experienced dome diver for an AN\SQS-26AXR sonar." And, as usual, it was the result of another bad decision on my part. If I had it to do over again...I wouldn't!

*****

During our next WESTPAC deployment the weather was less than perfect for much of the cruise. It started with a sea breeze that blew the wrong way.

During out transit from San Diego to Pearl Harbor we were tasked to perform a burial at sea for the ashes of a retired chief warrant officer. No one in the crew had ever served with the late veteran, but if there is one thing the Navy excels at, it is formal ceremonies. So the second day out of sight of the west coast, we had a rehearsal for the ceremony since it is very rarely done. A couple of divisions of the crew and the officers and chiefs ran through the ceremony. The next day we all put on white uniforms and fell in to do the actual burial. Attention was called and the CO read some nice formal words, and the gunner's mates of Second Division fired a rifle volley.

Then it was time to set the ashes adrift, and my roommate Todd Lowe had been designated to complete this task. During the walk-thru the day previously, Todd had moved to the starboard side of the flight deck and pretended to toss over the ashes. However, during the actual ceremony he felt more pressure to properly execute this formal duty, especially with most of the crew at attention witnessing his performance.

With great dignity and appropriate military bearing, Todd retrieved the decorated cardboard shoe box that contained the remains and then proceeded to his assigned spot on the edge of the flight deck. Then he did something that was unexpected and confused those of us standing at attention in our white uniforms.

Todd removed the lid of the shoe box and tipped the box slowly to dump the ashes into the water. We had expected him to drop the entire box with its lid into the water, knowing that the seawater would dissolve the cardboard box and scatter the ashes throughout the sea. By opening and tipping the box, a plume of human remains was blown back over the flight deck. In a matter of seconds all of us were standing there with the grey ash and tiny bits of bone of what previously had been a warrant officer covering our white uniforms. Todd turned his head and shut his eyes as the ash cloud hit his face. A couple of seconds later he gave up his attempt to scatter the ashes and dropped the box over the side.

The captain read the last words and dismissed the formation. Most of us went to the downwind, port side and dusted the warrant's remains off our uniforms and into the Pacific.

Okay, maybe it wasn't as clean as it could have been...but we got the job done.

*****

The weather was the reason I learned a lesson about command from Captain Almstedt. We were transiting in company with another frigate from Yokosuka, Japan to Subic Bay, Philippines. The CO of the other frigate was senior to our captain so he assumed duties as commodore of this very small flotilla.

Before satellite weather screens and GPS navigational systems, the bridge team on a Navy ship had to know how to keep a seaman's eye on the weather and to use celestial navigation as well as LORAN to fix our position. Well, I had an OOD from the "old school" train me when I was getting qualified and he had the habit of maintaining a half-hourly barometer log. So, I did the same during my OOD watches. The only time it paid off was during this transit.

The skies were getting darker around the half way mark of my morning 8-12 watch. I asked the quartermaster what the weather forecast was and he said there were no reports of heavy weather along our route of advance.

When the size of the sea swells grew two feet higher than when I had assumed the watch, even a dumb ensign was beginning to figure out that the weather forecast might not be too accurate. I waited until the bottom of the hour to get one more reading on the barometer. Since I had a practice of monitoring barometric changes while on watch, the rapid fall in pressure looked unusual to me. I quickly plotted the inches of pressure on a piece of graph paper and then put a call into the captain. I told him of the drop in barometric pressure and he came to the bridge quickly and reviewed my chart.

Holding the chart in his hand he put in a call to the "commodore" in the lead frigate and advised him of the unusually quick drop in pressure. The more they chatted on the primary tactical frequency, the more Captain Almstedt scanned the skies and sea state. Finally, he suggested to the "commodore" that we should consider turning right and heading to Kure, Japan which was a typhoon safe harbor. We could stay there until the bad weather passed. The "commodore" thought that was not necessary and he said the flotilla of two ships would press on to the Philippines

Captain Almstedt hung up the handset and sat in his elevated bridge chair. He sat there very quietly as he pondered his choices. I always assumed he was recalling the worst damage done to the American fleet during World War II. More ships were sunk and damaged due to a fleet steaming into a typhoon than in any battle with the Japanese. Whatever he was musing about turned into action about thirty seconds later.

He almost leapt from his chair and grabbed the PRITAC handset and called the other frigate. Once he got the "commodore" on the line, he said, "It just doesn't look right to me, Stan. We're heading to Kure. Out."

He turned to me and said, "Take me to Kure."

I responded with "Right standard rudder, come to new course 3-0-0." The course was just a guess based on where I believed we were at the time, but we had many miles to fine tune it.

Our captain had put the "commodore" in a very delicate position. If he had pressed on to the Philippines and sustained even very minor damage due to the approaching storm, then he would have a lot to answer for. If he made it to Subic unscathed, then he would "bilge" his fellow CO by making Almstedt look like a "nervous Nellie." Either way, it would be viewed as poor leadership on his part. However, if he turned and followed us to a typhoon safe harbor, then his peacetime caution would be understood and accepted.

The other frigate put its helm to starboard and turned to fall in line behind us.

What I saw evidenced in this little episode was how a CO must always think for himself and to do what he feels is right for his command and his men, regardless of what the chain-of-command might get wrong.

What I also learned on that day was how to maneuver and dock a ship in very tight quarters with very heavy winds setting you off the pier and into moored super-container ships parked across the tiny harbor. It took us nearly an hour to moor successfully alongside the other frigate and required the use of shot lines to get our mooring lines over to our sister ship. Then the only way we were able to walk the ship closer was by using our bow and stern capstans to wench into the wind.

Once again, it was a very long watch and sea and anchor detail.

*****

Later that cruise we had liberty in Kaohsiung, Taiwan. We were moored to a buoy in the harbor and went ashore using water taxis. Still being an ensign, I pulled the dock watch that first night. Two petty officers and I were stationed on the wharf where our sailors disembarked and re-boarded the shuttle boats. It was rather boring duty for the most part; helping drunk sailors get back to the ship without getting into trouble and ensuring no contraband was brought back from this seaport city.

There was a bright street light in the middle of the short wharf and our station was under that light. The light was so bright that it was like working in a spotlight on stage; you could see inside the circle of light, but your eyes could not make the adjustment to see anything outside the spot.

After a while I began to get so bored, I thought I would explore our surroundings a little. Another big mistake.

As I approached a pile of what I guessed was trash some merchant ship had dumped on the end of the wharf I thought I heard some men rumbling in the debris. I started to investigate by going towards the noise when I heard one of the petty officers shout for me to halt.

"I wouldn't go by that pile of trash, sir," he said as he reached me with his flashlight on.

"Why not?" I asked.

He shone his flashlight beam onto the debris pile and illuminated something that scared me! Looking back at us with beady eyes shining in the flashlight beam were six pairs of black eyes. Each pair belonged to the biggest rats I had ever seen. Each was the size of a very large cat...even bigger than some dogs I'd known...and they were UGLY!

I returned to the round circle of light beneath the street lamp and decided I would stay in this "hoop of safety" for the rest of the watch.

*****

The next day I had the chance to go on liberty in southern Taiwan and check out the sights during the day time. It was much less scary then. Although, I did have one experience that I can recall. We got ashore shortly before lunch and after awhile we decided to get food at a local restaurant. We chose one that was packed with Chinese using the road logic of stopping at the truck stops with the most rigs because that was where the best food was served.

By this time I was an experienced world traveler and I knew what to order. Remembering the advice I had received at the Iranian O'club, I ordered a dish indigenous to the whole world—chicken! The waiter asked me if I wanted a whole chicken or a half-chicken. Being hungry and figuring that Chinese chickens might be somewhat undersized, I ordered the whole chicken.

A short while later our food arrived. I had a plate of deep fried chicken and started eating. I was pleased that I had made a good choice as the chicken was crispy and plentiful. However, on about the third piece I heard a sharp crunch as I bit into it. I checked my teeth to see if the sound was a filling breaking off, but there was nothing wrong with my teeth.

I examined the chicken piece in my hand and that is when I noticed the beak and eyes visible under the deep fry coating. I was eating the cooked head of the hen.

I then understood the waiter's question. I had asked for a whole chicken, and I got the *whole* chicken.

I set aside the head and then located the giblets and feet at the end of the drumsticks and set them to the side and ate the rest. I was hungry and it was good eating.

*****

Another stop during this cruise was a two-week stay in Guam to get repairs and upkeep. There is not much to do on that island other than scuba diving and visiting (at that time) the world's largest McDonalds. In fact, prior to the opening of the island to the tourist trade which built luxury hotels and resorts, sailors used to ask, "You know what Guam stands for? Give Up And Masturbate."

But I discovered a little known treasure on the island. It was the Navy center for all movie distribution throughout the Western Pacific fleet. I visited the non-descript white building on Naval Station Guam and made a deal with the civilian clerk who staffed the front desk. Each night I could check out a film from his library of Hollywood classics.

The hull technicians and boatswain mates made a large movie screen out of a pipe frame with canvas stretched across it and laced to the outer edges. The screen was fastened to the side of the ship that was tied to the pier. At night we rigged a projector and showed these classic movies on the screen, and since the sailors were on the pier and not on the ship in a mini drive-in arrangement they could bring beer and popcorn to the show. We screened the Errol Flynn-Olivia de Havilland version of "The Adventures of Robin Hood" in wonderful three-strip Technicolor and we saw "Casablanca" on a big screen in an uncut version and "Stagecoach" with the Duke. Being a movie nut, I was impressed by the crew's reaction to these films and the other half-dozen I had selected. All of the movies had been famous before they were born and this was the first time many had ever seen them without commercials and "panned and scanned" for television.

Many crew members returned early from liberty to spend an evening under the stars enjoying treasures of the cinema at the "Schofield Theater."

What I did not know, was this expertise with the operation of movie projectors that I had developed on Guam would be valuable later in my career.

*****

The combination of rough weather and a suspect power plant made for a real religious experience during this cruise. I often think back to the late afternoon when we were caught trying to outrun the fury of a typhoon. The seas had grown to twenty feet and the tops of the swells were blown away in the fierce winds, encrusting the entire topsides in salt. I remember standing on the bridge wing, my eye-level over twenty feet above the water line and looking up at a twenty foot wall of water that loomed over my head. With twenty foot seas, the ship would ride up twenty feet above the normal sea level on the crest and then, when the waves had amplified their motion for a few seconds, we would sink into a trough with high swells on each side.

The only thing that keeps a sleek warship from rolling over and sinking is power to the stern. As long as we had the screw turning, we could steer the bow into the on coming waves and knife through them like a surfer paddling out to catch the big one. It was on this day that I actually agreed with the captain...the only important job in the Navy is the engineering ratings. If the turbines shut down or the boilers went off line, it would be just a matter of minutes before the seas turned us to where we were caught in a trough with mountains of water slamming against our superstructure. Combatants are built long, narrow and sleek to race through the oceans in order to project power rapidly anywhere in the world. They are not built fat and stumpy like Liberty ships that were designed to bob like corks in typhoons.

So that evening and through the night I am sure about 200 crew members were all praying to escape the massive strength and dominance of the sea...and that we maintained power to the stern.

*****

Just before I was promoted to lieutenant (junior grade) I was once again identified as the one officer the ship could afford to be without during a joint exercise. This time I was selected to be an exchange officer with the Royal Thai Navy.

Once again I found it challenging at meal times. The first night onboard before we departed for the five-day joint exercise, all the officers gathered for a welcome dinner in the wardroom. A main dish was steamed rice.

Now growing up, whenever my mother served rice there was always something to ladle over it, such as gravy or a vegetable based sauce. This meal had nothing like that to go with the rice, but I noticed that other officers were passing around a small bowl containing a sauce and each took a spoonful to spread over his rice. When they had finished, I reached for the bowl and spread a tablespoon of sauce on my rice. It soaked in rather quickly, so I took another spoonful and when the rice absorbed that one as well, I added a couple more spoonfuls. It was then that I noticed everyone at the table had stopped eating and was watching me. I figured they must be thinking that I was a real hog, so I stopped adding the sauce to my rice.

They all kept eyeing me until I took my first bite of the rice. WOWEE! I was raised in California and was used to spicy Mexican food, but this Thai sauce was a hundred times hotter! They all got a good laugh as I reached for my water and gulped it down while my eyes filled with tears. That was some real powerful spice I had consumed unknowingly!

For the next four days the chimes would ring and an announcement was made in Thai that the meal in the wardroom was ready to be served. Again, not knowing any Thai, I just associated the chimes and announcement with rice in the wardroom. So I would put down my book and shuffled down to the wardroom. When I wasn't observing in their Combat Information Center or on the bridge I often would lie in my rack and read a book I had picked up in Taiwan. The book was Five Years to Freedom by Major Rowe who was held captive for five years by the Viet Cong. I read the book in a very realistic setting. In it, Major Rowe described his hot, humid and bug invested captivity and how he survived by following one basic rule: "Eat rice and live; don't eat rice and die."

This pre-World War II destroyer escort that America had transferred to the Thai Navy had no air conditioning and when a cockroach fell from the ceiling into my food at the wardroom table my embarrassed hosts explained that the cockroaches were American and had come with the ship. So often times when I heard the chimes to call me to eat rice, I'd be lying in my top rack with by shirt unbuttoned to keep cool and flicking cockroaches that fell from the overhead off my hairy chest. As you can tell, I really was immersed in Major Rowe's story.

Three events during these days riding the Thai ship stand out in my memory. The first was the observation of a different attitude their crew had about immediate responsibilities. During the exercise, the Schofield was scheduled to shoot its AAW Tartar missile at a drone target. I was helping my hosts with translation of Navy tactical signals because I could understand the directives coming over the radio without having to convert the direction from English to Thai. They had a copy of an old Allied Tactical Publication with English written on the right page and the exact same information written in Thai on the opposing page. I would hear the radio call and then quickly flip to the right page and hand the book to the CIC Watch Officer. He would read the direction in Thai and then recommend to the bridge what course to take in compliance of the order.

Well, when the call came from the Schofield to standby for missile launch, I quickly excused myself to leave CIC and step outside so I could see the contrails of our Tartar spin up into the sky. I had never seen our missile fired while on another ship. When I got to the rail and started watching the Schofield, I noticed that I was not alone. Standing next to me was the one English speaking officer and next to him, lined up along the deck was the entire CIC watch team!

I asked my interpreter, "Who is monitoring the radio circuits in CIC?"

"We all want to see the missile shoot," he said as he smiled.

"But what if someone calls while we are all out here on deck?" I asked incredulously.

"Oh, don't worry," he answered, "They will call back."

I shook my head. That was a totally different attitude to the involvement we expected our watch teams to have.

Another strong memory was my visit to this destroyer escort's engine room. I mentioned that I wanted to visit the engineering spaces and my English speaking escort suggested that I wear my oldest set of work khakis I had brought with me. That seemed strange but I followed his advice.

I understood the suggestion as soon as I entered the engine room.

Before and during World War II many ships did not use steam turbines as primary propulsion. The old Victory ships and many merchants used what was called "triple expansion reciprocating steam engines." This old destroy escort had a triple expansion system. I felt like I had been shrunk to a three inch man and inserted into a cars crank case. The high pressure steam came from the boiler and was vented into a six-foot diameter piston. The steam would drive the piston on the down stroke and then the piston would rise as the humongous crankshaft below rotated. On the upward stroke the steam would be ported to a second piston. Since some of the energy had been lost driving the first piston, the second cylinder was larger than the first and it ported its used steam to a third, much larger cylinder. On this old ship, the seals around the lubricating system were leaky and the result was that the crankshaft was lubricated as much from the oil mist that floated all around the engine room as it was by the seal system. When I left the engine room my khaki uniform was spotted from the oil in the air and my face, arms and hair were covered as well. But it was neat to be *inside* a reciprocating engine!

My third memory of that time as a ship rider was the skillful ship handling expertise of the CO. Now I had a reputation as a bridge and CIC watch stander who could solve maneuvering board problems accurately and more quickly than most of my peers. I honestly had the ability to make that "mo' board" sing! A "mo' board" is just a graphing sheet used to add vectors to determine what direction to steer the ship to arrive at a new screening position around the carrier or to determine the direction and time to intercept another ship and problems such as these. I was on the bridge helping the OOD solve maneuvering problems because I could understand the English directions and then rapidly come up with a new course whenever the ships had to change positions in the screen. Confident in my abilities to quickly and accurately solve these problems, I was not shy about announcing my solution to the bridge watch standers. However, it wasn't long before I found I could just keep my opinions to myself.

We received a long signal to switch positions in a screen around the high value target. It was a complicated problem and it took me a full minute to arrive at a solution. While I was focused on this task, I did not notice the captain quietly say something to the helmsman. When I announced with great pride my solution for the recommended course I could see that I had beaten the other junior officers who were still working the problem. Then I realized just how salty this CO was after a decade of commanding this particular ship.

I said, "I recommend course 1-7-6 to new screening station!"

The English speaking officer got a grimace on his face as he ever so politely and with a touch of regret in possibly embarrassing me said, "Eh...the captain prefers course 1-7-5."

That old sea dog had solved that intricate vector problem of effective ship handling in his head and had given the helmsman an accurate course just seconds after the order was received. I did feel a little foolish in my false pride, but I was even more impressed by the ship handling skills of this seasoned officer.

*****

Foreign navies have different attitudes about many things that cause the U.S. Navy great concern. My department head went to a coordination conference with the South Koreans prior to a joint exercise. During this pre-sail meeting, the Koreans showed great interest in the practice missile launch that was on the schedule for the Schofield. We were to fire the Tartar missile in the surface mode at a target placed off the west coast of South Korea.

My boss, the Weapons Officer, asked a simple question that at first the Koreans had trouble understanding. He said, "Who is going to clear the range around the target before we shoot?"

The Koreans assumed puzzled looks and asked what he meant.

The Weapons Officer expanded his question, "Who is going to be sure that there is nothing out by the target that could be hurt?

"What do you mean?"

"You know," my boss elaborated, "like a fishing boat too near the target."

"No worry," the Korean officer said as he smiled, "we have plenty fishing boats."

My boss's eyes grew wider as he understood that any life taken by any error in military operations was a price the Koreans were willing to pay.

We arranged for our LAMPS helicopter to clear the range before we shot.

*****

Bad seas also got me kicked off the bridge on a second occasion...sorta.

One day I went to sleep in my rack with the world's absolute best excuse for any screw-up I might make. All I needed to say was, "Well, what did you expect? I'm only a dumb ensign?"

The next morning I woke up and all of a sudden I was expected to be the backbone of knowledge and competence in the destroyer navy. Onboard small boys, ensigns are too junior to know anything and lieutenants and above are department heads and they are too senior to do the daily grunt work. It was the lieutenants (junior grade) who had the experience to be expected to know how to do a job, but not so senior yet to get out of doing it.

I really was happy as a dumb ensign and I thought it was cruel that at the two-year point of commissioned service I was automatically promoted. I was sure it was a conspiracy to trap me into meeting higher expectations.

These increased expectations after being promoted led to my next opportunity not to impress the captain.

We were refueling from a carrier during a transit and "Romeo Corpen" (heading for the evolution) chosen did not take into account that a frigate rides differently than a flat-top. The course the carrier chose crossed the moderately heavy swells at a diagonal. The refueling station we were to use just happened to place our ship right on the bow wake of the carrier.

These conditions meant that we were rocking from side to side due to the sea state and we were in essence, "surfing" on the big ship's forward wake. We had to keep extra turns rung up on the propeller to overcome the drag of the wake. If we got just a few feet too far forward we would break through the wake and rapidly shoot ahead and be out of the perfect position.

The rocking back and forth meant that our spreader which held antennae to the stack could sway closer than desired to the carrier's lowered elevator as the two ships tilted towards each other.

I had the 7 -12 morning OOD watch and so when we went alongside the carrier at 11 AM I had the deck and the con, and I would retain it throughout the evolution. For the next fifty minutes I gave a constant stream of helm and lee-helm orders through the voice tube on the port bridge wing. It went something like this.

"Come left to 2-3-8. Add two turns. Come farther left to 2-3-6, add two more turns." Then we would break ahead of the carrier bow wake and I would almost shout, "Come right to 2-4-0, drop five turns!"

I had driven the ship alongside replenishment ships many times and I never had to work so hard and steadily to keep position. The combination of the refueling course, selection of refueling station, the carrier's chosen speed of advance and our ship's relationship to the carrier's bow wake made for constant work to successfully conduct this everyday operation of the U.S. Navy.

Add to these circumstances that I was tired from having already been on watch for over four hours and I was in no mood to accept criticism from anyone—even the CO.

The CO had positioned himself behind me prior to my approach to the carrier. He had his arms hanging over the side of the port bridge wing bulkhead and he stood on the deck plates while I was stationed eighteen inches above him on the raised platform around the compass repeater. The captain did not say a word for the first forty-five minutes as he observed me working my butt off to keep us on station.

Eventually, I was a little late in making a correction to keep our distance from the carrier at the desired eighty feet. As a result, we closed to sixty-five feet before I could move us out again. Just at this time both ships rocked towards each other due to the seas and there was only about thirty feet between the carrier's elevator and our mast spreader.

"SIXTY-FIVE FEET! WHAT ARE YOU DOING?" the captain yelled at me.

That is when I had had enough and let him know. Before I could think about what I was saying, I yelled, "WHAT AM I DOING? I'M DOING THE BEST THAT I CAN! IF YOU DON'T LIKE IT, GET SOMEONE ELSE TO DO THIS."

I did not muse over my rather blunt snap comment to the captain because I was tired and *busy*! I returned to my constant steam of orders to the helmsman and lee helmsman. A short while later I noticed the XO conferring with the captain behind my back, but I was too involved in keeping us on station to consider what they were doing.

Five minutes later, my boss, LT Hall stepped onto the port bridge wing holding a sandwich in one hand and wearing binoculars around his neck. It was obvious that he had been called to leave lunch and report to the bridge.

He said, "Bob, I understand you want to be relieved."

Now I knew what the CO had told the XO.

"Yes, I do," I replied between orders to the bridge team.

"Okay, I'll take over. Go get some lunch," Hall said in his casual Kentucky accent.

Captain Almstedt never mentioned my comments and I retained my OOD qualification and remained on the watch bill. I guess I had reached my limit that day and I have no regrets at being relieved early...none whatsoever.

*****

One day we were in port in San Diego, nested just outside of the USS Samuel Gompers once again. The Gompers was a newer Destroyer Tender and had a very high freeboard, its main weather deck being the same height as the 0-3 deck of the Schofield. I was making a tour of our main deck when I noticed Gunner's Mate Technician Chief (GMTC) Housdan supervising a test of the Mark 32 Torpedo Tubes on the port side, amidships. Chief Housdan was the senior ASROC petty officer onboard. He was in charge of the other ASROC gunner's mate technicians and the Torpedomen in Third Division.

Like most chiefs in the Navy, he preferred to do things the way he had been taught by his senior petty officers when he was coming up the ranks. I first realized this when I inspected the inside of the ASROC launcher and saw an inch of hydraulic fluid sloshing around the bottom of this sophisticated weapons system. I will always remember his answer to the young junior officer's inquiry on if that pool of fluid was normal.

"Sir, I was taught that when it comes to hydraulic systems, if it ain't leakin', it ain't workin'."

He wasn't trying to buffalo me with this answer. He actually believed what he was saying. It was what his chief had convinced him was the truth years ago.

As I came upon the torpedo tube test he was supervising with the two Torpedomen in the division, I knew enough to ask, "I see you have removed the three torpedoes from this port side launcher. Have you also removed the torpedo tube flasks from the starboard launcher?"

Knowing it would only take a small error to select the starboard vice port side on the launch console in the Underwater Battery (UB) Plot to fire the wrong tubes, procedures called for the opposite side launcher to be rendered unusable before a test firing of a torpedo flask.

"We don't need to so that, sir. We're only testing this side," the chief replied.

"Well," I said in a firm, but non-demanding voice, "how about you humor the JO and take out the starboard flasks just to be safe?"

He sighed, but stopped the test until the compressed air flasks that were used to fire the torpedoes out the tubes were removed from the starboard tubes. I left and went about my business, feeling confident that safety was ensured.

I happened to return just as the chief was about to give the order to fire the air from the flask being tested. I saw the three torpedoes sitting on blocks on the deck and the two flasks not being tested sitting next to them.

Pleased that everything was proper and ready for the test, I asked just one more question before the chief continued, "You did remember to remove the muzzle covers, right Chief?"

"Of course we did, sir."

The muzzle covers were made of marine plywood and were round discs that fit in the end of the tubes to keep salt water from entering the weapon systems when at sea. Each was attached by a lanyard to the end of the tube, but they were not visible when the tubes were cranked to the launch position, with the barrel end facing out to sea.

"Okay, then I guess all is ready to test the flask," I said to the chief.

A little exasperated that his division officer had made such an easy chore much harder than it had to be, the chief told the third class petty officer to relay the fire signal via sound-powered phone to the UB Plot.

Immediately a very loud "WHACK" rang through the harbor, followed by a series of "BANGS" as the muzzle cover was shot against the steel side of the USS Samuel B. Gompers and then bounced from ship side to ship side as it fell into the water below.

The chief and I immediately stepped to the side and looked down at the camel spacer tied between the Schofield and the tender. We were just in time to see the muzzle cover bounce off the camel and slide into the water.

There was a momentary pause and then the chief spoke, "Oh, by the way, sir, did I mention that we lost a muzzle cover during our last at sea period?"

"Then I guess you better order a new one from supply," I answered as I stared at the large mark and slight dent in the steel side of the Gompers.

Just then, as sailors on both ships started to arrive to investigate the unusual sounds, the chief and I thought it a good time for the test crew to take a break. We vacated the area and went on about our business.

*****

Unusual sounds in port occurred on occasion.

In the Navy, probably the most tradition-bound and formal service, there is a "rite" performed everyday when one officer assumes the duties of another. A formal recitation of exact words is used to pass the responsibilities to another at the end of the watch. It goes as follows.

Relieving officer says, "I am ready to relieve you, sir."

The officer going off watch replies, "I am ready to be relieved."

Relieving officer states, "I relieve you, sir."

The departing watch stander answers, "I stand relieved."

As soon as that statement is made, all authority and responsibility of the watch officer is transferred to the on-coming watch. It happens in an instant and there is no way to rewind the event and pretend it did not happen.

I know this, because of what happened in the first seconds of the very first watch I ever stood as the Command Duty Officer (CDO.)

I had worked hard to complete all of my qualifications to receive a letter from the CO saying I was fit and ready to act in his place should he be absent from the ship. That is the duty of the CDO, to meet the CO's obligations whenever the captain and XO might be ashore. A good example of the responsibilities of the CDO can be seen in the opening minutes of the John Wayne movie, "In Harms Way" when a LT (JG) gets his destroyer underway on the Sunday morning of the Pearl Harbor attack by the Japanese. The CO of the ship is chasing the destroyer in a small boat shouting for the ship to slow so he could rejoin his command, but the CDO ignores the captain because he felt it would endanger the ship to stop in the channel.

Just because I had finished the self-instruction program to earn my CDO designation, it did not mean I was confident in meeting the new and larger responsibilities. However, since the other officers wanted to add another watch stander to the watch bill to lift some of the duty load from them, I was immediately assigned as CDO on the very next Sunday after my final qualification.

I remember exactly how that duty day began. The off-going CDO and I followed the formal ritual. At the end I said the fateful words, "I relieve you, sir," and we exchanged salutes. By the time our arms had returned to our sides from the salute an extremely loud "BANG" was heard. It sounded like the five-inch gun had gone off. A look of dread and worry came over my frightened face, but a sly smile formed on the lips of the previous CDO.

"It's all yours, Bob," he said

What a way to start your very first watch! Besides the explosion, all the lights and power went off. I raced to the 0-3 level to investigate, as that was my best guess of where the bang had emanated. When I got there I found a sailor with a fire extinguisher knocking down a small electrical fire near where the shore power cables had been attached.

I came to find out that the source of the blast was when a shore cable failed and blew out of the outlet. The duty engineering department personnel got our auxiliary diesels on line and restored power. Later that day a new shore power cable was attached and things were back to normal.

However, that was the end of that khaki uniform because I was standing on the 0-3 level when the diesels lit off and the breeze was blowing from the fantail. The Schofield's diesels had the nasty habit of blowing small droplets of oil with their exhaust. My uniform now could join the ruined one I had worn on the Thai ship.

*****

Sailors sometimes do the stupidest things. One day I was inspecting our torpedo magazine and I happened to see a couple of dents on the warhead area of one of the fish. It did not take much investigation to notice that the indentations were a perfect match to a work hammer attached to the bulkhead. It was obvious that some sailor had been beating on the warhead with a hammer.

Now who would whack 97 pounds of high explosive with a hammer? Why would he do that? I tried to answer these questions, but I never found the answers and finally just had to chalk it up to: "Sailors sometimes do the stupidest things."

Of course we had to empty the magazine and inspect all of the weapons for any more damage. In doing this I learned that sailors can be rather ingenious as well.

The Navy procedure to move a MK 46 torpedo required the use of a chain hoist to raise the weapon and set it on an expensive, specially designed wheeled cart. The cart would then be maneuvered out of the large magazine door and wheeled to the torpedo tubes. The flask would be removed from the breech of the tube and then the cart would be positioned to permit it to be latched to the breech. Then once the cart is perfectly aligned with the tube, the torpedo could be carefully pushed into the weapons launching system. Then the cart would be unlatched and moved out of the way to permit the reattachment of the compressed air flask. When I watched this procedure performed by my two Torpedomen I was thinking about how difficult and time consuming this evolution would be if we had to reload at sea during combat. I doubted it could ever be done should the need arise to reload in a hurry.

It was during the emptying of the entire magazine that I saw how sailors had worked around the engineers' instruction manual to overcome this handicap should we need to reload in a battle. My Torpedomen did not use the chain hoist mounted on the ceiling of the magazine, nor did they use the awkward cart. Rather, they had two heavy nylon straps about thirty inches long with a loop sewn in each end that the boatswain mates had made for them. They would pass each one under the torpedo on either side of the center of gravity and grab the ends on their side of the weapon. With the sailors facing each other across the weapon and the loops around their wrists they would lift with their legs and then side step out of the magazine with the torpedo suspended at arms length. The torpedo weighed 500 pounds and two stout torpedo men, using proper leverage had no problem maneuvering it. When they reached the torpedo tubes they would lift the nose into the tube and slide the weapon in. Using this method a reload could be accomplished in under a quarter of the time taken when using the hoist and cart system.

I was once again reminded that sailors get the job done.

*****

Sailors also can make mistakes.

I had assumed duties as Third Division officer about two weeks prior to the day I met Chief Housdan descending the ladder near the ASROC magazine just as I was climbing up. He was soaking wet from head to toe. I made a small joke as I stopped climbing half way up the ladder.

"Wow! You gotta learn to get out of the rain, Chief."

"Sir, we've got big problems," he said in a low, serious voice with an anguished look on his face to match.

He turned and went back up the ladder and I followed closely behind. The armed ASROC sentry which was required to be posted 24/7 while we were in port had my access badge ready as I reached the top of the stairs. Today's sentry was a Sonarman from my division and had anticipated my arrival.

Two steps later the chief and I reached the aft door to the ASROC magazine. The forward door was a big hatch with sufficient room to move the large rockets in and out of the magazine. The aft door was a small personnel hatch that had its base about three feet above the deck and the top rim about four feet above the base. The chief entered first and then I lifted my leg and stepped over the opening to enter. I set my leg down into three-foot deep water. The magazine sprinkler system had filled the space with salt water in a matter of seconds. It was off now and the water was quickly draining from the magazine. I sloshed my way around the conventional weapons to reach the nuclear depth charges stored in the magazine.

Now ASROC nuclear depth charges are activated by emersion in salt water and then armed when a certain depth trips a trigger. Well, through a gross error, the first step in that firing sequence was completed when the bottom two weapons had been flooded by the sea water.

I knew I had better report this to the captain before I even found out how it happened. As the custodian of our nuclear weapons I knew that there was a special flash message that had to be sent to the military command center in Washington D.C. within fifteen minutes of any mishap with a nuclear weapon. There were three levels of this mandatory report. The first was a "Broken Arrow" report which means that an accidental discharge of a nuclear weapon had left a large mushroom cloud somewhere in the world. The next level was a "Bent Spear" which means the weapon was lost, or damaged sufficiently to require it to be returned to New Mexico to be rebuilt. The lowest level was a "Dull Sword" which was used to report something unusual or possibly news worthy about nuclear weapons.

As I bent over and stepped out of the aft hatch, I knew I was a little late in getting to the CO. In my vision was a khaki shirt collar with two stars attached. Next to this admiral that had instantaneously appeared on the Schofield was the captain.

The only word that came to my mind, but which I fortunately did not verbalize was "Oops."

The initial flash message was sent within the fifteen minute window, which was something to feel good about. Of course, we reported it as a "minor" "Dull Sword" incident. Turns out we were wrong in our classification because the weapons had to be shipped back to New Mexico to be rebuilt...but that was a week later when all the fuss had died down somewhat.

I added the experience of sending a "Dull Sword" to my prior captain's mast as something I was sure 99.9% of all officers went through their entire careers without doing. *Yeah Bob!*

The cause of this mishap was a lesson learned. Chief Housdan scheduled the test of the magazine sprinkler system and advised me he was going to conduct it that morning. It being a normal "Preventive Maintenance System" (PMS) check I thought nothing of it. The chief verified that the correct diverter test valve was selected by his GMGTs and then he stepped out of the magazine to verify that the hose which would dump the saltwater overboard was correctly placed. Unbeknownst to him, his petty officer had examined the diverter valve and come to the conclusion that it was too large for the planned test. He chose another one in the box and inserted it in the sprinkler intake pipe. When the chief returned, the diverter was installed and the overboard discharge hose was in place. So the chief ordered the sprinkler water to be turned on. The smaller diverter valve did not redirect the water properly and the magazine sprinklers did exactly as they were designed to do and promptly started to flood the weapons. By the time the chief had notified engineering to turn off the sprinklers, the water had risen higher than the two weapons stored on the bottom of the pile and had reached the base of the aft hatch.

The results of this error were many. Firstly, the Schofield crew had its qualification in nuclear weapons handling revoked until retraining could be completed. This meant we had to endure the embarrassment of another, still qualified crew from a sister ship coming aboard to remove our weapons for shipment back to the weapons station. Secondly, someone in charge had to be held accountable.

Our ship's office was always terribly behind in their administrative work. It was only because of this inefficiency that my career proceeded unaffected by this major mishap. As the division officer I should have been the witnessing supervisor of this test, however the letter designating me with this authority had yet to be typed by the yeomen. Consequently, the chief who had a qualification designation in his file got a formal letter of reprimand and I got nothing. The chief shrugged it off because he was just a couple months away from retirement and had no intention of vying for another promotion.

I was once again reminded of what my mother said of me...go in dirty as sin and come out smelling like a rose.

*****

On our transit back from Pearl Harbor to San Diego at the end of a seven and one-half month deployment, we conducted a Tiger Cruise. This is a special short cruise where male relatives of the crew are allowed to ride along. At about five days, the Hawaii to California transit is the perfect length. Approximately 35 civilians consisting of brothers, uncles, older children, and fathers rode with us. My dad was a Navy combat veteran of the Pacific theater during World War II and he was thrilled to relive the experience of going to sea on a big grey floating thing once again.

It was a special memory, but it was marred by something I had to endure during the transit. Early in 1975 the Navy approved the awarding of Surface Warfare Officer Insignia to ship drivers. The pilots had wings and the submariners had dolphins, so now the "surface skimmers" were getting their own insignia. A qualification program had been developed by BUPERs which was quite detailed. I had worked hard to complete all the requirements prior to our arrival at Pearl Harbor on the transit back from this latest WESTPAC cruise. There was only one more item to complete to be the first on my ship to earn the new insignia. I had to pass an oral examination board.

The board members consisted of the XO and the department heads on the ship. None of them had ever completed such a board or sat on an oral examination board, so they were totally new to this just as I was. I was confident in my knowledge of Schofield systems and fleet tactics and seamanship evolutions such as anchoring, mooring to a buoy, alongside and vertical replenishment procedures as well as the capabilities and employment of our armament systems. However, I was not ready for the attitude of the department heads.

This oral examination soon turned into an initiation with the primary objective of discovering what I did not know as opposed to discovering what I did know. Each of the department heads tried to show the others that he knew more about his department than his peers. I remember two questions that are perfect examples of the kind of minutia they quizzed me on. The chief engineer asked me what the energy was of the steam as it entered the low pressure turbine. No other officer sitting around that wardroom table could answer that question. I said, "Obviously the entropy of the steam decreased while driving the high pressure turbine, but I would need a Mollier Table to determine what the energy was as it entered the low pressure turbine. If you have one, I will show you how it is used to answer your question."

He just shook his head and gave an audible hiss through his teeth.

I was an Academy graduate and I knew the steam cycle and even how to utilize a Mollier Table and I could give the four functions of the De-aerating Feed Tank and diagram the entire fire room and engine room systems. But I did not have the precise answer to his obscure question. I got red under my collar when this type of question continued to be thrown at me, since I knew that the Operations Officer and Weapons Officer had never served in engineering and knew even less than I did about the power plant.

Next the Operations Officer asked me, "What is the Data Link between Marine ground units and naval aircraft?" Again, I knew the Data Link and its parameters that ships used between each other and with naval aircraft—but what possible need did I have to know what Marines in-country used? No where in the qualifications list of required knowledge factors was this mentioned. And once more I was sure that neither the Chief Engineer or Weapons Officer or Supply Officer knew the answer.

For nearly four hours I was grilled by the department heads on the particular subjects each was an expert in. Then I was dismissed from the room while they discussed my performance. Then they called me back into the wardroom. They temporarily failed me and said I would have to sit for another examination board in three days. I left that room humiliated. I had never failed in trying to earn a qualification and they failed me *with my father onboard!* He greeted me in my stateroom with a big smile and ready to slap my back and congratulate me on earning my SWO pin. Instead, I had to disappoint him and that honestly and deeply hurt.

Over the next couple of days I researched the minutia that had tripped me up and I screwed up my positive attitude and entered the wardroom ready to try again. This time the board consisted of the department heads, the XO *and the CO*. It went differently the second time.

Captain Almstedt knew my watch standing and division officer performance. He knew I had good study habits and had prepared well for this required step in earning my SWO pin and I came to believe the XO had briefed him on how the first board had been conducted. So this second examination did not take four hours. In fact, it barely took four minutes. I was asked three questions which I answered correctly and succinctly. The captain then placed both hands on the table and pushed his chair back.

He rose and said, "Well, I'm convinced he is ready for his pin. You guys can continue to ask him more if you like, but I've got other things to do."

He rose and left the wardroom. The department heads looked at the XO. The XO said, "Well, I guess that settles the question."

Everyone left the wardroom and I remained sitting there dumbfounded, but relieved.

My dad and I enjoyed the remaining days of the Tiger Cruise.

*****

After two and one-half years of standing up to drive the ship, I was ready to transfer from the fleet to a job where you could sit down while you worked. I completed an application to attend flight school.

Getting my department head's recommended approval was easy, but it took nearly an hour of discussion with the XO to obtain his recommendation. The XO tried talking me out of the request because he was sure that the CO would disapprove it. In the prior weeks, two other junior officers had made requests to transfer off the Schofield. One wanted an early out to attend post graduate school and the other wanted to attend Supply Officer School. The captain had disapproved both. The XO was sure my request would suffer the same fate.

It took a lot to convince the XO I was not trying to *leave* the Schofield, but rather I wanted to *go* to flight school. Eventually he agreed to send my request to the CO with a recommendation for approval.

I got the word the captain wanted to see me as soon as we moored after a five day at sea period. When I reported to his in-port cabin, the CO was sitting at his desk, both hands supporting his head. You could tell from his eyes that he had not slept for at least 36 hours while we finished the sea exercise.

I expected I would have to defend my request with even more earnestness than I had with the XO, but he did something that surprised me.

He turned to me and asked me only two questions. "Do you know how to fly?"

I had earned my private pilot's license in high school so I answered, "Yes, sir."

"Do you like it?"

I answered truthfully, "Yes, sir."

Without another word, he took my request and signed it recommending I be selected to attend flight school. The only proviso was that my relief had to check aboard before I departed.

I was stunned by how easy it had been to get his approval. So I tried to fill the silence by asking a germane question, "Do you think I have much of a chance of being selected?"

His answer has always stuck with me and I think, reflected his opinion of aviators, "Oh, they'll take you alright, but then they won't have a job for you."

At the time I thought he was referring to the post-Vietnam navy draw down, but upon recollection I think his point was that aviators were so plentiful it was hard to keep them fully employed in their ground jobs.

I discovered he was right.

Chapter Three

Flight School

When I had been in ASW Officer School an Academy classmate was attending at the same time. He had been a big football star at the Boat School and had chosen Navy Air as his service selection upon graduation. He had bilged out of flight school and was assigned to a ship when I met him in Point Loma where we were training. During the course of the class I heard him explain why he failed to finish flight school.

"I just couldn't put up with their chicken attitude about stupid stuff," was his explanation.

I remembered this comment on my first day at Pensacola and every time I was frustrated by the bureaucratic and rigid requirements of parts of the flight pipeline. The comment made me put my ego in a can and bury it deep within me. I was determined to get my wings and there was nothing the system could ask of me that would deter me.

The transition from operating in the sea going fleet to readjusting to a training command was not easy. One of the changes was the different responsibilities. A month prior to reporting, I drove a 3,426 ton ship with the lives of a crew of 220 in my hands, and I had my own nuclear weapons arsenal and I was totally responsible for the performance of the 25 technicians in my division. The day I reported to flight school I became responsible for the performance of only one man—me!

On the first day of flight school were two academic tests that all reporting student pilots had to complete. In order to commence training, new arrivals had to exhibit sufficient knowledge in math and physics to evidence they were ready to begin ground school. Practice exams had been sent to me prior to reporting day. Although I had been a history major in college, I had attended an engineering school where all midshipmen had to complete a ton of math and science in the curricula. However, my skill set in these subjects was very rusty, so I had spent many hours preparing for the exams.

I was still nervous when I reported to the classroom at NAS Pensacola and saw that I was the oldest student taking the exams. I got more nervous when a small group huddled around me asking if I knew how to use the slide rule I carried. They wanted me to show them how it worked! This frightened me, because for four years I had toted this thing to classes everyday. How is it that these recent college graduates had no idea how this "slip stick" even worked?

What a difference three years had made. All the other testers carried multi-function engineering calculators. I began to fret that maybe trying to compete with these younger guys might be tougher than I had anticipated, not only academically, but also physically.

A lieutenant entered the room and prepared to administer the tests. He asked if there were any questions before we started. I raised my hand and he nodded at me.

"How many decimal places in our answers are necessary?" I asked.

He looked at my slide rule and answered with a smile, "For you, just three."

"Okay then!" I thought, "I can do this! It isn't going to be so bad."

*****

The academics consisted of a lot of aerodynamics and reciprocating and turbine engineering and standard operating procedures. It did not take long for me to get back into my student mode and walk through these classes. However, the physical requirements posed a different challenge. I remember running the obstacle course and achieving a passing time on the first attempt, but since it was not a super time that would validate this event, I had to report after class to participate in physical training. That seemed unnecessary to me since I had already shown I could meet the standard...but I didn't complain. I wanted my wings and I would overcome whatever they put in front of me. I was going to keep a good attitude about this transition to becoming a Naval Aviator.

I experienced the same silliness in the swimming validation trials. We were required to swim four lengths of the pool using a different stoke for each segment: breast, crawl, side and backstroke. During my validation swim the comments of the enlisted instructor were like this.

"Great side stroke, sir!" Then, "real fine back stroke" and "wonderful crawl!" Then when I did the breast stroke he commented, "You are using a scissors kick. We want to see a frog kick. Turn your foot out." I did and he said, "Perfect! That's the way to do it!"

When I climbed out of the pool I expected to be placed with the few in the class who had validated the swimming classes. However, I was told I would have to report every afternoon to complete the two-week swimming instruction. I asked why, if all of my strokes were "perfect?" I was told by the third class petty officer, "Because I had to tell you to change your frog kick." Now the fleet experienced officer in me was ready to go to his superior and get this injustice corrected. But the flight school student in me who was going to do whatever it took to get his wings just walked over to the remedial swim group and spent the next afternoons in the pool.

When I was assigned two duty officer watches at the NAS Saufley Field BOQ because my name started with a "B" and they assigned the watches alphabetically by class, I did not complain. I seethed inside that I had previously stood more watches and duty days than the Aviation Officer Candidates (AOCs) had served in the Navy and yet they only got assigned one watch if their last name started with a "C." I kept this complaint to myself...because I was going to get my wings no matter what they did to me.

*****

This attitude paid off and I finished first in my primary flight training class at Saufley Field. Number two in the class that week was Jeff Grant, my Academy classmate who had also spent a full tour on a frigate before coming to flight school.

There were seventeen graduates that week and six of us had high enough scores to qualify for the jet pipeline. That week there were only four jet seats available. My first choice was propeller because I wanted to fly P-3s and my classmate had the same desire. After we had been given a high pressure sales job by the two primary squadron COs on why we should go jets rather than props, we were sitting around a table in the gedunk (snack bar) and sipping our diet Dr. Peppers when we were approached by the two AOCs who had finished fifth and sixth that week. Both wanted to go jets so badly that they were nearly in tears of joy when they approached us with a question.

"We heard that you two chose props and not jets. Is that right?"

Jeff and I nodded and said, "Yep."

The two soon-to-be officers nearly leapt in the air and gave out with a "Yoo-hoo!" Our answers meant two jet pipeline seats would be left for them. They floated out of the gedunk a foot above the deck.

About ten minutes later, the smarter of the two came back to talk with us. He approached these two Lieutenant (j.g.)s who each wore Surface Warfare Officer pins and asked a very intelligent question. "Why?"

It had dawned on him that maybe our fleet experience had taught us something he did not know yet.

Jeff and I smiled and told him the truth, "We don't ever want to be stationed again on anything that is big and grey and floats."

A frown came over the AOC's face that showed his confusion over our answer.

I took pity on him and added, "You're not married are you?"

He shook his head.

I continued, "I bet you have a 'vette or Datsun 240Z parked outside, don't you?"

He nodded.

"Well, outside is my car. It's a Volvo station wagon with two roll bars in its ceiling and a child's car seat strapped in the back seat. We have different goals. You want to streak through the air and pull mega-Gs and I want to spend time with my family."

At this point, Jeff joined in the conversation, "Do you know the deployment cycle for a carrier these days?"

The AOC shook his head again.

"Most carriers pull a nine month or longer deployment and then spend maybe six months in their homeport before they deploy again. Patrol Squadrons do six-months overseas and then pull a year at home before they go over again. We're going prop."

I guess we gave him something to think about because this time he did not float out of the gedunk.

*****

The work ethic initiated at the Academy and honed aboard the Schofield helped make flight school a real easy tour. I got my wings pinned on exactly one year to the day after I first reported to take those preliminary tests. And I like to say that the Navy crammed seven months of flying into that year. That is a true statement. I spent five months sitting around doing nothing while I waited to start different steps in the pipeline. The backlog of students meant that when you did start flying the system needed "completers" each week to make their graduation quotas. I had developed a system that meant this push to get "completers" worked to my advantage.

My system was simple. Since the ground school part of the curricula was self-paced program text type instruction, I had the discipline to work each day on the units in order to get ahead of the required syllabus completions needed before a flight could be scheduled. As an example, the schedules officer could not put you on the flight schedule for an instrument hop if you hadn't done the instrument ground school modules yet. I made sure that I was always academically ready for any flight that the schedules officer might need to fill.

The classrooms available for study to complete the units were open from 6 AM to 10 PM and a duty instructor was there if you needed help in understanding part of a module. So I arrived at 6 AM every morning and did ground school modules until noon and then went home to have the afternoon off. In my mind I was working less than half days. This flight school was sweet duty compared to 18-hour days on a ship. I got so far ahead in my ground school that in the intermediate phase of flight school I had all my ground school done before my very first familiarization flight.

Brand new ensigns would see my ground school modules marked as completed on the "big board" in the schedules office and seek me out to discover how I got so far ahead. I shared with them my system and invited them to meet me at 6 AM the next morning and we could study together.

Invariably, I would be sitting by myself the next morning until about 11 AM when the ensigns would finally show up at the classrooms. They explained that last night some guys had come by their BOQ room and invited them to hit the beach bars down in P-cola. By the time they flopped in their racks it was near 3 AM. They would struggle to get to the classroom by 11 AM and then usually a friend would come by close to noon and invite them to a beach picnic. They would spend the afternoon and late evening on liberty again and maybe get two hours of study in the next day. In their minds there was no hurry to finish ground school because they believed they had two months stashed in a pool of students to get it done.

Of course, I had a different attitude. I wanted to get my wings as soon as possible. I considered all of flight school as "dead time." The clock did not start ticking to complete your five-year Navy obligation until the wings were pinned on your chest. So I made sure I was always ready to take any syllabus flight the schedules officer needed me to fly.

Plus, of course, the advantage was that with all my ground school done, I could devote all of my preparation time to getting ready for the items to be covered on the next flight. Many of the flight school students in my squadrons had to rush through ground school modules to complete them before the next flight and this took away from prepping for the flight maneuvers.

*****

Flight instructors in primary school have some of the best stories. My instructor shared two with me that I remember as sounding true.

He was assigned to instruct foreign pilots who were being sent through the world's best flight training program by their respective governments. He shared how he was having trouble getting an Italian student pilot to believe he was ready to solo. So on his last flight before the solo hop, my instructor told the student to pretend the back seat was empty. Well, the student got flustered as he approached the 180 degree position where he was suppose to start his turn to final for landing. The student could not remember the four basic steps he had to complete. This ICS conversation followed as they flew away from the airport, totally disrupting the pattern for other flights.

"I must think. You take control," the Italian said.

"No, remember that I'm not here. You must figure it out for yourself," the instructor responded.

"No, you take control," replied the student.

"But I am not here. You must do it."

That is when the Italian culture of pragmatism came to the surface and he took both his hands off the controls and placed his palms on the canopy over his head. He yelled back to the instructor, "But you *are* here! *You* take control."

My instructor refrained from grabbing the stick and throttle and let the plane wander off over southern Florida for many minutes. The Italian never took his hands down from the canopy and finally, when the plane started to turn and descend on its own, the instructor started flying it. Needless to say, the foreign student had a couple of more hops before he was okay to solo.

Another nationality that underwent training when I was in primary flight training was the Iranians. It was always a little bit of a mystery for the flight instructors how the Iranian students could speak fluent English when at the BOQ bar after work, but they could not communicate when in the airplane. There was really a good reason for that. Most of them were not in any hurry to return to Iran. The longer they took to complete flight school, the longer they could enjoy American society, girls and freedom. Since the Shah had paid the U.S. government to train the pilots, it was nearly impossible for an Iranian student to flunk the program. If they blew a check ride, then they just got more training and did it again and again until they passed.

One example of the "failure to communicate" experienced by flight instructors was shared with me by my instructor. He had taken an Iranian student up to introduce him to spins. After many failed attempts by the student to put the plane into a controlled spin, the instructor began to think that the problem was that the student was afraid he did not know how to recover from a spin. So the instructor's solution was to put the plane into a spin and then talk the student through the recovery steps. Once the student was confident he could recover from a spin, then properly entering one should be a piece of cake.

The instructor explained his plan to the student and then he put the plane into a spin. Now during training, the T-34B Mentor was limited to three turns in a spin before recovery was initiated. Since the aircraft lost nearly 500 feet per turn, this maneuver was always attempted from a relatively high altitude.

Once the instructor had the plane at 5,500 feet and cleared the airspace below, he put the Mentor into a left hand spin. Well, what happened next was once again a clash of cultures. The instructor spoke via the ICS, "That's one turn....that's two turns...that's three turns, now start your recovery."

The student failed to move the stick or rudder and initiate recovery. The instructor continued in a mild, confident voice, "Okay, recover *now*...that's four turns, you need to recover by centering the rudder pedals and moving the stick forward."

Still there was no movement of the stick or pedals and no response from the Iranian. As they started their fifth turn, the instructor heard the heavily accented voice of the student in his ear piece say, "ABDUL NOT AFRAID TO DIE!"

"Well, I am! This ain't no test of bravery! I've got the airplane!" the instructor said as he recovered from the spin.

The Iranian got a new instructor after they landed.

*****

The memorable flights in intermediate training involved flying the T-28 Trojan, or as it was also known, "The Ensign Eater."

During my first bounce hop we were near the Middleton Field airport in Evergreen, Alabama when the instructor in the back seat keyed the ICS and said, "Look down between your legs. Do you see a red light on that's labeled 'Chip'?"

I answered in the positive and he took control of the airplane and we immediately landed at that small airport. The chip light indicates metal chards in the oil have been detected by a sensor. This means either there was "fuzz" that had accumulated from maybe the installation of a new cylinder or the engine was coming apart and chunks of the block or rings were dropping into the oil pan.

We landed and waited for the duty truck to drive the hour to the field and bring some mechanics to pull the sensor and see what was happening. They did and it wasn't fuzz.

In fact, that old bird was not worth salvaging since the engine was so blown on it. They towed it to the entrance of the airport and mounted it on a pedestal and to this day, it sits there as a reminder of the service that airport has given to Naval Aviation.

It was the slope that ran off the right side of Runway 19 at Middleton that became a sea story that illustrates the thought patterns of a "Nasal Radiator."

One of the duties a flight student pulled while in training was to stand the "Runway Duty Officer" (RDO) watch at outlying fields that were not controlled by towers. The RDO's job was to observe each Navy aircraft approaching to land. Now there is a true saying in aviation that goes, "There are only two types of pilots; those who have forgotten to lower their landing gear, and those that are going to." If an RDO saw a plane trying to land with the gear up, he was to shoot off a flare to warn the erring pilot. It was a very boring job...most of the time.

The famous story concerning Middleton Field was the time a T-28 pilot forgot to lower his landing gear and only realized his mistake too late when his landing flare just continued right to the deck. The solo student touched down and skidded down the runway until he departed the asphalt to the right and then flipped over going over the down slope. There was no fire or any major problems other than he was now sitting in an upside down aircraft. As the RDO and fire engines were approaching they saw a rather funny sight. The landing gear motors in the T-28 are electrically driven, so as they got nearer they watched the three wheels magically appear from the bottom of the fuselage and rise towards the sky. Only after he had lowered the gear handle did the student turn off his master electrical system.

There is another axiom in Naval Aviation...never admit to a fault. This student's story was that he had lowered the gear and he was going to stick to it. The lesson is always to be sure the switches are in the correct position before you evacuate the cockpit.

*****

The most challenging flights during the intermediate syllabus were the solo hops on Thursday mornings in 1977. This was because the television series "Baa Baa Black Sheep" aired on Wednesday nights.

The solo flights in the T-28 included practicing aerobatics. The student was to depart Whiting Field in Milton, FL and fly fifteen minutes south to the acrobatic operating area over Escambia Bay and then practice loops, wing-overs, spins, and barrel rolls. Or, since it was a solo flight, the student naval aviator could just motor around straight and level in the designated area and then claim he completed all the maneuvers when he reported the flight completed. I am sure some of the students took this way out on the first couple of solo acrobatic hops.

I made it a point to do at least one of each maneuver during these hops. But it could get crowded down in the south acro area and you had to be on the lookout for other T-28s sharing the space. This was especially true on Thursday mornings.

I remember doing my clearing turns before I initiated a loop. I put the nose over and gathered airspeed and then pulled the stick back to three Gs and fed in right rudder to maintain a true arc, then I saw the horizon disappear, then nothing but sky, and then the inverted horizon as I fell through the back half of the maneuver, then as my windscreen was filled with nothing but the ground, I concentrated on having the nose run right up the road I had picked as my reference line before starting.

Proud of actually completing a safe loop all by myself, the feeling left me very quickly when I heard someone shout, "ACK! ACK! ACK! GOTCHA!" in my helmet headphones. I banked right and jerked my head around in all directions until I saw another solo T-28 buzz by my tail. I wanted to chase him, but thought better of it. As I flew to the eastern boundary of the practice area I saw a sight that looked like a scene from "The Battle of Britain." There were four T-28s climbing and diving, yanking and banking as if in a mock dog fight and I'm sure each of the pilots thought of himself as Pappy Boyington.

As this was my first solo acro flight, I didn't feel confident just yet to play in their unauthorized game. I reversed course and did my other three mandatory acro maneuvers to the west and then went back to base.

*****

Intermediate flight training was the longest phase of the pipeline. Later, having mastered instrument flight and formation flying in the T-28, I did participate in a game with my flight instructor.

During our preflight one day toward the end of intermediate training, the instructor put me in the cockpit and had me lower the speed brake located under the fuselage belly. The then stuffed a dozen rolls of toilet paper that had been partially unwrapped into the speed brake and had me raise it again. We took off and climbed out over the Gulf of Mexico about a mile off the coast, then after checking to be sure no other planes were in the area and watching, we opened the speed brake and dropped all the toilet paper rolls. About four of them started falling with long streamers floating in the sky. Then my instructor and I took turns cranking that Trojan into tight turns to see how many times we could cut the streamers before we reached 1,000 feet.

It was a fun flight and a great diversion from the strict and graded syllabus flights.

*****

In addition to Navy lieutenants serving as our flight instructors, we also had a few Marine captains. I discovered that Marine aviators had a slightly different attitude than the grunt I had as a company officer at the Academy.

I was one of three flight students scheduled to conduct a solo night cross country flight. We would take off and keep a safe separation without trying to fly in formation and proceed on a triangle circuit from NAS Whiting Field over southern Alabama and then, hopefully, not be so lost we could find our base and make uneventful night landings. A Marine captain was assigned as our chase pilot. He would fly a thousand feet above and a mile behind the three little chicks and play mama hen to be sure we did not wander away and die in the black night.

During the pre-flight safety brief, the captain reviewed the course and landmarks to look for and radio frequencies and other pertinent information. Then he ended the brief with a review of emergency procedures. All three of us student naval aviators were diligently taking notes on what he was passing out. As he covered the most important last review of the worst emergency case, our pens were all writing feverishly to be sure we retained his advice.

"Okay, gentlemen, it is time to review the low altitude engine failure procedures. If your engine quits at an altitude below 800 feet you will not have time to go through restart procedures and you are too low to bail out. You must complete the following steps without hesitation or confusion.

"Number one, set up a glide.

"Number two, pick a field to land in. Since it will be pitch black tonight, your best bet is to pick an area that has no lights showing, that means there probably won't be a building there you will hit.

"Number three, make your 'mayday' call.

"Number four, prepare the aircraft to hit the earth by checking the gear up, mixture off, and master electrical switch off.

"The final step is more of a suggestion than a requirement. When you get down to a hundred feet off the deck, if you want, you can turn on the master electrical switch and then flip on your landing lights. Then, if you don't like what you see...turn the lights off."

I think two of us actually wrote down the last step before we got the joke.

Marine aviators have a little better sense of humor than grunts.

*****

About two months into intermediate flight training our first child was born at the NAS Pensacola hospital. My wife is very petite, barely five feet tall, and our son arrived weighing ten and one-half pounds. After an emergency C-section my wife developed a whole slew of complications that kept her in the Intensive Care Unit for days and then even more recovery days in the hospital. I had called the Training Officer in my squadron and he told me just to take care of my family and not to worry about coming back to a flight status until I thought I was emotionally ready.

Ten days later, Mary and the baby came home, so the next morning I got up and went to the squadron. When I walked into the Schedules Office to report myself ready to be placed back on the flight schedule I was greeted by the Schedules Officer with derision and confrontation.

"Nice of you to show up, Bartron. I thought you had dropped from the flight program," sneered this lieutenant Naval Flight Officer (NFO.)

"I was out while my wife had a baby. I was told—" was all I got out before he cut me off and snapped at me.

"That's right; your *wife* had a baby, not you. Look, as far as I'm concerned you have been U-A for the past week!" he said in a mocking, loud tone so all the half-dozen officers and enlisted personnel in the room could clearly hear him accusing me of Unauthorized Absence from my job.

Now, I had been humbled enough since my first day as a plebe so that I knew how to bend with the blows. But inside this malleable exterior is a rod of hardened steel that will not bend when pushed by a jerk.

Contrary to what Chief Williams believed, this is one time an Academy grad did not choose to take an ass chewing well.

"We need to talk about this," I replied through clinched teeth and looked for a place not as public. I moved my head to indicate that he should follow me into a side office. He did and once inside, I shut the door.

I got a foot from his face, and watched his complexion turn red as I did my best Jack Webb imitation, "What? Do you think I arrived during the mid-watch last night? Look at my chest, Lieutenant, I have crossed many seas, out run typhoons, defied death in seas larger than your house, led good men in very arduous and harrowing conditions and personally kicked a dozen sailors out of the Navy for misconduct. Do you really think I don't know what U-A is?

I took another deep breath and continued before he could do or say anything, "I had the Training Officer's permission to be absent, and I don't need to be embarrassed in front of other sailors by the *only* NFO assigned to a *pilot* training squadron who has never learned the first thing about leadership."

I stormed out of that office with my temper starting to get the better of me and climbed the stairs to the topside offices where department heads and XO/CO were located. I was headed for the Training Officer's office but if he was not there I would push my way in to see the XO.

Luckily for me, the Training Officer was in his office. I entered and shut the door behind me. He could tell by the look on my face and body language that I was really upset.

He motioned for me to sit down and as I did I began explaining why I had stormed into his office. I let him know that it was not the confusion concerning my absent status, but the embarrassment I experienced in front of the other students and sailors at the hands of what I considered a poor officer with limited or non-existent fleet experience.

Finally, after months of maintaining the attitude of "I don't care what little nuisances they put before me, I will do whatever it takes to get my wings," my frustration had boiled to the surface.

I remember the first words this fleet experienced lieutenant commander *pilot* said, "How's your wife and child, Bob?"

That question immediately told me that I was dealing with an officer who understood the basic tenants of leadership.

Without even hinting that the lieutenant Schedules Officer might be incompetent and assigned to the squadron just to complete his mandatory service before he was asked to take advantage of the opportunity to resign, the Training Officer assured me that I had not misunderstood him and that he would see I was put back on the flight schedule to resume my training. I thanked him and left his office feeling that things would be fine.

And I was on the flight schedule again...in fact, the Schedules Officer made sure I had the chance to fly anytime there was a dawn launch or a very late take-off time that he could stick me with until I transferred from the squadron.

*****

I went through intermediate flight training in the summer. It was a typical hot and humid Florida panhandle summer. In fact, it was so sticky that the line crew was authorized to go without their chambray shirts and wear shorts and a white T-shirt while directing aircraft on the ramp.

This being 1976, it meant that for the first time, women were assigned to the aircraft handler rating. Young women...shapely women...busty, well built women. It got to be dangerous on the flight line.

The "Ensign Eater" had a big 1,425 horsepower radial engine on its nose that rotated a very large three-bladed propeller. It was a massive single-engine low wing aircraft. If you taxied that beast into a person or another aircraft, death or damage would ensue. Total concentration on the task at hand was necessary to operate it safely.

I remember climbing up into the cockpit and strapping in for an afternoon hop while my instructor did the same in the rear cockpit. We went through the start checklist and then waited for a line person to arrive to standby the fire extinguisher while we cranked up that massive radial engine.

When this well endowed sailor arrived, she was not wearing a bra under her white T-shirt. This was absolutely noticeable because of the wet sweat making the fabric cling to her attractive form. The flight line had become an unplanned "wet T-shirt contest."

My instructor and I both tried to share our scan while we taxied from the parking spot between the plane's wing tips and hers. There were a couple of near misses, but we managed to make it to the runway without ramming anything.

The next morning, there was a sign hanging in Maintenance Control that read, "Bras are mandatory for those sailors who need them."

That ended the exotic shows by the women linemen, but it did open a door for harassment of a heavy set sailor who found a bra hanging in his locker, courtesy of his "funny" shipmates.

*****

It was on a solo cross country day flight that I learned in aviation, if something is different and strange...look around because you probably screwed up.

The day cross country flight of three students was launched, but no chase pilot was assigned. We were far enough along in the syllabus by then that we should be able to cover a couple of hundred miles flying a round-robin that took us from the Florida panhandle over Alabama and then into Mississippi and down to Louisiana before we returned to our home base.

We were to complete a couple of touch-and-goes at airfields along the way. On the first touch-and-go to an unfamiliar field, I positioned myself to land second and completed a very nice straight-in approach from our high transit altitude. My interval was good and I slammed it on the deck with a good, firm "Navy touchdown" (our training did not introduce us to a flare because we were all being prepared for the possibility of being carrier pilots) just as the first student lifted off the runway.

I raised the flaps during my roll out and then pushed the throttle full forward but the engine seemed to have lost some of its power. My speed was sufficient to get the plane generating enough lift over the wing regardless of this decrease in power. I completed my take-off rotation and put the nose in a climb position, but the plane did not streak into the sky as it normally did. The T-28 had such a powerful engine for its weight that it could beat an F-4 jet to 1,000 feet on take off. But not my T-28 on this day!

I lowered the nose which kept me from wallowing upward and then I reestablished a climb at a much more moderate rate. All the engine temperatures and oil pressure were normal and the horsepower and manifold pressure were normal, but I just sensed something was wrong.

I was trying to determine the cause of this reduction in performance of my aircraft when the lead of our flight keyed his mic and asked me a question.

"Bob, is there some reason you have your speed brake down?"

I immediately thought, "Yeah! The reason is that like a stupid jerk I forgot to raise it when I landed!"

But like all good "Nasal Radiators" I lied and said, "Just slowing to let number three catch up."

I raised the speed brake and, funny thing, the aircraft performance returned to normal!

And I retained the lesson learned...if something doesn't feel right, you probably screwed up somewhere.

*****

During Intermediate Flight Training, my system of getting the ground school work out of the way prior to the flight phase meant I had the time to "fly" each of the scheduled hops at least three times in the static trainers. This meant I was totally ready for the maneuvers I was expected to demonstrate on the hop. As a result, I finished first in my class again.

My proper prior preparation resulted in my chance to accelerate the syllabus a little. Upon landing, my instructor would call the schedules office to report that syllabus hop complete. A couple of times he would chat with the scheduler and then turn to me and ask what I considered a rather dumb question!

"You did well on that flight, Bob. It was the warm-up before your next stage check flight. Schedules wants to know if you want to count that as your check flight and move on with the syllabus?"

That is what I considered the dumbest question ever! I was being offered the opportunity to skip the endless study, gut-wrenching nervousness, and hours of waiting involved in the preparation and execution of an all-important check ride. Did he honestly expect me to say anything but "YES?"

When the squadron had a quota of pilots to turn out by the end of a month or quarter, I made sure I was available to fly. As I said before, I considered flight school "dead time" and I was anxious to graduate. In intermediate training my syllabus was shortened when my instructor and the training officer became aware of my desire to get assigned to P-3s. As a result, they thought it unnecessary for me to complete the entire seven flight sequence of formation flying. My instructor informed me that in P-3s if two Orions are flying in the same geographic hemisphere that was considered "formation flying" in that community. So my formation flying syllabus was shortened to three flights: the first an introduction and demonstration flight; the second a practice flight of conducting break-ups and rendezvouses; and then my third flight was the check ride.

The same speeded-up process was used to complete my acrobatic flights. So, my early completion of all ground school modules coupled with their need for "completers" meant my intermediate flight training phase was cut short by over a month.

*****

Advanced flight school for prop pilots took place in the S-2 Tracker. It had two 1,850 horsepower radial engines located on the high wing and only about ten feet from the pilot's ears when he was at the controls. It felt like it weighed twenty tons and could withstand a direct nuclear weapons hit. It was an old fashioned war machine...but slow. I think we cruised at 120 knots.

Its sturdy construction and robust landing gear meant it could operate from straight deck carriers and was great as a training aircraft used to introduce naval aviators to a multi-place cockpit. It could take a student's beating and shrug it off.

There was another good reason it worked in teaching multi-engine, multi-crew cockpit procedures for student aviators. For the first time, we were sent up on hops with two students and one instructor. One student would fly in the left seat and the other would sit aft and wait his turn to change seats and fly his hop. Students were quick to grasp the advantages to having two sets of eyes available to watch the sneaky instructors as they simulated emergencies by popping circuit breakers or purposely being slow to assist the student pilot at the controls.

Directly in front of the student sitting in the aft space was a torque tube that connected the pilot's wheel to the ailerons on the wings. A good flying partner would watch the instructor and if he did something to screw with the student at the controls, the partner would grab that torque tube and slightly shake it. A small wobble of the wheel would alert the flying student to look for something screwy. Of course, it was important not to make the shake too obvious so as not to attract the instructor's attention.

But sometimes this assistance was lost on certain pilots. During the instrument flying phase in advanced, I had a partner, Bill, who I referred to as the "Dead End Kid." If you are under the hood and have no reference of up or down or right or left except the instruments in front of you, then it is important to sense immediately any changes in attitude and airspeed with your "seat of the pants." You should never believe your feeling because it is invariably wrong. It may feel like you are in a right turn when in reality you have just corrected to straight and level. However, the sense that something has changed will initiate a thorough scan of all instruments to determine exactly what is different and needs to be corrected. Bill never sensed any changes in attitude or altitude or airspeed.

Try as I might by shaking his yoke to alert him to the need to correct the airplane's position, he would fail to respond. I could sit in the back seat with my eyes closed and feel that something had changed and then look at the instrument panel and see us descending or banking into a left turn or whatever had caused the feeling of change. But Bill was never alerted by this motion. I felt bad for Bill, but our instructor just felt frustrated. Bill most certainly had a harder time in this phase because he sat on a "dead end."

I discovered another way to increase my pace through flight school. I always volunteered to fly first on our hops. This was contrary to what most students did for a couple of reasons. The first student had to suffer through start malfunctions and taxi the great distance at NAS Corpus Christi to the runway hold short line. Additionally, most wanted to see what kind of instructor they drew for this hop and watch the first student do the maneuvers first to see what was expected. But I realized on my first flight that the S-2s were old and maintained by junior mechanics, so about a quarter of the time the flights had to be aborted due to a malfunction before the lessons were completed for both student pilots. It was not unusual for us to taxi in from a flight having landed early and the instructor radioing the squadron schedules office, "Bartron up and complete; Smith incomplete."

*****

Sometimes you drew a real good student partner. I remember Fred. He was about through the syllabus and very close to getting his wings and he was one sharp officer and pilot. I especially remember how he kept me from getting a "down" on one fight in particular...and saved us from crashing on another hop.

I was working hard to make a good instrument approach to Corpus Christi International Airport and the closer we got, the more it became apparent that I might have to take it around due to deteriorating weather. When I reached the Minimum Descent Altitude we had yet to see the runway so I started to move the power levers forward to give full power and go around.

In the S-2 the throttles, mixtures and prop controls are located on the ceiling between the pilot and copilot. The pilot flies with the yoke in his left hand and rests his right hand on the throttle levers near his helmet ear hole. On this day, I had failed to properly position the engine quadrant levers prior to my approach in actual Instrument Meteorological Conditions (IMC.) I had failed to put the prop controls to the full forward position so that in the event of a missed approach, I could jam the throttles forward and easily climb to safety. With the prop controls pulled back to a normal cruise position, if I jammed on full power it would over-boost the manifold pressure and could require significant engine rework.

Just as I decided to move the throttles forward to go around, out of nowhere a strange hand appeared near my throttle fist and shoved the two prop levers to the full forward position. It turns out that Fred had unbuckled his harness and slipped from the rear seat and climbed into the small passage that separated the cockpit from the aft cabin and he was there to fix my error without the instructor noting his assistance.

Now that is a good flying partner...and even though it may seem a relatively small thing to some, it taught me two things: what a good shipmate is...and to remember to always set the prop lever before moving the throttle!

It was about a week later that I happened to be assigned to fly with Fred once again. This time our instructor was a "plow back." Now over the decades, the Navy's opinion on plow backs has fluctuated immensely. When I was in flight school if an officer met the minimum requirements to earn his wings, but he was not deemed "fleet ready" just yet, he was plowed back into an instructor assignment in the training command so he could get "seasoned" to help him reach fleet standards. In fact, this system addressed that some pilots grow into the job at a different rate than others and it worked quite well. When I was in the fleet, some of the best pilots in my squadron had served as plow backs. If you could survive a couple of years of students trying to kill you in the air every day, you developed into one fine aviator! Later the Navy changed its attitude 180 degrees and to take some of the stigma from plow back assignments they limited the duty to only those students with the very best grades. The bottom of the class was sent to the fleet where they could meet the standards or be dropped.

On this particular hop Fred and I flew with LT (jg) "Smith" as our instructor. I flew the first hour and got my high work done and then Fred and I switched seats and he completed his high work before we descended to get in some dedicated field work. The weather was clear above the heavy clouds that were a common winter sight over the Corpus Christi area. As we entered the top of the overcast and left the warm sun behind it began to grow cold in the airplane. Smith decided to turn on the cockpit heater to warm his feet. That proved to be a mistake.

Fred set up to complete the instrument approach into Corpus Christi International and as he descended the entire airplane started to fill with gasoline fumes. The heater in the S-2 was just a heat tube that ran under the pilots' feet and gasoline was atomized and lighted to generate heat. The igniter was inoperable on this aircraft, so the tube just started to fill with raw gas. If you smelled gas and did not feel any heat, then you turned off the heater and the problem was solved. Unfortunately, the heater shut off switch failed to shut the fuel valve, and more and more gas was pumped into the tube below the rudder petals. The entire interior of the plane soon gave me the impression that I had stuffed my head into an open 55-gallon drum of gasoline and tried to live off the fumes floating from the top of it.

It was a bad situation...that soon got worse.

Smith decided he needed to take control of the airplane from Fred and get us on the deck at the civilian airport immediately. Sitting silently in the rear, I absolutely agreed with his decision and with his choice to send a "mayday" call to get us top priority in the airport traffic pattern. But then Smith began to scare me...and "I'm fearless."

Smith was all over the sky as he tried to shoot the actual approach to the runway. He was too low and then too high and so far to the right that the VOR needle was pegged to the side and could not move. Smith was most definitely not handling this emergency well.

I knew we were too low to bail out, but I felt I had to do something, so I slipped my arms through the parachute harness I was sitting in and thought maybe we could climb to where I could open the side door and give the aircraft back to the taxpayers.

We were getting close to the ground and off course and blinded by the thick clouds and rain with a poor pilot who was in over his head at the controls. Crap! I was hoping to make it through flight school without a crash! About this instant I realized that maybe standing bridge watches hadn't really been that bad.

Just then, Fred, who was still cool, calm and in control, said, "I see the runway. I have control of the aircraft." I saw

Smith's hands come off the controls and Fred bank us in a sharp left turn. Later he told me that he had lied and had not seen the runway, but he wasn't about to let Smith run us into the ground when Fred knew the runway had to be to our left.

Fred did some good flying and we landed on the runway and stopped there. When the fire trucks arrived, I was standing in the rain thirty yards from the parked S-2 wearing my helmet and parachute. Fred and then Smith were just crawling out the side hatch I had left open. Once again, I proved I was real good at evacuating aircraft.

I did not get much sleep that night. It wasn't the emergency landing that kept me awake. Rather, it was the thought that I should report Smith's performance to someone in the chain-of-command. That is not a student's responsibility, so I was bothered by the idea. I wrestled with it most of the night, and the next morning I found myself knocking on the door of Lieutenant Commander Wiley, the Training Officer.

I had decided not to report the poor performance I had witnessed from an instructor, but I had come to another conclusion. I politely asked Commander Wiley if it was possible for me to finish my flight training without ever having to fly with Smith again.

Wiley looked into my eyes and then did something I hadn't expected. He pulled open his right top desk drawer and pulled out an envelope. He removed a piece of paper from the envelope and unfolded it. There was a list of five names on the paper. Wiley wrote my name at the bottom of the list and then returned the paper to the envelope and the envelope to the drawer.

Wiley looked back up at me and said, "You won't,"

And I never did.

I sometimes wonder if any further action was taken to get Smith out of the cockpit before he killed someone. However, that was not my responsibility, so I just proceeded on in my quest to get my wings.

*****

One of the shortest flights I had in advanced training was also one of the most exciting and educational.

My flying partner for this hop was a fleet S-2 pilot who had been ordered to instructor duty in the training command. Before he could assume his duties he had to complete the IUT (Instructor Under Training) syllabus. We were teamed with another experienced fleet pilot who was nearing the end of his tour as an advanced instructor.

This time I was to fly second in the hop, so after the preflight I strapped into the aft seat and observed these two experienced pilots in what was my first exposure to how fleet professionals flew this aircraft. Up until this time, I had witnessed only student pilots and instructors complete the required checklists before start, taxi and take-off. It was always done methodically and with great concentration on the part of the student to ensure the proper responses were given. Now I watched how the professionals ran through the challenges and responses in about one-tenth the time a student took.

Before I knew it we were sitting in "position and hold" on the runway numbers. We were cleared to take-off and the IUT in the right seat watched as the instructor who was playing the dumb-bunny student naval aviator awkwardly moved the throttles forward. We lurched down the runway and lifted off a little early as the instructor pretended to do what a new student might do. As soon as we got to 100 feet, the cockpit went from a training make-believe environment to a real serious fleet cockpit.

"Loss of oil pressure, number one," the instructor said with an even, but authoritative voice.

"Roger," the IUT responded, "completing the engine shut-down checklist."

By the time we turned to climb to the downwind leg of the landing pattern in preparation to make a real single-engine landing, the engine had been feather and the checklist complete. The IUT made the appropriate radio calls to the tower and emergency vehicles were put on alert.

Their cool and calm teamwork truly impressed me, but what happened next really drove home to me the importance of all the drill and study we had been required to do during flight school. As we turned off the 180 and commenced the landing descent, the IUT called, "Loss of oil pressure on number two."

Now even a flight student can count and I realized that we were about to lose our only remaining engine. This wasn't good.

The instructor rammed full power to the remaining engine and ignored the falling oil pressure until we were over the threshold of the runway. He then pulled the throttle to idle and landed the S-2 as if nothing was wrong.

As we rolled out on the runway, the number two prop came to parade rest, the engine having seized.

The two fleet pilots up front chuckled and coasted the aircraft onto a taxiway. Then the IUT said to the instructor, "It's lunch time and I could use a drink."

The instructor nodded and they both exited the cockpit and passed by me as they climbed out through the side hatch. When the instructor reached the tarmac he asked me a question through the open hatch door.

"Are you brake rider qualified?"

I shook my head.

"Well, here is all you need to know. Keep both feet on the deck and only touch the brakes if you are going over the sea wall into the water or the lineman gives you the signal. Got it?"

I nodded.

"Okay, you're now brake rider qualified." And with that he turned and joined his IUT to walk across the grass to the Officers' Club.

The linemen and the tow tractor showed up later and hitched up the S-2 and towed the plane and me back to the squadron hangar which was across a busy road and down a quarter mile of sea wall. I kept my feet on the floor. When the plane was parked in the hangar, I went to the schedules office and asked to be rescheduled for my incomplete hop.

*****

Part of the final check ride for flight training was to complete the qualification to earn an instrument flying card. The Training Officer, Commander Wiley gave me my check flight and during that hop I noted just what an accomplished and professional pilot he was.

Later I would have the opportunity to fly with him again.

Chapter Four

First Patrol Squadron Tour

Between getting my wings and reporting to Patrol Squadron Fifty (VP-50) at Moffett Field, CA, I was ordered to attend what was normally referred to as the Replacement Air Group (RAG) where I was introduced to the P-3. This six-month school not only taught the new aviator how to fly the four-engine turboprop, but also the basics of sound propagation in water, submarine sensor systems, airborne and subsurface tactics and crew coordination of a twelve man team.

There was a lot to learn and a battery of flights and simulators to be completed. My flying partner, Paul, who was assigned with me on the syllabus hops, was a good guy and okay stick...but he was a nervous wreck during the preflight and planeside briefs. This was because no smoking was permitted on the flight line. By the time we taxied out to take-off his hands were shaking uncontrollably. If he was in the pilot seat for the first half of the hop, he always did something I never saw another nugget (brand new aviator—the junior most pilot in the fleet) ever attempt. The pilot under training was to take-off and fly the departure and maintain control of the aircraft until he was told to rotate out of the seat to let the other student fly.

What Paul would do caught all of the instructors off guard. As soon as we were airborne, Paul would call for the gear to be raised and then the flaps to be reset. Once the instructor in the right seat who was pretending to be the copilot had completed these chores, Paul would turn to him and ask a question.

"Can you take the airplane for a second?"

The instructor usually thought Paul's seat might have slid back as we had accelerated down the runway or some other out of the ordinary need had arisen. However, the instructor was usually taken aback when Paul used his free hands to fumble in his shoulder pocket to pull out his cigarettes and then, with shaky hands attempt to light one.

The change that came over Paul when he pulled his first long drag on that cigarette was impossible to believe unless you witnessed it.

He would immediately transition from a nervous Don Knotts character to a smooth Clark Gable voice as he said with a distinctive mellow tone, "Okay, I've got the aircraft back."

Give Paul a cigarette and his nervousness was flushed from his system with the very first breath he exhaled. It was an amazing transition to see.

*****

Included in the RAG syllabus was an extended over water cross country flight. In fact, four fellow nugget pilots and NFOs and I went to Cubi Point Air Station which was located adjacent to my old stomping grounds, Subic Bay Naval Station, the Philippines. We were scheduled to spend two days at Cubi and then make the transit back to Moffett Field, CA. However, sailors being sailors meant that "somehow" the plane broke which required us to remain four days in this enticing liberty port.

While we were waiting for the enlisted crew members to complete the "repairs," I was lying around the BOQ pool when the conversation with my fellow young pilots and NFOs became centered on the capabilities of different U.S. Navy ships. It was then that I realized that none of my fellow RAG students had ever been aboard a Navy ship. They had gone to AOCS and then straight into flight school and then got orders to a land based squadron of P-3s.

I felt it was my duty to expose them to an entirely different Navy than what they had experienced. They were eager to learn about the "other" Navy and all quickly donned their khaki uniforms and met me in the BOQ lobby. We took a cab down the hill to the Subic side of the complex. During the ride there, we reviewed how to board a Navy vessel, including what and when to salute and what to say.

We were dropped at the edge of the piers and I selected three ships tied against the pier as my examples of the "other"

Navy. The first one was a frigate and I happened to know one of the junior officers in the crew. He showed us around for ten minutes and then we went down the pier to a "Gator Navy" ship and boarded a LST. The petty officer first class standing the in-port OOD watch was happy to send this gaggle of lost officers on a quick tour led by his Messenger of the Watch. As we looked at the distance we had to walk to reach the supply ship I had picked for our last visit, the gang decided they had seen enough. So I suggested we stop into the Chuck Wagon club located near the piers for a bite to eat.

The lasting impression of the surface Navy for these young officers I believe was formed during out visit to the Chuck Wagon.

Now Naval Station Subic was a traditional, "old school" base with a traditional, "old school," stuffy officers' club. Patrons were expected to wear ties and jackets to use the dining room in the evening and a complete uniform was required at all other times. Across the street from the O'club was the informal officer's bar and dining facility called the Chuck Wagon. Here casual civilian clothes were okay and a lower brand of etiquette was tolerated.

The Chuck Wagon was in the shape of a "U" with a dining room on each side with a bar connecting them. We found a table and the five of us ordered hamburgers and sandwiches. In the far corner was a small raised stage and on this late afternoon a four-piece Filipino band wearing plaid shirts, jeans and neckerchiefs tied around their necks was setting up. Soon we were listening to "Your Cheatin' Heart" and "I Walk the Line" sung in a thick Filipino accent. But the drummer could keep a beat so it was fun.

Yet it seemed to raise the noise level of the patrons as they started to yell to be heard over the music. Soon, we were privy to every opinion of the Navy and world politics that this warrant officer held. Unfortunately, a lieutenant who had escaped the pressures of his ship for a couple of hours of beer drinking objected to some of the warrant's opinions. I watched the faces of my brand new ensign companions become more and more concerned as the disagreement got hotter and hotter.

When the warrant began to slur all aviators and submariners and Marines I leaned over and loudly whispered to my companions, "You might want to cover up or remove your wings about now."

They must have thought I was a real veteran of the harsh waterfront life when almost immediately a couple of LAMPS pilots sipping beers at a table across the room took offense at the warrant's drunken comments. Now the SWO who had been arguing with the warrant, switched sides and began to agree with him that aviators were a worthless drain on the resources of the Navy.

As we were outnumbered by members of the surface community I thought the best choice was to "clear datum" and get out of there before it accelerated into a physical confrontation.

The LAMPS pilots' table flipped over as the warrant and SWO charged it, but I don't know how the brawl continued because I left by the side door before it reached a peak. Looking behind me I was pleased to see that the ensigns had showed sparkling good sense by following me.

That was how our visit to the real Navy...to the waterfront of working men under great stress ended. My little gaggle of pilots had seen enough and I don't think they ever left the relatively civilized confines of the Naval Air Station for a great while.

*****

Survival, Evasion, Resistance and Escape (SERE) school starts in San Diego. Most people just know it as POW school.

Having completed a Surface Warfare Officer tour, I reported to SERE school as what I believed was the second senior student. The other thirty in the class were also new aviators or enlisted flight crew. At the time, just a couple of years after the end of the Vietnam War, all aircrew on the West Coast who would be deploying to the Far East were required to complete this POW school. The class met for Monday and Tuesday at a building on NAS North Island in San Diego. After this classroom training in identifying eatable and lethal shrubs and roots, we reported on Tuesday night to the beach on base. We spent the night as a group learning how to start fires and rigging a large tent from a parachute. That night was actually quite nice, if you ignored the hunger pains that were starting to rumble in your stomach. We slept in the sand and relaxed for the twelve hours we spent there.

On Wednesday morning we were loaded onto a bus and driven out to the Warner Springs area in southern California's high desert. For the next two days we received more survival training which meant no food while learning land navigation by trekking up and down the foothills in hot days and cold nights. By the time Friday morning rolled around we were all pretty weak and exhausted which was just perfect to start the evasion, resistance and escape portions of the course.

The first event of the POW experience is the evasion course. The class is spread apart at the starting line with about ten yards spacing. Then we are directed to transverse, without being detected, the course which is about a half-mile long and covered in underbrush. Roaming the course were the "tormentors" who had the job to find us and take us into custody. We had about three hours to crawl through the cover to reach the finish line. If you were successful, then you might get half a jelly sandwich and some water before you were transported to the holding area where those who had been caught were being held.

There is no escaping the prison camp experience, but staying out of the tormentors' hands for even an extra couple of hours was a prize worth seeking.

I thought I'd reach the finish line because as a youth I had played "army" with my older brother in a vacant field near out house with tall grass. This evasion course was going to be a piece of cake in my expectations.

It was going along fine for the first...ten minutes. There was a dirt road I had to cross and I successfully rolled over it just as we had been taught. Then I came to a small clearing, and since my fellow students were to my left and right, I felt it best just to sneak across it as quickly as possible. As I reached the middle, I heard the rumble of a truck coming down the dirt road behind me. Not wanting to draw attention to myself by moving, I did as we had been taught and froze in my position.

The direction we had received prior to the evasion course was always to freeze; just because you think you are visible that is not always the case to someone searching the woods. But if you move, you instantly draw the searcher's eyes to your position.

I froze right in the middle of my crawling motion, one foot off the ground, one hand in the air and my head looking forward. I must have looked like a natural history museum exhibit of a stuffed cougar about to pounce on its prey. I heard the squeal of the truck brakes as it slid to a stop on the dirt road. I heard the crunch of the tormentors' footsteps as they approached. But I remained in my frozen position just as I had been taught.

Out of the corner of my left eye I noticed the boots of an instructor who had the wonderful duty of pretending to be a communist enemy. Then I listened as he talked to the other petty officer standing next to him.

"Will you look at this, comrade?" he said in the worst Hollywood Russian accent, "This stupid American is trying to hide right in the middle of a clearing!"

The next thing I felt were the laces of the petty officer's boot against my cheek as he gently kicked me over onto my side. I finally decided that freezing in position had not worked.

The two tormentors grabbed me under my arms and pulled me to my feet. In a matter of seconds I came to realize that this school was unlike any other I had attended in the Navy. One of the petty officers stepped in front of me and asked me what ship I had come from. His accent was so overblown and terrible I guess I smirked a little in response to his theatrics. Suddenly, his right hand flew from his side and the meaty part of his palm near his little finger caught me right under my left jaw. He had cold cocked me to get my attention. The force of the blow knocked me off of my feet and onto the ground to my right.

Say!...these guys are serious! I began to think that maybe it was a little bit of a cheap thrill for these petty officers to have permission to beat the crap out of a lieutenant.

I had been punched square in the face on more than one occasion while boxing at the Academy, so I was used to quickly shaking the cobwebs from my brain. Just as my eyes and thoughts cleared, I was again yanked to my feet and hustled to the flat bed truck they had been driving. There, another tormentor waited and he was holding the rifles of the other two. I was thrown on top of the truck bed and a nylon sack was pulled over my head. I was positioned in a sitting position with my knees in my chest and my heels touching my butt. I had to use both arms to squeeze my knees close enough to maintain this mandatory position. To keep me upright I received help from the bayonet tips stuck against my shoulders by the tormentors. On the bumpy dirt ride to the holding area, I had trouble maintaining my balance so I got to feel the blade tips many times.

Upon arriving at the captive holding area, I was searched for any weapons. The bottoms of the pockets in my fatigue shirt were ripped out, and the pants pockets pulled inside out and then every orifice of my body was searched, including my nose, mouth and the requirement to drop trou and bend over and spread cheeks.

Satisfied I had been humiliated sufficiently for the time being, the next item was a standing interrogation. I had resolved before starting the evasion course that when I was captured I would keep it simple...the "big four, and nothing more." The Geneva Convention required all prisoners to provide their name, rank, serial number, and date of birth—the "big four." I would refrain from saying anything else. Or so the plan was.

The tormentors obviously had no idea of the kind of plebe year I had endured at the Academy. Their shouting inches from my face and insults did not have the desired effect on me as it just seemed to be old home week. But for some reason we got stuck on a simple question that drew a physical response.

"How old are you, war criminal?" both of the petty officers demanded.

"March nine, nineteen fifty one," I replied giving my birth date once again.

I guess my attitude needed adjustment, because no sooner had those words passed my lips when I felt simultaneous blows to my shins and both my feet were kicked from underneath me. I fell to my belly with my face just an inch from the dirt.

The next command was to write the current year in the dirt with my right hand. I reasoned that was not classified information, so I wrote 1-9-7-7. Next they had me write the year I was born underneath the current year. I wrote 1-9-5-1. They ordered me to draw a line under 1951 and then subtract it from the year written above it. I wrote 2-6.

With his hand on the back of my head a tormentor yelled in my ear, "NOW READ THAT NUMBER!"

In what was about my last great act of defiance I said, "Nine March Nineteen Hundred Fifty-one."

BANG! My head was slammed into the dirt and it felt like I broke my nose again. Before I could take proper inventory of my injury, I was jerked to my feet by two tormentors and this caused me to go light headed. It took a second for the blood to return to my eyes and when I opened them I was shocked by what I saw....shocked nothing, I was scared!

Standing before me was the shell of a man who just an hour before had been the perfect Arian Nazi model—six foot three inches with sculptured muscles and pure blond hair with shiny blue eyes. Now this junior officer looked like a frightened cat that had just been pulled from a raging river. He had a fearful yet vacant stare, hunched over posture and downcast eyes full of shame. He was a broken man.

"Comrade, tell this war criminal what will happen to him if he does not tell us what we want to know," the tormentor demanded of the wet ensign.

"Sir, they will put you on the water board," he said with a shaky voice and then added in a soft mumble, "and you don't want that."

Many thoughts quickly ran through my mind. "Could this guy be a plant? I mean, if he is, it is very effective. Maybe I should take his advice? Aw, but that would be just plain stupid. There are only two full lieutenants in this class and I am one of them, so it is inevitable that as a senior prisoner I will be water boarded at some point. What is it they are asking me now? What is my designator? Heck, I might as well go to the water board over that as it is as good as anything else they could ask."

As I was thinking, the biggest tormentor decided he had waited enough for an answer, "WHAT IS YOUR DESIGNATOR? WHAT IS YOUR DESIGNATOR?"

Now a funny thought crossed my mind as I stood there being yelled at over something that in real life would not be question. Officers in the Navy receive a qualification designator that tells the computer what your primary job is in the service. If I was captured in Vietnam I would be standing there in my flight suit with my naval aviator wings sewn across my chest. It would be rather hard for me to deny that my designator was that of a pilot. I don't think anyone who captured me would think I was a civil engineer or lawyer in the Navy.

Just like plebe year, I felt I had a limited number of responses on how to answer this question. I picked the best of the "big four" available to me, "Lieutenant, United States Navy."

I guess that wasn't the right answer because less than thirty seconds later I was being strapped to a water board device.

Over the last couple of years there was a lot of public discussion about how suspected terrorists were subjected to "enhanced interrogation techniques," specifically water boarding. The big cry was that America does not torture prisoners. I never understood the indignant shock of those who claimed it was torture. My definition of torture is that it must leave a scar on the body to qualify as such. And I failed to see how water boarding could be called torture if we used it on our own military as a training device.

So for those readers and journalists who have never undergone the experience, I will explain what is done and how you feel while it is happening.

I was laid on my back with my head at the lower end of an inclined board about five-foot long and shoulder width. My arms and waist were strapped to the board with nylon belts and buckles designed for that purpose. At my head, squatting so that I could see his head from an upside down angle was a senior corpsman or a real doctor who had the job of making sure I did not die from what was about to happen. (Note: I always have thought that these medical personnel must have been related to Dr. Mengele of the Third Reich...I mean what kind of doctor participates in this kind of treatment?)

Once I was in position, the medical person took a rolled up T-shirt and used it as strap across my forehead to hold my face in position for what happened next. Using a hose, water was shot at my upper lip so it went down my mouth and up my nose. At first I gagged on it as I tried to spit it out and move my head to position my mouth to the side where I might be able to draw in more air. Whenever I moved my head, even a little, the man holding the T-shirt harness would pull it tighter to where eventually I could not move my head at all.

Have you ever been horsing around in the pool with other guys and someone held your head under the water until you were out of breath? That panic you felt that made you fight your way to the surface just to be able to draw a breath is what you feel on the water board. However, unlike playing in a pool where you can soon reach the surface, your tormentors hold you in that panic as long as they want and there is no way to get any air. But you never pass out, because when the corpsman or doctor see you are about to lose consciousness they motion for the man with the hose to move the water stream a little to one side to permit you to gasp a little air with the water going down in your lungs. This will keep you from passing out so they can hold you in this panic for quite a long time.

My head was lower than my waist, so the chance of my lungs filling with water was quite remote...but knowing that intellectually was not a great help when physically it felt like I was going to die.

I thought of all the Jews who went like sheep to be gassed after being pulled from the trains "to the east." I always thought I would have chosen to fight back and die by a bullet than just accept my fate. So, as I lay there feeling like I was about to drown I had a change of attitude. Up to this point in this evolution I had complied with what the tormentors told me to do. I did not want to get them angry, fearing they might mistreat me more. Well, as I felt my lungs filling with water a thought hit me, "They're killing me! What more can they possibly do?"

So I decided to fight them. I was tall enough so that my heels just touched the ground as they hung over the elevated end of the ramp. I pressed against the ground and started bucking and arching my back as best I could. I was putting up a good fight.

And then I discovered there *was* something more they could do. The biggest tormentor standing nearby leapt onto my chest, mounting me like a small pony and at the same time the corpsman unfolded the wet T-shirt he was using to immobilize my head and covered my entire face with it. The water kept coming down on my nose and mouth that were now being suffocated by the T-shirt. Any remaining air I had in my lungs before I started fighting back left me immediately as that goon landed on my chest.

While the water is coming down, the senior tormentor is yelling questions he wants answered. What is my designator? What kind of plane do I fly? What is my squadron?

Well, let me tell you I did not hesitate to answer his questions in the hope I could get some air back in my lungs. I shouted out my designator...I told him I flew P-3s...I yelled out "VP-50"...heck, I even volunteered my new CO's name! If he had asked, I would have admitted to being Hitler's love child! Anything! Just let me breathe again!

And therein lays the failure of using "torture" to extract information from captives. Whatever intelligence you get is tainted and very unreliable, which raises the question of where is the need or wisdom in doing it?

However, the water board did achieve one significant goal...for at least fifteen seconds. When I rolled off that board having spilled my guts to get air, I felt like a total failure. I had started the day with an image of myself as a cross between John Wayne and Chuck Norris. Now here I was on my hands and knees crawling away a weak loser with absolutely no self-respect or pride left.

At this time I was a believer in the water board and I told myself that short of anything like signing a disloyal statement condemning the United States, I would do whatever was necessary to avoid going through the water board experience again. They had beaten me, and I was ashamed. And that was the real reason the water board was used. It makes prisoners more compliant and open to doing things they wouldn't have considered before they became "believers."

Then something very little happened that restored by high opinion of myself and re-sparked the pride I had when the course started. As I was crawling away to be put in a bamboo cage only three feet high, one of the tormentors yelled at me.

"Halt! Look at what you did, you Yankee war criminal!" he said as he pointed to a large wad of spit sitting in the dirt just ahead of my bowed head. "You spit at my brave comrades and me when you start your fun!"

From the position I was in on all fours with my mouth right above the spit I expected his next order was going to be, "Lick it up." Well, when I had that thought something inside of me raised its head from a feeling of shame to one of total defiance. I told myself that there *was* something other than signing a disloyal statement that I absolutely would not do to avoid being strapped to that water board again. I was never going to lick up that fellow's spit!

That instantaneous thought made me feel better about myself and I began to realize that I was still in the game and needed to start resisting again. So when he ordered me to pick up the spit and put it in my pocket...well, I was okay with that! I scooped up a handful of loose dirt that included the spit and shoved it into my jacket pocket...the same pocket that had its bottomed ripped out during the cavity search, so the dirt fell right back onto the ground.

After another hour of fun and games at the collection site, we were all transported to the POW camp. There we each were placed in our own box that measured about three feet high, three feet long and just wide enough for your shoulders to squeeze in. The front of the box was a board that slid up and down to enter and exit. We were directed to keep quiet and keep our nylon bags over our heads. When the guards came by and slammed a fist on top of your box you were to yell out "War Criminal Number Twenty" or whatever your number was. There was some debate over whether we should answer as self-admitted war criminals, but that is where a strict prisoner chain-of-command was a benefit. When our Senior Ranking Officer (SRO) shouted out "War Criminal Number Seventeen," then that was permission for the rest of us to avoid beatings by answering the same way.

I say "beatings" because some of us actually did have the opportunity to be physically punished. I recall three interrogation sessions throughout Friday night. The first one included a requirement that I rest all my weight against my two fore fingers as I leaned against a wall. Eventually strength in my fingers gave out and I fell to my knees. Once again, my experience of "hanging around and listening to music" as a plebe had prepared me for this sort of training and it was not that effective in extracting answers to their questions. As this "hard sell" questioning continued they tried another tactic to have me assist them. They brought in one of the enlisted students in the class and blind folded him and had him on his knees opposite me in this hooch. One of the tormentors pulled a .45 automatic pistol from his holster and pointed the barrel at the student's head. Of course, they said he would be shot if I did not cooperate. Well...they did not quite understand my lack of connection with these fellow class members. I had only met them four days earlier and really had not gotten close to any of them. My attitude was, "As long as the gun is not pointed at me, I'm cool with it."

Later they took another enlisted and tied him to a water board and said they would torture him if I did not answer their questions. I stuck with the "big four" because, quite honestly, my attitude was, "I survived it. He can too."

I never claimed to be a hero.

The next interrogation session was a couple of hours later. Luckily I heard the guards pounding on the top of other boxes as they approached mine because I was so tired that I was fast asleep. I was barely able to pull my bag down over my face just as the door rapidly slid upwards and two guards grabbed my feet and pulled me from the box.

I was led to a small room where there were two chairs, one on each side of a small wooden table. On the table were a loaf of bread and a pitcher of water with a glass. In the other chair was a civilian who invited me to sit opposite him. I sat down and then in a very quiet manner the "soft sell" session began. The first thing he did was offer me bread and water. The Code of Conduct says I could not accept any special treatment and although water was available to every prisoner the bread was not, so I politely declined the offer.

This guy was good! I made the mistake of engaging him in innocent conversation. Before I knew it I was drawn into discussing world politics. He said, "How is it that America only has ten percent of the world's population, yet it uses fifty percent of the earth's resources? Do you think that is fair?"

That had an easy answer. I said, "I've heard that said before."

Never agree and never disagree...just check and move.

Ten minutes later I realized that I wasn't as smart as I thought I was, and this guy was much better than me in verbal games. In fact, I don't know how he did it but eventually he asked me a question that if I agreed with him or disagreed with him in any way I would make his point. Luckily, I had been married for four years by this time and had learned how to dodge tricky questions my wife was excellent at asking.

I just sat there in silence and then after a very uncomfortably long pause, I asked, "Is that water still available?"

I caught a small smile come over the interrogator as he turned his head. I had somehow avoided his trap. About five minutes later I was led back to my box, having learned that talking with the enemy is a very dangerous game. Once again, I determined to stick with "the big four, and nothing more."

After the school was over we were introduced to this civilian interrogator. His name was Douglas Hegdahl and he was very good because he had been a prisoner in North Vietnam for two years and had lived through the real thing.

My third interrogation that long night was another "hard sell." In the middle of the compound was a tall metal fence covered in corrugated metal panels. One of the interrogators took me to the fence and started to throw me against it every time I failed to answer his question. On the first hit I discovered that the fence gave way against my weight, and even though the metal clanging made it sound like I was getting a terrible beating, it really did not hurt much. Not wanting him to proceed to anything that might hurt more, I made a big show of crying out and shaking every time he slammed me against the fence. It was my best World Wrestling Entertainment theatrics. However, it did not take long for a little short tormentor to catch on to my act. He stepped in front of me and assumed the slamming duties. His height and upper body strength meant his hold on the front of my shirt was right under my collarbones. When he lifted me, the pain was suddenly very real and I thought he was either going to break or dislocate my clavicles.

Along with the sunrise on Saturday came more fun and games. Our SRO had been removed due to injuries he sustained (I'm not sure just how.) That meant the duties of SRO fell to me, the next senior student. The biggest challenge in this job came when the students were separated with the officers in one group and the enlisted in another. One chief decided he knew better than the officers and when this happened he broke with loyalty to the chain-of-command and ordered the junior enlisted only to follow his orders. The chief wanted a harder line against the enemy and his orders were to stop working and to go on strike. This might be a fine strategy in a school, but such a decision in a real POW camp would get some prisoners killed. Of course, the instructors thought this was just great! One of the major objectives of the POW camp is to break the strength found in the chain-of-command.

So there I was, an American lieutenant and SRO standing in front of the assembled enlisted POWs explaining to them why they had to return to working for the enemy. It was one of the most difficult oratories I ever had to deliver! I guess it went okay, because at the start all the instructors were standing behind the sitting group of students and were smugly smiling at the tough—nearly impossible—position I was in. Ten minutes later the sailors agreed to return to following the officers' orders and every instructor behind them had a confused and incredulous look on his face.

The troops went back to work, but now the tormentors decided that the work was not going fast enough. Their solution? Take me in front of the assembled students and strap me to the water board again.

"Either you work faster or your officer gets the water board!" the enemy leader shouted.

I honestly didn't expect anyone to step forward and say, "Don't do it! We'll work faster!" So I just braced myself with the knowledge that I lived through it before and I will again.

The water started coming out of the hose and the tormentor approached my immobilized head...then all of a sudden one of the guards pointed in the sky and shouted, "AIR RAID! AIR RAID! EVERYONE TO BUNKER!"

I was released from the water board and joined the rest of the students in an underground bunker. And I fully admit that if I ever come across that Cessna 172 pilot who flew over Warner Springs that morning, I would kiss him or buy him a beer.

When we were rousted from the bunkers, the program moved on to the next lesson. We were all assembled in a tight group sitting on the dirt, cross-legged with our knees touching the student next to us and the student in front of us. Standing before us was our designated "chaplain" who was going to conduct the Geneva Convention approved religious service. The chaplain was a student officer who was given a Bible to read. I can't remember the verses he chose, but whichever ones they were, the guards did not like his choice. They rushed up and knocked the Bible from his hands. He picked it up and started to read again. This time the guard grabbed the Bible and ripped a chunk of pages from the binding.

It was obvious to me that the instructors were trying to get a rise from the students. We had demanded our rights under the Geneva Convention and we needed to fight for them or lose them one by one. Being the SRO, it fell to me to do something.

I was sitting on the end of the second row of huddled prisoners. I stood up as best I could with my feet still crossed and objected, "Under the Geneva Convention we are permitted religious ser—"

That was all I got out before a guard approached from the rear and using his fist like a sledge hammer struck me on the shoulder. With my feet crossed and knees bent it was easy for him to drive me to the ground just like a railroad spike.

I stood up again and repeated my protest, "Under the Geneva Convention we are permit—"

WHACK! He hit my shoulder again and down I went a second time.

I figured one more time might make my point, so I stood again and again I was pounded to the ground. I stopped, satisfied that I had made my point.

I may be slow...but I'm not stupid.

As that Saturday wore on, there was only one thought that kept us hopeful. It was Saturday and, despite their terrible accents, our instructors were sailors and their liberty did not commence until the training was done. Eventually the hope of getting to the boat and fishing or seeing the wife after a week in the field would override their disappointment in our class's performance.

Around 3 PM the POW camp was "liberated" by friendly Marines and we boarded the bus back to San Diego. Sitting next to me on the buss was the other pilot lieutenant. His ankle was swollen and his eye was black and he was really beat. As the SRO he had received special attention. I got to talking with him for the first time and discovered something quite interesting now that SERE school was over. This lieutenant did not know the difference between "Date of Rank" and "Date of Commissioning." On our first day in the classroom we had all filled out data sheets which asked for our "Date of Rank." I had been promoted to lieutenant about two months earlier and gave that date. This other lieutenant had mistakenly put down his date of commissioning which was four years earlier. In fact, he had made lieutenant about a month after me. Turns out that after the fact I discovered that I had been the SRO of our merry group.

I'd rather be lucky, than good.

*****

Immediately upon my arrival in Patrol Squadron Fifty (VP-50,) I became aware that I had transferred to a totally different Navy. The difference between a frigate and a land based squadron was night and day. Onboard the Schofield we had about 200 enlisted members and twelve officers. Of the dozen officers, I was the ninth Naval Academy graduate to check aboard. In VP-50 we had 300 enlisted and sixty officers, and I was one of three Academy graduates in the wardroom. I thought I had transferred to a reserve outfit that had been recalled to active duty. The formality between officers and enlisted onboard a ship was not present in the squadron.

The large number of officers in a squadron was due to having twelve aircrews with five officers on each crew. This meant that many junior officers had ground jobs that we had considered "collateral duties" onboard a ship with a small wardroom. In fact, the squadron had a whole department devoted to training while on the ship getting qualified in your assigned position was the responsibility of the individual officer. Legal officer on a frigate was a collateral duty assumed by an officer who led a division. In VP-50 it was a full-time ground job with the aid of another officer assigned as the "Assistant Legal Officer!"

Most of the aircrews were led by a lieutenant who only had experience in the patrol aviation navy. Being raised professionally in this community meant that some of the practices, in my way of thinking, were just too loose. Some Patrol Plane Commanders (PPCs) had the enlisted crew members calling them by their first names. For an Academy graduate from the surface navy, this sent a shiver up my spine.

I remember one new lieutenant (j.g.) who checked into a crew and was introducing himself to the crew as "Bill." He asked the chief petty officer flight engineer how it preferred to be addressed.

"Chief Vaneps."

Bill shook his head and said, "No. I mean what is your first name?"

"Chief," the old school leader said and turned and walked away.

I was one of the very few officers in the squadron with the first name of "Lieutenant." The crew never objected to my "formality," because I always gave as good as I got. I never addressed a sailor as "Smith;" it was always "Petty Officer Smith." I had learned years previously that sailors would rather have confidence in the competence of an officer than feel as if they had a new "friend."

I must say that despite this milieu of informality between ranks, I never witnessed a more professional unit than a well-led and well-trained P-3 crew in the air. When an aircrew was on station searching for and then finding submarines, it was a precise and beautiful dance of knowledgeable professionals performing to the highest standard possible. I often felt that all members of the crew had merged into a Star Trek Vulcan mind meld. The communication between the sensor operators and the flight deck personnel and the tactical coordinator and the ordnance man was done in short, one and two word sentences. Nothing more needed to be said because all were solving the same problem.

In pro football many great pass plays are only accomplished because the quarterback and receiver see and react to the same motions of the defense and adjust the pass pattern to succeed without a word being exchanged. That coordinated teamwork is a pale example of a twelve man P-3 crew in action.

Just as on the ship, I had to get qualified and earn specific qualifications. All nuggets start as "No Ps" (No Pilots) and then after multiple training flights and simulators, plus a three hour oral examination board you become a "Third Pilot" or "3P." After about a year in the squadron and another long oral examination board you earn your NATOPS (a ubiquitous Navy abbreviation for *Naval Air Training and Operating Procedures Standardization* –the "Bible" or "owners manual" for how to operate Navy aircraft) qualification in the P-3 and are designated a "Second Pilot" or "2P." About six months later, after completing even more study, you finish the Patrol Plane Commander (PPC) syllabus and sit for a long oral examination board on proper utilization of the airborne weapons platform. Then, most but not all, PPCs go on to earn their "Mission Commander" or "MC" qualification so they can not only have full responsibility for the safety of flight of the aircraft but also full tactical command, which more often is placed in the hands of the Tactical Coordinator—"TACCO," the NFO who runs the tactical problem. The MC oral exam centers more on "what if" questions, such as "What if you receive authorization to drop nuclear weapons, what must you do to ensure they are successfully deployed?" or "What if you are intercepted by a Soviet fighter, what do you do?"

As you note above, for the first two years of a three-year P-3 squadron tour you are constantly in training to obtain the next qualification. But that is not to imply that all pilot training was well thought out, thorough and documented precisely.

One day I was told that as a newly qualified 3P I was assigned as the duty taxi pilot for maintenance. If a plane had to be moved or taken to the end of a runway for a power check, the taxi pilot would be employed for these purposes. On my first day of this duty I was sent along with a second class petty officer who was undergoing flight engineer training and an airman to act as an aft observer to take a plane down for a high power turn at the end of the taxiway by the runway threshold. This was going to be fun...my first chance to be "in command" of a large plane all by myself.

We reached the high power area near the entrance to the runway and I parked the bird. We were just about finished with the test when two things happened. First, another P-3 approached and needed to get by our plane so it could take the runway to depart. However, I was blocking the entry. I needed to back up, but I had never done that before. The flight engineer trainee told me the secret to the maneuver. He said to place both feet on the deck and don't touch the brakes once I reversed the pitch of the props and started to roll in reverse. That sounded very familiar to me and once again I got qualified because the circumstances dictated the need.

"Be sure to use the power levers to stop the reverse movement and not the brakes," the flight engineer directed, "because if you slam on the brakes the weight in the tail will make it fall and strike the MAD boom into the dirt."

So I self-taught myself how to back up a four-engine turboprop, but I learned something else that afternoon. I learned that the lower the fuel level gets in P-3 fuel tanks the less reliable the gas gauges are. We had 1,000 pounds of fuel indicated on the gauge of #2 tank when the engine died due to fuel starvation. We used the fuel manifold system to get it restarted with fuel in other tanks, but I remembered the unreliability of the fuel gages at low volumes.

*****

It was during my first squadron deployment that I learned the difference between Navy and Air Force command and control philosophies.

A short time after VP-50 assumed the deployment site at Misawa Air Base, my crew's PPC and TACCO were invited down to the Headquarters of the 5th Air Force based at Yokota Air Base by Tokyo. The purpose of the meeting was to coordinate expectations between P-3 aircrews flying *Peacetime Airborne Reconnaissance Program* (PARPRO) missions and any support to be provided on these missions by the 5th Air Force should a patrol plane be intercepted by Soviet fighters.

PARPRO missions took an American plane closer to the Soviet and Chinese borders than normal. They were so sensitive that the duty officer at the National Military Command Center in Washington DC was kept advised of each take-off and landing. Position reports were made by the plane during the entire time it flew in the sensitive areas. The Air Force position reports were easy to transmit because their route of flight was precisely planned to include times, airspeeds, and altitudes at designated spots. Consequently, the tracking unit at the 5th Air Force could receive simple reports like, "Point Bravo" and nothing else was needed if the plane was flying its track precisely

Navy patrol flights did not follow a precise route. Unlike electronic intelligence flights, we gathered information about surface ships using the "Mark 1, Mod 0" eyeball. If we spotted something of value, such as a Soviet intelligence collection trawler then we would orbit it and take pictures and in some cases drop sonobuoys to record a specific acoustic signature of that hull. Of course, if we ever stumbled upon a surfaced submarine we would go crazy and spend whatever time was necessary to work up a complete acoustic profile of this target of opportunity. We did not know how far along our proposed track or what altitude or speed we might be when it came time to make a position report.

This really confused the full colonel who was conducting the meeting. He had trouble grasping exactly how we conducted our mission. According to my lieutenant PPC and lieutenant (j.g.) TACCO the meeting became an exercise in miscommunication because the two services had fundamentally different approaches to command and control.

"What do you mean you interrupt your route if you find something *'interesting'*?" demanded the colonel.

"If we see something interesting we investigate, and that means we stop following the designated route of flight until the investigation is complete," answered my PPC with appropriate deference to the senior Air Force officer's rank. A colonel is an O-6, or captain in the Navy, while a Navy lieutenant is just an O-3 and a jg is only an O-2, just one step above a dumb ensign.

The colonel was getting hot under the collar as he was losing his patience with these two junior officers the Navy had sent to this important coordination meeting.

"How do you know if a ship is *interesting*?" the colonel almost bellowed.

My PPC was getting flustered by the aggressive attitude of the colonel and responded with the truth, "We just know."

"HOW DO YOU *KNOW*? WHO TELLS YOU IT IS *INTERESTING*?" the colonel shouted.

The Navy lieutenant was confused by the questions. In almost a panic to give the colonel what he demanded, my PPC pointed to the O-2 next to him and said, "*He* does!"

The colonel almost popped a neck vein and swallowed his tongue at what he considered an inappropriate answer.

The lieutenant (jg) TACCO gave a dumb grin and cheerfully responded, "Yes. Yes *I* do."

The difficulty in communicating at this meeting was based in the fact that Air Force aircrews are controlled from headquarters. Someone up the chain-of-command must tell them to deviate from their route or alter their preplanned mission...or if a contact is *interesting*. That is because the Air Force came into being after World War II when instantaneous world-wide communications were available through HF radio. Naval heritage dates back to the days of sail, when a ship would leave American ports and sail over the horizon not to return for a year or more. Upon coming home, the ship's captain would report to headquarters about the battles he fought, revolutions he instigated, and trade routes he had swept clear of pirates. This empowerment of on-scene officers to make independent decisions was maintained in the way patrol crews flew PARPRO flights.

And it drove the Air Force batty.

*****

During this deployment it was time to have a change-of-command. The XO was going to fleet up to become the new CO, and the formal ceremony was going to be done at Misawa Air Base. Two days before the ceremony, my crew was launched to make a parts run to Guam.

The trip to Guam was uneventful, but we only spent an hour on the ground to refuel, get the part and to complete a McDonald's run. At the time, the world's largest McDonalds was located in Guam, and it was the only one in the entire western Pacific. Mickey D's is a taste of home. So we weren't going to fly seven hours across the Pacific Ocean and get that close to a McDonalds without getting burgers and fries.

Once the meals were picked up, we took off for Misawa. The quick turn around was because all members of the squadron were expected to be present at the change-of-command ceremony. Flying roundtrip from Misawa to Guam is long and tiring. In order for the crew to get some sleep prior to the ceremony that was scheduled to take place two hours after our landing, everyone slept on the transit home. Everyone except one pilot who was to "drive the bus." That pilot was me.

For most of the seven hour flight I was the only aircrew man awake in the plane. The PPC slept in the right seat and the FE in the middle seat and so it was a very quiet cockpit. It was night and we were over the deserted Pacific and it was *too* quiet. I was also tired, but since I was designated to be the bus driver I was exempt from having to attend the ceremony when we landed. My sole job, despite being totally exhausted, was to monitor the autopilot, watch for warning lights in the cockpit, and stay on course. But doing that proved to be a real challenge.

In the cockpit of a P-3 is a tactical display. It is a ten-inch diameter round tube with an aircraft symbol that tracks across the screen toward the next "Fly To" point that is entered by the navigator. On the left side of the tube is a display of your ground speed, the distance and your estimated arrival time to the next "Fly To" point. At night, it gives the impression of a video game where you drive the little airplane symbol around a digital world.

The quiet and fatigue made me struggle to keep my eyes open. Eventually, I lost that struggle. The last thing I remember seeing before I dozed off was "205 miles" as the distance to the next "Fly To" point. When I awoke with a start and panic, the scope read "345 miles." Since the "Fly To" points are entered about 350 miles apart for this kind of transit the plane must have captured the last "Fly To" point and computed the distance to the next one. A quick mental calculation told me that at 300 knots ground speed I had been asleep for about forty minutes.

I looked at the PPC and he was snoring. I looked at the FE, and he was snoring. I had a thought that maybe the navigator was fooling with me and had moved the "Fly To" point, but when I looked back in the tube, he was stretched out on the floor under his station snoring. The cold realization hit me that this plane had flown with no one at the controls for over a half hour. I woke up the PPC and told him I was having trouble staying awake and his only response was, "Quit being a wouse! We need our sleep to be able to attend the ceremony."

I was able to stay awake for another hour, but then my eyes became too heavy to hold off the inevitable. This time I awoke after about ten minutes, but what had happened scared me even more. When I awoke, I saw in the moonlight two gigantic thunderstorm cells, one to our right and one to our left. Both reached over 10,000 feet higher than our altitude.

I woke the PPC and the radar operator to help me avoid any cells ahead of us.

Of course, I never admitted to wandering into the line of thunderstorms because I was sleeping at the wheel...but I did say a little thank you prayer for our track being between the two humungous airplane killers.

Once again, I exhibited my preference to being lucky vice good.

*****

There are two other types of pilots in the Navy; those who have received a "down" on a check flight and those that are going to. I did not believe this adage upon graduating from flight school. I had never struggled with the syllabus and the thought of getting a "down" or flunking a check seemed far fetched to me.

I thought that much of myself...

Then I took my first P-3 full NATOPS check flight and at the end I was told I would have to prepare more and fly it again—I was given a "down!" It was shocking! How could that check pilot flunk the self-described "Ace of the Base?"

To this day I would argue that it was a "chicken" down because although I told him three times that I would flip a certain switch before I reached a certain speed in a ditching drill held at high altitude, I actually forgot to do it a minute later. Obviously I knew the correct procedure, I had just forgotten to do it...so he said I needed more practice...in what? Practice not forgetting?

Regardless of the reason, the "down" did me some good. I needed to be humbled once again, and since I always considered one of my "super strengths" to be my flying ability, a flight "down" was an excellent reminder that I was not the "end all, be all" in patrol aviation.

Regardless of this minor set back, I earned my PPC and MC qualifications and was eventually given my own crew. My first mission after being designated as a PPC was a flight out of Misawa, Japan.

We took off in some rather crummy winter weather and flew nearly due East out over the Northern Pacific. Using our forward facing surface search radar set at zero degrees depression angle our Sensor Three, the radar operator, was able to steer us around the really big thunderstorm cells as we transited to our search area. Our target this day was one little trawler that intelligence believed to be a Soviet spy ship. Our mission was to fly five hours east over the vast Pacific and locate the trawler and take pictures of it to confirm its real mission.

We found the tiny ship bobbing in rough oceans and descended to get our pictures. Now, just like the sailor's method of getting the torpedoes loaded at sea by ignoring the sophisticated tools provided by the Navy engineers, the same approach was used by P-3 flight crews when it came to photography. The correct procedure was to position a plastic grid on the pilot's and co-pilots side window by using ground personnel to determine the exact angle needed to fill the nose mounted camera lens with the target ship. I guess some pilots and crews might have actually tried to use this equipment. However, I did like most crews and simply placed a dot using a grease pencil on the window by my left shoulder. Then when you rolled into the photo run on a ship, you just drove that dot over the ship and clicked your pictures. Nice and easy peasy. I know it worked, because I won the "Silver Shutter Award" for the Western Pacific and the "Golden Lens Award" for the Eastern Pacific while flying P-3s.

As I approached the trawler from the rear I noticed it was going to be quite tough to drive that dot over the ship. The wind was blowing so hard that I had to crab the plane to the left about thirty degrees to maintain the path over the water I desired. The seas were so high and the winds so strong that salt spray was crusting on the windscreen as we flew at 200 feet. I wanted to get the pictures, but I was beginning to worry about the salt spray being sucked into the turbines. Even though it was very rough in the air, I smiled...because I was thinking how great it was not to be on that bouncing boat down below! This once again confirmed my choice to request flight school!

We got our pictures and started to climb to altitude to transit the five hours back to Misawa when number two engine developed a problem that necessitated shutting it down. In my mind that was par for my experience. Just like the shore power cables blowing up when I assumed my first CDO duty, I should have expected an engine failure on my first PPC flight.

Flying with one engine in the bag is normal for a P-3 as often times one is shut down to save gas and extend our time on station. And since landing with an inboard engine feathered did not present an asymmetric power problem, losing an engine on this flight was not that serious.

However, what happened next was extremely serious.

"Flight, Sensor Three," came the voice through my headset, "I just lost the forward radar."

The skies were full of big, dangerous thunderstorm cells that would rip us apart if we flew through them. It was nearly dark and we were in and out of clouds, so we needed that forward radar to get us safely home. Things looked really bleak at this point.

The In-Flight Technician (IFT) arrived in the cockpit about two minutes later. He was a brand new aircrew man, having just finished IFT School.

"Can you fix it? We need that radar to get home," I asked with as much control as I could muster.

"The only way to fix it is to swap a relay from the aft radar to the forward."

"Can you do that?" I asked hoping for a response like "no problem."

"Yeah, I think I can, but I'd have to enter the main load center to reach it," he said with honest hesitation.

Now I had to make a "command decision." The main load center is absolutely off-limits to anyone whenever there is power on the aircraft. It is a narrow closet on the starboard side of the plane fuselage that is only wide enough barely to fit the width of one man and is about ten feet long. It is off-limits with power on because there are exposed electronics on the back side of the main circuit breaker panels, which if touched when hot will electrocute the maintainer. It was dangerous to enter that load center when the aircraft was absolutely still and parked in a hangar. We were bouncing around in terrible weather and this third class petty officer was asking to enter the closet and perform a swap out of a relay.

I thought about it for five minutes and finally came to the conclusion that the chances of us penetrating a mass of thunderstorm activity in the blind was risking the whole crew, while permitting him to enter the load center was risking only one man.

I told the chief flight engineer to remove the escape rope from over the main cabin door and use it to tie around the IFT. I wanted to be able to pull the IFT, or at least his body, from the closet should the need arise without anyone else entering the danger zone.

I found what I thought might be a block of semi-stable air and held the plane as motionless as possible. I listened to the description of the action going on in the tube via the ICS. In a matter of three minutes I heard the radar operator report, "Forward radar working, come left thirty degrees to avoid the next cell."

A minute later the chief appeared in the cockpit with the third class technician who said, "Piece of cake."

The crew knew what he had risked for them and I don't believe that petty officer ever had to buy his own beer for the rest of the deployment.

*****

After a short stint as the Assistant Administrative Officer where a couple of yeomen worked for me, I got a job that fit my preferences much better. I was moved to the maintenance department as the Avionics/Armament Division Officer. In this capacity I had three branch officers and about 75 sailors working for me. There were three branches, each with a lieutenant (jg) in charge of avionics technicians, ordinance men, and electricians.

One Friday afternoon I had the chance to payback a favor done to me as a midshipman. During the spring of my junior year I had $75 which was enough to buy a one-way stand-by ticket from Sacramento, my hometown, to Baltimore. I had a week off for the spring break and if there was some way to get to California for free, I had just enough to pay my way back. I hitched a ride with a classmate to NAS Patuxent River, MD and the next morning got a seat on a reserve P-3 flying back to Moffett Field. Enroute a fellow passenger, a lieutenant commander catching a ride back to the west coast asked me how I was going to get to Sacramento from the San Jose area. I told him my plan was to hitchhike. He didn't think that was much of a plan so he went to the cockpit and had a talk with the PPC.

Soon, I was invited to the cockpit and the PPC turned his head to ask me, "Would you like to be dropped off at Mather or McClellan Air Force Base?"

Both were in the Sacramento suburbs so I said McClellan was closer to my house. The plane landed there and dropped me off.

Now seven years later I was walking along the hanger enroute to preflight for a scheduled "Dedicated Field Work" (DFW) flight when I heard a leading petty officer in my Avionics Branch complaining to a shipmate about his weekend plans. He was going to drive to Seattle right after work and then drive his mother-in-law back to San Jose in his car. Then next month he would have to find money to buy a commercial ticket and fly up to Seattle to pick up her car and bring it back home.

My flight today had one mission. It was the end of the month and end of the quarter which meant the squadron had to burn all its quarterly allotted fuel or the next quarter our allotment would be cut because we had not used all of it previously. To prevent this cut, the axiom was "Use it, or lose it." So my flight this day we called a "DFW—Dedicated Fuel Waste." I had no training syllabus flight to accomplish, rather my tasking was to burn five hours of fuel before I came back, which was usually done by flying from one airfield to another and doing multiple touch-and-goes to retain our "pilot proficiency."

I interrupted my leading petty officer's conversation, "Would it be easier if you just flew up to Seattle today and drove your mother-in-law back in her car?"

He nodded in response.

"Grab your gear, tell your chief you are excused from the shop this afternoon and meet me at S-G-0-5 in a half-hour. We've got nothing better to do, so we'll drop you off in Seattle."

And we did. It burned the five hours of fuel that operations wanted done and it helped out a shipmate. I pretended not to be aware that the Wing Commander had outlawed landing at any airport more than 300 miles from Moffett Field without prior Wing approval. We got into Boeing Field and out before anyone noticed.

Payback is good karma.

*****

Submariners lie...and I have proof.

On one of our crew's trips to Barber's Point on Oahu we were to spend the night. Rather than stay in the BOQ, I asked my brother who was stationed aboard a nuclear submarine in Pearl Harbor to take me home to spend the night with his family. He picked me up and as we drove off base we got to talking about our work, as brothers will do.

"Say, Bob," my brother and Academy classmate, Bill, asked casually, "How large are those SUS bomb-ettes you guys drop?"

SUS devices are what a P-3 slides out of the airplane through a free-fall chute in the aft cabin during training exercises to mark where it would drop a torpedo in a real war. There were two kinds in the fleet. The old Mark 64 model was a little explosive device to put a small burst of noise in the water. The newer ones, Mark 84, were safer and consisted of a small transducer that pinged a harmless sound into the water like a miniature sonar.

"Oh, I'm not sure, Bill," I replied, curious to the reason for the question. "I guess a Mark 64 might have an eighth of a pound of TNT or something like that."

He was silent for a couple of seconds and then said, "Well, that doesn't make much sense."

"What doesn't?"

"Well last week we were out operating with a P-3 and it dropped a SUS that went off directly against the sail of our boat. It sounded like it would punch a hole in us and we gave thought to doing an emergency surface to check for possible damage. I can't believe a charge that small would sound so serious."

I did not try to hide my smile as I confessed to an aircrew secret. "Now, Bill, I'm not saying *my* crew has ever done it, but I've heard of some crews taping three or four of those Mark 64s together before they slide them out of the chute."

"Sneaky aviators. That must have been what happened."

We drove on another five minutes and finally I had to ask how his boat evaluated the attack—close aboard, near, or distant?

Bill answered matter-of-factly, "Oh, distant, very distant."

I always knew submariners lie about their invulnerability and this was proof!

*****

VP-50 was one of the very first aviation combat units to have women assigned. As a shore based squadron, our ground pounders were not in combat, only the aircrews were exposed directly to any enemy action. So we received about forty women as a "test" of assigning women to combat units.

It may have been termed a "test" but the outcome of this trial was already determined. We had been ordered to make it work and then to report back on how the transition had been successful. No naval officer is about to report failure to his superior officer, so the "trial" was predetermined to be a wonderful success!

At the end of the first year I happened to be in the admin office and overheard the meeting in the XO's office discussing inputs for the mandatory report of women in the squadron. I popped my head into the office and offered my two-cents worth.

"XO, are you going to include in your report that every woman in the squadron aged 21 and younger got pregnant during the last year?"

"Not relevant, Bob, now get lost," the XO said without a smile.

I smiled because I knew that the report had to be totally positive so the fact that my division had been put under severe stress because of the pregnancy card was not going to be mentioned. We only had five aviation electricians in our shop and before we deployed two of those billets were filled with females. The week prior to our deployment it was "all of a sudden" determined that both the females had just started the second trimester of a pregnancy. Under Navy personnel policy at that time it meant they could not deploy with us for a six month stint overseas. Since we were leaving in less than a week, there were no available replacements and the day our first crew left for Okinawa, our priority for replacements went from the top of the list of Moffett Field squadrons to the bottom. So now our Electrical Shop was in a real bind. During the deployment we would have to send support detachments to different sites in Westpac, but you can never send just one electrician or other maintainer rating. You always need at least two; one to do the work and one to complete a Collateral Duty Inspection, the quality assurance check of the work. So with only three aviation electricians the shop was screwed.

Just another leadership challenge to be met, so why bother to mention it up the chain-of-command?

*****

Having women work in my division meant I had to learn about something that most men truly try to avoid...*feelings*. Here's an example.

If I found it necessary to have a male sailor stand at attention in front of my desk to receive attention about an area where he screwed up or needs to improve, there was a certain bit of theater I had learned to expect. Once I finished chewing his butt, he would leave my immediate area and after he was far enough away that we could both pretend I did not hear what he said, the sailor would express his emotions by kicking a trash can and mumbling something about my personal heritage.

The first time I called a female sailor to stand at attention in front of my desk and receive feedback on poor performance, something unexpected and unprecedented in my career occurred. She started crying.

Crying! "There's no crying in a squadron!"

At first this started to fluster me, as I have never handled my wife or daughter crying very well, but I quickly realized that she did not want to cry any more than I wanted to watch her tears fall. She was more embarrassed by it than I was. I finished my "corrective instruction" and then ordered her to, "Take ten minutes and go out to the parking ramp and get yourself together before returning to the shop. Dismissed."

This first instance of having sailors shed tears helped me understand that the crying was the exact same emotion as the sailor kicking the trash can and verbally expressing his anger at the situation. It was the same emotion; it just manifested itself in different manner.

*****

I had completed an advanced degree in butt chewing when I was an ensign and under the tutelage of Boatswain Chief Williams. The aviators who worked for me as branch officers had never been exposed to such a real world leadership training opportunity. I felt it was part of my duties as their division officer to at least introduce to them some basic techniques for use when it might be necessary to "correctively instruct" enlisted members.

A Patrol Squadron had a group of about fifteen or so technicians assigned to it that were perpetually absent from the squadron area. They worked on the black boxes the organizational level technicians replaced when a radio went bad or an instrument was no longer accurate. These items were sent to an Aviation Intermediate Maintenance Depot (AIMD), where bench techs repaired the part and returned it to the inventory for further use. Many of the bench techs at the AIMDs actually were assigned to the squadrons they supported and although they never worked alongside the squadron techs, they deployed with the squadron and worked at AIMDs overseas. This system was supposed to provide squadrons with integral intermediate maintenance support should a war start and the squadron deployed to non- supported locations.

In reality, it meant there were sailors in the maintenance department that very few in the squadron were aware even existed.

Well, one of our third class petty officers assigned to AIMD became a trouble maker. His daily supervisors who are permanent AIMD personnel got tired of dealing with this rebel, so they contacted our Maintenance Department Head, who told me to look into a solution. My Avionics Branch Officer needed to have a talk with this young petty officer and explain how the road he was on led to nothing good. The problem was that this NFO lieutenant had never led a hungry man into a restaurant in his life. He had graduated from AOCS and then went into the NFO training pipeline and then the RAG and then a job in the squadron Tactics Department. He was typical of first tour officers in a P-3 squadron. He had made lieutenant without ever having to lead anyone.

So I called Tom into my office and explained that I wanted him to sit on the sofa and remain quiet while I "counseled" this wayward sailor. I told him to observe closely all that he witnessed and then we would discuss it after I dismissed the sailor.

I had word sent to Petty Officer Krunkle to report to his division officer at 4 PM after work concluded at the AIMD. He showed at my office at 4:10 wearing his civilian clothes in anticipation of going on liberty after he had met with this division officer. He shuffled his feet as he entered the office and said, "Yeah? You wanted to see me?"

I kept him standing there and waiting as I reviewed a report on my desk. After thirty seconds, I lifted my head and with no emotion in my eyes or on my face said, "That's not the way you report to your division officer when ordered to do so. Now leave my office and change into an appropriate uniform and then return immediately with proper military decorum. Go!"

Krunkle came to attention and left my office in a hurry. Once he was gone, I turned to Tom and said, "That is rule one on butt chewing. Always do it on your own turf and immediately set the senior to subordinate relationship."

When Krunkle returned twenty minutes later he knocked on my open door and requested permission to enter. He had flipped a switch in his brain and reverted to his Boot Camp demeanor.

I kept him at attention in front of my desk as I asked his side of the stories I had heard about his screwing up over at AIMD. After listening to some typically lame excuses, I did what Chief Williams had taught me by example. I did a "push-pull."

"Petty Officer Kunkle, if you were in my position and heard excuses like you just shared, do you think you'd buy them as valid reasons for not carrying your own weight with your shipmates?"

I paused, but I did not expect an answer. Then I continued the push back.

"It sounds to me that you know what is expected of you over at AIMD. Yet you are having trouble getting your attitude right to meet those expectations. I'm not buying this whining about your supervisor is out to get you. You do the work well and then if he is still on your back, I will get involved and set him straight. But there is no way I'm going to bat for a sailor who can't even show he can do the minimum."

Having pushed back, now I needed to pull him to a place where he wanted to excel.

"I've looked over your record and it might surprise you to know that I see the makings of a very strong petty officer in you. You have the talent and intelligence to make master chief some day...but what you lack is the attitude. Stop behaving like some high school punk and show up to work with pride in who you are. You are a superior sailor if you decide to be. So make up your mind and get on with your work. I will know what you decide by the lack of complaints I will be getting from AIMD. I want to close with a promise that I have kept with many sailors over the past years. You work for me and I will work for you. You can have no better friend to your career than me. But if you continue to bring discredit on the squadron and on me personally, you will have no worse enemy than me. Now go and do good. You're dismissed."

Kunkle made a smart left face and marched out of my office. I spent the next ten minutes helping Tom understand the push-pull system of "counseling."

The best part of this story is that Kunkle's name was never mentioned by AIMD for the rest of that tour.

I share this success story only because 80% of the time similar tales ended in disappointment! Most screw-ups remain screw-ups.

*****

Rear Admiral Sinclair was Commander, Task Force 75, which meant that all the non-aviation ships in the Western Pacific were under his command. He was taking three ships into the Sea of Okhotsk with the expressed mission of just tweaking the nose of the Soviets. The Soviet Union considered the sea located between the Kamchatka Peninsula and the Russian coast to be their inland waters, similar to the way America considers the Great Lakes to be our domain. Every couple of years the United States sent a small group of ships to steam around the sea just to prove that the rest of the world considered the Sea of Okhotsk to be international waters. This evolution was called "Operation Free Seas, '79."

Part of the operation included air patrol support by P-3s stationed in Misawa, northern Japan. A P-3 Mission Commander was to be temporarily assigned to ride the flag ship with the admiral's staff to coordinate patrol aviation support. However, when the admiral visited Misawa for a pre-cruise meeting, he came across as one hard-nosed flag officer. In fact, he frightened all the MCs in the squadron who feared they might taint their career path by working for an admiral who cannot be pleased. So a phone call was placed to our squadron which was deployed to Okinawa at the time with the opportunity to provide a ship rider for this exercise.

As I was the only officer in our squadron who wore a Surface Warfare Officer pin along with my wings, I got nominated to be the patrol aviation representative on the admiral's staff. This was all done at the last minute and I was informed of my new assignment via a phone call from the Operations Officer around 8

PM to my BOQ room. Now prior to his phone call I had been in discussions about whether I would be taking my crew down to Diego Garcia in the middle of the Indian Ocean or if another, more senior officer would bump me to head the detachment of three planes we were keeping on that tiny, warm tropical island. My notification of the change of plans went as follows.

"Bob," said the Ops Boss over an unsecured telephone line, "There's been a change of plans and you will be flying out tomorrow morning early."

"For how long?" I asked.

"I'm not sure. Plan on a week...and dress warm."

"Okay," I replied thinking that now I would be taking my crew to Diego Garcia and then returning with another airplane that needed to be back for maintenance.

Very early the next morning I showed up at the hangar wearing my flight suit and carrying a small bag packed with a set of khakis, a swimsuit, shorts, flip flops and T-shirts. Five minutes before take-off the Ops Boss arrived and informed me that my destination was Atsugi, Japan where I would be transported to Yokosuka Naval Station to board the USS Bainbridge. That was all he knew, but he felt for sure I would be briefed by the staff at Atsugi with more details.

At Atsugi a staff member of the wing commander was astounded to discover I had no inkling of why I had been whisked from Okinawa. He had me change into my only khaki uniform while he gave me a ten minute brief on Operation Free Seas '79. It was then that I became aware that "pack warm" had meant prepare for cold weather, not tropical climate and that this trip would be over two weeks. Since CTF 75 had a very large staff, only the top members could accompany the admiral to ride the Bainbridge which had limited room. This meant that I would be the only lieutenant on his staff for this operation. Lucky me...nothing like being the low man in the pecking order again...like being a plebe or an ensign again...and making do with only one uniform.

The next couple of weeks were interesting and, to some degree, fun. I discovered that Admiral Sinclair was a very fair, level-headed officer that expected competence if not excellence in daily work. This might have appeared to make him seem tough to work for if you only met him for twenty minutes, such as the squadron in Misawa had done.

Every morning would be the admiral's brief in the flag wardroom and I always took a seat against the bulkhead behind the admiral, out of his sight line. Every morning I was ready with a list of flights and when they would be providing surface intelligence of surrounding Soviet ships. Every morning at some point during the brief he turned to me and asked me one question, "Are we getting the best use of our air assets?"

The first morning this happened I kept my carefully prepared brief on air operations in my lap and answered, "Yes, sir." He never said a word, but just turned back to face the table and take up the next agenda item in the brief. This went on for the entire exercise and since my two word answer had been satisfactory, I never saw any reason to burden him with my prepared brief.

Every evening, the admiral wanted to watch a movie. As the only lieutenant on the staff, it was my duty to pick the movie and to run the projector and to sit with the admiral while he watched it. The nights showing movies to the Schofield crew while in Guam had made me a rather fair projectionist.

My love of movies also was beneficial when I discovered that Admiral Sinclair would grow tired at the end of a day at sea. So invariably, he would fall asleep during the first reel and wake up when I changed reels. He would always ask me to summarize the action and plot and characters so he could enjoy the second reel. Of course, he would fall asleep during that reel and when the film was done he enjoyed my retelling what had happened. Since it was almost always just the two of us watching the movie in the flag wardroom, I had to hide a chuckle when he used a plot point of a movie to illustrate a tactical situation during one of the morning briefs. I was the only one who knew he had slept through those scenes and was relying on what I had shared when he awoke.

Since I was a qualified Surface Warfare Officer and the admiral's full staff had not made the cruise, the Chief Staff Officer (CSO) decided to put the aviator on the flag watch bill. One night I had the mid-watch by myself and I became *the "AB."* Alpha Bravo was the call sign for the officer in tactical command of the formation. On this quiet night, for a four hour period when everyone but the watch standers were asleep the night orders left by the CSO directed me to conduct tactical ship maneuvering drills, commonly called "tic-tacs.".

I remembered when the Schofield had steamed with the Bainbridge in the IO and the unfamiliarity the nuclear powered cruiser's OODs had with maneuvering close to other ships. So, I thought that of all three bridge teams steaming in this formation during this night, the Bainbridge OOD probably could benefit the most from the drills.

Consequently, I did something very rare. Whenever this nuclear propelled ship cruised with ships other than carriers, it was the "high value target" and remained at the center of any ship formations. It requires no effort to be the center of the screen. The challenge is when you must plot a new course to race to a different position in relation to the moving center. So I made the supply ship the center and ordered the cruiser and frigate to run to different positions in the screen.

The frigate, as expected, did this smartly and with ease. The Bainbridge, as expected, was clumsy and had difficulty properly finding their correct station.

I was having fun ordering the ships around the ocean and I thought the tic-tacks were going well and good training was being received. However, the commanding officer of the Bainbridge did not agree. Which was okay by me.

The CO of the Bainbridge was none other than Captain T.A. Almstedt, Jr., who had been my CO on the Schofield. He had maintained a great career arc and finally got command of his dream ship, a nuclear powered cruiser.

The door to flag plot flew open at around 3 AM and standing there with sleep and anger in his eyes was my former captain.

"Who built this formation with Bainbridge not in the center?" he demanded in his usual accusatory voice.

"I did, sir," I responded.

"And who are you to do that?" he demanded, even though I am sure he vaguely remembered Ensign Bartron.

"I *am* Alpha Bravo," I said with confidence that this was the only time where the shoe would be on the opposite foot.

Captain Almstedt turned and stormed out of flag plot.

The next morning at the flag brief, the CSO made an announcement to all assembled before the admiral arrived, "From now on, whenever tic-tacs are ordered, the Bainbridge will remain the center of the formation."

I never wondered where that directive was initiated.

*****

Working in the Maintenance Department meant I also volunteered to be a "Spintac" pilot to help maintain the department's reputation with the wing commodore.

Being a "Spintac" pilot was a very unofficial designation. It really could be considered a badge of idiocy. I don't remember what "Spintac" stood for, but it referred to a report that had to be sent to the wing by a deployed squadron anytime an airplane had not flown for thirty days. The motive behind the report was to ensure that squadrons were not working around the pitiful supply support they received by stealing needed parts from one aircraft to make another safe for flight. This practice was monitored by both a "cannibalization report" and the "Spintac" reporting requirement. What this emphasis did was basically put pressure on the maintainers to be creative in keeping the planes flying without having proper spare parts support.

Each squadron had nine aircraft, but on deployment, at the end of the supply chain, invariably one of the airplanes became the "hangar queen" or "spare parts locker." Yet, every thirty days enough equipment and parts had to be cannibalized from the eight flying birds to make the "hangar queen" flyable.

A "Spintac" pilot in the squadron was a volunteer to take the "hangar queen" airborne once a month. Most of these pilots worked in the Maintenance Department or were daredevils or both.

My most memorable "Spintac" flight was when I took off from Kadena Air Base on Okinawa with no inertials, no working altimeter, no working windshield wipers, and only two of three generators working...oh, yeah, and the pins remained in the landing gear because the hydraulic system was partially inoperative. But all four engines and props, one UHF radio and the flight controls worked, so what else was needed?

A minimum crew of four of us loaded onto this "hangar queen" and taxied to the end of the 13,000 foot runway and got permission to fly once around the pattern. We got airborne and five minutes later we were back on the deck. We logged 0.3 flight hours for the plane and nursed it back to the hangar. Mission complete.

I know of another "Spintac" crew that got airborne for an even shorter period. They ran down the runway and got light under the wheels after 4,000 feet and then landed in the remaining 9,000 feet of runway. Log it. Airborne for 0.1 flight hours. No report necessary to the wing; the plane had flown that month.

******

All aviators learn that there are three things that can never help you: the runway behind you, the air above you, and the gas you left in the truck. You will find multiple stories in this book that are tales about running low on gas, so here is one about "the runway behind you."

One of the missions VP-50 supported while deployed to Kadena in 1979 was the hunt for Vietnam refugee boats on the high seas. Usually these were flown by a detachment serving with the deployed P-3 squadron at NAS Cubi Point in the Philippines. We would depart Cubi and search for refugee boats enroute to a landing at Singapore. Then after a day or two of liberty at Singapore we would retrace our steps to Cubi, flying a search track enroute.

I flew as copilot for the XO on one of these missions. We were pre-flighting for the morning launch for the return flight from Singapore, when the XO and I hoofed the long, long way from the aircraft parking space to base operations at Paya Lebar airbase. We were surprised to find that the flight planning room did not have any aeronautical charts. It was then that we realized pilots were supposed to supply their own planning materials. I was about to start the long trek back to the airplane and retrieve the 3P bag which held all out navigation charts, when the XO noticed a National Geographic map of the world framed and hanging on the wall. To save time and my boot leather we constructed a route of flight using a string of latitude and longitude points we pulled from that eighteen-inch square wall hanging.

The flight plan submitted, we took the long walk back to the airplane. After the planeside brief, I climbed in the left seat and the XO took the right seat. We had a normal start sequence and I taxied toward the duty runway. It was late morning and the temperature and humidity was typical for that part of the world, hot and humid. We were sitting very low on the struts because of a maximum fuel load that was necessary to complete this mission profile.

As any pilot can tell you, maximum take-off weight and hot and humid weather meant it was going to be a real chore for the airplane to wallow into the air. Despite knowing this, we did something rather stupid.

We were unable to use the taxiway that led to the end of the northerly, 11,000 foot runway. So we entered the runway near the mid-point and were cleared to taxi to the end and takeoff. As we back-taxied on the runway, the XO asked if I was going all the way to the very end. Since a P-3 normally only needs less than 5,000 feet of runway to take off, I said I was going to turn around and start the takeoff with about 8,000 feet of runway in front of us. He nodded and watched as I spun the aircraft around and lined up with the centerline.

The flight engineer had computed the takeoff airspeeds based on using 11,000 feet so he had calculated that there was no "refusal speed" on this takeoff. "Refusal speed" is the point during the takeoff roll when you are going too fast to stop in the runway remaining should you decide to abort the takeoff. Once "refusal speed" is reached, you are going flying no matter what, as stopping just became impossible.

I advanced the power levers and told the flight engineer to set maximum takeoff power. We slowly started to roll down the runway...we slowly began to pick up speed...the airspeed indicator slowly started to creep in a clockwise fashion...however, the runway remaining was steadily dwindling...after 6,000 feet of runway had slipped under our gear we were nearing rotate speed, but hadn't quite reached it. The hot, humid weather and heavy load were making this normal takeoff rather exciting.

The XO finally said, "Rotate," and I pulled back on the yoke. It took a moment for the airplane to react, but finally we began tentatively to get air under the landing gear. I called for the "gear up" and when we passed over the departure end of that runway we were, maybe, twenty feet in the air. I continued the climb with full power and raised the flaps one setting at a time as the airspeed grew. Even with the plane now cleaned up, it felt mushy and unhappy to have "slipped the surly bonds of earth."

Less than five miles from the end of the runway was the Malaysian border. All planes departing Singapore were to remain outside Malaysia. As we approached the border while wrestling with our struggling bird, the tower operator kept demanding, "Turn right! Turn right! Do it now! TURN! YOU ARE ENTERING A FORBIDDEN AREA!"

Both the XO and I could care less about some line on a map at this point of our departure. Making a sharp turn at this airspeed and aircraft weight would have been disastrous. As soon as I felt it safe, I put in a shallow right turn, the radius of which took us over the border momentarily. As soon as we passed the magic border line, the tower went silent. That was disconcerting.

Ten minutes later the P-3 had gathered sufficient airspeed to feel normal and we continued upwards at a usual rate. We contacted Singapore radio and got our clearance to altitude to begin our track to the east.

Before he slid out of the seat to put the 2P in it, the XO informed the flight engineer and me, "In case you guys didn't know it, we had a refusal speed on that takeoff. Bob, if you had tried to come back on the power to stop, I wouldn't have let it happen."

We both nodded and then turned our attention to the mission ahead of us.

And after that scare, I have always taxied to the end of the runway before takeoff.

*****

After being the Av/Arm Division Officer, my next assignment in VP-50 was as Pilot Training Officer. This meant I completed the IUT syllabus and became the most senior first tour instructor. I really enjoyed this assignment. The ground job was mostly administrative; the meat of the assignment was instructing newer pilots in qualifying as a 3P, 2P and PPC.

One day my crew was assigned to fly to Hawaii in order to drop exercise torpedoes on a calibrated range off of Kauai. Since we were to be gone for four or five days to earn this crew qualification, my wife drove me to the squadron on our departure day so she could retain my car. At Moffett Field cars would drive across the aircraft parking ramp to reach the two large blimp hangers on the operational side of the field. As my wife drove me across the flight line we passed right next to SG-05. I knew that was the plane my crew would be taking to Hawaii later in the day, so I had her stop to permit me to throw my luggage onboard, thus saving me from having to lug it across the wide ramp later. My wife remembered the plane's number. It was the only time she ever knew the number of an airplane I flew in the Navy.

We transited to NAS Barbers Point, but the next day foul weather at the range site meant that our torpedo exercise was postponed, but other than a high sea state on the range, the weather was clear all over the islands. Most of my crew wanted to use the unexpected day off to visit Waikiki and hit the beach. I wanted to sightsee from the air and called back to our squadron and got permission to burn five hours of fuel, which they were happy to grant because it was getting close to the end of the quarter. My only problem was that both the other pilots in the crew had not been to Hawaii before and had no interest in flying around the islands. Being an instructor pilot meant it was permissible for me to fly with any military aviator in the other seat. I was not restricted to use only squadron pilots. So I called over to the Wing Commander's staff and got the safety officer there to come along as my copilot. The crew flight engineer and the TACCO had both visited the islands many times, so an aerial sightseeing trip sounded interesting to them.

We took off from NAS Barbers Point in SG-07, having switched aircraft with another VP-50 crew who was enroute to Pago Pago, American Samoa to participate in an air show there.

SG-07 had repairs being completed that morning which would have delayed the other crew's take off, so we gave them our plane to continue.

We flew down to the big island, Hawaii, and switched from IFR to VFR rules so we could zoom around the beaches and the volcanic craters. In fact, I got a little carried away in my desire to get a good view of the active volcano. A great portion of the island is covered with lava from previous eruptions and the landscape made it look like we were astronauts skimming the moon's surface. There was a 200 foot minimum altitude when we were on station over the Pacific Ocean, but when flying over the United States the FAA rules are a minimum of "500 feet from ol' lonesome Joe." This can be measured vertically or horizontally. So I took us down into the crater low enough that the tourists on the rim were pointing their cameras down to get pictures of our plane. At the end of the crater I made a ninety degree turn to the left to fly up another valley. There in front of me was a small airfield and I was about to fly through its pattern. I popped the P-3 up and got to 700 feet above ground level as I flew right down the runway. To exit the valley I had to turn around and fly over the runway once again.

Fifteen minutes later, as we approached Hilo Airport to land for a lunch stop, the tower responded to my initial call with, "Navy 1-2-3 report downwind for runway eight. And say, are you the P-3 down here flying through restricted areas today?'

I gave the standard Naval aviator response, "No, wasn't us."

The tower replied, "Eh...sir...you are the *only* P-3 down here today."

It was agreed that I would call them on a phone as soon as I landed.

Once on the phone with the tower personnel, the conversation went like this.

"Do you guys remember flying through the control zone around an Army helo airstrip earlier?"

"Oh, I thought for sure I avoided that by staying to the south," (a midshipman does not lie, cheat or steal...but there are times it is better to utilize discretion before admitting to anything.)

"Just a minute," I heard the FAA civilian say, and then I heard his half of a conversation he was having on another phone, obviously in touch with the Army. "No, the Army is pretty sure you flew right down their runway at a low altitude."

"I didn't know their restricted area was active this afternoon. Was there a NOTAM out on that?" I said trying to find some excuse for being such an idiot.

"I think the tower operating schedule is written on the sectional chart," the FAA civilian replied.

I decided it was time to just come clean and hope for the best. "Well, we're stationed in California and I was unaware of their active restricted area. I'm sorry."

I heard the FAA civilian mumble something in his other phone and then he got back on the line with me, "The Army says if you promise not to do it again, we can forget about the whole thing."

"I promise!"

Having escaped that flight violation, I left the flight engineer in the parked aircraft with the Auxiliary Power Unit on to keep the electrical systems and gyros up and running. Then the rest of this little band of sightseers walked into town and got a late lunch at a small cafe. Then we passed a florist on the way back to the airport and I saw a "Bird of Paradise" plant I thought my wife might like, so I bought it.

As we approached the plane, the flight engineer was standing in the doorway at the top of the ladder waving his arms frantically for me to hurry. As soon as I stepped into the cabin he told me the bad news.

"Ground control has been trying to reach you every five minutes for the last half-hour. They want you to call them immediately."

I thought, "So much for the Army dropping the restricted area issue."

When I made contract with Ground Control they told me to immediately start my engines and depart on a direct flight to NAS Barbers Point. When I asked why, they said they had no idea, but our operations center was very anxious to have the plane and crew back.

We quickly got airborne and once we got close enough to Oahu to use the UHF frequencies I had the TACCO connect us with the clear voice ops circuit at the Tactical Support Center (TSC.)

I reported our position and ETA and asked why they wanted us. The reply gave me a sick feeling in my stomach.

"Navy 1-2-3, land immediately. Do not go to the fueling pits or the bird bath. Park in the VIP spot in front of the tower. The duty truck will be there to bring the PPC to the TSC."

That sounded an awful lot to me like, "Go directly to jail. Do not pass go. Do not collect $200. Go directly to jail."

I decided to comply with these terse directions and not mention that I would have to let a non-squadron pilot taxi the bird back to the VP ramp. I figured he should have known about the restricted area and warned me since he was the Wing Safety Officer, so if he banged up the aircraft during the taxi from the VIP spot then he could deal with that.

The TACCO on this flight, who had come along as a tourist, was Lieutenant Commander "Fast Eddie" Booth. Since it seemed that I was being called to judgment for a flight violation it made sense that the Wing had no need to talk with the senior NFO onboard. The directions were for the PPC to report to the TSC.

The duty truck was there and I climbed in the passenger side. Fast Eddie slid me to the center of the bench front seat and climbed in the shotgun seat.

"I want to know what happens," is all he said. I was appreciative for the company so I didn't object.

As we drove along to the TSC, I tried to get a heads-up on why I had been summoned so I asked the driver, "So do you know what's going on?"

He shook his head as he answered, "I don't know, but everyone is sure hopping about something."

Oh, great...maybe I will lose my wings as well as my PPC designation.

I knew what the driver meant as soon as we walked into this secure installation. The TACCO and I gave our ID cards to the duty petty officer and waited for him to find our names on the access list and issue us visitor's badges. Just then the Wing Chief Staff Officer (CSO), a full captain, walked by the entrance lobby.

"Are you the PPC for Navy 1-2-3?" he asked sternly.

I nodded.

"Come with me," he directed

"I'll get my badge and follow you, sir," I said.

"You don't need any badges. Just come with me," again he talked in a dry, flat stern voice.

He maintained this tone while making conversation as Fast Eddie and I hustled to keep up with this captain in a hurry.

"Went down to the big island today?" he asked.

"Yes, sir," I replied meekly.

"Maybe got some lunch?"

"Yes, sir," I said, my eyes getting wider.

"Maybe bought some flowers for the wife?"

Now it was getting spooky. How did he know all we did?

Before I could answer, we arrived at his large office. He motioned for us to enter and wait for him to return.

I was on edge and my temper was starting to rise. I did not like the cat and mouse game this senior officer was playing with me. I turned to Fast Eddie and said, "If he's going to pull my wings I wish he would just do it and quit these games!"

Just then the captain returned and went to his desk and as he sat down he motioned for us to take two chairs facing his desk. Then he spoke, "Sit down. This isn't going to be very pleasant."

I sat there expecting to be told of repercussions for flat-hat stunts and busting a restricted area, but what he said next hit me in the side of my head like a ball coming in from left field when I was facing right field. It completely blind sided me.

"Your squadron's SG-05 crashed in Pago Pago, killing everyone onboard. We need you to get your crew together and be ready to ferry the accident investigation team down to Samoa as soon as they land about 2 AM tomorrow."

My mouth dropped open and I almost said out loud what I was thinking, "No! That's tragic! You're supposed to be chewing me out for a dumb stunt where no one got hurt—for flying through a restricted area!"

But I wisely kept my mouth shut except to respond, "Aye, aye, sir."

The next morning we had SG-07 pre-flighted and ready to depart as another VP-50 aircraft parked next to us and lowered its ladder. Down came the accident investigation team consisting of our squadron safety officer and many members of Commander, Patrol Wings Pacific staff as well as investigators from the Naval Safety Center. As I saw the number of the team members it became clear to me that most of my crew would have to deplane and remain in Hawaii. The P-3C we flew only held 23 persons. I had my TACCO, two sensor operators, ordnance man, and IFT get off the plane. That left a flight engineer and a second mechanic to rotate in the cockpit middle seat, three pilots, our navigator and radar operator. But once the entire investigation team boarded, I still had too many passengers. Since there were pilots in the investigation team, I had my 3P get off and stay behind. I still had one too many, so I had the navigator stay behind since the investigation team also had qualified NFOs on it.

Then I got a radio call from the Hawaii CSO who informed me that the commodore wanted his flight surgeon to join the investigation team. I told him I did not have room to take one more passenger.

I always remember his odd question after I had declined his request, "Lieutenant, are trying to tell me that your aircraft is incapable of lifting off the ground because you would have another 200 pounds onboard?"

Talk about pressure from a senior officer to do the wrong thing...if it was a matter of weight, I could off load a couple hundred pounds of fuel and still have nearly 60,000 pounds of JP-5 in my tanks. NATOPS set the limit at 23 persons on the P-3C because their were only 23 ditching stations with seat belts and 23 spots in the life rafts should we ditch.

I felt I was being pressured to ignore the rules to accommodate what the commodore and his CSO wanted done. I hesitated, and after a long pause replied, "I'll leave my second mech behind. Send over your doctor."

I figured it would take about nine hours to transit to American Samoa and the flight engineer would just have to gut it out. Besides, I had no plans of getting out of my seat for the entire flight either. I had logged ten hours in the seat more than once previously so it seemed like a good way to extradite me from this dilemma.

It was a relatively easy flight monitoring the autopilot over the Pacific. When we arrived at the airport, the accident investigation team left in a chartered bus, while my minimum crew and I remained to button up the aircraft.

I will always remember the cab ride from the airport to the mishap site. As we rounded the last corner prior to arriving at the only hotel on the island the smell of JP-5 jet fuel assaulted my senses. Not only could I smell the fuel, but I could taste it, the odor was that pungent.

As we pulled up to the hotel we discovered that the aircrew had crashed right into the only accommodations on the island. The crash had totally demolished the aircraft so that the largest piece that could be seen was a panel of aluminum shaped like a triangle measuring about five feet wide at the base and fifteen feet long. The only other items that were recognizable as being part of an airplane were two of the heavy crew seats sitting upside down in the rubble and a couple of large masses that had once been engines.

Seeing the remains of a plane I had flown just two days previously gave me a chill as I thought about just how true the flippant saying we regularly used in aviation really was: "I'm going out to defy death and gravity today." Sometimes both refuse to be defied.

This crash site was the most unique that any of the investigators had ever visited. Normally, they had to trek up mountains or into jungles to inspect a crash. However, this crash happened right at the hotel. The ensuing fire had burned three of the four wings of the hotel, but the investigation team was given rooms in the remaining wing so they had only to exit their hotel rooms and walk fifty feet to be at the crash site.

What the investigators discovered was the crash was due 100% to pilot error. Al Glenny was an Academy graduate who started at quarterback and graduated after I did. He had submitted his resignation papers and was beginning to transition to civilian life when his request was approved to lead the crew to Pago Pago to help the Samoans celebrate Flag Day. His job was to ferry a group from the Army's Tropical Lightening Parachute

Club down to the island and then provide the platform for them to parachute down in front of the holiday crowd as part of the celebration show.

I had also volunteered, as had about every other squadron PPC, to take this assignment because it was rare to get an all-expense paid vacation to an exotic island with nothing to do but show off. But I had to pull my request when our crew was scheduled to drop exercise torpedoes on the Kauai range...and my wife made it clear that there was no way I was going on a boondoggle and leave her with our son if it was voluntary.

After successfully dropping the parachutists, Al decided he wanted to give the crowd a thrill by making a low pass down the harbor. However, he failed to get low enough to fly under a tramway cable or high enough to fly over it. The cable hit the top of the cockpit just above the windshield and slid to the back. When it reached the tail it sliced off the vertical stabilizer and the smaller tram in-haul cable wrapped around his number four prop. This caused the tethered airplane to be pulled right into the courtyard in front of the hotel. It killed all six aircrew aboard and one civilian on the ground.

I had nothing to do for the five days that my minimum crew and I remained on the island. I took tours of the sites and spent time observing the investigation team. Two memories stand out about this trip.

I was observing a JAG officer and a Supply Officer who were members of the investigation team. They set up business at a folding table in the hotel ball room that had been only partially damaged. All the tourists who had missed being killed by the crash and fire because they were assembled downtown to watch the Flag Day show, lined up to enter the ball room one at a time. I watched as they each made a claim against the government for the personal items they had lost due to the crash and fire. Most were quite honest in their estimate and the Supply Officer would agree to their claim if they would sign a waiver the JAG officer had prepared for them. If they signed the legal quit claim, the Supply Officer would count out cash in fresh twenties and pay them on the spot. If they thought the amount being offered was unfair because they had lost "three business suits at $900 apiece and four pieces of jewelry valued at $2,000" (an actual claim I heard one man make!) then they would get nothing and could sue the government at their leisure. I even saw the Supply Officer disagree with a couple of gentle ladies and change their claim...he *raised* the amount due them and sent them out happy with funds to finish their planned vacation in Hawaii. I was impressed by how fair and understanding both these staff officers were as well as efficient in tying up the loose ends of the crash.

The other specific memory was the conversation I had with Lieutenant Commander Gary Woy, our squadron Safety Officer. One night I was visiting his hotel room and he seemed quite bothered by something. That was unusual because he had a well earned reputation as the best stick in the squadron and the kind of easy going, level headed department head that junior officers could approach about anything.

He asked me a question that was bothering him, "Bob would you ever take it upon yourself to violate the NATOPS rules about passengers on your aircraft?"

That question upset me! Was Gary now going to lecture me on how I should have ignored the rules and just loaded the doctor onboard without kicking off my second mech?

"Look, I don't know what that captain told you, I think his request was way out of line! I stand by decision!"

Gary gave me a queer look and shook his head and asked, "What are you talking about, Bob?"

I explained to him how the CSO had wanted me to bust NATOPS rules and add his flight surgeon to my aircraft manifest. Gary's attitude actually improved a little when I told him the story.

It seems he had been upset because he had just found out that Al Glenny had taken a cross-county hop some months earlier to his hometown. There Al took his father up on an unauthorized local flight. This was totally illegal and it upset Gary because he had thought he had a special relationship with the junior pilots and now he was just hearing about this kind of stuff. Why didn't the other members of Al's crew report him? Why did they go along with such a hot dog move?

While I was flying around the Pacific and seeing new places, my wife had a different experience. The wives "jungle drums" are a very effective communication system in the Navy.

Mary heard about a squadron plane crashing in Pago Pago and knowing that I had expressed an interest in taking that mission, she thought it best to check on my status. So she called the Squadron Duty Office and had the following conversation.

"Hello, I understand that a plane crashed. Which one was it?"

The Duty Office was a mad house at this point and she had been lucky to get through on the telephone. On the other end was a junior enlisted standing watch as an assistant to the Duty Officer.

Before he gave it much thought, he replied, "SG-05."

Mary's world stood still and her heart stopped for a second. SG-05 was the aircraft she had seen me board prior to my departure two days earlier.

She was able to force out just one more question, "This is Mrs. Bartron, can you tell me when my husband will be coming back?"

The petty officer had just heard that my crew had been tasked to ferry the investigation team to Pago Pago and he had no other estimate of what might happen next, so he answered my wife with, "Ehhhh....your husband won't be home...for...a *very* long time."

At that point she was disconnected.

In her mind I was dead. And I remained dead for another hour until she could get clarification from the Duty Officer.

Let me tell you, when I finally did get home I could do nothing wrong!...for at least the first twenty minutes anyway....

Back at Moffett Field sometime later higher authority held a JAG investigation. Since I was nearly a contemporary of Al Glenny's I was called as a witness.

It was just like most Naval Aviators thought such procedures would be. I was called into a conference room at wing headquarters and there in front of me was a very long and wide table. The table was covered in a green felt cloth and on one side were eight chairs with eight senior officers sitting in them. In front of them were water pitchers and glasses. On my side, the witness or accused side, was one chair...and no water.

Unlike my experience with Captain Matthews and cutting chapel, this time my testimony was one of the very shortest they heard.

They asked me if I knew of Al's poor choices in violating NATOPS standards or doing things against wing policy. I told them the truth. Whenever I had flown with Al he had been a stickler about the rules. I gave an example of how one of his copilots had flown with me and when I directed the young aviator to commence a climb before we received permission from Air Traffic Control, he said Al would never let him do that, even when we were solo over the Pacific in clear weather, five-hundred miles from the coast and not in radar contact. Now I thought that was taking things a little too seriously.

After about ten minutes of this honest report on my part, the senior member of the Board of Inquiry said, "Lieutenant Bartron, the person you are describing is very different that who the other witnesses described." Obviously they thought I was closing ranks and protecting another Academy graduate, which was not the case.

"Well, maybe that was because we didn't fly together that much, being that we were peers."

"You're dismissed, Lieutenant."

And they never asked me back...and never offered me any water.

*****

Then there was the time I spotted a UFO.

We flew an operational mission in the Yankee Patrol Area (YPA) which was located about a thousand miles off the California coast. Listening stations that rimmed the Pacific would detect a Soviet Yankee class ballistic missile submarine on patrol and then feed the general location to a P-3 base. Our job was to go out and find the submarine, track it and sometimes gather acoustic intelligence about that specific hull on patrol.

These missions were the primary contribution of our community and we did them very well. If a hot war was starting, we had a very good chance of sinking the Soviet sub on station before it could launch nuclear destruction on America's west coast. During the Cold War it was fun just to have the opportunity to play with the Commies.

These trips to YPA were long and tiring, especially if you drew the middle of the night time on station. A typical flight would start at 4 PM with a detailed briefing, followed by a four hour preflight of the airframe, engines, and sensors to include loading a full belly and internal racks with sonobuoys. Take-off would be at 8 PM and then we'd transit the four hours to the YPA, spend another 4 hours searching for the submarine, and then fly the four hours back to NAS Moffett Field. After this twelve-hour mission came the two-hour debrief where the crew would be quizzed on why they turned right instead of left seven hours earlier. The Patrol community had a habit of eating their young in these debriefs which always included a grade being given. So a YPA mission would mean a minimum of an eighteen hour work day.

It was on one of these flights that the cockpit crew got scared. We had been flying at about a thousand feet practicing gaining attack criteria on a Soviet submarine and had just started our climb to transit altitude when a bright light appeared in front of the airplane's nose. It was the first external light we had seen since leaving the coast line of California. There was a high overcast that blocked our view of any stars or the moon, and a low overcast that prevented us from seeing any boats on the water. For nearly eight hours we had been flying inside a black cave, having absolutely no outside reference.

At first we thought we may have another aircraft flying high above our route of flight, but that was discounted immediately as the light zoomed up, down, right and left at a speed and with an agility that no man-made craft could achieve. Our total focus on trying to identify this mysterious craft nearly got us killed. We were in a climb with no horizon and when I looked down at the airspeed indicator to backstop the 2P in the left seat I noticed we were nearly at stall speed. I pushed the yoke forward and we re-established a normal rate of climb, but our total attention was once again on that light racing from the left to the right and high then low.

The biggest problem was that the three of us in the cockpit all agreed that we saw the light and we all agreed that it was moving too erratically and swiftly to be a plane...but also all agreed that none of us wanted to report seeing a UFO. You land with a story like that and you could have your wings yanked off of your chest and be sent home without a pension. So we were in a real bind.

What does any good Navy pilot do when he is in a bind? You call for help from a NFO.

"Nav, Flight," I said into my headset, "come up here. I want you to see something"

The navigator left his station in the tube and stepped into the cockpit.

"See that?" I asked as I pointed to our mysterious light.

"Oh! Yeah! Thanks! I was hoping to see Venus this morning. I wanted to try a celestial fix on the way home," the navigator shared with unexpected enthusiasm deep into a very long flight.

"I thought you might need it," I lied with great confidence.

Once the navigator left the cockpit, the pilots and flight engineer had a good nervous laugh.

It didn't take long to figure out what had happened. We were flying due east, just before sunrise. Cloud layers below and above us prevented seeing any man-made lights. But the sun just over the horizon was reflecting off Venus which was rising very low in the sky ahead of us.

The reason the light moved so erratically was due to two factors. The first was that our aircraft nose and attitude were changing in reference to the single light. Our own aircraft movements made it look like the light was moving.

The other reason was something we had learned in flight school. As part of the course dealing with aviation physiology we were taken into a classroom that had no windows. The lights were turned off and we were directed to focus on the only light source in the black room. The instructor's voice was heard asking if we could see him moving the single light to the left and right. We all saw the light moving. Then he turned on the classroom lights and we saw that the light in the front of the classroom was permanently attached to the wall. We had just experienced autokinesis. We had learned that our brains could not hold a single light steady in space without another light to give it a reference. I had totally forgotten that demonstration until that night climbing off-station over the Pacific Ocean.

And that was how we explained away the UFO we saw...that's our story and we're sticking to it.

*****

A few weeks after the loss of SG-05 in Pago Pago, I was assigned to a six-week detachment to Adak, Alaska. Pacific Fleet patrol squadrons maintained a three plane detachment on the far end of the Aleutians Islands. I was assigned to fly with another crew for this detachment because their PPC/MC was a lieutenant commander and would remain on the ground as the Officer-in-Charge of the detachment. I would act as the PPC/MC for his crew whenever they flew.

Our arrival to the island did not go well. I was in the right seat acting as copilot and the crew's PPC was in the left seat flying. His name was LCDR Armando Wiley...the same Armando Wiley who had given me my winging check flight in S-2s at Corpus Christi. He was an experienced, fleet S-2 pilot who could make that aircraft sit-up and beg! However, this was his first tour flying P-3s. By the time he joined the squadron I was already an instructor pilot in the Orion and had many more actual hours in the airframe than LCDR Wiley.

It was obvious to me that Wiley was still adapting his superior flying skills to this much different and larger beast. As we approached Adak the weather had closed in and we were required to make an instrument approach. As I sat there watching Wiley fly, I noticed he was "far behind the airplane," ...meaning he would see the need to correct his flight path or descent a few seconds after the optimal time to do so. As a result, we failed to be in a position to land at the end of the approach. I watched him make two attempts and we got very close to breaking out and being able to land each time, but we had to wave off and drive around the instrument pattern once again.

On the third try, Wiley offered me the chance to fly the approach. I did so and immediately became aware of the unique challenges found in flying out of Adak. The runways are situated on a patch of flat land that is surrounded by hills which direct the heavy winds in funny ways. As you fly the precision approach there is one stretch where the wind is funneled across your flight path with such velocity that you have to adjust your heading substantially prior to reaching that spot and then take out the correction very quickly once you pass through the blast of high winds. The winds are swirled around so much over the runway that it is not uncommon to have a twenty knot direct cross wind from the left at the approach end of the runway and then have a twenty knot direct cross wind from the right by the time you roll out to the far end of the runway. Another challenge of flying out of Adak was "White Alice." At the exact end of the main runway was located Mount Moffett which you somehow had to avoid if you failed to touch down flying in from the sea and then had to go around. If the Navy had built the airport, we would have sent some EOD types up there and blown off the top of that mountain to give the pilots a little more leeway if a bad situation developed on the runway. But the Air Force (Army Air Corps) had developed the airfield and instead of blowing the top off of that mountain, they erected a large antenna. The aircrews had dubbed that obstacle, "White Alice," and no pilot ever wanted to see "White Alice" up close.

I flew a good approach despite the challenges...but not so good that we were able to land. So we climbed to altitude and started for our divert fields. There were two located in the eastern part of the Aleutians, but both of them had worse weather than Adak. So we continued on all the way to Elmendorf AFB in Anchorage.

Now when you intend to land at Adak, you are required to have at least 23,000 pounds of fuel upon arrival to ensure you have enough fuel to make a divert field should it become necessary. We had that much upon arriving at Adak, but we burned a lot of fuel in attempting three approaches. So as we transited towards Anchorage we did some serious fuel use calculations. The best we could figure it, we might have enough to make one approach and get on the deck before the engines flamed out due to fuel starvation. It didn't make us feel any better when the Anchorage weather was reported to be below approach and landing minimums.

I sat there in the right seat and asked myself a question that I would ponder multiple more times in my aviation career. How can a plane that carries 60,000 pounds of fuel ever run out of gas?

The closer we got to Elmendorf the more critical our fuel consumption grew. I had just finished another estimate using the "whiz wheel" all pilots carried, when I happened to look down through the solid under-cast below us. Through a hole in the clouds I saw the lights of what obviously was a runway. The navigator confirmed that we were over King Salmon, Alaska, a coastal fishing village with a big, beautifully long runway there to support a small jet outpost of the NORAD system. That was all I needed to hear. Even before we requested permission from Air Traffic Control or before I asked Wiley to come to the cockpit, I pulled the power levers back to idle, lowered the landing gear and a couple notches of flaps and pushed the nose over into a spiraling emergency descent. I wanted to keep that runway in sight, so from 27,000 feet in the air, I kept the nose low enough to watch the runway lights get bigger and bigger as we penetrated the weather from that high altitude. When Wiley was able to crawl forward to the cockpit, he was supportive of my instant decision. We switched to VFR rules and contacted the tower at King Salmon for landing instructions.

The tower was surprised to hear from us and could not get a visual on our plane. I told him to look straight up, and eventually he spied us. We got immediate clearance to land. Keeping the field in sight, we swung out over the small bay there and made a good Navy short approach to a firm Navy touchdown. However, when the nose gear touched down all of us in the cockpit heard a loud "pop."

As we rolled out on the runway we were directed to switch to ground control. I called ground control and discovered I was speaking to the same controller as there was only one man staffing the tower at night. He asked if I had stopped to get a load of salmon, since it was the busy season there because the salmon were running.

The thought of picking up a small box of fresh salmon to take with us to Adak had appeal so I mentioned that we might be interested in loading salmon. His comeback question surprised me. He asked, "How many *tons* do you want?"

I felt like we had landed in the old west. It was about 8 PM but still quite light out and the airport was really hopping. As we got directions on how to taxi to the small Air Force side of this civilian airport, bush planes were crossing in front of our nose and under out wings and tail. There really was no true "ground control." It was every pilot watching out for his own plane.

After we parked, all four pilots, both flight engineers, and maintainers who were onboard to support the aircraft during the detachment closely inspected the nose gear. Nothing unusual was found and we figured the "pop" we had heard was when a sleeve of ice that had built up around the strut as I penetrated with the gear down came loose when weight on the wheel compressed the strut.

The next morning we all went to breakfast at the Air Force galley. It was a breakfast I will always remember. It was my intention to diet while in the Aleutians and drop ten pounds to make it easier to meet the weight standards during my next physical exam. Since this breakfast was my last real meal for six weeks, I made it a big one. I had cold and hot cereal, pancakes, bacon, waffles, bear claws, four glasses of orange juice, corned beef hash with fried eggs on top, and a western omelet just to finish it off.

The crew pilots did a thorough preflight while I waddled over to the portable trailer that was used as the flight operations office. I filed the flight plan and as I was leaving I noticed something I had never seen at a military air base. Sitting on the counter was a display of Mutual of Omaha Flight Insurance applications. I grabbed a handful as a joke to give to the crew during the planeside brief. Later, they didn't think it was too funny.

All gassed and ready to go, we had a nice departure from King Salmon and a quick flight back to Adak. The weather at Adak was temporarily good, but it sat in the middle of a large circle of clouds that was shrinking by the minute. In another twenty minutes the field would be covered in fog and clouds.

We got clearance for a straight in approach from a high altitude in order to beat the weather noose tightening around the runways. I was in the left seat and Wiley was in the right. I have always admired his intelligence and lack of ego in letting me fly the plane to our destination. If this had been an S-2 he could have flown circles around me, but in a P-3 on this particular day I was the better pilot. Recognizing this and remembering the events of yesterday, Wiley put me in the left seat to make the landing. That decision evidenced to me that he would rather do the professional thing for his crew than insist on his ego being fed. LCDR Wiley impressed me more as a pilot and an officer every time I flew with him.

I called for the gear down, and all I heard from Wiley and the flight engineer was, "Uh-oh" instead of the expected, "Gear down."

"Unsafe gear indication on the nose," were Wiley's first words.

Sure enough, a barber pole sat in the nose gear indicator. It was then that I realized a typical oral exam problem was not as realistic as we thought it was. Whenever you have a gear problem the standard answer is, "Delayed emergency. Pull out the NATOPS Manual and read the steps to me." We never had to memorize the emergency procedures for a gear malfunction. We just had to remember to pull out the NATOPS and look up what to do. However on this particular afternoon, I needed to get through the emergency trouble shooting steps in a hurry to beat the incoming weather. I made a mental note to modify my flight instruction technique to simulate these conditions when conducting drills in the future.

The first step was to cycle the gear to see if it would snap into place on a second attempt. When we raised the gear, the cockpit personnel heard a crunching sound, so we lowered the gear handle and decided not to try that again. Next I pitched the nose up and down in an attempt to lock the nose into place. That was ineffective so we accelerated in an attempt to have the wind blow it back to a locked position. When that did not work, the next step was to fly by the tower and have them examine the gear to see if maybe it was down and the indicator was the problem.

I rushed these steps as I watched the fog get closer and closer to the runways. The tower had said the nose gear appeared to be down all the way, so I moved to the east to establish a normal approach to the runway. While doing this, we had a discussion about what might happen should the nose gear collapse on landing. We were carrying a lot of fuel, twenty-three souls onboard, and a bomb bay full of crew luggage for the six-week stay we expected. I was convinced that the inboard props would come into contact with the runway if the nose gear collapsed. By this time other squadron aircrew men had arrived at the tower and were available to join in the discussion. One officer who was assigned to the TSC said he had been on a P-3 that landed without a nose gear working. When he told us that the inboard prop tips did not strike the asphalt I thought that was not logical. I asked him how much the aircraft weighed when that had happened and he said he did not remember. That seemed odd to us, because a pilot would remember a fact like that. So we ignored his input and decided to come up with our own procedures. As it turns out, we later discovered that our suspicions were right as that officer was an NFO who had ridden in the back for the event.

We decided that the flight engineer would fuel chop engines two and three when I directed on very short final. We wanted to get the energy off those blades before they might strike the runway. Of course, this meant that if I screwed up the landing and we had to go around, it would be on two engines at maximum landing weight. Getting by Mount Moffett and White Alice would probably be impossible, so I had better not screw it up on short final.

If the gear did collapse, then we would feather the outboard engines. We specifically did not want to feather the inboard engines because the blades being perpendicular to the forward motion of the aircraft could snap off the tips when they hit and fly back into the fuel tanks right behind them.

Now there is not a lot to do on little Adak for the military, civilians and their families. So when a P-3 calls in with a gear problem it means there could be a nice show on the runway...if you liked to watch crash and burns. Consequently, there was a big crowd gathered with their cameras on both sides of the runway when I approached.

After the fact, I was able to get a couple of snapshots of my landing and I was so relieved on what the pictures showed. As an instructor pilot I had spent hundreds of landings demanding that the student needed to land 1,000 to 1,500 feet down the runway in a nose high attitude, on the centerline. *That* is the way you land a P-3 properly. I was more relieved than pleased when I saw that in the pictures I had done exactly that.

I would rather be lucky than good.

In the cockpit I made another mental note. We had moved the TACCO and navigator to rear seats because their stations were right in the arc of the propellers. If pieces of the props did come off we didn't want them fragging the NFOs. I had all aircrew onboard don their helmets. Tube rats did this for landing, but we never did in the cockpit. My mental note was just how different the sensation was when landing this beast without hearing your normal aural cues due to the ear protection in the helmet. I decided I would have pilots practice a few landings while wearing helmets when I got back to the squadron.

We fuel chopped the inboard engines on short final and set down on the main mounts. I followed the book procedure and slowly lowered the nose to the deck with constant pressure to keep it on the deck and not let it bounce. The purpose of this was to keep pressure on the over-center locks that could possibly initially engage and keep the gear upright, but if weight was removed from the gear the locks would pop open and the gear come down.

As the nose gear reached the deck there was a slight hesitation in the nose's fall. The flight engineer let out a yell loud enough to be heard despite the helmets being worn.

"Yeahhhhhhh!" he said. But then the nose started its fall again to the deck and his cry changed to, "Noooooo!"

A couple of seconds later it got very loud in the cockpit as the nose started scraping along the runway.

I shouted, "FEATHER NUMBER ONE AND NUMBER FOUR!"

It was then that I noticed the flight engineer had rigged his seat for crashing. It was lowered all the way and slid as far back as possible. In this position his arms were not long enough to reach the feather handles directly in front of him. Later he told me that he saw that mountain rapidly approaching in the wind screen and he had a choice to make; he could release his locked harness and try to reach the feather handles, or just let the pilots grab the handles and do it themselves. He chose the latter, and for the only time in my career I had the chance to pull out the long feather handle. Wiley saw me do that to number one engine so he pulled out the handle for number four.

I had all my weight pressing on the rudder toe brakes and not caring at all if I happened to blow a tire doing it (I didn't.) I just wanted these 50 tons of aluminum to stop so I could run away. With the nose dragging on the deck, it did not take long for the ship to come to a stop. Just as we stopped moving, the cockpit appeared to fill with white smoke. I opted not to complete any checklists and slid my seat back all the way, unfastened my harness and stood up. Wiley and the flight engineer did the same. The flight engineer pushed through the cockpit seats and started running aft. I had the same training as he did and we both knew that any fireball would be racing to the front of the airplane due to our abrupt stop, so the best way of escape was by running aft and getting through it quickly.

I made eye contact with Wiley who motioned for me to go first. And I did! I never pretended to be a hero...I hadn't signed for this airplane, I was just the "guest pilot" on the crew, so I had but one thought—"GET OUT OF THIS PLANE BEFORE THE SMOKE TURNS TO FLAMES AROUND ME!"

I expected to find the fuselage empty when I reached the over-the-wing hatches. To my surprise there were three sailors lined up at each exit. When I saw why it was taking so long for them to evacuate I was astounded! These were maintainers and they were bred never to cause damage to an airframe. So as one reached the exit, he took the hatch and handed it to the man behind him, who in turn carefully handed it the next sailor. I did not have that much reverence towards this hunk of junk that was trying to kill me, so I grabbed the hatch and threw it down the length of the tube and yelled, "JUST GET OUT OF HERE *NOW*!"

Less than five seconds later, it was my turn to climb out onto the wing. I slid off the flap and started sprinting to the rear. In fact, there is a series of pictures taken of my escaping the plane. The first one shows me hitting the deck in a perfect sprinter's crouched form. The next picture shows me catching up with the rest of the crew who had evacuated before me. The last picture shows me thirty feet in front of the gaggle of crew members.

I like to say there is proof that I won the "Adak Sprint Championships" that year.

The cause of the mishap was a hairline fracture of the nose gear connecting rod that led to it parting and not being able to set the over-center locks. The only way it could've been detected was through an x-ray.

There was no smoke in the cockpit. The concrete dust kicked up by the plane's nose had filled the small space when we stopped.

Normal procedure is to determine the eating and sleeping habits of pilots involved in a mishap, however the accident investigators did not believe me when I listed all I had eaten in the last 24 hours. They thought I was confused when I listed my breakfast, thinking I had given them a whole week's list of food.

After a ten minute debrief and quick check over by the flight surgeon of all passengers, we were put on the flight schedule and flew an early morning flight the next day.

Later that afternoon, ground personnel inflated a big bladder under the nose to raise the plane up. Then the nose gear was lowered and pinned in place and the plane towed to a hangar to begin repairs. In fact, the inboard props had struck the ground on roll out and about five inches were sheared off on each blade. The pieces from number two engine damaged number one and the pieces from the number three engine penetrated the fuselage and ripped into the luggage stored in the bomb bay. As poetic justice would have it, the only two bags with damaged contents were Wiley's and mine.

About the biggest worry of the day was "Who was going to tell the wing?" This was a few weeks after Pago Pago and no one wanted to be the goat to tell the wing that another VP-50 aircraft had crashed.

Chapter Five

First Recruiting Tour

By 1980 I had been in uniform for eleven years, but during those years I was with my girl friend/fiancé/wife for much less than half of that time. Now we had a son and planned on more children and I was tired of being gone. Since commissioning, I had yet to have shore duty, so when my detailer started outlining how to get me back into an aviator's normal career path I was less than thrilled by his plans. He wanted to send me to Naval Post-graduate School at Monterey for two years to study astrophysics (he must have been desperate to fill that slot to suggest it to a history major) then send me back to sea in some sort of education "pay back" tour for two years. Then I would be the right seniority to roll back to another squadron tour for a department head assignment, and then with a little luck I could screen for an immediate follow-on XO/CO tour. In essence, he had my career planned so that by the time I was a couple of years from retirement I would have had only two years of shore duty.

Now maybe Boatswain Chief Williams loved being at sea that much, but I was very tired of sea duty and the family separation that was organic to it. Plus, I knew myself well enough to know that if I went to post-graduate school I would take the time from my family to study forty-hours a week outside of the classroom to strive for an "A" and not settle for any "B" grades. Oh boy...some good shore duty that would be!

So I decided to leave the Navy and pursue a dream of owning and operating a Fixed Base Operation (FBO) on a small airport near my hometown of Sacramento that included providing general aviation maintenance and flight instruction services. I still had over another year of obligated service I owed for getting my wings. So I asked my detailer if there were any flying billets in Northern California that did not incur any additional obligated service.

At first he told me the only job close to matching my desires was a tour as a RAG instructor right there at Moffett Field. I would have enjoyed that and it would of kept me "in community" with my airframe. However, at that time it required a two year commitment to accept those orders and I only had fourteen months left before I could resign.

He was in Washington DC and I was calling him from California. In response to his comments I said something that, in hindsight, truly did change my career and life.

I asked him, "Don't you have *anything* in Northern California? Not even something like ...*recruiting*?"

I heard the rustle of papers on his desk and the tenor of his voice grow excited as he answered, "Navy Recruiting District (NRD) San Francisco has billets for three pilots and they only have two."

We agreed that I should investigate what the position required of a pilot and call him back with my decision about the vacancy in four days. I had been under the misconception that the primary job for pilots in recruiting duty was to fly the T-34B trainer to introduce aviation candidates to Navy Air. A couple of phone calls to actual recruiting offices quickly enlightened me on a pilot's real duty. Aviators were in recruiting districts to work as full-time salesmen and only part-time pilots.

I called my detailer back and intended to discuss other possible options. The conversation did not go as planned.

"Hello, Denzel, this is Bob Bartron and as we agreed I am calling you back—" He cut me off before I could finish.

"Oh, thanks for calling me back and your timing is perfect. Your orders to NRD San Francisco are being cut and you should receive them tonight," he informed me with glee in his voice. It was obvious to me that the pilot billet in NRD San Francisco had been vacant and a thorn in his side for a long time.

"But I thought we were just *talking* about maybe getting orders to recruiting?"

"Well, they always want volunteers, and you did volunteer."

"Volunteer? How did I volunteer?"

"The word crossed your lips first."

Gee...maybe I should of let "White House Fellow" slip through my lips if that was all it took to get a new set of orders.

Well, that is how I became a professional salesman.

*****

The Navy, in typical Navy fashion, established a very effective school in Orlando, FL to teach knuckle-dragging boatswain mates and lost pilots how to become slick, effective used car salesmen. It was one of the tougher Navy schools I attended. The classes required a lot of memorization and labs where you practiced one-on-one interviews with potential applicants. After retiring from the Navy I attended other civilian sales training programs and none of them held a candle to the intense and thorough Navy sales training.

After the month long recruiting school, the pilots were sent to Pensacola for a two-week refresher training in flying the primary trainer. Here it was drilled into us that as independent pilots out in the field we would not have the support of a squadron to assist us in insuring proper aircraft maintenance and in keeping our "hot dogging" tendencies in check.

Enroute to NRD San Francisco I called the Officer Programs Officer (OPO) prior to my arrival to let him know my moving plans. He interrupted a meeting of all his officer recruiters to take my call. I will always remember my introduction to how recruiting managers thought. I learned it by the very first question he asked me.

"Bob, do you happen to know a Black female dentist with a Hispanic surname?"

I guess such an applicant would be a quadruple counter in the District competition system.

This transfer once again removed me from the Navy I had known to another, "new" Navy. Recruiting duty was not the "real Navy." I discovered that the informality of the command was even more pronounced than in the VP Navy. The CO called his top enlisted recruiters by their first names and even expected me to address him by his first name. I could never bring myself to address a Navy captain as "Jim." I got around his request by avoiding using his name when in his presence or substituting the informal "Skipper" or "Cap'n."

I discovered that in recruiting duty there were two phrases that explained how things operated. The first one was, "Volume covers a multitude of sins." If a recruiter was a top producer and consistently wrote a lot of contracts each month, he could lip off to officers or the Commodore and it would be tolerated...because he produced contracts!

The second truism was "Hero to zero every month." You could write 150% of your goal this month, but come the first of next month you were back to zero and you had to earn your reputation all over again. In the real Navy a sailor was assigned to a three-year tour in a command, but in recruiting you were given thirty-six one-month tours.

This became crystal clear to me about five months into my first recruiting tour.

*****

I was initially assigned to the OPO office in San Jose, CA. One of my biggest markets was the student body at San Jose State University. The great challenge was getting the state college to cooperate with military recruiters. I discovered over the next decade that university administrators, on the whole, had been anti-Vietnam War protesters before they began their rise through academia. Many were determined to "save their students from immoral jobs such as serving in the military"...however if a graduate could get a job with Lockheed or Boeing, that would be wonderful! It was okay to build weapons, but not to actually sign-up to protect their freedom to choose what college to attend.

Naval officers hate to fail...in fact, we invariably find a way to overcome obstacles and achieve success. To present the option of a wonderful, secure, career-oriented job upon graduation to San Jose State students we needed a way to contact them. We requested through proper channels a list of juniors and seniors in the engineering and science departments who had at least a 3.0 GPA and were U.S. citizens. Now the school would sort their digital database and provide similar lists to civilian employers, but they would flat out refuse our requests.

We got around this by old fashioned "dumpster diving." One of the candidates we did sign up was the son of a professor at San Jose State. The other officer in my office took the father to lunch and there presented our problem concerning the ability to contact potential candidates. The father said he had access to the database and could sort it for us, but if the administration discovered he had passed that along he would be in hot water. However, if he happened accidentally to print out a copy of such a list and throw it away, then there was no way it could be connected to him.

Based upon an "anonymous tip" my coworker just happened to be behind an academic building when trash was deposited in the dumpster. As soon as the janitor returned inside the building, the lieutenant, dressed in whites, climbed into the dumpster and sorted through the trash until he found a large computer print-out.

We used that list to prospect the junior and senior classes for the next two years.

*****

After a few months, I had an intra-district transfer request approved by the NRD commanding officer. I was sent to recruit out of our OPO office in Sacramento, my hometown. It was there that after hours I was establishing my new FBO business with my father. Soon after my Sacramento arrival the NRD had a change of command and Commander Rodgers became my new CO.

A couple of weeks later, the CO made a trip from the District HQ in Oakland out to our Sacramento office. I had just received the results of the promotion board and had learned I had been selected for lieutenant commander. So when Commander Rodgers visited and he asked me a question, I was full of myself and figured a lieutenant-commander was nearly on a par with a commander and so I gave him a brutally honest answer. Big mistake, again. How was I to know that the promotion board was about to make him a captain a year early?

He asked me, "What do you think of recruiting duty?"

I answered truthfully, "Skipper, it is different than most of my experience. In the big picture it is not the same as operational requirements. I mean, I've had jobs where my performance was monitored by the Joint Chiefs of Staff because the sensitive nature of the flight could actually impact national security. But here in recruiting, if I leave at 1800 on a Friday and a kit isn't quite done until Monday, what really happens? Some college kid gets commissioned maybe two days later?"

That was not the answer this captain-select wanted to hear. He left my offices with his jaw screwed tightly shut.

It was that month that I "rolled a donut," meaning I submitted zero new candidate applications. As was my normal experience, my timing was all wrong. The new CO was looking to "hang a crow" on the fence in the OPO department and I gave him the perfect crow. Captain Rodgers was a surface warrior who was un-impressed by our previous one-on-one discussion, so I should not have been surprised when the new Officer Programs department head gave me a letter of probation from the CO. I was to submit six new applications within the next month or he would start the process to have me relieved for cause.

That was a shock and unique to recruiting duty. Here I had done well at the Academy, graduating in the top ten percent of my class, had a great record as I earned my warfare designation as a SWO, finished first in flight school and was ranked the number two of thirty-five lieutenants in my squadron. Yet all of that counted for nothing because when you get relieved for cause, your career is over. Eleven years of excellence wiped out by one bad month as a used car salesman.

Yeah, recruiting was not the real navy.

The normal production expected from an officer recruiter was less than two new applications per month. Yet the CO said I had to produce three times that amount in the next four weeks.

I reverted to my "1.94 GPA" mode and kissed the wife good-bye as I practically moved into my office for the next month. Some good shore duty this was!

I had my pipeline of applicants full so it wasn't like I was starting from zero. Unlike enlisted contracts that can be completed in a matter of hours, it took weeks to assemble a complete officer application. I had identified applicants and had them in process, but due to some unusual factors, none of the applications had been ready to submit during the previous month.

The fact of the matter is that I really did not do any special prospecting to meet the extremely high target the captain had set for me. However, I was able to have six applications to the Recruiting Command (CRUITCOM) Officer Selection board before my deadline.

And to finish this story with a good ending, by the end of that recruiting year I was named as the "Recruiter of the Year" for the District and the entire western United States.

I was able to do this because it had not taken me long to figure out that you can never sell anyone on becoming a naval officer. It took about six months for the application process to be completed and then the first weeks of AOCS or OCS before you got credit for an accession. Your applicant could quit the process at any time during this long period and you would not get credit for a valid accession. I had learned early that to be a successful officer programs recruiter, you had to sell the Navy your applicant. A successful recruiter prospected enough to where he could identify the kind of applicant the selection board would pick. Then he would package that applicant in the best wrapping paper he could find to get a valid job offer from CRUITCOM. This technique meant that at the end of my three years "carrying a bag" as a recruiter on production I had put over 115 officers on active duty, which was double the national average. What was even more impressive was that I had managed to get 117 job offers which meant only two of my applicants ever failed to follow through on the decision to join. The national average was closer to 30% drops per recruiter.

Yeah...I was that good...

*****

I was so good I got the reputation as the "pervert recruiter"...and I earned it!

I once interviewed a pastor of a local church who was interested in becoming a chaplain. Our interview highlighted to me that he had two strikes against him. First, he only had a 2.1 GPA from a small seminary. How do you complete graduate school with less than a "B" average?

His second strike was much more substantial. He had been convicted of exposing himself to children!

I asked if maybe it was a mistake, like the time our high school track team bus got pulled over by the police of a small nearby town because sprinters were "mooning" the populace as we left the city. Just a high school prank...right?

No, this applicant, we'll call him Maurice, said he'd had a problem showing himself to kids in a park. He underwent counseling and the judge let him off of probation if he would join the Marines. Maurice served as a sniper with the Corps in Vietnam. After coming home he had a deeply religious experience and used the GI Bill to get his bachelor's and masters of divinity degrees. After a number of years in the ministry, now he felt God was calling him to serve the spiritual needs of Marines.

To be hired as a chaplain in the Navy you have to be approved by three different chains-of-command. First, the minister's home denomination must endorse his application to fill one of that denomination's allotted slots in the Navy. Secondly, the applicant must pass scrutiny by the CRUITCOM process to determine if he is officer material. The third approval must come from the Navy Chief of Chaplains. The Chief of Chaplains personally gets to choose who joins the Chaplain Corps.

Maurice got the endorsement from his denomination and I managed his application through CRUITCOM, but I thought it would truly be a miracle if he could get approval from the Chaplain Corps. They can be very selective and Maurice's low seminary GPA and conviction probably meant his request was doomed.

I set up his interview with three Navy chaplains over in the San Francisco Bay area. When he came back I asked him how he thought it went.

"Oh, at the beginning it seemed pretty cold," Maurice shared with me, "but then they seemed to get excited about having me join the Chaplin Corps."

"Why do you think that was?" I asked.

"Well, when I mentioned that I felt God was leading me back to work with Marines, they all seemed to lean forward and sit up straighter."

I figure these chaplains must have thought, "WOW! We actually have a *volunteer* to go with the Marines!"

Whatever their thinking was, Maurice passed the chaplain interview and was selected for Officer Indoctrination School in Newport RI. When he completed this "knife and fork" school of how to be a staff officer, he received orders to report immediately for a one-year unattached tour on Okinawa with the Marines.

For the next six months I got calls from his wife who had to stay in Sacramento, where the only Navy she knew was me, her husband's recruiter. I tried to help her get an ID card and learn about family medical care and commissary privileges. She felt I "owed" her because I had yanked her husband from the family and sent him overseas.

Her attitude only changed when one day as she told me how it was entirely my fault that she had been "abandoned," I responded with the truth, "No, I didn't send your husband off to Okinawa. God did."

And I truly believe it took an "act of God" to get Maurice into the chaplain corps.

My other experience of recruiting a pervert sounds like a twisted tale, but in the end it proved to be beneficial and I am proud I did it.

I asked "Dan" what his major was at Chico State College. He answered forestry. His GPA was only 2.7 and he was 30 years old with only slightly above average officer test scores. Truly a plain vanilla applicant; nothing special and a relatively poor chance of being selected to attend OCS. Despite that, I took his case to act as his voice before the Selection Board. There was a saying in recruiting, "a contract is a contract is a contract." I was only mildly surprised when my "packaging" of Dan was sufficient to get him an offer to go to OCS.

I was about to leave my Sacramento office to visit an enlisted recruiting station in Chico to ask for referrals from those they saw with college degrees when I received the enlistment papers for Dan in the mail. Only two times did I ever visit an applicant's home. I always figured if they were really serious about joining the Navy they could make the time and effort to come to my office. I wasn't about to make house calls to help them get a wonderful job. They had to prove they were worthy before I worked with them. This was fundamentally a different approach than most other recruiters who thought it was necessary to spoon feed applicants so they wouldn't back out. However, since I happened to be traveling right by Dan's home I decided to alter my way of doing business and bring along his enlistment papers to save him a trip down to Sacramento.

Since I so very rarely visited the home of an applicant, the memory of Dan's home is easy to pull up. It was a ranch house in the middle of a barren acre, far removed from the closest neighbor. I met his wife and stepson and then administered the enlistment oath and gave him his orders to report to Newport, RI for OCS.

Months past and I never gave another thought about Dan...until my phone rang. On the other end of the line was a JAG officer at the Naval Station, San Diego legal office who wanted to talk to Dan's recruiter. I identified myself and asked why he was calling. What he shared made me sick, and then glad.

It seems that Dan had been sexually abusing his pre-teen stepson for years. The sick S.O.B. even took pictures of him violating this boy. Dan had been at OCS for four months and when he returned home he tried to start up his perverted relationship with the boy again. However, the months that the boy had been free from the oppression of his stepfather had given the youth a chance to gain a better perspective. This time he did not buy the threat that the police would take the victim to jail if he told anyone. The boy told his mother. She notified the police and they arrested Dan and found his photo albums.

The JAG officer wanted to advise me that the Navy was letting the civilian authorities have first crack at convicting Dan, but he wanted me to track the case and let him know the outcome. If the civilians did not put Dan in prison for a very long time, then the Navy would make sure he was punished.

Dan was locked away by the civilians and after I reflected on the horror of having recruited such a pervert, I gradually came to realize that my supporting his selection for acceptance to OCS was a good thing. If Dan hadn't been removed from the home to give his stepson the opportunity to gain a proper perspective there is no telling how long he would have abused the boy.

*****

Not all the weirdo visitors got the greeting they hoped to receive. One day, while we were having some remodeling being done to our offices, a man about 35 walked in. He wanted to talk to an officer programs recruiter. I was standing by the reception desk and offered my services to answer his questions. He was nicely dressed in a cheap suit and carried a brief case. Accompanying him appeared to be his nine-year old son. I escorted this potential applicant down the hall to the testing room I was using as my office during the remodel. Our recruiter with front desk duty looked after his son.

He told me his name, Kent, and then I proceeded with the blueprinting segment of a normal sales interview.

"Where did you go to college?" I asked.

"Chico State."

"What was your major?" I inquired.

"Auto shop," he replied. I gave him a quizzical look and he continued, "Well, they called it Automotive Engineering, but it was really just auto shop."

"What program are you interested in applying for?"

"I thought maybe I should go on ships," came his vague reply. At this point I was having uneasy feelings about this gentleman.

"How old are you, Kent?" I said as I continued the basic blueprinting of this contact.

"Thirty-six."

I put down the pen I was using to take notes and looked in his eyes, "I'm sorry but the law has set an age limit of thirty-five. You're not eligible for any of our programs."

Upon hearing this he lifted his brief case and clutched it to his chest. His eyes grew wild and intense. After a brief pause he stated in a low voice, "Oh, I think they will make an exception for a Nobel Prize winner."

"Do you know one?" I said trying not to sound too sarcastic.

"I am."

"Really? What field did you win it in?"

"Physics and Peace."

Keeping my cool I played along for another question, "Really? What year did you win these prizes?"

"Well, I haven't got them just yet but I will later this year," Kent said as his knuckles turned white and he tightened his grip on his brief case.

I had just read in the newspaper about nominations for the Nobel Prize being announced, so I asked him, "Really? Who nominated you?"

That question threw him off his story. Obviously he had never heard that you must be nominated to receive a Nobel Prize. After a short pause he did something that crossed the line of my patience.

"You don't believe me, do you?" he demanded.

"Let me ask you a very basic question," I said as my jaw tightened, "Just why would a double Nobel laureate want to become an ensign in the Navy? Surely there would be a much better way for a man of such intelligence and achievements to serve mankind than floating on a small ship in the middle of the ocean."

Now he almost yelled his next challenge, "I can prove I am telling the truth! I will leave my briefcase here, and if you can figure out how to open it you will find half the formula in it!"

I popped to my feet and opened the office door as I said in my best no-nonsense command voice, "If you leave that briefcase here I will put it in a bucket of water and call the bomb squad and get a warrant for your immediate arrest. Now clear out of these offices right now."

Kent got up and huffed down the hall and out to the parking lot. I watched through the office front windows as he loaded his child in the car where a woman was waiting in the front passenger seat and then he drove away. As he disappeared from the parking lot, Chief Sheppard who was staffing the reception desk that afternoon told me that as I had interviewed Kent his son had continually marched up and down the hall like a stiff, tin solider and the woman in the car seemed continually to talk to herself.

I was about to call the police and report the odd event when the phone rang. It was the security police office at the main gate of Mather Air Force Base. They wanted to give us a heads up that we might be visited by a nut who had tried to get on base while clutching a brief case to his chest. When they had turned him away, he mentioned he would take his discovery to the Navy. The first listing for any Navy office in the Sacramento phone book was our office.

To be safe, I notified the other recruiting offices in the city. Nothing more was heard from Kent, so the day went on. Just another odd visit to a recruiting office.

*****

Not only was I the pervert recruiter, I also could be labeled the "smarmy" or "slimy" recruiter.

The California State University, Sacramento was the largest officer market in the area, yet it would not assist the military in offering career opportunities to its graduates. We tried getting a list of potential applicants from the Dean of Engineering and from the Mathematics department and Career Services, but all said it would be against campus policy to provide that information. I had trouble with that policy because we were talking about college students who should be mature enough by their junior year to be able to say "no" to a military recruiter if they were not interested. It was not like we wanted to talk to high school freshmen.

As I stated before...naval officers hate to fail.

On campus visits I made sure I spent time engaging the middle-aged administrative assistant to the head of Career Services. I chatted with her as I waited to talk to her boss and I stopped by and talked to her as I left my meeting with the department chair. I made a point to thank her for helping me get in to see her boss, even though I was flatly denied a contact list of students.

Two weeks later I gave a ten dollar bill to a stash ensign and sent him to a cut-rate florist located in the same office park as our office. They sold a dozen ("day old") roses for $10. I had him pick up a dozen roses and drive the ten minutes to the Sacramento State campus to deliver them to the secretary in the career services department. With the flowers I had him take my business card with a hand written note that said, "Again, thank you for your assistance the other day. Happy birthday!"

Before the ensign was able to return to our office the phone rang. It was the administrative assistant who thanked me for the flowers but informed me that it was not her birthday. I replied that I must have noted her birthday incorrectly, but I was glad she enjoyed the unexpected bright spot in her hard working day.

Two weeks later, I gave another stash ensign another ten dollars to get another bunch of flowers and had him deliver them to the secretary. This time the note read, "Now I know I got the date right this time! Happy Birthday!" I directed the ensign to hang around her office and place some recruiting brochures in the career services library after delivering the flowers.

Once again she called my office and we spoke. She thanked me for the flowers and kidded that I had better stop giving her gifts or her husband would start to think bad thoughts. I laughed and made nice. Then she asked a question I had hoped she would verbalize.

"Bob, just what is it you want anyway?"

"Well, since you asked...I could use a list of all juniors and seniors with engineering, science or math majors with at least a 3.0 GPA and are U.S. citizens, along with their address and/or phone numbers."

"I'm not supposed to do that."

"Oh, I know. I just want to be sure all the Sac State grads have the chance to learn of career opportunities as a naval officer."

She hung up on me.

But a half hour later the ensign returned to our office with a computer print-out that had taken her maybe a dozen key strokes to build. That gold mine helped me write contracts for the next two years. Twenty dollars well invested.

Make that thirty dollars. A week later I sent her another dozen flowers with a note that just said, "Thank you!"

*****

I really enjoyed only one part of my recruiter job. That was the opportunity to become proficient in the T-34B. Three pilots in NRD San Francisco shared the use of one plane that was stationed about thirty minutes from the recruiter in San Jose and the same distance from the recruiter in Oakland. It was about seventy-five minutes from my office in Sacramento. Yet I usually logged twice the hours of the other two pilots. The other two would schedule their flying for afternoons and go to their offices in the morning. Because I never went to the office before I went to the airplane, I never got caught by an "urgent" matter that would entice me to postpone the flying I had scheduled on my calendar.

The supposed purpose of having 52 T-34s assigned to CRUITCOM and spread around the nation was to test the "aeronautic adaptability" of applicants for naval aviation officer programs. In actual fact, the airplanes were there to get pilots to accept recruiting orders. All pilots had to make certain "gates" of serving in flying billets or they would lose their flight pay after a dozen years or so. A three year tour in recruiting if they were not flight orders would wreak havoc with a pilot's career progression. And CRUITCOM wanted relatively junior pilots as recruiters because invariably their outgoing, confident personality traits made them some of the most productive in the field.

I developed a system to block two or three days on my calendar to be out of the office and out flying. For the first two years I would schedule six flights per day. I would spend a half hour briefing the applicant and strapping him into the back seat and fly a demo ride for one hour. It wasn't until my last year in recruiting that my attention was drawn to regulation that set the limit of three flights per day for a single-piloted aircraft. Being that I came from the P-3 community, flying six or more hours per day was not a burden. However, it was tiring and as the day wore on my patter to the guy in the back seat changed substantially.

On the first flight of the day I would talk the applicant through each maneuver. For instance, "This is a wing-over. Note the altitude, heading and airspeed as I begin the maneuver. At the end I will be at the same altitude plus or minus ten feet, the same airspeed plus or minus two knots and heading exactly 180 degrees in the opposite direction plus or minus two degrees. Naval aviation is *precision* aviation. Everything must be done with precision."

Then as I started the maneuver, I would continue the stream of words as we flew, "Notice that as I raise the aircraft, the highest nose attitude is obtained as we pass through the 45 degree portion of the turn and the angle of bank is changing at a constant roll rate. As we reach the 90 degree point of the turn my airspeed is now between 75 and 80 knots, the fuselage is parallel to the earth and the wings are exactly perpendicular to the horizon. As the nose drops, the roll direction is reversed but remains at the same rate and when we are at the 135 degree point of the turn we experience the lowest nose attitude. As I roll out of the wing-over please look at the airspeed, altitude and heading. You'll notice that they are exactly what I said we would achieve. Naval aviation is *precision* aviation."

I would give the same detailed patter for the loop, barrel roll, aileron roll, half-Cuban eight, split-S, Immelmann, and then a stall to a three-turn spin. On the first flight of the day that is. By the last flight I was so tired my patter was reduced to, "Here's a wing-over," and "Here's a loop," and "Here's a spin," etc.

Coming out of flight school the only maneuvers I knew were the loop, spin, barrel roll and wing over. The other maneuvers I had to teach myself. I would go up solo and get plenty of altitude and then refer to notes I had transcribed onto my kneepad from reading about the maneuvers in a book I had purchased at a small airport gift shop. With enough practice and experimentation I was able to get pretty good at performing these. The toughest thing was mastering how to make left and right turns while in inverted flight. And, of course, I made errors during this process, like the first time I entered an inverted spin while trying to climb when upside down. The nice thing about the "Teeny Weenie" was how forgiving Beechcraft had designed it. Whenever I got into something unintended, I just had to let go of the controls and the plane would eventually come around to a position I recognized and could recover from.

The typical applicant flight I gave started with the front canopy open and a climb out from Sacramento Executive Airport to the south. I would let the applicant take the stick and rudders and fly as we headed to the area off airways where I would introduce aerobatics. This would keep the air in his face and usually have the applicant so focused on what he was doing that despite being nervous, he was not overcome with airsickness. The next part of my demo ride was to introduce the wantabe pilot to the world of TACAIR (fighter jet stuff) with all of its "yanking and banking." The last maneuver I performed was a spin to get us down to lower altitudes. Then I would go to maybe fifty feet off the ground as I flew with the canopy open and skimmed the foothills on a path from the Rancho Seco Nuclear power plant, south to Comanche Reservoir. I kept my speed up so in the event of an emergency I could trade airspeed for altitude and get over the hills surrounding us and reach flat land in the valley. I would tell the applicant that he was getting an introduction to the attack community which flies missions at this low level. We would arrive at Comanche Reservoir and I would pop back up to 200 feet over the water and tell him this was the typical view in the P-3 community, low and surrounded by water and all alone. I would zoom over the dam and the ground would fall away from us and put me at the right pattern altitude for one of the many uncontrolled airfields located at sea level in the Sacramento Valley.

Previously, when we were doing maneuvers at high altitude I had pointed out Franklin Airfield below us and had the applicant notice just how small the runway numbers appeared from that height. Now as we approached this airfield I told them that we would do five touch-and-goes and that I would land *on* the numbers, *on* centerline every time; not a foot long and not a foot short, but on those small numbers *every* time because *naval aviation is precision aviation* and a Naval aviator is able to set his aircraft down precisely on any fifty-foot patch of steel deck or asphalt he chooses.

And in over two hundred flights or 1,000 landings I never missed...except for once. Well, that is what all the applicants thought. There are two factors that made my boast possible. First, the T-34B has certain characteristics that make it very controllable in close to a runway. If you get it flying on the back side of the power curve for the last fifty yards of the approach you can motor over the end of the runway a foot off the deck and when you get to the spot you want the main mounts to touch, you just close the throttle and it drops instantaneously from the air. The second reason the applicants believed me when I would say over the ICS as we touched down, "There! Perfect once again!" is because they were sitting in the aft cockpit. Their vision of the runway and the numbers was blocked by the wing below them. They could never tell if I was lying or not.

Now, about that time I did not hit the numbers. I was flying this jerk of an applicant out of Reno for the chief who was stationed there and recruited officers. This applicant was on my bad side when he showed up at Reno Airport. This was the second time he had been scheduled for his "aeronautical adaptability" ride. He had been a no-show the previous time. Right there that told me about his motivation. Whenever I asked one of my applicants if he had ever been upside down in an airplane before, he invariably shook their head. Then when I would ask, "Do you want to?" their eyes would grow wide and heads nod enthusiastically. These guys would miss their own mother's funeral for the chance to fly in a Navy plane.

Well, this jerk came across as timid and he barfed twice during the straight and level transit to an area where we could do the high altitude portion of the demonstration. Once again, before we spun down, I had him look at what appeared from that altitude to be tiny numbers painted on the Douglas County Airport.

I was to find out soon that, in fact, they *were* pretty small.

On my first approach to a touch-and-go things were normal, but as I got to the end of the runway I noticed that the numbers had been painted only two feet from the edge of the asphalt. Normally the numbers are 75 feet from the end of the pavement. I motored over the end of the runway and took my power cut. As expected, we fell from the sky and slammed onto the ground...only I was four feet short. The main mounts hit the dirt and then ran into the five-inch high curb that was formed by the end of the asphalt.

We hit so hard that I was sure the landing gear was going to collapse. Yet that solid Beechcraft that had been built to survive years of primary student screw-ups didn't give an inch. I gingerly taxied to the ramp area and then climbed out and inspected the gear. It all looked good so I left that jerk applicant standing by the fuel pumps as I gave a rough taxi test to the gear. I made sharp and drastic turns at high speeds to see if I could get the gear to collapse. There was no maintenance at this facility, but I was determined to regain my confidence in the ability of the gear to take a landing before we departed.

That bird took the beating without complaining. I flew back to Reno and flushed the memory of my error to the back of my mind.

*****

My usual flight profile for an applicant flight was such that I felt some civilians might see a small plane with "Fly Navy" in Blue Angel Blue and gold on the wings and object to their tax dollar frightening picnickers at the Rancho Seco Park or boaters on Comanche Reservoir. To develop allies in case such a call might come in, I discussed my mission profile with the Flight Service Station (FSS) personnel located at Sacramento Executive Airport. In fact, I offered to take one of the FSS federal employees up for an hour to observe my usual flights. One guy took me up on it.

A year later a call did come in to the FSS wanting to know why a Navy plane buzzed a car driving in the foothills. When I was informed by the FSS personnel of the complaint my heart sank...similar to when a cop pulls you over for running the red light when you're a teenager. I guess the guilt was all over my face because the FSS counter person broke out in a big smile and laughed at my expression.

"Don't worry I told the guy it was an official Navy low altitude training flight. He was satisfied."

I said, "Thank you"...and meant it.

*****

I had an ensign in my recruiting office on no-cost temporary orders for a month while he waited for his flight school class to begin after completing AOCS. I always had an ensign or five working part-time in my office. In fact, I made it a point to recruit ensigns to come back and help our Sacramento team if they had to endure a pool status awaiting training.

A lot of them wanted to complain about the menial tasks I had them doing, such as stuffing flyers into envelopes for a local direct mail campaign. However, I realigned their attitudes by sharing a simple fact. Although they were now officers and gentlemen, they should not feel they were being asked to do E-3 (seaman) work...rather, they were doing O-4 (lieutenant commander) work, because if they didn't do it, then I would have to!

I made it a habit to get every stashed ensign up in the T-34B for some fun whenever possible. One time I took this ensign up with me and we had a memorable flight. Our first stop was Columbia Airstrip in the Sierra Nevada foothills. You can walk to town from the airport and the city fathers had recreated a street of Gold Rush stores and cafes. We had our diet sodas and ice cream and then returned to the airport. As we sat by the porch of the FBO offices we noticed a Cessna 152 trying to land. Obviously this was a student pilot on a solo cross country hop and had never been to Columbia Airstrip before. The runway sits in a valley surrounded by hills on all sides. Many pilots misjudge their altitude above the ground on short approach because the hills rise up from the end of the runway. Pilots have to ignore their normal altitudes on final or they will arrive over the threshold way too high to get down in the runway remaining.

After three attempts, this student pilot finally got the Cessna stopped on the runway. When the aircraft was parked, the pilot hurriedly exited and made a bee-line straight for our plane. As we were just finishing our walk around, the pilot called out and asked, "Is this a real Navy airplane?"

The ensign and I turned around and discovered that the student pilot was a very attractive woman about 25 years old. We talked a bit and soon I realized that we had killed her fiancé. It turns out that she had been engaged to the copilot on the P-3 that had crashed in Pago Pago. My squadron had killed her fiancé. Jill related how she was determined to "fly Navy" herself and planned on submitting an application for AOCS as soon as she got closer to finishing the Aviation Management program at San Jose State University. She was in Columbia completing her required solo 100-mile cross country flight for her Private Pilot's license.

I offered to sign her log book to verify she had actually reached Columbia and then I had a thought. I asked her, "Have you ever been upside down in an airplane yet?"

She was excited about the chance to go up for a demo ride and I figured, in my opinion, she was a bona fide potential applicant for officer aviation programs, so why not?

I never had a flight like this before or since. I pulled the spare flight suit we kept for applicants from the luggage compartment and she slipped it on over her clothes. Then she climbed into the back seat and I supervised her adjusting the straps on the parachute which we were required to wear. Often times I would just grab the chest straps and yank them to the right position when strapping in applicants, but I hesitated to do it with a woman. I watched as she struggled to make the straps stretch to reach a position where they could be snapped together.

Her difficulty was because she was an extremely well endowed young woman. She wiggled her shoulders and adjusted her seat in an effort to get the straps to meet. In the middle of these efforts she stopped and looked up at me with big doe eyes and smiled as she said, "Now I know why they call this a T-*34*...I don't fit in a 34."

The flight was fun, because rather than the normal smell of nervous sweat and puke floating to the front from the aft cockpit, I smelled her perfume as it rolled forward. She was unaware that I could hear her talk even when she did not depress the ICS button and I could watch her with a small mirror mounted on my windscreen. So throughout all the acrobatic maneuvers she would scream in near ecstasy. I would key the ICS and ask how she was doing, and her answer was always quiet and affirmative, being very polite not to let on just how excited she was.

Yeah, you just don't fly applicants like Jill everyday.

*****

Another story also illustrates how sturdy the T-34B landing gear was. I took another stash ensign out visiting local airports and we stopped at Grass Valley out in the foothills. It was a long dirt, but well maintained, strip. When we took off we proceeded on the westerly facing runway, down a small decline. I had my canopy open because it was a warm, sunny day. Just as we lifted off the grass and I was about to raise the landing gear I looked to my left and spied a beautiful young woman sunbathing in her backyard which was just off the runway. She was sunbathing in the nude...on her back.

I mentioned this to the ensign in the aft cockpit and then dipped by left wing so he could enjoy some eyeball liberty. We had a good laugh about California girls and then proceeded to fly out of the foothills and into the big Sacramento Valley. Since the ground was falling away as we headed westerly, I did not have to pull the nose very high to increase our altitude. Soon we were high enough to do some acro.

I first warmed up with a series of wing overs and barrel rolls, both are about 1G maneuvers. Then I put the nose over to enter a loop. We had to attain a minimum of 150 knots for loop entry. This would give us about 90 knots at the top of the loop. I lowered the nose to reach the entry speed but something was wrong. The nose attitude was very, very low and much steeper than normal. Eventually I reached 150 knots and pulled back into a 3 G loop. When I reached the top I noted our airspeed was only 65 knots and we were approaching an inverted stall. I managed to get the nose to fall through on the back side of the loop and made a mental note to myself that I needed to get the compression of the cylinders checked as this old 225 HP engine was acting very tired.

When I spun down from altitude to enter the landing pattern at Lincoln Airfield I noticed the control was actually pretty responsive in this old bird. When I reached the 180 degree position abeam of my intended point of landing, I reached to lower the landing gear...and then I knew why the plane was acting squirrelly.

The gear was already down and locked...my distraction on takeoff caused by that nude woman had broken my pattern and caused me to fail to raise the gear.

I immediately thought back to when I left the speed brake down on the T-28 and wanted to kick myself. Hadn't I learned anything from that experience? Why hadn't I investigated the sluggish performance before?

However, right then I had another concern on my mind. The maximum speed authorized in a T-34B with landing gear extended is 100 knots. I had gone 50% greater than that limit when I entered the loop. Was the gear damaged? Will it stand up to the impact of landing?

I continued my approach for two reasons. First, I really had no other option. I was going to have to land sometime, so why not now? And secondly, I understood that the speed restriction was more about not raising or lowering the gear at high speed. The gear doors attached to the mounts were flimsy and moving them at high speeds could cause them to come loose and then foul the gear in the raised position.

So I landed softly at Lincoln Airfield and then gingerly taxied to a parking spot. I climbed under the aircraft and visually inspected the gear doors and shook them as hard as I could to ensure nothing had come loose. All seemed okay, so we continued our fun day playing with the airplane.

Another day flying without adult supervision in the Recruiting Command.

*****

There was real danger in flying independently without others in a squadron working with you to keep you from doing some stupid stuff.

As the cruising speed of the "Teeny Weenie" was only 130 knots it could take more than a little time to fly around all of Northern California and Nevada. And after you get your fill of yanking and banking, you get bored and are tempted to try other things.

One beautiful clear day, I was flying from near the Oregon border back to Livermore, CA where we kept the airplane based. I was scooting along at around 1,500 feet with the front canopy in the open position enjoying what I referred to as some "convertible time." Then I got an idea that turned into an urge. I wondered what it would be like to stand up in the cockpit and get a little experience similar to what wing walkers had back in the barn storming days.

So, leaving my parachute securely attached, I released my seat harness. I grabbed the top of the windscreen and pulled myself to a standing position. As soon as my head got higher than the windshield I realized I had made another bad choice.

The 130 knot wind flew into my helmet which pulled me backwards with great force. My back was pinned against the top of the canopy rim behind my seat. My hands had slipped off of the windshield and I was stuck in this dangerous position. I needed to pull myself back down into the seat, but the only thing readily available to grab was the control stick. I refrained from grabbing that because it would just pull the nose up and, with my luck, complete the start of a loop. The last thing I wanted to do was make up a story about how I had engine trouble and had to abandon the plane to explain why I was standing in the middle of a farmer's field with a deployed parachute around my ankles.

After a long minute squirming from side to side I was finally able to grasp the throttle and side of the fuselage and pull myself into my seat.

That had been scary. I learned my lesson.

If you are going to stand up in an open cockpit, be sure to remove your helmet before you do. Following that rule, I logged about thirty minutes over the next couple of weeks of "free standing" flying.

*****

Boredom also led to giving into the impulse to herd sheep and cattle from the air. It wouldn't take much to get the sheep to start running; just a low pass at twenty feet. But the cattle usually just took a step to the side and ignored me.

However, the commodore didn't ignore these silly deviations from NATOPS minimums.

Somehow word got to him about some of his pilots chasing the livestock and scaring drivers on country roads. We had a regular quarterly Area safety meeting at the commodore's headquarters. After a couple hours of boring lectures and round-table discussions, the commodore came into the meeting to personally address the twelve pilots assigned to him. He made some general comments about safe flying, and since he was a pilot himself he knew how to make his points.

One point in particular got my attention. I was sitting at the end of the conference table, right next to where the commodore was standing to address the group. When he got to one issue he bent over, made eye contact with only me and wagged his finger in my face as he said in a very stern voice, "I want you all to observe the minimum altitude restrictions. If I hear of any pilot flying below 500 feet except for landing and taking off—I WILL TAKE HIS WINGS!"

Gee, Commodore, why give me so much individual attention?

After that meeting I adjusted my normal applicant flight profile and I no longer flew below 500 feet except for landing and taking off.

Of course, I do have to admit that sometimes it took me about twenty miles eventually to climb to 500 feet after taking off.

Chapter Six

Staff College

Recruiting is not the best shore duty possible. However, like every job in the Navy, once you master the assignment it can become good duty. Compared to other shore duty I could have drawn, I found elements of recruiting to be unique and educational.

If you make or exceed your monthly goals, you are left alone. It truly becomes independent duty. I wrote my own calendar and set my own working hours. I made time to enjoy flying often and any tour in the Navy when you can make time to watch your son's soccer games in the middle of the week is good duty. For the first time in my career I could plan on being home for dinner during the week and making family events on the weekends. I only worked "half days" (twelve hours) from 6 AM to 6 PM, Monday through Friday. I lived fifteen minutes from the office, so I was able to sit down to dinner with the family at 6:15 PM most nights. Yep...pretty good shore duty.

And to my surprise the Navy was offering a bonus equal to a year's pay if I would sign up for another four years. Pilots were getting in short supply, so for awhile bonuses were offered if you agreed to stay in.

The thought of going to the same job every day for the rest of my life began to drag on me. I went to my father and explained that I was thinking of closing down the business we had got up and running so that I could take the bonus and stay in the Navy. To my surprise he was elated with the idea. He had wondered why I would leave a job that catered to the foot disease I had inherited from him. He was born with "itchy feet." After holding any job long enough to master it, he got itchy feet to move on and find something new. He thought the Navy was a perfect match for me because they gave me a new job every couple of years...and medical and retirement benefits that weren't lost when the job changed.

I began to think about how I could extend shore duty one more year and then return to a patrol squadron at the right seniority for a department head tour. A good place to kill a year that looks good to promotion boards was attending a war college. Being that my career was already tainted as non-standard by not starting in aviation and then leaving the P-3 community for shore duty, I didn't see any reason to attend a normal war college. I began to research foreign Navy war colleges.

The Royal Navy Staff College in Greenwich, outside of London looked very interesting to me. So I signed on to receive the bonus and began maneuvering to make myself the best choice to fill the one American billet at the college.

Recruiting taught me that all leadership is sales and all sales is leadership.

The best leaders empower their sailors to reach decisions they thought were the product of their own choices. How do you think a civilian is convinced to accept a job where they shave your head, scream at you, have you clean a urinal with a toothbrush, possesses the possibility of death during your enlistment and you can't quit? Every new recruit must think it was their independent decision to join.

All leadership is sales and all sales is leadership.

My goal was to convince the foreign war college placement officer in Washington DC that she should pick me. I reverted to my "smarmy" recruiting methods. I called her and chatted her up, laughing at her jokes and empathizing with her trials. I became a good phone friend who "understood" her. I even sent her a birthday card on her real birthday. In essence, I was not above flirting with her to make her think positively about me as a candidate to attend the Royal Navy Staff College.

I thought myself quite the charmer when I received orders to attend the school. Of course, as usual, I was delusional. Years later this female officer retired and I discovered that she had caused a little heartburn with her commodore when she invited her lesbian partner to attend the retirement ceremony. I actually had doubts (for a minute) that maybe my flirtatious charm was not as powerful as I had thought.

*****

My introduction to serving with the Brits set the tone for the next eight months. Not sure of when they might "commence ship's work," I decided to arrive at 7:15 AM. on the first day. Most American Navy commands begin work at either 7 or 7:30 AM, so I figured I would be smart showing at 7:15.

It was cold that January morning as I sat in this old Austin Maxi I had purchased for 250 pounds. I waited...and waited...and waited, but nobody showed and the big doors to this 18th century building remained locked. Finally at 8:55 AM a janitor showed up and unlocked the doors. A minute later a car drove up and out stepped a British commander.

As I walked towards him, dressed in a Royal Navy pull-over uniform sweater I had been issued a week before, he smiled and asked, "You must be the American, right?"

I nodded and said, "Yes, sir."

His next question surprised me. "When did you arrive? Seven or seven-thirty?"

"Eh...seven-fifteen," I answered sheepishly.

"Well, the first thing you must learn at this school is that no gentleman arrives at work prior to nine o'clock."

He wasn't joking. The Staff Course schedule was not hard to adapt to. Normal class days started at 9 AM and we attended lectures and group discussions until 10:30. Then we broke for coffee until 11 AM. There were more lectures and discussions until 12:30 when we went to lunch. We did not start the afternoon syndicate meetings until 2:05 PM which went until 3:30 when we broke for tea. Our last session of the day was from 4 PM to 5 PM.

Of course this "arduous" schedule was modified on Mondays and Fridays. On Mondays, we did not start the class until after the coffee break, 11 AM, because they did not want to cut into weekend liberty. And on Fridays, you had to attend tea, but nothing was scheduled after 4 PM because they did not want to cut into the weekend.

It was becoming apparent to me why Britannia no longer ruled the waves.

*****

I caused a stir at the school without trying to be difficult. I was the first American Pacific sailor to attend in a decade. As a result, I did not give the expected answer when I was asked many times during the first weeks, "So how do you feel about the condition of the Alliance?"

I was not being flippant when I responded, "What alliance?"

These British naval officers nearly swallowed their tongues and did a spit take with their whiskey and waters in response to my answer. They were shocked that a United States naval officer did not eat, sleep, and dream of NATO daily.

"NATO, of course!" was their response.

I admit that I rarely missed an opportunity to tweak the nose of someone who came across as puffy, and many British naval officers had a tendency to be that way. So my response was usually, "Oh, *that* alliance...you know we have mutual defense pacts with nearly twenty-three nations. I just didn't know which one you had in mind."

*****

My "Americanisms," as my fellow students referred to my phases I expressed in discussions, became a subject in themselves when the Brits gathered around the bar.

One day I was passing the bar on the way to the lunch room when a Brit commander saw me hustling to get in line for my food. Now the "lunch room" at the Greenwich staff college was the main hall which could seat a couple of hundred at formal dinners. It was like eating in the Sistine Chapel because its fifty foot high ceiling was painted in beautiful murals of famous naval battles. Lunch was served from a small buffet set up on folding tables. If you dawdled too long at the bar, most of the food would be picked over by the time you made your way to the lunch room. So this commander had to practically grab my arm to stop me from racing by...I have always enjoyed lunch.

"Bob—oh! Bob!—May we have a short word with you?"

I slowed to a make a quick stop as the commander continued, "I was just telling these chaps about what you said in syndicate this morning."

"What? What did I say?"

"Oh, you know, about 'taking names and kicking arse,'' he said as everyone smiled.

I had forgotten that I had used that phrase during a discussion about the use of naval forces in the Persian Gulf. A snotty Royal Navy lieutenant-commander had made the statement of how our carriers could not effectively operate in those waters because cruise missile gunboats could hid behind islands there and then speed out to the open to fire their missiles. He claimed that the U.S. wouldn't dare put their huge and expensive carriers in such a vulnerable predicament. I had listened to this know-it-all prattle on for a good ten minutes while I sat there saying nothing.

Finally, the syndicate leader turned to me and asked, "Well, what do you think of this opinion?"

I responded honestly and with just a couple of sentences, "I don't think the lieutenant commander has ever steamed with an American carrier, because if he had he would know that the carrier never goes anywhere without an umbrella of air cover protecting it. No island is going to hide patrol boats from naval aircraft. And if a carrier task force decides to enter the Persian Gulf during a hostile period, you can be assured that it will just wade in there, take names and kick ass. End of discussion."

I never knew what I might say in normal conversation that the Brits would find amusing. However, it was an American Air Force officer who uttered the best "Americanism" I heard while in England.

One week during the course, the students from the Royal Navy Staff College joined with students at the British Army and Royal Air Force staff courses for a week of joint training and planning. Teams were made consisting of members from each service and then each team was given the same military problem to solve. In essence, we were to devise plans on how to invade Albania using NATO resources stationed in Italy and Greece. At the end of the week each team would give a presentation of their solution to the other teams. Those teams observing the presentation would try to find fault with the solution.

This very condescending RAF wing commander listened to the solution briefed by the joint team that included the USAF exchange officer.

As part of the brief, the American lieutenant colonel was excitingly briefing how the allied airplanes would fly down in this valley on the first night and take out the bridges so the enemy could not bring up reinforcements. This American reminded me of George C. Scott as General Buck Turgidson in "Dr. Strangelove." He was really into this plan and was irritated when the wing commander interrupted him.

"Excuse me, yank!" the wing commander said in a nasally, high pitched very proper English accent, "but you forget that this plan must only include the use of our equipment, and we don't have the kit to enable us to fly down that valley at night."

The smug expression on this RAF officer's face disappeared as the American pilot's response was applauded by the assembled group. In his best John Wayne voice the lieutenant colonel said, "Aw, kit hell! All you need is moonlight and guts."

*****

The Brits were wonderful hosts, but that did not stop them from taking good natured digs at their allies. It seems every officer had an opinion that I had to hear about how America and the American Navy were screwing up the Cold War.

I discovered that the best defense to these verbal assaults was to just agree with the accuser and then blame it on the difficulty inherent in commanding large units.

I'd say something like, "You're probably right, but sometimes it is hard to move around such a large worldwide force. You must remember that while you have a fifty frigate navy, we have that many sitting in mothballs waiting to be called back into service if our other two hundred are not enough...and, you know, the U.S. Marines have more aircraft than the entire Royal Air Force, but we don't usually count them as part of our order of battle."

Yep, having a west coast sailor in their midst was something new for these Eurocentric sailors.

*****

Probably the most interesting experience I had while serving with the Brits was the trip to their nuclear submarine base in the Firth of Clyde in Scotland. I was the only foreign student of the dozen in the class permitted to view the nuclear ships and visit their tactical training center. The obvious reason was the special relationship between America and Britain. Luckily, this gave me the opportunity to hear a passive sonar recording that was made of the sinking of the Argentine cruiser General Belgrano by HMS Conqueror during the Falklands War. What was of particular interest to me was what happened after the captain had sent two torpedoes into the hull of the old American-built cruiser.

It was eerie listening to the ship break up as it sunk. It sounded like wind chimes as the bulkheads collapsed. But the next part of the recording taught me not to discount the training I had experienced while serving two tours in Anti-Submarine Warfare.

Commander Wreford-Brown, RN was in command of the Conqueror and after the successful attack he made the assessment that the biggest threat to his ship and crew was posed by the cruiser's two escort ships. Consequently, he ordered the submarine to clear the area as rapidly as possible. I could not believe it when the sonar technicians explained that the noise I heard for the next twenty minutes on the tape was the sound of water rushing around the hull as the submarine ran away at twenty knots at the same depth and on the same course.

In the fog of war, Wreford-Brown had weighed his options against his understanding of the threat and did something any ASW officer would think impossible. He increased his speed and maintained a steady course and depth to escape the area. A submarine running at twenty knots puts enough noise in the water to be detected by any and all listening devices in that hemisphere of the ocean. Developing attack criteria to drop a weapon from an airplane would be "easy-peasy" for even the most inept P-3 crew in the fleet against a submarine maintaining a constant course and depth.

In fact, I was informed that once the submarine slowed to listen to what was going on around it, two splashes were recorded. The Argentines had used old S-2 Trackers to attack from the air. Only their poor quality of weapons prevented the Conqueror from experiencing its own tragedy.

When I took this information back to my next squadron, few believed me because it was hard to fathom how a professional, talented nuclear submarine commander would make those choices. It was even harder to believe since we all held the abilities of the Royal Navy to be so high. What it taught me was to put faith in our sensors and tactics, even when what we might see does not make sense. Even the best COs can make unexpected decisions in wartime.

*****

The Royal Navy is quite traditional and conservative. They don't give medals for doing your job well. The U.S. Navy and Marine Corps are quite tight about giving medals to sailors compared to the Army and Air Force. But even the American Navy is not as strict in this as the Brits. In fact, once or twice a year the Queen's Honor List is published and then the very few military members being awarded a medal are recognized, some in fact traveling to Buckingham Palace to get it pinned on their chest.

I had checked out of NRD San Francisco before the approval to award me a Navy Achievement Medal was received. So my previous command forwarded the medal and citation to my new command along with a note to "conduct an appropriate ceremony" in presenting it. Well, when the Brits got this letter and medal they assumed it was something pretty important and not just the lowest personal decoration a sailor could receive. In fact, it was my first personal decoration and I was a lieutenant commander at the time. Later in my career I discovered that it was not unusual for a reserve corporal in the Army to have two or three achievement medals without having even to leave the base. This educated me on how the different services award decorations differently.

I did not expect any special recognition from doing my job, so I was gob smacked when the entire staff course class was called to attention at the start of a mandatory lecture and the First Sea Lord of the Admiralty (their top admiral) arrived unexpectedly. He ordered everyone to sit down and then he called me to the front of the room.

Captain Pentreath, the CO of the school held the medal case and handed the admiral the citation that accompanied it. As I stood at attention, the First Sea Lord read aloud the medal citation for my tour as a bag carrying recruiter.

About two-thirds the way through the very long paragraph he noticed something that astounded him. He had been reading how I had achieved 110% of this goal and 130% of that goal and 112% of another recruiting goal when he stopped and looked up.

He looked me in the eyes and with a small grin said, "Now I knew you could do a lot with statistics, but I didn't know you could earn a medal with them."

I wanted to shout, "Just give me the stinking medal and let me sit down! This is embarrassing!"

But I just kept my mouth closed and quickly sat down after he pinned the medal on my chest.

Chapter Seven

Second Patrol Squadron Tour

After I completed the staff officers' course I took a few weeks enroute to my next assignment to drive the family around the continent. Then, I reported to VP-31 to undergo RAG refresher training before I reported to VP-40 at Moffett Field, CA. One of the first things I had to do was get a new flight physical as I had missed my annual one while assigned with the Brits. Passing that exam got difficult.

The Moffett Field flight surgeon found a lump on my throat and ordered me to get it checked out. I was referred to Oak Knoll Naval Hospital where the otolaryngologist ran some tests and determined I had a fluid-filled sack on my thyroid. No big deal, but he wanted to drain it and have the lab check the fluid. I remember him having me lay on a back on a table and putting a large pad under my neck so my head was tilted back, exposing my throat. Then he retrieved something from a cabinet and held it behind his back as he approached me. I made the mistake of looking at what he was hiding. It was very, *very* long needle. He positioned it over my throat and stuck the tip into my exposed neck.

Then he said something that is still remarkable to me today. He said, "Whatever you do, don't swallow."

Of course, as soon as he said that my saliva glands jumped into overdrive and my mouth became so full I thought I would drown before he pulled that thing out.

A week later the lab results came back and I got a call from a Navy surgeon who had a very direct, if not calming bedside manner.

"Bob, we have only had one other case with a similar lab result and it turned out to be malignant cancer. So, I would like to crack you open and see what's in there." His exact words.

Three days later they had given me a Valium to calm me before they wheeled me to the operating prep room. Never having taken such a drug, it had a mellow effect on me. I remember everything seemed funny to me. I recall the corpsman laughing himself to tears as we waited for an elevator to arrive. I was on a gurney, covered by a sheet and smiling at everyone. An elderly couple stood next to us as they also waited for the elevator.

"Psst! Psst!" I said to get their attention. When they looked down at me I said in a loud whisper, "Do you wanna know a secret?"

They each got a quizzical expression and then I continued in a much louder voice, "I'm naked under this sheet!"

For some reason I thought that was hilarious. When I got to the prep waiting room, they parked my gurney next to another one that held a woman who was obviously quite nervous over her imminent procedure. So I got her attention and tried to have a conversation.

"Say, lady, I'm naked under my sheet. Are you naked under your sheet?"

I thought it funny, but then five minutes later I don't remember anything else until I awoke in the recovery room five hours later.

That night I was returned to my private room. All through the night, about every hour or so a nurse would wake me up by scratching my forearms and lightly slapping the backs of my hands.

The next morning the surgeon was making his rounds while trailing three doctors-under-training as Oak Knoll was a teaching hospital. My doctor stopped at the foot of my bed and addressed the trainees as if I was not there or deaf.

"Now what we have here is a 33 year old aviator we operated on yesterday," he began his mini-lecture and then went on to explain what he had done to remove my thyroid and the cancer he had found in my neck. Then he ended his instructional session by saying, "Now when you have a patient who has had this trauma done to his vocal cords don't expect him to be able to speak immediately. So, be sure to only ask questions he can answer non-verbally."

He then moved to the head of my bed and addressed me. "Commander Bartron either shake your head for no, or nod for yes. Are you in much pain this morning?"

He almost lost his balance when I answered him in a strong, but slightly lower than normal voice, "Actually, Doc, I'm feeling pretty good this morning. How are you doing?"

The doctor should have known it would take a lot more than what he did to keep a Bartron from talking. After all, I had earned the nickname of "Big Bad Babblin' Bart" as a midshipman and it stuck with me for good reason.

He asked if I had any questions and I said, "Yeah. Why are the nurses constantly coming in here and slapping my hands and scratching my forearms?"

"To make sure we left you a parathyroid. You remember, we talked about that."

"No, Doc, you never mentioned anything about a parathyroid. What is that?" I asked innocently.

"Well, people have two to four parathyroids located right behind the thyroid, but they can look like fatty tissue when we're operating, so they are testing to make sure we left you one," he explained.

I asked the next obvious question, "What's a parathyroid do?"

"It regulates your body's calcium level."

"Is that important?" I asked and then continued with a more personally serious question, "Can I still fly if I don't have one?"

"Oh, I'm afraid you won't be getting anywhere near a Navy cockpit if we didn't leave you one. In fact, you probably won't live the rest of your life very far from a VA hospital."

I immediately started scratching my forearms and slapping the backs of my hands as I urgently asked, "What am I looking for, Doc?"

"Don't worry; it looks like we left you one or more."

*****

A month later I was back at Oak Knoll for follow-up radiation treatment. It was December 26 when I entered a room in the Radiation Medicine Department and took a seat. Five minutes later three corpsmen arrived wearing long lead aprons, long rubber gloves, and Plexiglas face masks. Two of them were carrying a very heavy orange painted box with radioactive symbols stenciled on the sides. It was a cube with each side being about 18 inches in length. They set the box down in the middle of the room and carefully unlatched its three-inch thick, solid lead cover. The two biggest corpsmen carefully lifted it and set it to the side. This revealed a solid lead box with a small hole in the middle of the top. It was about the size of a pickle jar. Inside the hole sat a small vial about the size of prescription bottle. In it was an eighth inch of clear liquid. The third corpsman took a bottle of distilled water and squirted it into the vial to fill it. Then another corpsman, dressed in all this protective gear took a glass straw and set it in the vial in the lead box.

Then he turned to me and said, "Drink it."

Right! You guys have got to be kidding to think I'm stupid enough to drink that obviously dangerous crap.

They I smiled and drank the "kool aide."

I spent the next week as the only guest in a four-man room. As it was the week between Christmas and New Years, the hospital staff moved all the patients from my floor in the east wing to the west wing. This meant less staff was needed over the holiday as they could close the east wing nursing station. I was in isolation with brown paper rolled on the floor to make a path from my bed to the in-room head. I was not to get off the paper if I got out of bed. In the head was an orange bag stenciled with "Nuclear Waste" hanging under a port-a-potty seat. A bottle was supplied as a urinal and it was marked "Radioactive" as well.

I thought this was all quite dramatic and comical at the same time. As the doctors and corpsmen left my room they placed yellow police tape across the door that read "Quarantine, Radioactive." I asked them what I should do if I needed any assistance. The doctor started to tell me just to push the call button by my bed, but then he remembered that there was no one at the nurses' station in this wing. So he looked around the room and came up with a plan.

"Just toss this trash can down the hallway and yell. But whatever you do, *don't leave this room.*"

I read a good book and watched a lot of television that week. It was a little boring, but quite peaceful. Three times a day a corpsman would bring me a tray of food and leave it sitting next to the door on the opposite side of the large room. After he had left, I could go retrieve my meal.

On Thursday of that week I did receive a couple of visitors. Two ladies in their eighties arrived at my door. Both were hard of hearing so it was easy to hear their shouted conversation.

"Gladys, this is Frank's room. I know it is. He was here last time," yelled one.

"I don't see him. What is all this yellow tape?" Gladys answered, "FRANK! FRANK! YOU IN THERE?"

"Oh Gladys I'm sure he's in here. He's probably just using the toilet. Let's get this silly tape down!"

I had been yelling to them from across the room while they discussed where Frank might be, "LADIES, YOU CAN'T COME IN! THIS IS A QUARENTINE ROOM. STAY OUT!"

But they were focused on only one thing; they were determined to visit Frank. I tried to get them to understand that I was radioactive, but they did not seem to grasp what I meant and just kept pulling the tape down.

Finally, I had an idea that women who were adults in the 1950s might understand.

"LADIES HALT! I AM THE ATOMIC MAN!"

That did the trick and they went scurrying to the other wing to find a nurse...and Frank.

*****

After the surgery and radiation treatment I remained grounded until a Medical Board could clear me for flight status again. This took several months, during which time I attended Aviation Safety Officer School at the Navy Post-graduate School in Monterey.

Eventually, I was cleared and returned to a flight status. I caught a military charter flight and flew to Keflavik, Iceland where my squadron had deployed. This was a rare "cross deck" deployment of a Pacific squadron working from an Atlantic base.

The difference in this deployment was drastic. In the Pacific as much flight time was expended doing large ocean surveillance as it was hunting submarines. The water conditions in the Pacific make finding any submarine a real challenge.

Gaining contact on Soviet submarines transiting from their bases in the Barents Sea through the Greenland-Iceland-United Kingdom (GIUK) gap was like shooting fish in a barrel. In the Pacific we would deploy a 16-sonobuoy pattern in the hope of getting a sniff of a submarine. In the GIUK gap you could detect and track a submarine with one or two buoys at a time. Since VP-40 flight crews were used to having to aggressively search in the western Pacific to generate "on top" time over a submarine, we launched missions into the GIUK gap with the same urgency and delight as a hungry fat man being locked overnight in a candy store. We jumped on every hint of a Soviet submarine contact even when the Tactical Support Center personnel recommended we pass on a contact because we could "always fly on it when it returns to the Barents Sea." As a result, when VP-40 completed the six-month deployment to Keflavik we set the record for the most submarine contact time ever accomplished by a deployed squadron up to that time.

*****

Arriving in mid-winter and staying to the summer meant we had very long and dark days to start the deployment and very long and light days by the time we rotated back to California. At times, it seemed to be dusk all day and night long.

I recall trekking across the tundra fields from the BOQ to the TSC located within the hangar complex and hustling all the way there because I knew the pre-flight tactical briefing was scheduled to start at four o'clock and according to my watch I had only ten minutes to arrive on time.

The scheduled flight was to be our crew's fourth in a long series of ASW flights in a six-day operation against Soviet submarines in our area. We were flying ten or twelve hours and then getting the minimum required crew rest before we flew the next flight. When you get in a cycle like this, it is very easy to lose track of the days,... and as I discovered, to become confused on whether it is morning or night.

As I hustled to make the brief on time I looked around the base and noted that it was dark enough to be either four o'clock in the morning or four o'clock in the afternoon. I got in a serious argument with myself on whether the brief was a morning or afternoon event. I honestly had no idea which it was, but I knew what I hoped it might be. A 4 AM preflight meant the farther south we flew to get on station, the lighter it would get and flying in daylight is always preferable to an all night flight. A 4 PM brief meant this event would be a dreaded dark, all night challenge.

When I arrived at the brief seven other members of the crew were in their seats waiting for the TSC briefer to arrive. The first thing I did was ask everyone what the time was—4 AM or 4 PM?

After a few minutes of give and take the vote came out; four said it was morning and four of us said it was the afternoon. When the briefer entered the room we asked him to settle the debate. He stood there with a blank face and concentrated very hard. However, all the hours of his work days had run together as well. He hadn't left that secure building for three days and had no idea of the time. So he went to the computer terminal and pulled up the brief and read the brief time in military time. It was 1600. A noticeable moan echoed across the room. Crap...an all night flight.

I believe it was on this night flight that I saw something scary and almost unbelievable. We had been tracking a Soviet nuclear submarine for several hours when we received a message from the TSC noting that soon it would be time for the submarine to maneuver closer to the surface to trail a wire antenna to use in listening to a blind high-frequency broadcast sent from their operational headquarters. The Soviets did this on a regular enough basis to allow our TSC to estimate when their next listening session would occur. Normally we kept an altitude on station high enough to minimize any noise we might generate in the ocean. Our goal was to track the submarines without them knowing it. But on this night we were given permission to "ball bat." We could drop to 300 feet over the water and use our Magnetic Anomaly Detector (MAD) to find the submarine's exact location. In other words, we were given the rare chance actually to play with a Soviet submarine.

Here would be a good time to mention the five things I liked about flying the P-3 in the Cold War. What I really liked was engine #1, engine #2, engine #3 and engine #4. To this day I get nervous flying over oceans in commercial planes that have only two engines. The fifth neat thing about hunting nuclear submarines back then was that they did not carry any weapons that could shoot back at an airplane. So I was fearless in descending to low altitude and tweaking the Russian Bear's nose.

There was almost a full moon that night as we yanked and banked an airliner-sized aircraft just above the water to place us in an attack position. The first step was to refine the sonobuoy fix on where we thought the submarine was. We did this by flying over the suspected spot near enough to where the 1,000 foot range of the MAD gear might detect it. I was sitting in the right seat and the 2P was flying the plane. As he made a steep turn to the right I looked down at the water and couldn't believe my eyes. I saw a very long cigar shape that was glowing with effervesce...I had actually seen a submerged submarine from the air...at night! I notified the TACCO to drop a "mark on-top" symbol on the computer and then I took control of the aircraft and flew around to that spot again. It took three more passes, but eventually my copilot and flight engineer also got a visual on the target.

It was eerie and impressive actually to see the entire outline of the submarine from the air. The darkness, its effervescence and the speed which we passed made it look like a super giant mutant Great White shark. It did in fact, (once again) "scare me a little...and I'm fearless."

*****

While flying out of Iceland I was able to add a qualification as a "Blue Nose" to my previously earned "Shellback" status.

Every month the deployed squadron to Keflavik was tasked to "show the flag" by flying into NATO allied countries and participating in some cross training. Enroute to Bodo, Norway our crew flew into the Artic Circle and this necessitated a little ceremony onboard the plane that included the painting of our noses with blue marker and an entry in our service record that we were now officially "Blue Noses."

Which, of course, was better than becoming a "brown nose."

During this visit we flew into some beautiful fiords as we took a little airborne sightseeing liberty. The scenery was spectacular and unforgettable.

One morning during our visit the crew officers were directed to be in the hotel lobby to meet our Norwegian counterparts for a tour of their operations center. We all piled into this unmarked van and headed out of town. Sometime later, when we Americans were tired of riding and had seen enough trees to last a long time, I remarked how well built this highway was. One of our two hosts explained to me that certain stretches of highways in Norway were built to withstand the weight of fighters. In time of war, a designated stretch of straight highway could become a temporary air base. Support facilities could be brought in by tanker truck, maintenance, spare parts, and operational trailers could be quickly grouped to support a mobile squadron. Sounded like a land-based carrier concept to me.

Eventually the van turned into the small parking lot of a low, commercial building. We were under-impressed by our ally's facilities and it made us doubt how secure the northern flank of NATO was when the entire operations center could fit into a 7-Eleven.

However, we did not park in front of this building. Rather, we crossed the parking lot and exited along a single lane gravel road that proceeded towards a couple of large mountains in the distance. When we arrived at the end of this road there was a small dirt parking area in front of a run-down shack that sat nestled against the base of the mountain. The driver stopped, but left his engine running. Our hosts had us exit the van and enter the shack. I noticed the driver quickly left the area and headed back down the one-way road.

Inside the shack was a modern desk with a uniformed member of the Norwegian Air Force wearing a side arm sitting behind it. He took our military ID cards and checked our names against a previously received clearance list. He issued us badges and then buzzed open a very thick security door located on the back wall which was, in reality, the rock face of the mountain. As we were led down a long, cave-like hall we all felt as if we had just entered the world of James Bond. At the end of the slightly uphill climb the stone walls turned to brick and then to drywall as if we had entered a business building and not a mountain. Another security check point greeted us and our IDs were checked once again by armed sentries located behind bullet-proof glass.

A large door that looked like it belonged on a bank vault opened and we were led down more hallways and up and down stairs. Eventually we came to a room that looked familiar to us. It was filled with computer screens and status boards and radar displays, all very similar to a Tactical Support Center on a P-3 base...only quite larger.

I guess you really should not judge a book by its cover.

*****

I became the Safety Department Head in the squadron. Next to the Admin office, it was the smallest department in VP-40. Working for me were a flight safety lieutenant and a ground safety officer and NATOPS standardization experts for each aircrew position on a P-3. Counting me, the department totaled eleven sailors; about the smallest unit I ever led.

VP-40 was one of the very first west coast squadrons to receive the P-3 Update III model of aircraft. They were sweet to fly. Unlike regular P-3s that had been in the fleet for years, the Update III was brand new and everything worked rather reliably the first year. However, there was one great challenge in having a new airplane. The sensors were all improved, the computer software was all upgraded and air crews had to learn the new equipment and the right buttons to push in the new program. It was similar to a new NFL head coach coming to a team with a new offensive system that had to be learned. A lot of study of the "playbooks" was required by the tube rats to master the new systems. Of course, pilots were not that challenged as all the new software and hardware dealt with tactical systems; the flight controls, hydraulic, pneumatic, communication and electrical systems were the same so all we pilots needed to master was a couple of buttons on our cockpit tactical display.

PATRON (Patrol Squadron) Forty was due for a Chief of Naval Air, Pacific (CNAP) squadron-wide written test for every aircrew position. These are comprehensive examinations and for a squadron to receive a passing grade at least 60% of the aircrew positions must have at least 60% of the sailors who man those positions pass the exam. These don't sound like tough standards until you know that no squadron in Moffett Field history had ever received a squadron pass grade after receiving new aircraft. There was that much new to learn.

My team set up a detailed training program to prepare the squadron to pass this tough NATOPS examination. Classes were held everyday by the NATOPs evaluator assigned to the Safety Department for each crew position. Only through such a detailed and thorough preparation plan did we have the slightest chance of getting a squadron pass on the first testing date.

The team did very well and to the surprise of the wing and our CO we came very close to passing. In fact, it came down to one answer to one question on one In-Flight Technician's (IFT) exam. It was an ambiguous question and you could argue that there were two answers that were correct. If this IFT was given credit for a right answer then he would get a passing grade and that would give the IFT position a positional pass, and if the IFTs passed, then the squadron would achieve 60% passing of all positions. It all came down to this one question with possibly two answers.

The IFT positional NATOPS evaluator in the squadron was Petty Officer Second Class Johansson. He took the CNAPS evaluation team into the back room of the Safety Department office. I have no idea what he said or what he did behind closed doors, but when they emerged from that room twenty minutes later, the IFT was given credit for his answer so he passed and that meant the IFTs achieved a positional pass and that meant the squadron became the first in the history of Moffett Field to pass the CNAPs standardization examination after getting totally new aircraft systems.

The next day, the CO called me into his office and thought he would impress me with his leadership. He told me that since we passed, he was going to give me the job I truly desired in the squadron. He was going to make me the new Maintenance Officer (MO.) There are about 60 officers and 300 enlisted in a P-3 squadron; twenty-two officers and 200 enlisted are assigned to the Maintenance Department. I was going to get another chance to lead a large group of sailors once more.

I left the COs office pleased but also disappointed. I thought he should have called me into his office the day *before* the CNAPs examinations and told me of his decision. He was aware of the excellent preparation program that the Safety/NATOPS staff had planned and executed to give the squadron the best chance to pass. There was no way I could take the exams for every aircrew member in the squadron, so I really did not have any personal control over the ultimate outcome of the tests. I thought the CO should have considered the preparation plans and their execution and then called me in and said, "Bob, regardless of what happens tomorrow, I don't think we could be better prepared. I've been impressed by your thorough work and I want you to be the next MO."

As with all my COs, I learned something from this one as well. If I had the chance in the future, I would look for a way to recognize good work regardless of an uncontrollable outcome.

*****

During this second tour in P-3s, I once again was designated an Instructor Pilot (IP.) I enjoyed flying in this role, but I retained my "non-hero" status. This was reflected in my planeside brief before every syllabus hop.

After the Naval aviator undergoing instruction gave his formal, exact brief on emergencies, I would add the IP brief of, "The mission today is to come back alive. Any training that might be done is purely icing on the cake and could very well be no more than an unattended bonus."

And I actually believed that! In many flights as a P-3 IP you have a rookie in the left seat and the middle seat. The Instructor Flight Engineer stands behind the rookie in the middle seat and can not always stop the FE under training from doing something incomprehensibly wrong. I figured the trainees had me out numbered two to one, so my primary goal was to keep them from killing me.

On more than one occasion I came close to failing in this quest. I remember when this new squadron pilot, fresh from the RAG, was making a simulated two-engine landing on Runway 32 Left at Moffett Field. This was simulated by me bringing the power levers of engines number one and two to flight idle and letting him use the two engines on the starboard side to land. He was a little low, but his airspeed was okay and it looked like we would do a successful touch-and-go. He flared just a few feet too high, which was okay because he had the speed to fix his error and return to flying the main mounts to the deck. But then he did something that surprised me—no...it terrified me it was so unexpected! On a two engine landing all your thrust is generated by half the available engines so you need to carry twice the normal horsepower on the operating engines. Just when this nugget should keep his power on to adjust his attitude and overcome the slightly early flair, he takes a cut! He pulls his two remaining power levers to the fight idle position! Suddenly the entire bottom dropped from this approach and we sank like a rock in blue water. I reacted by using the palm of hand that was resting on the center console behind the FE levers to jam all four power levers forward in an attempt to arrest the sudden descent. We smacked the deck hard and bounced a good foot into the air, but before we could slam the pavement again, the powerful P-3 propellers grabbed chunks of air and flew us out of the mess.

The only problem was that by ramming my hand forward as quickly as possible I failed to move all four power levers at the same rate. The starboard engines came on with more power than the port engines and shoved our nose to the left. Our flaps were in the Maneuver position which is an option for a two engine landing, and so our lift was less than normal for this airspeed low to the ground. I was dancing on the rudder pedals and wrestling with the yoke in an attempt to straighten us out. As I did this, we zoomed over the many P-3s parked on the RAG's ramp and we were heading right for Hangar One at about 100 feet altitude. That was bad because Hangar One is an old blimp hangar and is 200 feet tall.

The P-3 is a multi-place cockpit for a reason. It is not easy to fly it solo, but that was what it had devolved into. The nugget and IP in training were no help whatsoever. I was able to adjust the power levers so the engines were pulling evenly and to get the flaps to take-off position and the landing gear up and to bank the aircraft to the right to avoid the hangar and establish a normal climb. All in about four seconds. I got us established on a crosswind leg in the pattern and gave the plane back to the nugget. On the downwind leg I once again pulled number one and two to the flight idle position and directed the nugget to do it again.

The FE in training had looked up at the wrong time during the last attempt and all he had seen was his life flash before his eyes as the hangar was rapidly approaching. When he heard me say we would try it again, the FE looked at the FE Instructor and asked in a pitiful voice, "We're not going to go through that again are we?"

The FE instructor thought it was time to give his student a break, so he assumed the middle seat.

We didn't die on the next attempt either. Mission successful.

*****

In the P-3 community you had to successfully pass multiple oral examination boards to earn your qualifications. Many of these boards were more in the form of an initiation than a valid examination of your fitness to be given the next qualification. I became quite popular with pilots preparing for their next board, because if I sat as the senior member of a board I would not tolerate the asking of what I considered "initiation questions." These were questions that junior board members asked because when they sat before a board they had to know the answer; even if the question was useless information.

An example of a useless question was a standard one asked at nearly every 3P systems board. The applicant would be asked, "What temperature brings on the 'fuselage duct hot' light?"

Whenever a junior officer asked that question I would forbid the applicant from responding and then show my displeasure that such trivia was being perpetuated in our community.

I would ask the junior officer who raised the question, "Why should he care? If he sees that big red alert light on the dash board glow, what does it benefit him to know what temperature made it come on? What if the sensor was not accurate that day and came on three degrees too soon or two degrees too late? How would he know? Why would he care? Here is the only valid question concerning the 'fuselage duct hot' light—what do you do when you see that light? Knowing what temperature brings on that light is useless, but knowing what to do if it comes on can save your life and the lives of your crew!"

As I said, I was asked by many pilots in the syllabus to sit as the senior member of their oral boards because I had no interest in conducting an initiation...but I also was known as the lieutenant commander who had no patience for anyone being under-prepared for the exam.

*****

I relieved my classmate as the VP-40 MO. He was a good officer and leader; however we had different approaches on how best to do the job, just as different football coaches have varying ways and systems to bring out the talent of their players. Rory wanted to be involved in nearly every decision made by every supervisor in the department. For example, he required the chiefs who ran Maintenance Control to gain his okay before they released a plane for flight.

I had a different approach. I figured that 97% of the time the Maintenance Control chiefs would make the same decision that I would make, and I was willing to bet that the different 3% would not occur during my tour. I reasoned the chances of me knowing some special circumstance that might impact their decisions was slight enough to allow me to sleep through the night without constantly being interrupted.

My approach got me more sleep during that year as MO...but Rory made captain and I did not...so maybe his way was more effective.

During the first week in the job, I was receiving regular calls in my office and at home throughout the day and night from Maintenance Control supervisors. They had been trained not to scratch their butt without first checking with the MO. I was dumb enough to think this was the way it was supposed to be done. However, I changed my mind when I got mad on a Sunday evening. Why was the weekend duty shift calling me for permission to list an aircraft as "up and ready?" Why couldn't they just list it as such and inform me in the morning? For that matter, why would I care if the standard was met in getting aircraft to their supposedly normal state—"up and ready?" If they were going to be unable to have sufficient aircraft ready to fly the flight schedule, *then* I should be advised.

So that Sunday evening I went out to my garage and found a small piece of half-inch thick scrap wood and cut it into a two-inch square. Then I spray painted it black and after the paint dried, I used a white marker to write "555-4040" across the top. I screwed a small clip to the back, and then I went to bed. The next morning I attended the day shift shop supervisors meeting in Maintenance Control. I watched as the day-watch chiefs assigned job priorities and observed the give and take of truly professional sailors.

Once the meeting had adjourned and the department had "turned to and commenced squadron work," I approached the Maintenance Control desk and had the following conversation with chiefs in the shop.

"How are you doing this morning, MO?" the senior chief asked me.

"I'm doing great, Senior Chief. In fact, it promises to be another beautiful California sun-shiny day and I have big plans. I think I'll take the afternoon off and head across the street to the base golf course and play a round," I said only to make a point, because I was not a golfer.

"That sounds like a good plan, MO. Hope you have fun, but how will we contact you if we need to?" the senior chief asked.

"Oh, that's no problem. I'm carrying a beeper now. Just call me if anything comes up that you feel I need to be involved in. Of course, if you call me it's because you *failed* to handle it yourself," I answered and then paused as the emotional word "failed" sunk in. Using that word with these professionals was like waving a red flag in front of a bull.

At first my statement brought just a momentary confused look on the three chiefs behind the counter, but after just a couple of beats, two of them set their jaws and understood my meaning. I knew they got my point and would only call me if an entire wing fell off an airplane...and only if they were unable to reattach it in a timely manner.

The third chief who was totally conditioned to seeking the MO's approval on every little decision was slower to grasp my meaning. As I turned to walk out of Maintenance Control he called to me and with his pen poised over paper he asked, "But what's your beeper number, MO?"

I returned to the counter and set my block of black wood in front of him.

It was silent for just a passing second and then all three chiefs had a small laugh. The senior chief ended our morning's conversation with, "Have a good day, MO. We'll take care of everything around here."

And I did, and they did...for the next twelve months...and whenever I wasn't on the flight schedule I got plenty of sleep through the night.

*****

My next challenge was to get the Material Control branch officer to stop constantly bombarding me with computer print-outs. The MO was required to review the inventory status of parts and equipment on a regular basis. My predecessor was very intelligent and would look at every line of these massive print outs and question why the inventory changed for radar relays since the previous week. I had a different approach.

I called in the Material Control officer who was a professional aviation maintenance restricted line officer and told her I required her to submit one additional piece of information with her weekly reports. I demanded that she place a post-it note with an "up" or a "down" arrow in the upper right hand corner of the top page. If I saw an "up" arrow that meant the report did not contain anything that required my personal attention and so I could initial the report without having to check every single line. A "down" arrow meant both she and I probably would be going to jail.

She thrived when I placed so much trust in her that I, in essence, was letting her determine the rest of my career. However, one late afternoon I returned from a flight and entered my office and threw my flight gear in the locker that was located in front of my desk. I turned and noticed a computer print-out sitting in the middle of my desk with what, at first glance, appeared to be a "down arrow" on it. My heart sank and my eyes grew wide as fear bubbled inside me. I rushed around my desk to sit down in my chair before I started to review the report. It was then that I realized I had been looking at the print-out upside down.

I called in the Material Control officer and added one small condition to our system to keep me from having a heart attack after a long, tiring flight. I directed her to draw a line under the bottom of the arrow so I could tell at a glance whether I was going to jail soon.

The only way this system worked was by a little habit I had that would backstop these reports. Just as I had in previous jobs, I spent a lot of time actually in the shops. I would keep my eyes open during these informal visits and if I saw something I did not expect or did not see something I did expect in their spaces and back rooms, I would go to the Maintenance Master Chief and discreetly inquire about my observations. On more than one occasion the Master Chief had the shop chiefs or leading petty officers conduct a thorough and supervised inventory of every piece of gear and spare part found in the branch.

I always preferred a real live leader to be responsible for our gear and parts, and not some computer generated system.

*****

Some of my predecessors found that being head of the largest department impacted their flying opportunities. The Ops Boss and MO traditionally had a back-up PPC or TACCO assigned to their crews to enable the department heads to remain on the ground to manage their men and mission. This was the same with the CO and XO. During our next deployment to Kadena Air Base in Okinawa, I flew as the PPC on the XO's crew. He was an NFO and so we had another TACCO permanently assigned to fly with us. I had no back-up PPC so I flew all of our crew missions...and I was well pleased for the chance to do it. Unlike some of the NFOs in the squadron, I was not a "sea gull"...that is, an aircrew man who, like a sea gull, you had to throw rocks at to get them off the ground.

I had a fantastic Maintenance Master Chief and superior Aviation Maintenance Duty Officers who were non-aircrew and I was happy to let them run things while I flew with the crew. I had learned one of the best differences between the surface navy and aviation was the ability to "get airborne and leave all your troubles on the ground." Flying kept my approach to being MO in balance and prevented me from getting caught up in matters that could be handled just as well by someone lower in the chain-of-command.

And there were some interesting flights on this deployment. One beautiful day we ran up on a Soviet Sverdlov class cruiser transiting south of Taiwan. We did a full-rig on this combatant which means we got port, starboard, bow, stern and overhead pictures of it using out nose camera. Doing a full-rig was not our usual practice; normally a view of each side was sufficient, but we had never seen a large Soviet combatant steaming by itself before. So, we took advantage of the opportunity.

As we made our initial pass from stern-to-bow along its starboard side at 200 feet altitude we noticed a little Cold War game being played by the cruiser captain. Every gun on that ship was pointed at us and tracked us the entire time we made passes. And on the Sverdlov class that was a lot of guns! She carried twelve six-inch guns and another twenty-plus anti-aircraft guns. It did not dissuade us from completing a full-rig, but I did wonder if the Soviets were like the Americans who steamed without weapons loaded or like the Taiwanese who always had a war reserve round in the barrel ready to pop out. On that flight, I hoped it was the former.

*****

There was a flight where we actually did carry a war reserve weapon and shot it. Our crew was selected to load a real Harpoon anti-ship missile and then fly out to a lonely patch of Pacific Ocean east of the Philippines where the old diesel submarine, the USS Grayback, had been towed and left to drift on the surface. Three Harpoons were taken from inventory and one each loaded on a P-3, a nuclear submarine, and the USS New Jersey. All were to be launched from different compass points and distances to arrive at the Grayback simultaneously. If all worked well, then the three missiles would sink the orange painted diesel submarine with one giant multi-warhead explosion.

Of course, like most exercises, all did not go as planned. I had to maneuver the P-3 to hit a launch point and altitude on a specific heading at a specific time to release the weapon. I made four passes at four different times because just as the TACCO was about to push the launch button, we got a call on the radio from either the battleship or nuclear submarine telling us to delay because they needed to refine their fire control solution. Ours had to be the first of the three to launch because ours would travel a farther distance. While the ships were messing around with their navigation and fire control problem I was burning holes in the sky and watching my remaining on-station time shrink. I was determined not to return to base with this real weapon still hanging under our wing. We had something that went boom and we had a real target. I wanted to fire the thing!

On the fifth approach to our launch point, the altitude, timing, speed and heading were all perfect and no one yelled "abort!" in my ear, so we launched the weapon. What happened next gave me a sick feeling. The Harpoon fell from the wing and went straight down. I just knew we had screwed up when loading it and forgot to attach a cable to fire off its engine.

Just when I was trying to come up with a believable excuse, I saw two A-7 jets scream under my nose and head out in the direction of the Grayback. They were the chase birds who had the job of trailing the missile to keep it in sight to observe its performance during this test exercise. I looked ahead of the jets, and down right on the surface of the ocean I saw the Harpoon running toward the target which was over the horizon.

A few seconds later came the "abort" call from the battleship. They were not able to launch as planned. In response to that call, the submarine came on the line and admitted they needed more time to launch correctly. Both units were afraid my Harpoon might sink the target and that would ruin their day.

They needn't have worried. The A-7s reported that our Harpoon had passed to the right of the Grayback and then crashed into the sea. The aviation wing staff riding in our plane immediately started coming up with someway to place the fault of the miss on the weapon and not on the aircrew. After all, aviators will never admit to a mistake or failure to surface warriors or submariners.

As it turns out, the textbook footprint of the Harpoon acquisition radar showed that it should have acquired the target...in the lower left corner on the very edge of the sensor 's supposed capabilities. Of course, in the real world the foot print is not a perfect square; the edges are jagged and affected by many things. The weapon would have worked as advertised had I launched it sufficiently to put the target right in the center of the radar footprint.

The next day my TACCO and I plotted our fifth attempt to launch on the exact second we needed to make the "time-on-target" perfectly. It turns out that in all my yanking and banking to get us around to the exact launch spot I missed the first gate established by our computer system. Lesson learned: you must hit the first gate to line up your aircraft correctly when you launch the weapon at the firing gate....oops.

But this event wasn't over yet. We flew back to base to drop off the observers which included the CO and some civilian technicians in addition to the wing folks. Then we refueled and ran back out to the exercise site. Our mission on this second flight was to clear the range as a safety precaution before the next two missiles were launched.

Radar found that there was a contact just inside the safety circle. So we flew over to check it out. It was a medium sized freighter heading Northeasterly. If it did not change course, it would take a good hour for it to transit from the safety zone. I reported this to "Alpha Bravo" and a minute later I was told to get the ship off the range because the submarine and battleship were *finally* ready to launch their Harpoons.

I used the VHF radio to call to the ship in the blind, but as expected, there was no answer. Merchant ships steaming in the middle of nowhere on a clear day, rarely have a full or any bridge watch.

Now what to do? If you are in an airplane and you want to get a ship to change course in the middle of the ocean, there are not a lot of options open to you.

I decided to have the ordnance man break out four smoke buoys and prepare to drop them through the free-fall chute. Then being careful not to cross the bow of the merchant because that is an international distress signal requesting the ship follow you to a life raft or a burning ship or some other sailor's emergency, I flew up the ship's starboard side at 200 feet altitude. I had the ordnance man shove one smoke out as we got even with the bow and then I entered a shallow right turn and had him drop the other three. It took a couple of minutes, but the ship understood my suggestion and made a starboard turn. Fifteen minutes later it was almost out of the safety zone. I called the battleship to report the range was clear.

The admiral's answer surprised me, "Tango Echo, this is *Alpha Bravo*," the new voice on the secured radio net said. I understood exactly to whom I was now speaking. It was no longer the air controller or the duty officer or the ship's captain. Rather, the admiral had grabbed a headset to talk to me, "Tango Echo," personally. He continued, "How did you get him to move? You didn't do anything stupid like drop smokes or anything like that, did you?"

Crap Admiral! What did you expect me to do? You wanted the range clear and now it is clear!

I wasn't about to admit to making a "stupid" move so I used the one response that wasn't taught at the Academy but was a staple of fleet communications. The scrambled circuit we used to talk securely between operational units only worked if the transmitter and receiver were synchronized. So the standard response to report when this was unsuccessful seemed to be my best choice on how to answer, "This is Tango Echo; dropped sync; say again."

So the admiral, thinking I had been unable to hear his question, repeated it. I gave him the same, "Dropped sync; say again" reply. He tried twice more and then I like to think he caught on to my dodge and gave up.

Lesson learned here? You never have to lie to an admiral if you can pretend not to hear the question.

*****

All pilots screw up sometimes. Often it is because of over confidence in doing your job. Even a self-described ace-of-the-base like me can screw up.

To the northwest of the long runways at Kadena Air Base are a couple of hangars and buildings that comprise the "Navy and Marine Corps enclave" within this massive Air Force installation. Included in those buildings is a flight operations office where pilots can get a weather briefing and file flight plans. However, because this office only supports two Navy and one Marine squadrons, it only operates from 6 AM to 10 PM. If a Navy flight crew has a scheduled pre-brief during the hours it is closed, the PPC and/or 2P must drive the three miles around the runways to the Air Force side to get the weather and file a flight plan at base operations.

Our crew was scheduled to load four simulated mines under out wings, take-off from Kadena and fly all the way from Okinawa to the northern tip of Honshu Island where there was a calibrated range where we could practice dropping mines. Our scheduled take-off time was 5 AM, so it was necessary for my 2P, LT. Steve Bross, and I to drive to the Air Force Base Ops to file our flight plan.

Pilots love to drop things from airplanes, so Steve and I were in a good mood when filing our flight plan. Our positive mood even grew upon entering the base operations building. It being the main western Pacific hub for Air Force logistics, the Kadena operations building was a happening place 24/7. The first thing we did was go to the snack bar and order a couple fried egg sandwiches with Fanta red cream sodas. We ate our breakfast as we watched AFRTS on the television. Then we found the foosball table and played a couple of exciting games whacking that disc back and forth. Having enjoyed a mini-liberty while the crew completed the aircraft preparations to include loading the mine shapes on the wings, Steve and I checked our watches and realized we had better do what we came to do. We blew into the flight planning room and quickly scratched out a flight plan and took it to the weather office. There the meteorologist on duty told us that the weather should be good all the way to the tip of the Japanese main island. Based on this brief and the length of the flight, I called back to our squadron and had them inform our flight engineer of my desired fuel load for the mission. Based on my quick mental calculations using the fuel flow and ground speed of a typical flight and then adding another 8,000 pounds as a reserve, I had them pass along to the flight engineer that all we needed for fuel was to "fill the wings."

The P-3 had four fuel tanks in the wings and a larger belly tank, but for a flight like this the four tanks in the wings would be more than sufficient. I knew this because I had hundreds of missions in the Orion and I was extremely familiar with how it operated. I had gotten so familiar with the plane that I needn't bother referring to the procedures found in the NATOPS manual for such a cake run as this.

Famous last words...

Steve and I finished enjoying our play time at Air Force Base Ops and showed up at the airplane with just enough time to do a good walk around before the plane-side brief. We then climbed into our seats and taxied for take-off. We climbed to our transit altitude and when I ordered the Second Mech who was sitting in the Flight Engineer's seat to "set max range cruise" as the power setting, Steve and I got a shock and a sinking feeling.

The Second Mech pulled out his NATOPS manual and looked in a graph buried deep inside this three-inch thick book. He then announced that our "max range cruise" airspeed was 182 knots.

I responded with, "What? You mean 230 knots, right?"

"Sir," he explained, "not with this drag configuration. Those mine shapes have changed our configuration from the normal Bravo to the Delta category. So our max range cruise is about 45 knots slower."

Steve and I looked at each other and we both knew there was no way we could transit the approximately 1,000 miles at this speed and still have enough fuel to return to Okinawa as was required by the flight schedule. There were two reasons why we couldn't turn back and quickly load on more gas. First was our scheduled time on the range. We would miss it if we took another hour to return for fuel. Secondly, and more to the point, we would have to burn off a major portion of our fuel load to be light enough to land. So we were committed to going north. It was rather obvious that I was going to be forced to admit my improper flight planning and make an unscheduled stop for fuel at Misawa Air Base near the mine drop range. That was going to be very embarrassing...but better a red face than running out of gas.

Then two things happened to cover my error. The weather brief we received was totally bogus. A hundred miles from Okinawa we flew into clouds and stayed in them for the rest of the flight. When flying in visible moisture with the outside air temperature below ten degrees, the P-3 must use engine anti-ice and this results in a nine percent increase in fuel flow. That in itself I could use as an excuse to land at Misawa to get more gas.

When we finally did reach the mine range, the best reason to land at Misawa developed. The poor weather had closed the mine range. Even with all five fuel tanks full on take-off a P-3 does not have enough gas to carry those big honkin' mine shapes all the way up the length of Japan and all the way back down.

I'd rather be lucky than good...what did my mom say? I go in dirty as sin, but come out smelling like a rose?

We diverted to Misawa Air Base and requested a holding pattern while we burned off the last bit of gas we needed in order to reach our maximum landing weight. Air traffic control had us enter a holding pattern slightly southeast of the airport. So we got our expected further clearance time and entered a standard orbit around our designated holding point. As we circled in the air, I decided there were some distractions coming up when we landed so I wanted to move from the right seat to the left seat. We had been up since midnight, flown nearly the entire flight without outside visual reference, and we were going to land in an unfamiliar configuration with four mine shapes hanging from the wings at a distant field where I was the only pilot onboard with experience operating from Misawa. As an instructor pilot, I had mastered flying from the right seat and even doing well enough to demonstrate unusual landings to a student while sitting as the copilot. But, I still was more comfortable in the left seat, and under these conditions I felt it best I be as comfortable as possible.

Steve, as the 2P, relieved me in the right seat and the 3P climbed out of the left seat. I climbed in the left seat, fastened my harness and adjusted my headset. I took the yoke and pedals and told Steve I had the aircraft. Just then we reached our designated holding fix and I rolled the airplane into a thirty-degree bank as I turned left. In a flash my entire windscreen went from snow and white clouds to the grey belly of an airplane about to hit us. If I hadn't initiated my left turn already, we would have collided.

Before I could react, two things happened. The other plane was turning away from my direction and so it passed within ten feet of our right wingtip without touching, and my flight engineer pointed out the windscreen and yelled, "That's a P-2-J!"

To this day I remember how impressed I was with his aircraft recognition! In fact, he was absolutely right. It wasn't a P-2 like the American navy had flown before the P-3; it was the Japanese Maritime Self-Defense Force model that had been retrofitted with two additional jet engines mounted next to the two prop engines. The FE saw the plane, nearly nose on for less than one second and was able to make an accurate determination of the type and *model* of the airframe!

In my mind I had a picture of what was happening. It was obvious to me that the Japanese air controller had assigned the same holding altitude and fix, but with a different orientation to this P-2 as he had previously given to us. So if I kept my turn in and did another turn in holding it was likely that we would both come around and take another pass at each other in the totally blind, instrument conditions. I was not going to play this game of chicken again.

Steve, as copilot, handled the radios during the flight. I directed him in a very no-nonsense tone, saying, "Tell Misawa approach what just happened and advise them I'm leaving five-thousand feet and commencing the ILS approach to Runway 2-5."

Steve was in momentary shock and had trouble forming a complete sentence. I was too mad that some guy sitting safely in an underground, windowless room was trying to kill us to be in shock. I took control of the radios and got the first call out to approach control as I descended to intercept the glide slope and commence the approach.

We didn't get any static from the ground controllers and we were cleared to commence the precision approach.

Now a good, well trained crew knows how to respond to situations without being told everything. I came on the ICS speaker system for the tube and said, "Set five NOW!"

In Condition Five the aircrew in the tube are to prepare for landing by donning their helmets and strapping into their seats. Normally, pilots announce when to "set five" and then after about three minutes or more, the TACCO replies with "Five set aft" once everyone had made it to their spot.

There must have been something in my voice the way I said, "Set five NOW" that day because less than five seconds later the TACCO called me on the ICS and said, "Five set aft. What's going on?"

By this time Steve had snapped out of the amazement of nearly dying and told the TACCO why we were immediately making our approach.

Now, in my flying career, I have made some rather sticky approaches in real bad weather. But this approach and landing stick out in my memory as the one that required all my skill as a Naval Aviator to be keenly focused in order to set the beast on the runway. And I couldn't do it by myself.

The first odd thing I noticed upon establishing the airplane on glide slope and course was the amount of power it took. With those big mine shapes hanging under the wing I had to carry nearly twice the normal shaft horsepower to control my descent. There was a crosswind that necessitated a crab to maintain the correct path over the ground and adjusting to this was slightly different because the plane's responses were sluggish.

However, the real challenge was the blowing snow from the right in the thick overcast that gave the impression that our path of flight was creeping to the right. I had to stay on instruments all the way to decision height, 200 feet above the ground. As I was approaching this point of decision where I had to take it around or continue if I had the runway environment in sight, an odd statement came through my headset.

"Navy AB123, land long. Men and equipment on approach end of runway."

What? What! You gotta be kiddin' me!

Before Steve could even roger for that information the FE called out, "I got lights dead ahead!"

I looked up from the instruments and saw the flashing center line lights running towards the runway threshold like a little scared rabbit we were chasing. We were descending through 200 feet and I had to decide in a millisecond if I could get it on the runway or if I should attempt to take it around with maximum power due to the mine shapes on the wing. There was only one way I could make the transition from instruments to visual flying. I could not return my scan for even a split second to the instruments. I had to follow the lights and try to figure out a horizon so I could land this beast.

What happened next is remarkable to me. Steve was a good stick and he proved it right here. In a P-3 cockpit, if the pilot says, "Call my speeds," then the copilot will normally reply with two speeds that are determined by a chart over his head based upon aircraft weight. The first speed is the target for flaring if landing with approach flaps and the second is the speed for flaring with land flaps. There is a massive configuration change when the flaps are dropped from about 17 degrees to over 40 degrees so the speeds reported by the copilot might sound like, "145, 131."

I was working feverishly to keep sight of the approach lights and maintain sufficient visual reference to determine my altitude on short final. I did not dare look into the cockpit to check the rate at which my airspeed was slowing. So when I said to Steve, "Call my speeds" he responded perfectly. Rather than repeat the two speeds he had read from the chart as we started the approach, he gave me exactly what I needed.

"Passing 142, 140, 138, 135..." he called out as I neared the flare rotate point.

Sometimes flying in a multi-place aircraft is a real blessing.

We skimmed over the trucks parked on the approach end of the runway and I got the main mounts on the deck, on centerline...I think. With the nose high in a flare attitude I lost sight of the runway due to the blowing snow. I was not sure how far we had rolled down the runway when I got the nose wheel on the deck, so I quickly brought the prop levers into full reverse to stop our roll. Immediately we were in a complete white out. The props were blowing a snow cloud in front of us as we tried to get stopped. After a short while, my muscle memory told me I should bring the props out of reverse because we should have stopped by now. When I did I discovered that we had not only stopped, we were rolling backwards!

Now relaxed that we were safe on the ground, we taxied over to the end of the runway to a safe area and shut down the engines. We could not taxi to the ramp until we safe'd the mine shapes by putting pins in the pylons. While the ordnance man and second mech were doing that, I looked at the FE and 2P. They were both exhausted. I felt the same way. It had been a long day.

I said to the flight deck crew, "Once we get gas we need to fly back to Okinawa this evening so ops can use the plane for tomorrow's flight schedule."

Both these sailors dropped their heads and were searching their minds and hearts for enough energy and will to continue. Frowns covered their faces.

Then I added with a smile, "But I'm the PPC and it is my call that we need to hit the club and relax tonight. I'm going to call ops and tell them to work around the missing aircraft because we won't be back until tomorrow. It's a safety issue, don't you know."

They smiled and the thought of liberty replaced the dread of another long flight tonight. They both knew no one could tell the MO and former Safety Officer to ignore his best judgment and get airborne when safety was a concern.

I must have been getting old at age 35, because the only relaxing I did on that night of liberty was to eat a good meal and then early to bed for a long sleep.

*****

Just as in NATO, we also "showed the flag" with our allies in WESTPAC.

My crew and a select number of ground-pounder maintainers drew the four day flight to U-Tapao, Thailand. Upon arrival where at one time acres of B-52s were stationed during the Vietnam War, ours was one of only six aircraft on the Royal Thai Air Force Airfield. The massive parking ramps and taxi ways that had supported the bombers and KC-135s only fifteen years before were now overrun with weeds growing through cracks in the pavement. It was like landing at a ghost town.

The senior enlisted crew member was the flight engineer who had just put on his chief anchors, so I put him in charge of getting the air crew and maintainers over to Pattaya Beach and checked into the hotel. Pattaya Beach was a resort city frequented by European jet setters and it specialized in the sex trade. I had visited there when aboard the Schofield and knew it to be a wild liberty town for sailors, so I knew my men would need appropriate adult supervision. I stressed this to the new chief and he promised to watch over our young sailors.

After their bus departed, I led the five officers in the crew to the O'club for a short coordination and planning meeting and a buffet lunch. When we walked into the O'club the ghost town feeling was greatly amplified. The place was huge, but most rooms were empty with the lights turned off. In a small back room was a single folding table with food set on it. We discussed the planned flights for the next two days with our Thai hosts and then we were given a ride to the hotel in Pattaya Beach.

Now the chief had said during the entire flight from Okinawa that since it was past the "PCOD" he was going to be "good" in Thailand. "PCOD" stood for "Putang Cut Off Date," meaning it was too late to partake of hookers and still have time for a series of anti-VD shots to be complete before seeing your wife during the mid-deployment leave period. Each crew was given a ten day leave period once during the deployment and many either made the long trip home to visit for a couple of days, or met the wife in Hawaii for a short vacation, or some officers even brought their wives to Okinawa for a couple of weeks. Our crew's leave period would commence one week after we returned from Thailand.

Knowing sailors very well, I had a recent article from the *New York Times* copied and distributed to everyone making the Thailand trip. The article stated that there were statistics that indicated that nearly half of the hookers in Pattaya Beach were HIV positive. I didn't think it would convince any of them to visit the historical monuments instead of the bars, but I hoped maybe, at least, they would try to be careful and "safe."

When the officers arrived at the hotel, I dropped my bag off in my room and then went to find the chief to make sure the men had all been billeted appropriately. I found his room and before I could knock on the door, I heard the sounds of a rumpus from inside. It did not subside, so I went ahead and knocked...loudly.

Soon the chief opened the door. He was standing there buck naked and behind him was the second mech chasing and being chased over the beds and around the room by two hookers. All three of them were naked, too.

"All the crew got checked-in okay, Chief?" I asked.

"Oh, yes sir, I have a list of their room numbers if you need it," he answered with no modesty even pretended.

"No, you just keep track of them," I answered and then I smiled and added a question, "You being good, Chief?"

"I'm tryin', MO, I'm tryin'," he said with a smile and then I left.

The next day the ground pounders were free to enjoy liberty after they helped us launch for a surface surveillance mission in the Gulf of Thailand. We carried with us five pilots from the Royal Thai Air Force so they could observe how a P-3 operates. I am afraid it was not the most pleasant experience for these guests. There were a lot of targets to buzz and get pictures of, so we did some rather serious yanking and banking for patrol multi-engine platforms. Most of the guest pilots got airsick.

When we were above 5,000 feet I told my copilot to get out of the pilot's seat and I invited the guest pilots to take turns flying. I was extremely surprised by their reaction. No one wanted to take the opportunity to fly this new airplane! Finally, the most senior pilot coerced the most junior to accept the invitation. I sensed that none of the pilots had ever flown an airplane this big and none wanted to lose face by screwing it up. Better not to try and keep your pride than expose yourself to ridicule...understandable attitude, but completely opposite of an American Naval Aviator.

The next day, the three pilots on our crew got to fly a hop with our hosts. While the rest of the crew enjoyed liberty, we got to fly...which was very preferable to me!

We boarded the Royal Thai Air Force Fokker F-27 and flew out over the Gulf and tooled around a little. Then we landed at an airfield on the Malaysian Peninsula portion of Thailand. Our hosts took us out to town and bought us lunch at one of their favorite cafes. During the lunch, I noticed that two of the pilots slammed back three bottles each of tall Asahi beers. I just figured they were not returning with us to U-Tapao and didn't think anything of it until I saw then strapping into the pilot seats preparing to take off. Now, in the U.S. Navy we have the "twelve hours, bottle to throttle" rule, but I guess the Thai's don't.

On the flight back two things happened that still strike me as funny. After we were over the Gulf, the senior pilot on the crew climbed out of the left seat and invited me to sit there. Always wanting the best seat in the house, I naturally jumped at the chance and slid into the pilot seat. The copilot did not speak English so he just smiled and nodded. I guessed that meant he wanted me to take the controls and fly, which I eagerly did.

As I was making a couple of gentle turns to get the feel of this F-27, the copilot pointed down and indicated by reference to the altimeter that I should descend to one thousand feet. Or at least I think that is what he said. I pushed the nose over and then took a little throttle out to keep my speed from zooming away from me. Just then, I noticed the copilot climbing out of his seat and going aft to the main cabin. I figured he was getting out to let the more senior pilot have the seat. At least, that is what I thought...

As I leveled off at 1,000 feet I was still flying solo. No pilot came to the cockpit. I guess they had ridden with me yesterday and figured if I could push a P-3 through the sky then this twin-engined bird was no challenge for me. Just like their judgment to drink and fly was faulty to my way of thinking, betting their lives on the fact I could fly their plane seemed faulty as well.

After nearly fifteen minutes, the senior pilot finally slid into the right seat. Twenty minutes after that, my crew copilot replaced me in the left seat. Soon we were back at U-Tapao and I folded down the jump seat just behind the cockpit to watch my copilot make his first ever attempt at landing a Dutch made aircraft. His approach was good, but his airspeed got away from him and we overshot the runway and took it around. I made a mental note that this airplane, unlike a big fat P-3, will continue to race through the air when you decrease power.

Knowing that little fact made it 100% easier for me to take my turn at trying to land the plane. By starting earlier to decrease my airspeed I was able to have a better set-up on final. As we descended through 500 feet, the Thai pilot did something that again, in my book, was real faulty judgment.

He took his hands off the yoke, raised them over his head and put both feet on the floor. Then he turned his face towards me and said, "You do good! You land!"

If I went by this guy's breath, he was definitely under the influence. If I had a match, I could have lit his breath! Based on his trust of a pilot he had only flown with once, I think his actions would also qualify him as being suspiciously under the influence. The aircraft was easy to land so we all lived despite his poor judgment.

The next morning before dawn we gathered at the bus to be taken back to the airfield from the hotel. At the scheduled bus departure time we were still missing one shipmate. No one had seen this third class petty officer since he hooked up with a young woman at a bar last night. I was getting irritated when a police car drove up and parked next to the bus.

Out of the car stepped the policeman, a mama-san and my sailor. I got off the bus and talked to the trio. I discovered that my sailor had the choice of paying the mama-san twenty dollars or going to a Thai jail. Like an idiot, this young sailor was refusing to pay "on principle." He had paid the hooker and he had paid the bartender to get her out of the bar and he had paid for the hotel room, but he had neglected to pay the mama-san for her girl's service.

I asked the sailor if he had the twenty dollars and he assured me he did. When I suggested that he pay the mama-san and get on the bus, he objected saying he couldn't do it because it was "the principle of the thing." I questioned his principles if it was okay to pick up a hooker, but not okay to pay the market rate for her service.

When he still refused to pay, I pulled out a twenty and gave it to the mama-san.

"You can do that, sir," the sailor said with emotion, "but I'm not going to pay you back—it's the principle!"

When we got to the airfield it was just before full sunrise. We were dropped off about a hundred yards from where the plane was parked. We grabbed our gear and started trekking across the weed covered ramp. About ten yards in front of my 3P and me walked the two acoustic sensor operators. As they stepped over another line of weeds in the pavement all of a sudden the line moved! You've never seen two sailors jump so high from a flat-footed start! An eight-foot long snake had been lying across the old taxi way and moved when aroused by the clumping of the flight boots.

The rest of us immediately dug out our flashlights and started carefully scanning the ground in front of us.

We flew back to Kadena and the next morning I was sitting at my desk when the Maintenance Master Chief stopped in to update me on what had happened while I was off the island for four days. He started by asking how my trip had been.

"It went fine, Master Chief," I shared, "except for..." and then I casually shared how I had to shell out twenty dollars to keep one of our maintainers out of a Thai jail.

Smoke started coming out of the Master Chief's ears and his jaw tightened like a large torque wrench had been applied to it. He was so embarrassed by the actions of one of *his* sailors that initially he could not say a word. The idea that a sailor would not be totally supportive of his own department head was totally foreign to a professional such as the master chief. It was obvious to him that there was a junior sailor who needed a lesson in pride of his department, MO, and squadron.

When the Master Chief reached into his wallet and slapped a twenty on my desk I was not surprised. What he said was not a surprise either, "MO, I'll take care of this. He will pay...boy will he pay."

"Thanks, Master Chief," was all I said and then I let him do what master chiefs in the Navy do.

That sailor had the opportunity to ponder the structure of the chain-of-command for many hours while he completely repainted the entire Navy Batchelor Enlisted Quarters on base all by himself...and he never left the island again until we rotated back to Moffett Field.

I think he learned that you never embarrass the master chief.

*****

There were a couple of other things I recall about that trip to Pattaya Beach. The officers on the crew spent one night out investigating the entertainments offered on the main strip. The one place I remember was this open air joint situated on a pier jutting out over the water. It had a thatched roof and the sides were half-walls of bamboo. It was full of European tourists as well as many locals. It was more of a club than a restaurant. And it had a floor show.

In the center of the table area was a wooden stage about one foot higher than the pier floor and about ten yards square. It doubled as a dance floor as well as the stage for the floor show. Everyone took their seats and out came a group of modestly dressed Thai women dancers. They did what I thought might be a folk dance of the region, but soon it devolved into something else entirely. As the music moved from a waltz pace to more of a rock-and-roll beat, the dancers started to shed some of their costumes. Soon, it resembled the midnight girlie show at a Las Vegas hotel. The women retained their pasties and G-strings and high heels, but not much else.

As the music died down so did the lights. The troupe of girls exited and a single dancer took center stage in a spotlight. She was dressed in a G-string and attached to her nipples were eight-inch long tassels. The new music started and it consisted of nothing but a drum. The beat began slowly and then as her dance progressed it got faster and faster and her gyrations kept pace with it. Just as she got the tassels swinging to the beat, both going clockwise in a fast circle, the spotlight faded to black. In the darkness she lit the tassels and all you could see was the flaming tassels swinging full circles. The twin flaming tassels first circled clockwise, and then they reversed and went counter-clockwise. Then, with the crowd really hooting and hollering, the tassels started to twirl in counter-rotating directions! And then they reversed and twirled in a counter-rotating fashion the opposite direction! This performer was talented and would have been a top billed act in the old burlesque shows.

Something to remember...but the night wasn't over and there was another memory ahead.

In the Philippines they are called Jeepneys, which is a Toyota pick-up with bench seats built in the truck bed and a roof built over the top. They are a form of taxi and you hire them like you would a cab. In Thailand the same thing is called a Baht Bus. The currency of Thailand is the Baht, hence the name of the local transportation.

After the floor show on the pier, it was past midnight and so our little gang of five officers flagged down a Baht Bus to carry us back to our hotel. We had learned that since there were no meters in these local cabs, it was important to negotiate the price before you departed for your destination. It was my turn to pay for the Baht Bus so I asked the driver the charge to take us to the Hilton. He said forty Baht. That equated to about $1.25 so it seemed a fair price for this one mile ride. We all piled in the back of the pick-up and he took us directly to the hotel.

Upon arrival, the other officers got off and walked into the hotel. I went around to the driver to pay him. I started to get out my money when he said, "That be fifty Baht."

If he had said fifty Baht before we had departed I would think it fair, but he had quoted forty Baht and his attempt to extort another ten from me hit a nerve. He was the last in a long list of street merchants who had been pinging on me for the past couple of days, and his was the straw that broke the camel's back. The fact that I had intended to give him a ten Baht tip was not important to me...it was the "principle" of the thing.

I told the driver, "No! You said forty Baht. It is forty Baht."

He replied, "No! Fifty Baht."

I started to restate my side of the argument when I noticed that his buddy sitting next to him in the cab took the term "riding shotgun" quite literally. Beneath his legs he pulled out a sawed off shotgun and pointed it at me.

Suddenly I had no "principles." A quick risk-benefit calculation in my head determined that it wasn't worth getting shot over thirty-three cents American.

I gave the driver fifty Baht plus another sixty Baht tip. It seemed worth it to me at the time.

*****

While deployed to Kadena, a couple of typhoons came across the island. When this happened the hangar queen and two other birds were housed inside our hangar. The other six birds had to fly away to another location not in the track of the typhoon. All work would be stopped by those left on the island and many would hunker down to ride out the storm in very popular "typhoon parties."

The night before the arrival of one typhoon the Air Force closed the runway as they ran a drill. Unfortunately, we had a plane out on a mission and when it returned, the runway was closed. The PPC landed the plane at Naha Airport, the civilian air terminal on the southern tip of Okinawa. The crew was bussed back to the air base and the plane remained secured on the civilian's flight line.

The next morning we needed to retrieve the plane for two reasons. First, a typhoon was expected to hit late that afternoon and second, the Japanese were really unhappy to have an American military plane parked on their airport due to a strain in international relations at that time.

I gathered a copilot, flight engineer and after-observer and the duty vehicle took us to Naha commercial airport. We planned on a ten minute flight to Kadena Air Base and then to lodge the bird in the hangar before the terrible weather hit. All other airplanes except the hangar queen and one other had been flown away, so once we got this bird back in the barn and shut the doors we were ready to ride out the typhoon.

During the preflight I had second thoughts about this simple plan. The winds were so heavy that the airframe rocked rather substantially while still tied down and in the chocks. The wind was coming from the north and blowing right down the Naha runway so I figured if I could safely taxi to the end of the runway, takeoff would be a piece of cake. My concern was the direction of the Kadena Air Base runways. They were oriented fifty degrees to the east, which meant a strong northerly crosswind upon landing.

It took a little time to safely taxi at a slow, controlled speed to reach "position and hold" on the runway. Once I had clearance for takeoff and released the brakes, the plane leaped into the air as soon as the power levers started moving forward. The aircraft's light weight and the strong nose wind made this 45 ton assembly of aluminum and steel behave like a paper kite in a heavy breeze.

At the end of the runway I made a climbing right turn and switched from Naha Tower to Kadena Tower for permission to make a straight-in visual approach to Runway 5. As every other flight was grounded due to the worsening weather, it was no problem getting clearance.

I saw the field and started my descent and completed the landing checklist. However, the cross winds seemed to be exceeding the maximum permitted for a P-3 landing. The winds had grown since we had left Kadena and made our trip to Naha. Earlier it had been a steady crosswind of 45 degrees at 10 knots, gusting to 20. My crab necessary to maintain the right track over the ground as I flew towards the runway told me that it was now a lot stronger and more from the side than before.

The maximum crosswind for the P-3 is determined by how much upwind wing can be lowered to keep the airplane from being pushed off the side of the runway. The challenge on this landing was to maintain centerline without dipping the upwind wing so much that the #1 propeller struck the pavement. When that happens, it is never a good thing. The maximum angle of bank to prevent this is only about ten degrees.

As I got lower and neared the runway threshold I kicked out my crab and lowered my left wing to maintain my direction in the crosswind. It was then that I noted the real possibility that today the crosswinds might be exceeding the NATOPS limits on this airframe. I had to hold at least thirty degrees down wing to track over the runway.

About this time, my options were rather limited. Naha had the wind down its runway, but it was seriously doubtful that the civilians there would approve my request to return. Fatema Marine Air Base was also on Okinawa, but its runways were aligned the same direction as Kadena's so it would have the same crosswinds. I did not have enough fuel to divert to another island somewhere and I could not stay aloft waiting for the weather to improve as the typhoon was quickly barreling down on Okinawa.

So, I tried the only option I felt I had. I continued my approach and had the copilot call out anytime my angle of bank exceeded ten degrees as we got in the flare. The tower was reporting crosswinds to be steady at 22 knots with gusts to 35. I could land this thing with a 22 knot crosswind...so I just had to get lucky and time it to touch down between the irregular gusts.

I started my flare right over the numbers and then it was "Mr. Toad's Wild Ride" for the next half minute until I could arrest the left to right drift with less than ten degrees angle of bank and then take that moment to plant the main mounts on the deck...something we called a "firm Navy touchdown." As soon as the gear touched the asphalt I closed out the power and pushed the nose wheel down.

Despite being very similar to the delicate taxing that I had done at Naha, being safely on the ground made the challenge of getting the plane back to the hangar this time seem much easier.

Two hours later the squadron hangar and offices were all buttoned up and the typhoon parties were under way at the billeting buildings.

*****

During this Kadena, Okinawa deployment we had to maintain a small detachment at Misawa, Japan to augment the deployed squadron there for a few weeks. Our crew terminated a mission at Misawa and then secured for crew rest with the expectation of being put on the flight schedule the next afternoon.

I got a call before sunrise from my classmate, Rory, who was the detachment Officer-in-Charge at the time. He asked me to come down to the squadron spaces to discuss a special flight. Upon my arrival he asked if I would be willing to ferry one of our squadron's brand new P-3C Update III aircraft to Atsugi, Japan so senior Japanese defense officials could inspect it.

It was a simple enough request except for one thing. The plane had to be in Atsugi by mid-morning and the current weather was so bad that no take-offs or landings were permitted at Misawa. That is, no take-offs were permitted by instrument rated pilots holding a "Standard Card." A minimum ceiling and visibility requirement is normally required for take-offs so that the plane can return to land at the field should something go wrong.

Rory had called me in to ask if I would attempt the flight because I was the only squadron pilot currently in Misawa with a "Special Card." A "Special" instrument qualification (or as it was usually called, a "Blue Card"—because it actually was printed on blue stock) allowed the pilot to take-off with no weather minimums being imposed. However, NAPTOPS regulations clearly stated that take-offs only should be attempted when the weather is below minimums *"if loss of aircraft and crew is considered an acceptable risk."* In other words, don't do it just to save face with our allies by getting a static display into position and avoid having to reschedule the event. The option to use a Blue Card to take-off in zero/zero weather was there for wartime or emergency situations.

Rory knew this when he asked if I was willing to try to fly the mission. Rory also knew that I would probably seriously consider the challenge. I had no problem ignoring the restriction on when to use a Blue Card because it seemed rather silly to me. After all, *every* time a plane is launched you accept the possibility of potential loss of the aircraft and crew. The only way to avoid that danger is to park, chock and chain the birds and never "break the surly bonds of earth."

So I went over to base operations and got a good weather briefing and filed my flight plan to fly down to Atsugi. The weather forecast was for clear flying once we moved south of the fog and low ceiling hanging over the Misawa area.

I told Rory that I would load up with a partial crew and then taxi down to the end of the runway. If I thought the weather was good enough to take-off based upon what I saw and felt, then we would go. Otherwise, I would just taxi back to the ramp and he would have to send the Japanese our apologies. He was pleased with that plan, so we called in a copilot, flight engineer, aft observer, and a NFO to act as the host at the event. Just as we were finishing loading fuel onboard, Rory came to the plane with a Navy captain in tow. The senior officer was wearing a khaki uniform and a flight jacket. Rory wanted to know if the captain could bum a ride down to Atsugi as he needed to return to his job. I said, "No problem" and had the aft observer give the captain a brief on P-3 safety procedures.

We strapped in and taxied to the end of the runway. The weather was not any better, so I waited there as I hoped a thin spot in the fog and clouds might drift by. After ten long minutes I thought the visibility had improved to where I could see a hundred feet down the runway. I rolled onto the runway and started our take-off roll. We hit eighty knots and the engines were working just fine. A few seconds later I was starting to shift my entire scan to the instrument panel in order to rotate which is when I would lose all outside reference, when suddenly I heard the aft observer shout through the headset, "Bird strike number two engine!"

The flight engineer spoke just one word over the roar of the engines, "Confirmed."

I said loudly, "Abort!"

I pulled the four power levers back and lowered the nose wheel back to the deck. As I could not see the end of the runway, and although I was certain we had sufficient length remaining to stop, I continued to pull the power levers over the ramp into the ground operating range and went to full reverse thrust. Simultaneously, my left hand transitioned from the yoke to the ground steering wheel by my left knee. Soon we were stopped and taxied back to the hangar area.

I notified Rory of the bird strike and told him via radio that once the maintainers had inspected the intakes and we did a high power check, I would give it another shot.

Once parked by the hangar, I went back to the galley area to pop the top on the diet Dr. Pepper I had put in the refer. I needed something sweet to help pull me out of my early morning, minimum-sleep funk. As I did this, the Navy captain asked what had happened.

Having a bad attitude that morning, I answered him flippantly, "It just didn't feel right. I had no good vibes so I stopped."

He gave me a confused look before I continued.

"Actually, we had to abort due to a bird strike," I informed him.

Then this captain wearing an aviator's jacket asked a question that surprised me by being so snarky, "Do you mean to tell me that a tiny little bird would cause this big airplane any trouble?"

I was tired and in a bad mood, so I instinctively did not let that slam pass unchallenged. Here was this obvious jet jockey from the carrier down in Yokosuka trying to tell me how to fly my airframe! How typically arrogant of those "holier than thou" rocket riders! So I said, "I don't know how you do it in your community, but we always abort if we can after we ingest a bird because I like to fly with all four engines working."

Then I turned and stomped back to the cockpit. The last thing I needed this morning was some stuck-up know-it-all TACAIR hotdog sniping at the way I flew this aircraft. My attitude was, "Go ahead. Say something more and you'll be riding the train back to the Tokyo area."

The maintainers did their thing and we passed the power check and once again took our spot at the end of the runway. Once again I waited until I thought I saw a break in the weather and then we raced down the runway. This time we got airborne and after only fifteen minutes we were flying under blue skies all the way to Atsugi.

It was on the transit south that I learned that the captain's question was not meant as a dig from one aviator to another. It seems he was wearing a flight jacket, but in reality he was a Surface Warfare Officer. He really did not understand aviation procedures regarding bird strikes.

But I still didn't apologize.

I was tired and in a surly mood.

*****

Buddy Catron was the Operations Officer (OPsO) and I was the MO. Buddy was a "transfosite" pilot. He had been an NFO and then was selected to return to flight school to earn his pilot wings. We got along well together and many in the squadron referred to us as the "Tron Brothers." We were the last two squadron pilots left when it was time to take the last airplane home to Moffett Field, which of course was the hangar queen.

Patrol squadrons relieve each other on deployment over a ten day period. On the first day, two planes depart from the deployment site for home at the same time two of the relieving squadron aircraft depart for the deployment site. Two days later another couple of aircraft make the switch. This goes on every other day or so until there is only one plane left in each squadron to make the switch.

The benefits of this type of phased turnover are twofold. It keeps sufficient airplanes and crews available at the deployment site to fly regularly scheduled missions, and it provides a means to get the hangar queen back into flying shape. This is done by cannibalizing the first airplane that makes it back to Moffett Field. The parts needed to make the hangar queen airworthy are stripped from the first plane that returned home and transported to the deployment site by the relieving aircraft flying out to WESTPAC.

Now, traditionally for many years, P-3s returning from WESTPAC would take two days to return to Moffett Field. The first day they would fly to Barber's Point Hawaii and go through customs and spend the night. The next day they would fly to California and meet their loved ones after being gone six months.

Buddy and I questioned why we had to add an extra day to the deployment with the stopover in Hawaii. There were two reasons given for this procedure. The first was "no families want to stand around in sight of their sailors and wait while customs officials check everything being brought back on the airplane. The second reason was really the main cause of doing it in two steps..."because it had always been done that way."

So, Buddy and I went to the CO and presented our plan for the deployment turnover that eliminated the stop in Hawaii. Our plan was to preposition the returning aircraft the day before we were to leave the 7th Fleet area of operations by flying them to Misawa, Japan. The jet stream at that time of year was such that it was easily possible for a P-3 to depart northern Japan and fly non-stop across the Pacific and arrive on top of Moffett Field with the necessary 8,000 pounds of reserve fuel. We had investigated the possibility of completing the customs inspection right at Moffett Field by having a customs official drive down from San Francisco International Airport. The customs officials were more than willing to do it and make it a "non-problem."

As the OpsO and MO we hit the CO with a coordinated, enthusiastic proposal. Our skipper was an NFO who did the math and he was the kind of officer who was open to doing something differently. He approved the plan and our first two aircraft and crews flew to Misawa the day before the turnover was to begin. The next day they successfully made the over ocean transit and arrived with sufficient reserve fuel to prove the feasibility of the plan. Upon arrival at Moffett Field the good people at Customs cleared each flight completely in less than five minutes each, so the families had no wait to meet their returning sailors. Thus, VP-40 became the first squadron in memory to return from deployment "non-stop."

Things worked well for the first eight aircraft. The relieving squadron maintainers assisted the few mechs and techs we had left at Kadena to patch together the hangar queen. The relieving CO took responsibility for VP operations out of Kadena and 23 VP-40 sailors boarded the last plane and flew to Misawa. After being away from home for six months, all of us were quite anxious for the next afternoon to arrive for it was then that we could board our plane and start the last step to our wives, girl friends, kids and/or favorite bar.

However, we were in the hangar queen, so the preflight in the late morning of our last WESTPAC hop did not go smoothly. There were many little problems that we could get resolved, but two of the preflight hiccups promised to be deal breakers. The P-3C has two inertials used for navigation over water. Both of ours failed to align during preflight. Technical assistance was provided by the squadron deployed to Misawa, but it looked doubtful that either of them could be fixed, and we were required to have at least one to fly non-stop from Japan to California.

The other issue was more problematic. In the port wheel well gas drops were noted. This meant gas was coming from the internal wing tank. As the PPC and MO, I had to decide if the gas was from a leak...or if it was just a "seep." A "leak" would mean at least a four day delay in heading for home. The plane would have to be de-fueled one day and then the tanks vented for at least 48 hours before a mechanic could crawl inside to conduct an inspection. Then the repair would be at least a day, if it was possible.

If it was only a "seep," well then, it was not a downing gripe and we could takeoff and have it checked when we landed at Moffett Field.

The difference between a leak and a seep was the rate at which the drops formed and fell from the underside of the wing. If less than four drops fell during a thirty second period then it was a seep. The flight engineer and I watched the drops form and fall as we counted to thirty...*very, very* quickly. Guess what? Yep, it was a seep.

Through some magic with paperclips and rubber bands our IFT with assistance from the couple of ground pounder maintainers we had onboard was able to get one of the inertials to align. He told me he was not sure how long it would stay on line, but it did pass the preflight check now. I asked the navigator how his celestial navigation skills were over the open water at night. He was married to a good looking wife whom he was anxious to see again, so he assured me he could make the HO-249 Celestial Sight Reduction Tables sing and dance better than anyone in the fleet. With that assurance I told the CO we were good-to-go and we taxied to the end of the runway.

The hangar queen met the minimums for flight and nothing more. All the really important stuff worked, but some of the other items that aircrews were used to having did not. One of the inoperative pieces of equipment was the autopilot. To many pilots who fly smaller airframes, the loss of the autopilot does not sound like a big deal. However, flying a dozen hours, mostly at night, at high altitude in a P-3 with no help from the autopilot is extremely tiring. The Orion has a natural waddle at cruise. It pitches like a big boat in a sea with long waves and rolls in a systematic pattern with the pitching. Maintaining precise altitude and heading are a constant chore without the autopilot. On this long flight, that chore was shared between Buddy and me, as we were the only two pilots onboard.

Another challenge of cruising without the autopilot was the length of the fuselage. With 23 persons onboard, every time two of them walked from the aft to the front of the tube it was like a quarter-ton pallet sliding the length of the airframe in a cargo plane. The long moment arm associated with this cargo shift would immediately impact the pilot's attempts to hold a precise altitude. And sailors being sailors, once they observed this condition, four of them started running together from the aft galley to the navigator's station near the cockpit. Ha...ha...great joke. After a couple of laps and a few choice words from the cockpit crew and CO, the game grew boring for them and they stopped.

I flew the first hour and Buddy the next. Our rotation at the controls soon decreased as our fatigue increased during this night flight. By the end of the flight we were passing control back and forth ever ten minutes due to lack of energy to maintain focus for any longer without a break.

We flew the great circle route from Japan to California. Near the halfway point we had a decision to make. If the Jet Stream tailwinds were less than predicted there was a point about midway where we could make a left turn and fly to Adak in the Aleutians to get gas and spend the night. Just as the previous eight crews had experienced, when we reached the decision point, our tailwinds were super and our fuel flow right on target, so we pressed on towards California.

About 500 miles beyond the decision point we noticed our 100 knot tailwind starting to decrease. Before long it was only twenty knots on the tail. Our ground speed was correspondingly slower as a result. So Buddy and I pulled out our "whiz wheels" and calculated how much gas we would have upon arriving on top of Moffett Field. Our calculations resulted in an estimate of only 6,000 pounds of reserve, which was low but not critical.

We continued on with this reduced ground speed for the next 1,000 miles and as we flew into the rising sun and the comfort of daylight, we began to anticipate the homecoming just 500 miles ahead. Then this good situation started the transition to bad and in quick fashion it became ugly. The tailwind of twenty knots moved around to a crosswind of twenty knots. We re-calculated our fuel usage and now the result was an estimate of just 5,000 pounds of reserve upon arrival.

For hours we had been committed to reaching Moffett Field. There was no other option closer. So when the winds swung around to become a thirty knot headwind with 500 miles yet to go, we knew we were screwed.

I requested a climb to higher altitude from air traffic control and received clearance to 29,000 feet. The higher you fly, the less gas it takes to keep our turboprops spinning. The service ceiling of the P-3 is 30,000 feet. Planes flying on an easterly heading are assigned odd altitudes so as not to run into westerly heading aircraft flying at even altitudes. So we were as high as we could legally fly.

But the winds were not any better at this altitude. And worse yet, clouds were directly in our path at this altitude which meant if we entered them we would need to switch on engine anti-ice with its associated increase in fuel consumption. We needed to go higher.

Here was when all that study and oral examination boards' preparation on aircraft systems paid off. Buddy and I knew that the service ceiling on the P-3 was due to the efficiency of the Engine Driven Compressors (EDC) and not to any prop, engine or control limitations. Above 30,000 feet, the EDCs just could not pump enough air into the fuselage to maintain a cabin altitude of less than 10,000 feet. This was the maximum altitude you can fly without oxygen. The crew only had seven walk-around bottles of oxygen that lasted 22 minutes each available to be shared by the twenty sailors in the tube. However, the cockpit oxygen system was sufficient to supply the pilots and flight engineer with three hours of good air. Knowing from our rather detailed training that a pilot without oxygen can fly for a couple of hours at altitudes up to 13,000, Buddy and I had no problem ignoring the NATOPS service ceiling imposed on this flight. We figured it was better to bet on the EDCs working than to follow the letter of the law and land on the beach short of San Francisco Bay.

I requested a higher altitude from ATC. My request was denied. Once again, our training worked to our advantage. We knew ATC tried to keep maximum separation between jets flying at fast speeds at high altitudes, so breaking the 30,000 barrier by a slower prop aircraft would screw up their system. More importantly, we knew ATC kept these big distances between high flying jets because there was no radar following hundreds of miles out over the Pacific.

I ignored the ATC rejection of my request and told Buddy to keep us above the approaching cloud layer. We eventually settled at a VFR altitude (as if there was one that high) of 33,500 feet. And that P-3 still wanted to climb higher if we would let it. Of course, not knowing exactly just how far out the ATC radar reached, I did take the precaution of turning off our IFF altitude reporting instrument.

We successfully flew over the cloud layer for 100 miles and then descended to our assigned altitude once we had passed the clouds and "radar contact" was reported by ATC. By this time the CO and navigator were spinning their "whiz wheels" and trying to act casual when they entered the cockpit to read the fuel gages and fuel flow instruments. They began to sweat bullets like Buddy and I had been doing for over an hour. Now the "whiz wheel" magic showed us on top Moffett Field with less than 4,000 pounds of gas.

I didn't share it with the others, but I had a memory in the forefront of my mind that bothered me. I was remembering the day as a 3P when I taxied down to the end of the runway to conduct a high power check and an engine flamed out with 1,000 pounds of fuel being indicated on the tank feeding it. I remembered how on that day I learned that our fuel gages become unreliable with low fuel in the tank. Let's see...four engines and only a total of 4,000 pounds of fuel in four tanks...uh-oh.

By my calculations we could very easily run out of fuel just as we crossed over the Coastal Mountain range that separated Moffett Field from the Pacific Ocean.

WOW! Once again I was asking myself, "How can you run out of gas in a P-3 when you start with 60,000 pounds?"

I told ATC that we did not want to descend until the very last second and they acknowledged by passing us to Approach Control. On my initial call to Approach Control I requested direct to Moffett Field. In response to this request we were directed to turn right as they were vectoring us to the initial point for the TACAN approach to Moffett Field. That was Hooks intersection and every west coast P-3 pilot knew it well. Hooks was thirty miles out on a straight-in approach to Runway 32 at Moffett Field. That meant we would have to motor thirty miles out from the field and then thirty miles back to land. We did not have the gas for an extra sixty miles.

When I insisted that ATC just give us direct vectors to Moffett Field and let us enter the VFR pattern, I got push back from the controller and he directed us to turn and go to Hooks. It was then that I declared "minimum fuel" to the controller.

"Are you declaring an emergency?" he asked.

If I said yes, then our homecoming arrival would include fire engines and ambulances rolling out to meet the aircraft. That would be embarrassing.

"No, I said 'minimum fuel,'" I replied clearly and then added, "We don't have the fuel to go to Hooks and back. Just get us over the airport and everything will be just fine."

He gave a direct vector to Moffett Field and we switched to the tower frequency. Initially the tower had trouble getting a visual on us because we were about three times as high as the normal pattern. But they cleared us to land and Buddy did a great job getting dirty, slowing and setting down in the first third of the runway. As soon as we cleared the duty runway, we shut down two engines and fed all the remaining gas to the inboard engines. I expected them to flame out at any second, so when the line man—my own departmental shipmate!—directed us the long way around the hangars so we could park with our exit right in front of the cheering dependents and the commodore with his staff who were all there to greet the last plane returning home from deployment, I got nervous. It would be extremely embarrassing to run out of gas while trying to taxi to the welcoming spot.

I directed the shut down of #2 engine and all the remaining gas be fed to the one remaining engine running. Much to my surprise our #3 engine kept running until we parked and lowered the ladder. Before I could finish the shut down checklist, the TACCO came forward and reported that the customs official had already been aboard and cleared our arrival; we were okay to deplane.

The CO got off and was greeted by the commodore and escorted to the big sheet cake on a table set up at the hangar entrance. A couple of very short "welcome home" and "well done" speeches were said as our aircrew and passengers rushed to the arms of their loved ones.

This was my sixth deployment and I knew my family would not mind if I finished the job before our homecoming. When I reached the bottom of the ladder I turned right and went straight to the port wheel well. It was easy to enter. Normally you have to duck your head to miss the open gear doors; this time I could walk right in because the airplane was so light the landing struts were fully extended. I examined the interior. It was totally stained by the red dye present in JP-5 aviation fuel.

I guess maybe, it had been a leak after all.

I was joined by the Maintenance Master Chief who smiled and nodded.

His only words were, "Welcome home, MO. I'll take care of this."

I nodded and went to greet my family.

Chapter Eight

More Recruiting Duty

After being selected for promotion to commander I had a good counseling session with the XO of the squadron. Previous choices I had made during my career meant the realistic chances of me being selected for a command tour in patrol aviation were slim to none... "and slim has left town." Like many communities in the naval officer corps, patrol aviators were expected to follow a very rigid career path. It went like this: flight school, first squadron tour, RAG instructor or similar shore duty, then a disassociated sea tour on a carrier, then war college and then a second squadron tour as a department head. Do well there and you will make commander and get screened for patrol squadron command, then perhaps do a Washington DC tour before returning to community to command a squadron. My career path was much different. Heck, I couldn't even go to the regular Navy War College in Newport, RI; I had to go to a foreign one! Everything about my choices of assignments made me the odd duck and the members of command selection boards took a dim view of applicants who strayed out of the community and odd choices.

So the XO and I decided the best next step was to take a negative in my background and make it into a positive. I requested duty on the staff of Commander, Navy Recruiting Command (COMNAVCRUITCOM or CNRC) in the hopes of getting sufficient "face time" with the admiral to earn selection as a commanding officer of a recruiting district. Following that plan, I was ordered to DC to work in the CNRC Plans and Policy department.

My first staff assignment was to be the "I gotta guy..." officer. Out in the field if a recruiter found an applicant he wanted to enlist but the guy had something in his background that made him ineligible for naval service, the recruiter could request a

CNRC waiver to enlist him. I was the officer they called to tell me the hard luck story of this potential sailor and to ask for a waiver. Invariably the first words out of the recruiter's mouth were always, "I gotta guy who..."

I had just settled into this job and was learning its requirements when the Executive Assistant (EA) to the admiral called me down to his office for a personal, individual conference. The EA was a captain with an office right outside the admiral's door and I was still a lieutenant commander and brand new to the staff, so this order initially gave me a little stress. I took comfort in the fact that the EA was from the patrol aviation community and was not a nuke like the admiral.

"Bob, you've been selected for 0-5, is that right?" the EA asked as I stood before his desk.

I nodded and he continued, "You were MO in your last duty, right?" I nodded and then he asked more questions, "Ever work in admin?"

"I had a short stint as the assistant admin officer during my first squadron tour, sir."

He smiled and put a check on a list in front of him. Then he asked, "Ever split or combine branches in a division?"

"Yes sir, I had a spare jg who needed a ground job so I split the AMEs and PRs into two branches."

"And the Material Control officer worked for you, right?" the EA wanted to know. I nodded and he asked, "Did you guys ever go to jail?"

I shook my head and he checked off another block on his list.

"One last question, Bob," he asked, "Have you already made any plans for over the Christmas holidays? Like a deposit on a cruise or you bought plane tickets back home for the family?"

I knew something was coming around the bend and straight for me, but I had no idea what it could be. It was only October so his asking about Christmas plans struck me as funny.

"Here's the story, Bob. The Chief of Naval Personnel was tasked to supply an officer to work on a special Joint Chiefs of Staff project. He passed the requirement down to us. "

As he was telling me this, I immediately recognized that as the new lieutenant commander on this staff I had become expendable...again...just like I was as an ensign when the Schofield had to supply an exchange officer or send an officer to shore patrol duty.

"JCS has tasked each service to send a specialist in human resources, financial management, or organizational development to serve on this new task force. Bob, from where I sit you are a friggin' specialist in each of these areas!"

That was the typical Navy attitude about supplying officers to wear a "purple suit." The traditional Navy did not trust officers who had left the cocoon of Navy Blue and worked with other services. Later things would change to where a joint tour was necessary to get promoted, but in 1987, we did not send our best and brightest to have their thinking corrupted by the Air Force and Army. But since my career path was already so screwed up, being assigned to a Joint Chiefs of Staff (JCS) task force couldn't hurt it much.

The EA then asked what my security clearance had been when I left the squadron a few weeks earlier. I told him it had been Top Secret/Special Intelligence but that I had no need for that level of clearance working at CRUITCOM so it had been pulled.

He looked at his watch and said, "Consider it reinstated effective immediately, paper work to follow. Now you had better hustle over to the Pentagon because you are already late for the Task Force initial organizational meeting."

Reverting to my plebe disposition, I answered, "Aye, aye, sir." Then as I turned to leave, I asked two basic questions. "What is the function of this JCS Task Force?"

"Oh, those civilians in the State Department finally finished years of negotiating the INF treaty with the commies. Now it has to be initiated in less than ninety days. It takes State six months to decide which commode to use in the head, so the start-up assignment was given to the military to get it done."

"Captain, I have one other immediate question. Where do I go to report in as a member of the new team?"

"JCS spaces at the Pentagon."

"Aye, aye, sir," I said with totally false bravado, which the EA was wise enough to sense.

"Bob, you ever been to the Pentagon?"

I shook my head.

The EA smiled at the thought of a fleet officer being thrown into the Pentagon world for the first time and said, "Just find the signs to the north parking lot and then use that entrance to the puzzle palace. Ask for directions to JCS spaces."

"Thank you, sir," I said as I departed to gather my sack lunch from the break room and my hat and blouse in my office. Finding the Pentagon would be easy because I passed it every day on my commute to CNRC headquarters located in Ballston. I was over 21 and an officer in the Navy so getting to where I was expected to be was not a problem for me.

However, I did have a rather significant problem. I had no idea what the "INF Treaty" was or what the JCS could possibly want some commander-select from CRUITCOM to do.

In the next four months I learned how business was done inside the beltway. I arrived at the JCS spaces and the designated conference room. The INF Team meeting had just broken up when I entered the room. As the others were hurriedly leaving the room I saw a familiar face. The task force was composed of two or three officers from each service. The other sailor was Bill Evans, an Academy classmate. He had just enough time to tell me that everyone was moving to a new headquarters for the task force located at Buzzard's Point in the Coast Guard Headquarters building by Fort McNair. I had no idea where that was located, but a city map and an ability to "follow my nose" to find things got me to the right spaces.

A meeting was scheduled to start ten minutes after my arrival. I used the time to pump Bill for a little background on what we were supposed to do. He got me up to speed on the INF Treaty with the Soviets. Its real title was the Intermediate-Range Nuclear Forces Treaty and it would require the United States and the Soviet Union to destroy all their short- and intermediate-range nuclear missiles in Europe. This treaty had been in work for nearly seven years when all of a sudden agreement seemed imminent. The implementation of the INF Treaty required that a baseline inspection and inventory of all the American and Soviet missiles be conducted within 90 days of ratification. The only government entity that had the capacity to move that quickly was the military. Our task force was created to meet the standards set by the treaty.

The organizational meeting we had was something I can never forget. A bunch of tables in a deserted office space were pushed into the shape of a rectangle. At one end of the room sat an Army brigadier general. Around the remaining tables were two Air Force lieutenant colonels, one Marine lieutenant colonel, three Army lieutenant colonels...and the two junior officers in the group, Bill and me, both lieutenant commanders. It was at this meeting that I learned the Army technique of "line-of-sight-tasking."

The general started right into assigning duties to each task force member. He would almost shout, "I need an inspection team guru!" and then he would point to an officer and say, "That's you." Next, he assigned team leaders for escort duties with the Soviets, and then he picked an officer to find spaces for the new On-Site Inspection Agency that was being established to continue the work of the task force after the first ninety days. He was nearing the end of his point and select method of assigning officers to different areas he thought would be needed. Personnel identification and administration and other specific duties were handed out. Bill, who was a member of the Navy Civil Engineer Corps, was given what I thought an appropriate assignment based on his background. He was in charge of locating office space in the U.S. and in Europe.

The last subject to be shouted by the general was, "I need a finance king! A money man!" I smiled upon hearing this because there were Air Force and Army officers around the tables who had plenty of experience in getting, spending and reporting about money floated between DOD departments. I was thinking how being this general's finance king would be the worst assignment possible, especially for a fleet pilot who had never played with money inside the beltway.

As I was thinking about the unattractiveness of such an assignment I noticed that every other officer around the table was all of a sudden counting their own shoe laces. All had their heads down and avoided eye contact with the general. So his eyes fell on me and since I seemed to be the only choice he had, he pointed at me and said loudly, "YOU! You're the finance king."

As naval officers are too well trained and ingrained with deference to higher ranking officers, the thought of complaining to this one-star that I was a terrible choice never entered my mind.

"Aye, aye, sir," was all I said.

*****

I believe that meeting was on a Monday afternoon. The general called me into his office and told me he was scheduled to be in the JCS tank and give a brief on the cost of this Treaty to DOD on Friday afternoon. The "tank" was the room all the four-star heads of each service used to meet. A one-star could really do damage to his reputation and possible promotions if he screwed up his "face time" in the tank.

I did not want to embarrass "my" general, but I was totally in over my head. The only thing I could think to do was to take a blank piece of paper and mimic what I did every month with the family budget. I listed all expected expenses by category and started making wild guesses on how much money each would require. Of course, when making this new federal agency budget I added five or six zeros to the numbers I used at home.

The Marine came over and saw me doing stubby pencil work trying to put this budget together. He was just finishing his masters in computer science and he volunteered to help me by bringing in his personal computer and building a spreadsheet for me. I had never seen a computer spreadsheet before, but I was real quick to see how I could drastically change the bottom line by making small alterations to my assumptions. If I raised the estimated cost-per-foot for office space leasing or changed the amount of space we estimated might be needed, the bottom line could be changed by millions...and all without me having to add or subtract or multiply with my stubby pencil.

I got input and suggestions from each of the other officers concerning how much money they felt might be needed to pay for their portion of the treaty implementation. Then I played with these inputs and generated a detailed budget that called for $80M to do the job right. I took my budget into the general on Wednesday night. He shook his head and said I was off.

I had no idea how he knew that and where I may have made my mistakes. So I just stood there in front of his desk, totally confused.

He finally looked up and said, "I saw an estimate last year put together by Sandia Labs and they estimated it would take a lot more money."

"Can you give me a hint on how much more?" I asked.

"About 120 million give or take, I believe," he said as I took the spreadsheet back from him.

"Let me work on this again and I'll bring it back in the morning," I said as I departed.

The next morning I gave him a budget that called for $143M to be spent on the treaty. He looked at the figures I had estimated and smiled and nodded his head.

"That looks good. Now take it to the DOD Comptroller and see what he thinks before I have to brief it in the tank tomorrow."

I got in my car and drove over to the Pentagon and the Comptroller squeezed me into his schedule. He had a good laugh at my budget, which obviously had been created by a DC amateur. I had taken my line items out to the nearest dollar. At his level they usually lopped off the last five or six zeros when estimating costs. But he liked it a lot and gave his blessing to go forward with the planned spending.

So, I created a 140 million dollar budget for a new federal agency from a blank piece of paper in under four days. This working in DC wasn't that hard.

*****

Once again I had transferred to a totally different military than I had been raised in. The Air Force and Army officers had a tendency to let formal military courtesy get lax. My classmate, Bill, the Marine task force member and I came from a much more formal service. Our fleet habits just could not be turned off and on.

The general had the only office with a door on it. The rest of the task force officers sat at desks spread around an open floor. Whenever the general left his office and approached a team member's desk the reaction of the officer sitting there would vary by his service. Air Force and Army officers were used to working around senior officers in the Pentagon and so they would remain seated and ask the general what he wanted.

This seemed very odd to we members of the Department of the Navy. Every time the general approached one of our desks we would pop to attention and present ourselves for tasking. Whenever a senior approached you in the Navy, you never remained sitting in his presence. It was not proper naval etiquette.

Well, one day the general came to my desk and I popped up. He asked his question and then returned to his office across the open floor as I sat down again. Once there, he turned around and returned to my desk. I popped up again to greet him. He claimed he forgot why he had come to my desk and he left. I sat down again. He immediately returned again so I popped up again. He said something that elicited a standard response of, "Aye, aye, sir." He turned his back to me and looked over at the Army and Air Force officers and mouthed, "Aye, aye" while he wore a big grin. I could see what he did in his reflection in the window of his office. The other officers started to laugh because he had included them in the joke. He thought it was fun to have the Navy officers and Marine pop up over and over again, and I guess it could be viewed as rather funny in their experience. And our use of "Aye, aye, sir" as a natural response to tasking tickled them with its quaintness.

But neither Bill, the Marine nor I could stop ourselves. It was just ingrained in us always to offer proper military courtesy to flag and general officers...and I never understood the familiarity the Army and Air Force officers showed around them.

*****

The guy who has the money gets to sit at the head of the table. That's what I learned over the next few months. I attended a half dozen meetings with different offices wanting money to pay for their contribution to implementing the INF treaty. At more than one meeting there were general officers sitting at the side of the table while the Navy lieutenant commander sat at the head of the table. I had the money so I got treated best.

It also helped that some rather high ranking people on President Reagan's staff wanted this arms treaty to be a success. Specifically, there was a letter signed by Colin Powell that basically said, "Give this officer what he wants." During this time I came to understand how Lieutenant Colonel North was able to wield so much power in trying to help the Contras.

One small example was when the general approached my desk and suggested that I might need help in setting up a disbursing system to distribute the millions of dollars that had been approved per the budget we had created. He suggested that I take a trip down to the Army Material Command (AMC) headquarters near the beltway and look up a certain Army captain.

I found Captain Leon at his desk in an open bay arrangement surrounded by civilian workers at the AMC. I approached him and asked if he wanted to spend the next few months working on a special project with the Joint Chiefs of Staff. He said yes, and with no further explanation we rode the elevator to see his boss's boss in a corner office high in the building. I explained that I needed Captain Leon to assist me and with no further discussion, this colonel released him to the task force. Leon and I rode down the elevator and returned to his desk. I told him to take everything he did not want to leave behind because the chances of him returning to this job were very slim.

Leon had already been selected for major and had seven years experience inside the beltway working with Army finance matters. He was invaluable to a Navy fleet pilot who knew nothing about how the world operated in the nation's capital. He pointed out the land mines before I tripped over them and he directed me in ways to get around regulations that might hinder our fast track project.

He was along on one of my trips to Langley to coordinate with the CIA. After going through the metal detectors and being hand screened, Leon and I were led to a small conference room deep in the interior of the building. The purpose of the meeting was to determine how millions of dollars necessary to fund counter-intelligence operations during the treaty inspections would be transferred to the CIA.

The CIA employees took the conversation to areas that I was sure were of a much higher security classification than I had and most definitely was much higher than the "confidential" clearance Leon had. They were talking about the *many* front organizations they had which could be used to receive money from the new agency and how some of that money would fund different planned black operations. I stopped them twice when they started to run on about these matters and advised them that Leon and I did not have the security clearance or the need-to-know to hear what they were saying. Both times, the senior official present agreed and admonished the group to keep the conversation at a "confidential" level. That lasted for five minutes and then they were back to discussing too much detail about their organization and operations. I figured I had done my part by voicing my concerns twice, so I just shut up and listened. It was truly fascinating.

At the meeting they made a pitch that they needed at least five million dollars to start and probably more later. I was totally non-committal about how much they might get or when.

It was lunch time when the meeting broke and the assistant deputy director, or whatever his title might have been, who was senior at the meeting invited Leon and me to lunch in the executive dining area.

It was like a four-star restaurant with great eye appeal, and great service by uniformed waiters. I ordered a thick, half-pound medium-rare hamburger and it was delicious. As we chatted about the meeting, I finally told our host that he could count on receiving three million from our funds to pay for CIA involvement. He was well pleased and we both smiled as we shook hands.

That was the most expensive hamburger I have ever eaten. Three million dollars for lunch is a lot...but what our host did not know was that the general had authorized me to give them up to five million. If he had known, I imagine he would have insisted I order the lobster.

*****

The EA had been right when he asked about my Christmas plans before he offered me up as one of the naval officers to this task force. The assignment went months into the New Year and I had to beg CNRC to pull me back to a blue uniform. Every officer on the task force was getting their temporary orders modified to permanent assignment to the On-Site Inspection Agency (OSIA). Those of us who wanted to leave the "purple suit" duty had to fight hard to make a good escape. I still wanted command and I was not interested in keeping my new title of OSIA Comptroller.

Upon return to CNRC it was time for me to don my commander stripes. I was assigned as the Aviation Officer Programs Officer in the operations department. My job had two components. I was head of the selection board that chose which applicants would go to Aviation Officer Candidate School (AOCS) in Pensacola and I had responsibility for the safe operation of the 52 T-34Bs assigned to recruiting districts around the United States.

Only in the American Navy can you go from being a bag carrying recruiter to becoming head of the selection board just a couple of years later! In my new job, two lieutenants, one a helicopter pilot and the other a P-3 NFO, and I comprised the "selection board." We would closely read from 3,000 to 4,000 application packages each year to select the "best qualified" 400 to 500 candidates to attend AOCS.

One day, an application packet came across my desk after having been reviewed by the two lieutenants. Each of them had given this fleet applicant a "down arrow," meaning they did not recommend him to attend AOCS. The name on the application looked familiar to me. When I opened it to read the half-inch thick pile of papers I recognized who it was.

I asked the two lieutenants, "Did you guys note who signed this sailor's evaluations in his last squadron?"

They both presented lame reasons why this sailor wasn't ready to be made an officer, but it was obvious that they were pulling my leg. They knew perfectly well that I had been the reporting senior for Petty Officer Second Class Johannson...the same Petty Officer Johannson who had convinced the inspectors to accept the answer on the IFT CNAPS exam that gave VP-40 the first ever new plane squadron pass.

He went to AOCS and was commissioned.
Once again, payback is good karma.

*****

One day my Academy classmate, Kai, and I were ordered to present ourselves at the admiral's office. Kai was a nuclear trained submariner and he headed the selection board for Officer Candidate School in Newport, RI. Upon reporting to the Admiral we were transported with him to the Navy Annex near the Pentagon. There we were ushered into the office of our admiral's boss, Vice Admiral Boorda, the Chief of Naval Personnel (CNP.)

Admiral Boorda had enlisted in the Navy while still underage and because his chief had completed the paperwork for him, he was selected for OCS. He always identified with the "white hats" and he had insisted that Kai and I come to him and explain our methodology in selecting candidates to go to officers training.

CNP asked Kai what standards he used when reviewing fleet applications for OCS. Kai gave a typically dry, nuke officer answer; something about not being able to vary the standard because in the future these selected applicants would be tested as officers, especially those who became nukes and, of course, especially because "when a nuke has a bad day, the whole world has a bad day."

I could tell that was not the answer CNP was hoping to hear. So when he turned to me and asked the same question, I gave him a typically dramatic aviator's response.

"Admiral, I have a real attitude problem whenever I review a fleet application." Boorda clinched his jaw and his ears started to turn red, obviously starting to get upset by what I said. But I continued, "You see, when I review a civilian application I have a switch that is hard wired to the no position. It will take something very special and outstanding for me to break the wire and flip that switch to yes. However, whenever I review a fleet application, the switch is hard wired to the yes position and there has to be something pretty bad in his record for me not to select him for AOCS."

CNP slapped his hand on the conference table and smiled and yelled, "YES! THAT IS EXACTLY WHAT I WANT!"

Our one-star admiral was happy that the three-star admiral was happy and I was just glad to get out of there on a positive note.

*****

Our admiral was a nuke. He honestly did not like aviators. There were two aviators in my chain-of-command between the admiral and me. None of us were well received by the one-star. That was especially true the day I had to show up early to join my boss's boss in briefing the admiral about a crash of a T-34B in the Rockies that killed two officers.

When the admiral arrived at 7 AM I had already been there for two hours. I needed time to compile the reports from the recruiting district in Denver and to prepare charts and maps for use in explaining what had happened out west. A half-hour before the admiral's arrival, Captain Grotenhuis met me in my office. He had been my CO in VP-50 when the plane crashed in Pago Pago and now he was head of all CRUITCOM operations. He was one of the very best COs I ever had and it was a real pleasure to be working for him again.

Late the previous night the report of the crash had been received and the admiral notified. As head of the recruiting T-34B program, I was to brief him immediately upon his arrival the next morning. Basically, the admiral wanted to know what happened and also why it happened, which was the more difficult question.

It was during this briefing that I once again realized that there are many different "navies" within the United States Navy. As Captain Grotenhuis and I were discussing the accident and how we might want to change our training program for pilots being assigned to high, mountainous regions in under-powered aircraft, the admiral just sat there staring at us. He was not referencing the carefully prepared maps and charts that I had laid across his wide desk. Captain Grotenhuis and I were pointing to the accident scene as we discussed the causes and possible measures to prevent a reoccurrence, but he admiral just sat there with wide eyes filled with a mix of confusion and anger.

After a short while, he interrupted our conversation with comments that neither of us initially understood, "Look at you two pilots...you act like this is normal! In my entire career I have never lost a sailor due to an operational reason. You two just accept this. I don't get it."

I was confused and did not know how to respond to his comments. I looked at my old squadron commanding officer who looked tired, but full of compassion for this admiral who had enjoyed a career sheltered from the operational deaths of his men.

"Admiral," the captain said in a soft voice, "It comes with the wings. Bob and I and all aviators know shipmates who have died in crashes. It just comes with the job."

It was silent as I believe for the first time, this nuke admiral fully realized how different Navy Air was from his own experience. Then he expressed his honest feelings.

"We should shut down the program. No one should die in this command. We don't need this program," he said as he turned his attention to the maps in front of him.

"These are not the first deaths in recruiting, admiral," my boss replied. "We lose a couple of recruiters or staff each year to traffic accidents."

"Yes, but you have to drive a car to get this job done. We don't need these airplanes to make goal."

I did not like to admit he was right, but in all honestly we did not need the T-34B program to make our aviation officer goals. However, I loved the program and attributed the ability to get airborne and leave the petty demands of the job on the ground as a key factor in my retaining my motivation and effectiveness while carrying a bag. I was able to keep the program funded and running through my tenure, but my relief finally had to close the program a year after I left.

*****

My job at CNRC was classified a flying billet. I kept my flight pay because the lieutenant pilot in my office and I would use the local NRD Washington's T-34B to get our flight hours. Funny thing, but as head of the national program, I had no trouble at all getting the local recruiting pilots to make the plane available when I wanted to fly...go figure.

I volunteered to fly the plane from Washington DC down to South Carolina when it had to be delivered to a civilian contractor to receive an overhaul. I enjoyed flying VFR and finding my way via ground reference, so I looked forward to this distraction from my office job.

However, I discovered on this flight that community pride does not run very deep in parts of the south.

The weather was good visibility with a layer of scattered to broken clouds at 2,000 feet. Since it was a long flight with a couple of refueling/rest stops, I initially climbed to 4,500 feet as my cruising altitude. About an hour into the flight as I was approaching southern Virginia the clouds below me started to form a solid layer. This hampered my ability to navigate visually, so I had to find a hole to drop below the weather. I did not get under the clouds until I was down to about 1,000 feet, but visibility was good and there was no rain underneath so I trucked on with confidence.

My biggest problem was I did not recognize any landmarks I could see and the cheap VOR was not working...let's face it, I was lost. I followed one railroad line to what I hoped would be a major road that might be on the sectional chart. But it took me somewhere else and I was even more lost. So I reverted to a technique I had used when flying the little Taylorcraft I had owned years before. I found a small town with a community water tower. I buzzed the tower in order to read the town's name painted on it. I read "Conroy." Even though I searched the sectional chart thoroughly I could not find a town named Conroy.

I continued to fly in a general southerly direction until I saw a second town with a municipal water tower. I buzzed that tower, but there was no name painted on it. I continued to work my way south until I found another town with a water tower. I was able to read the name on the side of this one. The only problem was that it read "Conroy."

Either I had circled around to fly past the original town again, or there were two Conroys near each other...or the names on the sides of the towers were not the towns' names but that of the tower manufacturer. Realizing that the third option was the truth, I began to wish these country folk took more pride in their community.

I next tried to give a very low pass over a road sign in the hopes it would give the distance and title of the next community. All I found were signs for directions to roads not on my map. I had plenty of gas, but not knowing where I was exactly made me think that I might pull another stunt as I had in Hawaii and unknowingly fly through another restricted area. So when I saw a small airport near the horizon to the west I diverted course and entered its uncontrolled pattern. I landed and taxied to the small building located near two parked general aviation planes. I expected to see the airport name painted on a sign above the building, but there was none. So I shut down my engine and exited the aircraft. No one was around. I walked to the building and circled it looking for a location or name.

By the time I returned to the front of the building, two pick-ups had pulled up and the drivers were approaching my airplane. This was a normal occurrence when flying the T-34B. With its "Fly Navy" paint job and a pilot wearing a flight suit and helmet many pilots and aviation enthusiasts would come out of the woodwork at small civilian airports to inquire whether it *"really was a Navy plane?"*

I got to talking with these two farmers who had left their fields to investigate the strange plane that had unexpectedly landed at the nearby airport. It was around early lunch time, so I ended up riding with one of them to a small roadside cafe and sharing lunch with him. We chatted with the waitress and other customers and had a good friendly visit. For an hour I was a celebrity in their working world and they felt proud to see their tax dollars actually coming to their neighborhood. It was like the old barnstorming days after World War I. I remember the unplanned stop with fondness and I recall the warmth and strength of this rural community. They didn't have a water tower, but they did have civic pride.

Oh, yeah...I also found out where I was and which direction to fly to get back on track.

*****

My last four months at CNRC I spent as the head of all Officer Recruiting Programs. This was a captain's billet, but I filled in as a commander when there was a gap in officer assignments. I then requested to be assigned as a NRD commanding officer and the admiral sent me to Albany, New York.

I had fun as CO. I am not sure my recruiters had that much fun.

Normally when a new sailor checks into a command he meets with the CO for a five-minute, "welcome aboard" session. However, when new recruiters checked into NRD Albany they got a 45-minute philosophical lecture on how to succeed in their new, different-from-the-fleet assignment.

Basically I would tell them the "good news" and the "bad news". The good news was that they had arrived at one of only three districts of the 32 nationwide where the CO had ever actually sat across a desk and personally put someone in the Navy. The good news was that I had spent three years carrying a bag and having to make monthly goals. I knew that a recruiter could do everything right one month and still "roll a doughnut." I had been there and so I didn't worry about a hiccup in a month's production. I expected him to do his best and use the training he had been given and then things would work out for him and the district.

Then I told him that if the good news was that I carried a bag for 36 months...then the bad news was that I carried a bag for 36 months. I knew enough to never accept lame excuses like "there's no propensity to enlist in my area," "they can't pass the test in my area," or "the Army recruiters have poisoned the well for us." I would not accept that kind of crap because I knew the job and that it is quite do-able for any sailor that truly tries.

We did extremely well during this tour, ranking as the #2 of 32 districts because of the Chief Recruiter (CR), XO and a strong cadre of Career Recruiting Force (CRF) senior petty officers. I think Master Chief Siewing, the 30-year sailor who led all enlisted recruiting as the CR, would have appreciated meeting Chief Williams. For it was Chief Williams who had properly trained Ensign Bartron so that now, Commander Bartron was smart enough to get out of the Master Chief's way and let him run things.

I think the best story that illustrates our super work relationship deals with how we treated a serious error by one of our second class petty officer recruiters.

Drinking and driving a government car meant career death when on recruiting duty. However, we experienced one occasion where a set of circumstances had to be taken into consideration when determining the best course of action.

Our XO received a report from an Army recruiter in Amsterdam, NY that one of our Navy recruiters, Petty Officer "Jones," had been drinking wine at a city function and then drove the government vehicle assigned to his station. Upon closer investigation the XO determined that technically our recruiter had used alcohol within twelve hours of driving the government car. But the circumstances meliorated the seriousness of the crime.

All the Amsterdam local recruiters from all the armed forces attended a small reception given by citizens to support the local military. At this reception our recruiter took two sips of wine and then remembered he had arrived at the event in his government ride. According to his story and many witnesses at the event, Jones left the party three hours later and drove the government car the five blocks back to the recruiting station.

I wondered why this came to our attention. Why did the Army recruiter report another service member who worked in the office right next to his? It didn't take much digging by the XO to find out the reason. It seems our recruiter had a one-night stand with the soldier's wife. The soldier had been waiting to catch our sailor doing something that might impact his career progression. That civilian reception had given the Army recruiter exactly what he wanted. There was no way the Navy chain-of-command could ignore the report about something that was an area of extreme emphasis by our admiral and his bosses.

I was scheduled to hold Captain's Mast on our young recruiter to determine his future in the Navy. Under current directives concerning drinking and driving in CRUITCOM I had three options on what to do. I could process Jones out of the Navy or have him transferred out of recruiting duty and back to the fleet or I could award local punishment if I felt I had a case strong enough to justify such minimal action up my chain-of-command. I wanted the Chief Recruiter's input on this decision.

Master Chief Siewing came into my office and I asked him to shut the door. That alerted him that we would be talking some serious stuff. I explained the situation and outlined my options at Captain's Mast. Then I asked the Master Chief's recommendation.

He gave it serious thought for a few seconds and then answered, "Keep him, CO. He's a good sailor."

I nodded in response. As the CR opened the door to exit, he stopped and turned towards me to add one little request. He said, "But make him cry."

In order to give the full effect of what I had planned, I called in the Admin Chief and told him I wanted an office trash can with a clean plastic liner in it set next to the lectern to be used for the mast. That request had the chief puzzled but he left to insure it was done.

Ten minutes later I marched into the conference room that had been emptied of all tables and chairs. Towards the center of the big room was the lectern with a waste can sitting next to it. In the room were the XO, CR, Enlisted Programs department head, Jones' senior chief Zone Supervisor, his Station Recruiter-in-Charge and a couple of admin petty officers.

After I took my position behind the lectern, I nodded and the Admin Chief left the room to retrieve Jones, who then marched to a spot directly in front of me. Jones saluted and removed his hat. I left him at attention, purposely not putting him at parade rest.

Three minutes later all the preliminaries of a mast procedure were done and I was ready to give my decision. I started off speaking low and slow, but as I continued my voice got louder and meaner and I spoke with dramatic conviction and intensity. I think it was one of my better acting jobs during my Navy career. I was getting so worked up that I began even to scare myself.

I was coming to the climax of my little show and practically shouted, "Look at this Petty Officer Jones!" I held up his service record in my right hand. "Do you see this? It is the record of an excellent sailor—a sailor with the potential to rise to the highest pay grades—a sailor with a great start in the Navy—

but do you know what *you* did by not thinking and pulling this dumb stunt? DO YOU?"

His bottom lip started to quiver and I saw a tear form in the corner of his eye as I dramatically raised his record over my head and then threw it into the trash can.

"*THAT* IS WHAT YOU DID TO YOUR CAREER!" Everyone in the room was stunned by my fierceness in ripping this sailor a new one. I let the silence sink in for a couple of seconds, and then continued.

"As far as I'm concerned it can stay in the trash! As far as I'm concerned you called the tune and this is what the piper demands for payment! As far as I'm concerned I want to process you out of my command and out of my Navy." (Another dramatic pause here.) "But I'm not going to do that...and there is one and only one reason why I will not do that this time. Do you know why I'm not going to do it? It is because of *that man* standing back there—because Master Chief Siewing believes in you and asked me not to ruin your young career. Only one man is responsible for this." I bent over and pulled his service record from the trash. I tried to continue my little drama, but I was momentarily distracted by the heavy glob of goop hanging from the bottom of his record as I raised it up and set it on the lectern in front of me.

Much to my shock, the liner in the trash can was new...but just before it was brought into the conference room the third class yeoman had used too much gel on her hair and flung the left over into the trash can.

I tried to keep my intensity as I used my forearm to wipe the corner of his record at the same time I tried to keep from smiling.

I distracted the shell-shocked Jones by pointing to the back of the room and saying, "Turn around and look at that man! You owe that man!"

Then I quickly fined him $50 per month for two months and told the Admin Chief to march Jones out. I retired to my office and a few seconds later the master chief knocked on my door and entered.

He summarized the mast in a typically direct manner as chiefs do. He said, "I guess I won't have to wash my car for the next year."

*****

Like most every NRD commanding officer, there was rarely a waiver request I saw that I didn't find merit in. Our job was to help the recruiters and the district to make goal. Sometimes you had to trust the system to take some pretty raw material and mold it into a good sailor. I can only recall one waiver request that I turned down.

I knew something was amiss when a recruiter from a station in Connecticut arrived at my office in Albany, NY with his applicant needing a CO's waiver and asked to see me before I interviewed the potential recruit.

My recruiter entered my office and shut the door behind him, which in itself indicated that what he had to say was important.

"Captain," he began in total earnestness, "I have Johnny Smuckatelli outside. He's an applicant who wants to be a corpsman but he admitted to prior marijuana use and needs a CO's program waiver."

I nodded in response and after a pause he continued, "I strongly recommend that you do *not* grant the waiver."

This was a first in my recruiting experience! A recruiter who did not want his applicant to enlist! I asked him why the strange recommendation.

"Sir, I just spent two hours in the car driving him up here and after that experience I have concluded that this guy is a nut case. He's nobody I ever want as a shipmate. Just talk with him and you'll see what I mean."

I could have denied the waiver request just on the recruiter's recommendation, but since they had driven all the way to the NRD headquarters and my curiosity was peaked, I had the applicant ushered into my office.

It did not take long for me to see what my recruiter meant...this guy had a very serious psychological problem. On paper he looked like a good potential enlistee. He graduated from high school, had a clean police record, was physically fit, and motivated to join. The only spot on his application was experimentation with marijuana two years ago, something we ignored in most applications. However, since this guy wanted to become a corpsman and work around drugs, he needed to be personally interviewed by me.

I asked the standard questions about the facts of his drug use and his motivation for experimenting with it. So far, pretty standard answers; then I asked an obvious question and got anything but a standard answer.

"So tell me, Johnny, why do you want to become a corpsman?" I put out there.

"Well, in all truth I really think it is neat to watch someone die."

I had been around sailors for twenty years and had heard many odd things and weird ideas, but this was something new for me.

I did not react to his statement. Rather, I asked a follow-up query, "Have you seen many people die?"

"Oh yes. My mother is an ambulance attendant and whenever she is called to a gruesome crash, I find out and rush out there. I've seen a lot of people die."

I really was not interested in asking why he liked to watch people die. His reasons did not matter to me. My thoughts were of the corpsmen who had helped me in the hospital a few years before; the idea that one of them might be an "angel of death" was enough to make my decision about his waiver rather easy.

"You do know that liking to watch people die makes you abnormal, right?" I asked as I was beginning to notice my voice getting louder and sterner.

"I don't think I'm abnormal," he said matter-of-factly.

"I can prove that you are abnormal," I stated with my best CO's voice of invincibility, "If I had every person in this building step out of their offices and then I went down the hallways and asked each one of them if they liked to watch people die, you would be the only one to answer yes. Your answer would not be normal. That makes you abnormal."

I stood up and directed my recruiter to take this candidate back to Connecticut. Waiver denied. Next I went down the hallway to the Chief Recruiter's office and opened his door without knocking. He was conducting a Zone Supervisors meeting which I rudely interrupted. In the meeting was the classification supervisor who maintained and reviewed all the delayed enlistment contracts.

I pointed to the chief classification supervisor and said in a rather angry voice, "I want Johnny Smuckatelli discharged immediately. And I mean at this very instant."

"Aye, aye, captain," he said as he quickly got out of his seat and went to his office to comply with my urgent directive.

Master Chief Siewing had not seen this side of my personality for quite awhile. He gave his zone supervisors a coffee break and then asked if there was anything he could do. I shared what was bothering me and he just shook his head as he listened. The more I talked to the master chief, the more I convinced myself that I could not just drop this situation without doing one more thing.

I retrieved Smuckatelli's home phone number from his records and returned to my office. I called his home hoping to speak with his father.

I obviously had not thought this action out completely. I mean, how do you call up a man and tell him his son is crazy and in need of serious mental treatment? However, I did not hesitate to pick up the phone. One of the lessons a recruiter learns early is "don't think, just dial." The weak recruiters worry too much about what they will say when making a cold call. It is better just to dial the phone than to sit there practicing what you might say.

Johnny's father answered the phone and I tried to gently tell him that his son was nuts. I shared with him how my waiver interview went and that I had denied his son permission to enlist in the Navy. There was a long pause after I stopped talking. Then the father spoke words from his broken heart.

"Yes, his mother and I know Johnny has troubles. We have tried to get him help but it hasn't worked. We were hoping the Navy would be the answer."

"I'm sorry, Mr. Smuckatelli, but that is not what we do. I wish you and your family luck," I said before we exchanged good-byes.

That day after work I went home and hugged my three normal children...and I appreciated them especially that evening.

*****

My command tour ended a couple of months early. In another CRUITCOM reorganization (which happens every couple of years it seems) NRD Albany was being closed. Our recruiting territory was being absorbed by the NRDs in Boston and Buffalo.

I took advantage of this command closing to ignore some of the limits placed on commanding officers. Normally, sailors who transferred from a command received a plaque to commemorate their service. Well, since the command was leaving the sailors in this instance, I authorized the purchase of plaques for everyone. Additionally, a commanding officer is normally only allowed to award five Navy Achievement Medals to stellar performers in one fiscal year. I figured no one would be checking the administrative records of a command that was banished to the archives, so I issued eight that year.

My people had done very well which made my command tour look very good. This led to my next assignment. As part of the CRUITCOM reorganization, the Area Commands were reduced from six to four nationally, which meant each Area had a larger span of control than previously. In order to assist the commodores with their larger areas, a new position was formed on the Area staff. I was selected to be the first Deputy Commander of Recruiting Area One.

I sought out these orders for one primary reason. Our oldest child had been in eight different schools spread all across America and overseas during the first eleven years of his education. Now he was about to start his senior year of high school as I was up for another transfer. By being selected to work on the Area One staff, we could continue to live in the same house. My commute would lengthen from fifteen minutes to forty-five minutes, but our son and his siblings could stay in the same school through his graduation.

The Deputy's job was something new in recruiting, so when I reported to the Area commodore, we both had to define my responsibilities. Eventually, it boiled down to assignment of recruiting goals and training. I was to train the Area department heads how to make the numerical goals I had set and to train the new District commanding officers on how to better meet their unusual responsibilities.

When I reported as CO to NRD Albany, there were six districts in the Area. Five of the six commanding officers were male. During my tour the "Tailhook Scandal" took place in Las Vegas and suddenly the Navy had to address the way it had treated women officers. This resulted in a change in the gender of the majority of NRD commanding officers. When I finished my tour at Albany, the Area had been enlarged to eight districts and only two of them had male COs.

This reaction to the scandal had been a long time coming. For decades, women officers had been treated by the chain-of-command as second class officers. They had been limited in the type and expanse of the leadership billets they could fill. Most were classified as "General Line Officers" which meant they had not had the opportunity to earn a warfare specialty. The women filled positions that offered limited leadership opportunity. In fact, the 44 enlisted men that served under me in my first division as an ensign aboard a ship was more than most female officers had under their command before they made commander.

I had led a district that made goal every month, which was a very unique occurrence in the Northeast. For years while on the staff of CNRC I had lobbied for a "historical factor" to be added to the complex goal formula used to assign targets to every Area. I had kept asking why it was that "all the poorest recruiters are sent to the Northeast?" It was nearly impossible to make goal in the "Peoples Republic of Massachusetts." While down in the South they must have been assigned the best recruiters in the nation because they always seemed to make 115% of goal. As all the recruiters were drawn from the same pool, could it be that maybe it is harder to attract enlistments in Boston than in Columbia, South Carolina?

Unfortunately, the success of NRD Albany, which included western Massachusetts and Connecticut, did little to help my argument; although it did make me look like an "Ace" recruiting manager. This reputation and the lack of leadership experience of his female COs had given the commodore an idea of just how he was going to employ his new Deputy.

I was called into the commodore's office the third day I was in the job. My new office was still being assembled by the supply department so I was using a clipboard as my desk. So, I reported to the Commodore's great big office carrying my desk with me.

The current commodore was retiring after a full career which had included many years of recruiting duty at the district, area, and national levels. In fact, Captain Diman had been my boss during my assignment as Aviation Programs Officer at CRUITCOM as well as my commodore during my command tour. His relief, Captain Jim Dolle, was also a veteran of multiple recruiting assignments. These two aviators, as well as I, were the "old hands" of recruiting who had left our initial Navy communities and, along with the senior enlisted Career Recruiting Force members (CRFers,) made CRUITCOM work. Recruiting has very unique challenges that are quite dissimilar to other jobs in the Navy, and we all three knew this.

The change of command ceremony was scheduled to take place in about a week. So I was not surprised to see the new commodore in the office with Captain Diman when I entered.

I was not invited to sit down. Rather, Captain Diman motioned for his civilian secretary to come in and hand me an envelope.

"Bob, I'm not sure what to do with you yet, but Jim and I have an idea. What we do know is that there is no crying in command," he said to paraphrase Tom Hanks character in "A League of Their Own", "but I just got off the phone with the CO in Pittsburgh and she was crying. They haven't made goal over there in six months. Here are your tickets. You leave in two hours to fly to Pittsburgh. It is an open ended ticket. Don't come back until you can tell me how to fix Pittsburgh."

"Aye, aye, sir," was my only reply and then I took the tickets, turned and left the office. I quickly packed a bag and made the flight.

Three days later I returned to Albany. It had not been difficult to pinpoint the District's problems. I had found that the CO was a very competent officer who had been put in charge of 150 sailors for the first time. Couple her inexperience with leadership in general, and in recruiting specifically, and it resulted in missing goal for a half year. Her inexperience was her primary excuse for the poor performance of the district, but it was the lack of professionalism by her Chief Recruiter that practically sabotaged her efforts.

I arrived in Albany late Friday night and spent the weekend preparing my report. I did it by using a VCR. I made a short tape of two scenes from two favorite war movies. The first was from "12 O'clock High" where Gregory Peck tells the general that the "jinxed unit" was really just a failure of the commanding officer—"it is always the commanding officer." The second clip was from "Patton." It was the scene where he had over extended his lines in an attempt to beat Montgomery to Messina and he was on the road to encourage his commanders to make their objectives. At one point a lieutenant colonel gave an excuse on why he was bogged down and Patton replied, "You're fired! Major, you are now in command and if you don't break through in four hours, I will fire you!"

I ran the five minutes of video. The old and new commodores nodded.

I said, "Some butt kicking is necessary in Pittsburgh. The CO can do the job, but she needs to be trained. The chief recruiter is not doing his job and should already know how. He needs to be replaced."

After the change of command, Pittsburgh became my little project and neither the CO nor CR was fired. The CO was quick to pick up what she needed to do to understand her "daily numbers" which are a must in recruiting and all sales. The CR had to undergo re-training with the Area Command Master Chief, which neither enjoyed...especially the CR!

In two months, Pittsburgh made goal and did so through the remaining months of the CO's tour.

*****

I was on the road traveling across the Northeastern quarter of the United States for the next two years. I was able to help COs new to command and recruiting to get a quick handle on how to be successful because we could sit down as peers and discuss the challenges. If the commodore wanted me to "put on his shoulder boards" and let the CO know that the words might be coming across my lips but the voice was the commodore's, I made that rare occasion very clear at the start of the conversation.

For many of these trips I was accompanied by the Area Command Master Chief. He was one of the top six Career Recruiting Force leaders in the Navy and carried great weight with the district CRs. It wasn't long before the supervisors and recruiters in the field had labeled the Area Command Master Chief and me as the "commodore's castration crew." If we showed up unannounced, somebody was going to lose something...and it wasn't heads that were going to roll.

The Master Chief knew every trick a recruiter might use to make goal...illegally. On one visit to a recruiting station that had gone from marginal performance to super-star status, he showed up unannounced and walked into the station. The first thing he noticed was how anxious the two recruiters in the office became upon his arrival. The next thing the Master Chief noticed were two footprints on the top of a recruiter's desk in the middle of the room. The Master Chief looked directly above the footprints and noticed that a couple corners of the acoustic tiles in the drop-down ceiling were broken. He went to the closet and grabbed the station's broom. Using the broom handle, he hit the tiles in the ceiling to displace them. When he did, a stack of blank printed high school diplomas came floating down.

The Master Chief was as angry over the footprints as he was the forging of enlistment documentation. He had no tolerance for stupidity, and he thought any sailor smart enough to find a way to print good diploma forgeries should have been smart enough to wipe the top of the desk after climbing on it to reach his stash. Stupid sailor.

There were other ways that could be used to make you a success in recruiting that did not require busting the regulations. I proved that in Philadelphia.

The CO at NRD Philadelphia took six weeks maternity leave to have a baby. Normally, the XO would fill in during the CO's absence, but the XO was a new lieutenant commander and early in her first tour in recruiting. More importantly, Philadelphia had consistently missed goal for the past year. So the commodore figured I was expendable from his staff for an extended period and sent me down to command the NRD during the CO's maternity leave.

It was the end of November when I arrived. The first thing I did was have the CR and statistician brief me on their best and worst producers. Then I hit the road. I spent at least an hour in every one of the fifty or so recruiting stations in the district which covered eastern Pennsylvania, parts of New Jersey and Delaware. I gave the same "rah, rah" speech in each one. It was something I had perfected while in Albany and dealt with my expectations of each sailor. This was my fourth tour in recruiting and I had served at every level from bag carrying recruiter to the national headquarters. In fact, I had re-written the procedures manual for recruiting. I had instant credibility with these sailors and I was about the only CO they felt actually did know more about the job than they did. I used this circumstance to my full advantage.

It was unfair in many aspects. Their regular CO was a woman. For nearly every sailor in the command, this was the first time they worked for a woman and it frightened them. She was a mystery to them. However, when I walked into their office it took them five seconds to know who I was. A quick glance at my uniform shirt and everything they needed to know was obvious. I wore wings and a SWO pin and ribbons that said I had sailed the same seas and flown in the same sky as they had back in the fleet. My big ol' honkin' recruiting badge surrounded by stars representing 20 Gold Wreath awards for sustained superior recruiting told them I was not new to this game. These were advantages that set the sailors at ease and immediately raised their morale...and unlike their current CO, I was *there* in their offices. Their CO only saw them when they would attend some command-wide function held at headquarters.

I had tried to train their CO in "Big Bad Babblin' Bobby's Ten Secrets to Success as a NRD CO" but she resisted things that sounded dangerous to her. Like many female officers, she wanted to be sure her boss never received anything that could put a shadow on her command or wasn't 100% perfect administratively. This meant that nothing could leave the command without her personal okay.

I had experience in breaking this kind of command mentality when I empowered the chiefs in VP-40 Maintenance

Control by making my phony beeper. When I showed up at NRD Philadelphia, it took me about five minutes to size up the XO. She was a talented officer and there was no reason I couldn't hit the road and leave all headquarters decisions and paperwork in her very capable hands. I wanted to get face-to-face with the bag carriers and infuse some excitement and acknowledge their contributions.

For the first time in a year, NRD Philadelphia made goal that month. The admiral was impressed and made a personal call to me to give me an "attaboy." I accepted it, but in my mind I had to laugh.

For nearly two years NRD Albany had exceeded goal each month and not one time did the admiral think it sufficient performance to pick up the phone and praise my team. I did it once in Philly, and now it is worthy of special recognition? But what was the real joke? Before I came to Philly, I had set the monthly goals for each of the eight districts in the Area. Of course I knew I could make goal in Philly—I had lowered it sufficiently to make it nearly a sure thing!

I was the slimy, pervert recruiter and that never changed!

*****

The women not only took the majority of command spots in the Northeast, they also took over the entire recruiting command. My last year in the Navy we had a new COMNAVCRUITCOM. It traditionally had been a nuclear trained admiral's billet, but in 1993 he was replaced by a female general line admiral.

Something else happened in the early 1990s. We won the Cold War. And what happens to the military after every war is over? It is drastically cut. So many officers were being told, "Thanks for winning the Cold War; now go home!"

It was the time of Selected Early Retirement Boards (SERBs.) The Navy was being cut by 30% so a lot of officers needed to be cut. The Navy takes care of its own, so the attitude was, "let's get the guys with over 20 years in and currently retirement eligible to leave and that way we won't have to tell some officers with 17 and 18 years in that they cannot stay until retirement."

That made sense to me, but just because it made sense didn't make it any easier to accept that after being in uniform since 1969...after paying all the dues to earn a position senior enough to start getting the perks of the service...that I was going to be asked to go home before the "payoff."

The first round of SERBs sent officers home who nobody expected to be selected. Commanding Officers of cruisers and heads of training schools were told they had six months to clear out. When these stories circulated around the fleet, morale in the officer corps plummeted. If these officers in prestigious command positions were being selected, then no one was safe from being "fired" at the end of a good career. The chatter in the fleet was, "Just whisper to me that you want me to go home and I'll retire. Just don't tell the world you found me expendable and forced me to retire. Let me leave with my pride."

My timing for promotion stunk. It was the year with the lowest percentage of promotion from 0-5 to 0-6 in forty years...unless you were a woman. The Navy had a lot of catching up to do with our female officers so post-Tailhook was a good time for a woman seeking promotion. In fact, every one of the female NRD commanding officers in our Area was selected for captain and nearly everyone deserved it. Yet, not one male CO was promoted.

My wife helped me overcome my keen disappointment and depression when I failed to promote for the first time. I was moping around the house when she asked, "Are you doing a commander's job?" I nodded and she continued, "Are you getting a commander's pay?" I nodded again and she said, "Then what's your beef? Just snap out of it!"

There was so much negative feedback from the first rounds of SERBs that BUPERS made a change to policy. Any officer who wanted to submit a letter requesting retirement could now submit it up to two years in advance. Previously it was only permissible to do it one year in advance. Seeing the handwriting on the wall, I opted to take advantage of this policy to keep from the embarrassment of being told by the next SERBs that I had to go home. I submitted my retirement request two years prior to my leaving the service.

Once your retirement letter has gone up the chain-of-command, you become "ten foot tall and bullet proof." No more worries about how your performance will be reflected in your annual evaluation, no more concerns about ticking off co-workers or superiors. It can actually be quite freeing!

The admiral came to Area One to meet with the staff and district COs. The eight COs, the commodore and I sat around the conference table and the admiral stood at the head of the table. She was a tall woman, at least six feet. The commodore and I sat at the head of the table, to her right and left. During the course of the meeting, the admiral passed along current Washington rumors, new policy changes and then we took a break for ten minutes. Upon our return she was going to make herself available to answer any specific questions the commanding officers might have.

During the break the commodore and admiral adjourned to another office. The COs had a heated discussion among themselves about how no one thought the new enlisted commissioning program she mentioned had any long term merit. I agreed with their assessment and suggested that someone use the Q & A session that followed to give the admiral feedback about how this program was being viewed from the field.

The admiral and commodore returned and the meeting resumed. The admiral opened the floor for questions and not one of the COs spoke. After a long, awkward pause that was embarrassing to the admiral, I felt I should get the ball rolling.

"Admiral," I said to break the silence, "There was some discussion during the break about the introduction of a new enlisted-to-officer program. Basically, the consensus was that it is a stupid program and should not be rolled out."

"Stupid" is another of those words like "fail" that carries a lot of emotional baggage with it. I was reminded of this by what happened next.

The admiral made the quarter-turn to face me and with fire in her eyes and her finger wagging in my face, she said sternly, "That is *not* a *stupid* program. *I* want it because it is *needed.*"

Okay, so I had no idea that it was her personal pet project. I looked across the table at the commodore and he was using his hand to cover the big smile on his face. He was having great trouble in keeping from laughing out load at my error of stepping in moist kimchi. I looked at the other commanders around the table and all of them had gone from vocal supporters of my position during the break to being keenly interested in counting their shoe laces. All of them stealthily slid their chairs away from mine as none wanted her white uniform to be stained by my blood spatter. It was obvious that I was on my own. However, as I already had my retirement letter submitted, I saw no reason to back off my assessment of the new program. I gave her a couple of suggestions on how to improve it before implementation which she did not think had merit and then we moved on to another topic.

Two months later something unexpected happened. I went to a civilian job interview just to get practice on how to perform at one. Unexpectedly, I was offered the job at well above my current Navy salary. However, my new employer wanted me a year before my approved retirement date. This meant I would have to get a request to change my retirement date approved by the chain-of-command.

Our Commodore, Captain Dolle, always took care of his sailors and he recommended approval of my request to leave early in order to get a good job. He hand-carried my request to the admiral on his next trip to Washington DC.

When he returned I was anxious to learn of the admiral's decision. When I asked Captain Dolle, he started laughing out loud. He said her initial reaction had been, "Is this the officer who called me 'stupid?'"

"Technically," the commodore had replied, "he called your idea stupid, not you."

He said she took the letter and enthusiastically favorably endorsed my request.

So the last lesson I learned while in the Navy was never to call an admiral stupid.

You'd think that would be a lesson that didn't need to be taught.

ABOUT THE AUTHOR

Commander Bartron is a retired Navy pilot and education administrator. During his 25 years on active duty he accumulated over 5,000 hours in the air and survived one crash and five emergency forced landings. He earned his Bachelor's degree (History) from the U.S. Naval Academy and Masters degree (Film) from Empire State College, SUNY. His wife and he have been together for over 45 years and have three grown children and three grandchildren. Commander Bartron and his wife live in Sacramento, CA.

Made in the USA
San Bernardino, CA
06 March 2018